T0072570

The Rebbe's Army

The Rebbe's Army

INSIDE THE WORLD OF CHABAD-LUBAVITCH

SUE FISHKOFF

Schocken Books, New York

Portions of this book were originally published in slightly different form in
Moment magazine and *The Jerusalem Post*.

Library of Congress Cataloging-in-Publication Data
Fishkoff, Sue.
The Rebbe's army : inside the world of Chabad-Lubavitch / Sue Fishkoff.
p. cm.
Includes bibliographical references and index.
ISBN 978-0-8052-1138-2
1. Habad—United States. 2. Hasidism—United States.
3. Judaism—United States—History—20th Century. I. Title.

BM198.54.F57 2003
296.8'3322'0973—dc21   2002075763

www.schocken.com

Book design by Johanna S. Roebas

First Paperback Edition

145820445

When it all began, Heaven was here on Earth.
The physical plane, more than any of the higher spiritual
    worlds, was the place where the Divine Presence yearned to be.

But Man, step by step, banished the Divine Presence
    from its home, with a tree of knowledge, with a man who
    murdered his brother, with all those things that human
    beings do. . . .

Since Man chased it away, only Man can bring it back.
And this began with Abraham, who proclaimed Oneness for
    all the world.

And it ends with us. Our generation will bring Heaven back
    down to Earth.

——FROM THE 1951 INAUGURAL DISCOURSE OF RABBI
MENACHEM MENDEL SCHNEERSON, AS ADAPTED BY TZVI
FREEMAN IN *BRINGING HEAVEN DOWN TO EARTH* (ADAMS MEDIA
CORPORATION, 1999)

Sooner or later we'll land an astronaut on Mars, and he'll
    be met there by a Lubavitcher shliach.

——PROFESSOR VELVEL GREEN, BEN-GURION UNIVERSITY

CONTENTS

The Rebbe's Army

PROLOGUE

It was a rainy November afternoon in 1993 when I got the phone call from Lubavitch headquarters in Crown Heights, Brooklyn. I was in my second year as the *Jerusalem Post*'s New York correspondent, and although I had reported briefly on the Lubavitcher Rebbe's illness, I had not yet been to Crown Heights and I knew very little about the Hasidic movement he led.

The voice on the other end of the line belonged to Zalman Shmotkin, ad hoc spokesman and press liaison for Lubavitch in New York. "Can I come to your office?" he asked. His voice sounded strained, as if something were weighing heavily on his heart.

Zalman showed up a few hours later, a young red-haired man with a wispy beard and wire-rimmed glasses, dressed in a plain white shirt, dark suit, and black hat. I had never met a Hasid before. I'd seen them many times—on the streets of Jerusalem and New York, on the subways, on Forty-seventh Street, in the camera stores near Penn Station. I'd studied about them in Jewish history classes, I'd read Martin Buber's *Tales of the Hasidim,* I'd seen *Fiddler on the Roof.* The image I'd come away with was of a shadowy, insular world filled with Shabbos tables, dietary restrictions, and one-way conversations with God. I'd grown up in a secular household in New Jersey, and Hasidim were very far removed from my reality. They were intriguing, mysterious, but ultimately alien.

Zalman began to talk, telling me about his rebbe. Menachem Mendel Schneerson, the ninety-one-year-old grand rabbi of the worldwide Lubavitch movement, had suffered a debilitating stroke twenty months earlier and was no longer able to speak. He was being cared for and protected by his closest aides who, themselves devastated by their leader's incapacitation, were struggling to keep the movement together while fending off a dangerous messianic tendency that was fast gaining ground among the Rebbe's followers.

But Zalman wasn't talking about that. He spoke to me, instead, of his rebbe's teachings. He told me what this holy man meant to him personally. He spoke for more than an hour, passionately, openly, talking about the nature of the human soul, the fabric of existence, the love God has for all creation. His eyes, already reddened when he arrived, filled with tears. He let them run down his cheeks, uncaring. As I listened to this Hasid lay bare his soul in front of me, I was deeply moved. Who was this Rabbi Schneerson to inspire such devotion? Why did I feel so stirred, so strangely elevated by the ideas this young man put forward in his name? We were from very different worlds, he and I, but in that moment I felt deeply connected—to what, exactly?

A few months later I spent a Sabbath in Crown Heights. It was, during those years, almost a required trip for Jewish reporters who covered the New York area, and it was arranged by Lubavitch headquarters: Shabbos with a Lubavitcher family, going to the great synagogue at 770 Eastern Parkway, staying up late Friday night singing Hasidic songs, and making l'chaims around the holiday table. It was supposed to show us, of course, that Hasidim are people, too, so we shouldn't disparage them out-of-hand in our reporting. But it's also part of Lubavitch outreach; if they're looking to kindle the spiritual sparks in every Jew, why not in Jewish reporters?

When I stepped out of the subway onto the corner of Eastern Parkway and Kingston Avenue, I was taken aback. There I was, right in front of 770, Lubavitch central. It was late Friday afternoon and people were rushing here and there, finishing their last weekday errands before sunset brought a halt to all work and Shabbat descended on Crown Heights. I saw crowds of men in black hats and suits, going in and out of the synagogue, and I felt very exposed. I didn't fit in here. Surely they were all looking at me, wondering what I was doing in their neighborhood. This was not my home. These were not my people.

Since that first visit I've been back to Crown Heights many times and have reported on Chabad activities around the world for *Moment,* the *Jerusalem Post,* and other Jewish publications. I discovered that no one in the Jewish world is neutral about Chabad. Everyone has an opinion, and much of the time it's not very flattering. One editor of a Jewish newspaper called me to say Chabad was "taking over the city" where she lived. What does that mean? Are they running the other rabbis out of town with shotguns? Are they multiplying so quickly that they're skewing the Jewish demographics? Hardly. And yet over and over I've heard the same warning, sometimes delivered in a whisper, sometimes in an exasperated shout: They're taking over. But what exactly are they taking over? And who's letting them do it?

I spent more than a year researching this book, traveling to Chabad Houses throughout the United States to spend time with Chabad *shlichim,* the movement's outreach emissaries. I spent weekends with them, sleeping in their homes, sharing their food, playing with their children. Without exception, they opened their lives to me with incredible generosity. More than once I slept in rooms crowded with cribs and toddler beds and realized the youngsters I'd displaced were bunking down with older siblings, or sleeping in their parents' beds while I was there.

I began watching my clothing—am I modestly dressed? Is my skirt long enough, my neckline high enough? No Lubavitcher would expect me to adhere to their fashion dictates, but I wanted to indicate my respect, and—it's true—I was also hoping to lull them into revealing more of themselves than they would to a casual outsider. I doubt that it worked, but I'll never know for sure.

As the year passed, I became more and more impressed with the shlichim I met. I admired their devotion to family, their work ethic, their optimism, and their openness to the world. Unlike other Hasidim, Lubavitchers aren't insular at all. They adhere to a very strict set of Jewish ritual observances, but they live very much in this world and are able to converse with anyone about anything. They know who they are, but they don't reject me for what I am. That combination of high personal standards and a nonjudgmental attitude toward others is compelling.

Some of the Lubavitchers I met activated within me what they would call my Jewish soul. After countless meals in Lubavitch homes, I've become more aware of the food I put in my mouth. I don't keep kosher—yet, as a Chabadnik would insist—but what used to be unthinking habit has now become a conscious choice that I'm forced to reevaluate every time I eat.

One rabbi sent me a *pushke,* a tin can with a hole punched in the top for dropping in coins, a traditional Jewish method of giving a little bit of charity—*tzedaka*—every day. My grandmother used to keep a blue-and-white *pushke* from the Jewish National Fund on her kitchen counter, and I remember seeing her put pennies and nickels into it when I was a small child. But I'd never had one myself. Now, because this Lubavitcher whom I'd met only once thought to send me one in the mail, I, too, give *tzedaka* daily. And when I drop in my coins, I feel connected in a very real, physical way to the generations of Jewish women who have gone before me. It's the first time I've felt the link between the action of doing a mitzvah and the spiritual benefit it's meant to deliver.

I, and many of the non-Chabad Jews I interviewed for this book, have been touched by how Lubavitchers incorporate into their daily lives the Jewish values to which most of us give little more than lip service. They visit the sick. They comfort the grieving. They take care to avoid embarrassing others. Whenever I visit a Lubavitch home, I am urged to stay for dinner, if not for the entire weekend.

I'm sure most of the Chabadniks I visited have no idea how impressed I was by these simple actions. To them, it's just part of life. But I'll never forget the day Minnesota shliach Rabbi Moshe Feller, a man in his late sixties, dropped me off at the Minneapolis–St. Paul airport. As I was waiting for my flight back to California, I perused the sandwiches at the deli cart for something to take on the plane. All they had was ham and cheese, and whereas ordinarily I wouldn't think twice, this time I hesitated. It felt wrong, somehow, after spending a weekend with Chabad to eat *trayf* so soon. Maybe that's silly, but I just couldn't do it.

As I walked back to my gate, I saw Rabbi Feller running around the waiting area, clutching a small brown paper bag to his chest. Seeing me, he ran up and thrust the bag into my hand. "I got home, and my wife couldn't believe I let you go without giving you lunch," he apologized. "Here, please, you shouldn't go hungry." Inside the bag were neatly wrapped slices of kosher cheese, some bread, a cookie, and a bottle of juice. I almost cried.

Certainly, part of Rabbi Feller's motivation was his desire to enable a Jewish person—me—to perform the mitzvah of eating a kosher meal; but the major impetus was simple, Torah-inspired hospitality.

There's much about Chabad I don't like. The women's *sheitels.* The rejection of modern culture—movies, television, music, literature. The messianism. The excessive veneration of the Rebbe. The refusal to recognize Reform or Conservative Judaism. The arrogance of a theology that teaches that only Jews have an additional godly soul and are thus privileged, above other people, to make the world a holy place. I reject the right-wing political stands taken by the Chabad movement in Israel— their refusal to consider territorial concessions to the Palestinians, their obstinacy in the "Who is a Jew?" Knesset debate.

Some of what I can't accept about Chabad is standard Orthodox Judaism. I won't sit behind a *mechitza,* the partition separating men and women in any Orthodox synagogue. I won't be barred from the *bimah,* from standing next to the Torah on Saturday morning and chanting the ancient Hebrew blessings. I believe in a participatory, egalitarian Jewish practice, and no matter how articulately the role of women in Orthodox Judaism is explained, it will always feel second-class to me.

But it's the same Torah and the same Judaism, and Chabad has a lot to teach most Jews—and non-Jews—about both. The remarkable thing is, they want to do it. They devote their lives to this mission. And they've been tremendously successful. In the past few decades, Chabad-Lubavitch has developed an enormous international presence, opening outreach centers in close to a thousand towns and cities around the world, pulling hundreds of thousands of Jews into their extensive network of adult classes, Hebrew schools, summer camps, and holiday programs. If not exactly setting the Jewish agenda, Chabad acts as a constant barb, pricking the rest of the Jewish world to do more, in opposition to, if not always in imitation of, their own work.

Who comes to Chabad programs? Who sends their children to Chabad camps and schools? Who gives money to fund Chabad outreach centers? To an overwhelming extent, it's Reform, Conservative, and unaffiliated Jews, Jews whose lifestyles are far removed from the Lubavitch empire they help support. This book is an attempt to understand how that happened.

There's a lot this book isn't about. It's not about what is wrong with Chabad. One can find criminals and ne'er-do-wells in any group. Chabad is no exception. This book is not about the movement's political involvement, in Israel or elsewhere. I don't purport to provide a comprehensive history of Lubavitch Hasidism, or a deep explanation of its theology.

There are other books that serve these purposes. Some of them are listed in the bibliography, and I urge anyone who is interested to consult them.

This book isn't about Chabad's work in other countries. Such a book would become too unwieldy, as Chabad's story in every land is colored by the local cultural and political setting. In some places, like England and Australia, Chabad rabbis fill more than half the pulpit positions and are major players in their country's Jewish communal affairs. In the former Soviet Union in particular, Chabad has become the dominant Jewish voice, shaping the future of this newly emerging Jewish community in a way they have done nowhere else. A separate book would be needed to discuss that monumental outreach effort.

This book is about Chabad outreach in North America, the Jewish community I know best. It's an attempt to describe how this small group of Hasidic Jews from Russia spread out across the land and became players on the American Jewish scene. Above all, it's about the shlichim, the young Lubavitch couples who leave their home communities and move to places with little or no Orthodox presence, just to devote their lives to bringing Jews back to their Jewish roots. Who are these people? What motivates them? This book is their story, and the story of those who support their efforts.

One day near the end of my research, as I stepped out of the subway at the Kingston Avenue stop, I realized that something was different. I looked around at the men in black coats and hats walking hurriedly down the street, the women in long dresses pushing baby strollers, the children laughing and chattering in the yards. And it looked familiar, no longer alien. These *are* my people. Like any family, we may squabble and grumble and kick each other under the table, but at the end of the day we are part of the same long chain of Jewish history. And that, I believe, is what Chabad is trying to teach.

Yes, Chabad is about lighting huge menorahs outside the White House. It's about star-studded telethons and multimillion-dollar girls' schools and fancy marble mikvahs and Lag B'Omer parades. But for me, Chabad will always be about a short, white-bearded man in a long black coat running back to an airport terminal to hand me a brown paper bag with a kosher lunch inside, so I shouldn't be hungry on my flight.

Pacific Grove, California
July 2002

CHAPTER I

FROM BROOKLYN TO
YOUR LIVING ROOM:
Cornering the Jewish Outreach Market

The lights were dimmed in the Grand Ballroom at the Brooklyn Marriott, but two things were still visible—a sea of black coats and hats crowded around more than a hundred linen-bedecked tables, and a makeshift *mechitza* separating dozens of elegantly dressed women from their husbands. It was the gala Sunday night banquet of the International Conference of Chabad-Lubavitch Shlichim, or "emissaries," and more than 1,300 Lubavitcher rabbis had flown in from their postings around the world for a weekend of study, networking, and morale-boosting.

The roll call, the evening's highlight, was beginning. "Argentina! Australia! Austria!" Rabbi Moshe Kotlarsky, conference chairman and director of development for Chabad's international emissary network, was reading off the names of more than sixty-one countries around the world where the movement maintains permanent outreach centers. As each name was read, one, two, sometimes a dozen, men would spring up from their seats to a smattering of applause.

"Panama . . . Paraguay . . . Peru . . . Romania!" The clapping got louder as the shlichim congratulated their colleague who had just opened Chabad's newest center in Bucharest. Kotlarsky paused dramatically.

Then, in a booming voice, he shouted "Russia!" Almost three dozen young men—one-quarter of Chabad's 130 full-time emissaries in the former Soviet Union, a place where Jewish education was banned for seventy years, where Jewish activists were routinely harassed and imprisoned until the collapse of the Soviet state in 1991—jumped out of their seats to thunderous applause and raucous cheers. The room broke into a spontaneous *hora,* with clapping and singing and wild, boisterous dancing that went on and on—a giant pep rally without the pom-poms, a political convention without the TV cameras. Pure joy. Pure passion.

This is Chabad-Lubavitch, the 250-year-old Brooklyn-based Hasidic movement that pundits predicted would collapse following the death in June 1994 of its seventh and last Rebbe, Menachem Mendel Schneerson. Schneerson, or, as his followers call him, the Rebbe, had been the heart and soul of Chabad for forty-three years, its spiritual leader as well as its intellectual and organizational fulcrum. He shepherded Chabad from a small postwar community of Russian-born Hasidim into a worldwide, highly public movement as well known in Congress as in Crown Heights Brooklyn.

But in January of 1994, the frail ninety-one-year-old Rebbe lay dying in Manhattan's Beth Israel Medical Center. He left no children and had designated no heir to take up the reins of his international empire. Around his sickbed swirled succession speculations and rumors of power-grabbing, complicated by the emergence of an almost desperate messianic strain among some of his followers that threatened to tear the movement apart. But it didn't. Today, Chabad is stronger, bigger, richer, and more popular than ever, with more than 3,800 emissary couples stationed in 45 U.S. states and 61 foreign countries, dedicated to bringing Jews back to Judaism. It's almost as if the movement forced a shot of adrenaline into its collective arm after Schneerson's death, just to prove—to the Jewish world and to itself—that his legacy would survive him. "All the 'ologists thought we'd run to California and jump off a cliff when the Rebbe left us, or shave off our beards," says Rabbi Yosef Langer, Chabad emissary in San Francisco. "But they don't understand the relationship of a Hasid to his rebbe."

Chabad is a fascinating phenomenon: a deeply religious Hasidic movement whose members adhere to a strict interpretation of Torah law, but which sends out its best and brightest young married couples to live and work among non-observant Jews all over the world.

Perhaps half, maybe two-thirds, of the Lubavitchers in America continue to live in a handful of Lubavitch communities, the largest number in Crown Heights, the group's spiritual and administrative center. These Hasidim send their children to Lubavitch schools, shop in Lubavitch stores, and visit their Lubavitch friends in the evening and on the Sabbath. They live in a kosher world. But a sizable chunk of Lubavitchers have chosen to leave their home communities to live in places where they are certainly the only Hasidic, and sometimes the only Orthodox, family. They set up Chabad Houses to spread their teachings among the general Jewish population. The Jews who attend their prayer services, who show up for their Chanukah parties and Torah classes, and who end up giving them money, are not Lubavitchers. Most are not even Orthodox. For the most part, they are non-observant or even unaffiliated Jews, or perhaps members of Reform or Conservative congregations, who are responding to something in the Chabad message.

It's a new entity: an ultra-Orthodox Jewish movement that attracts mainly non-Orthodox Jews.

Chabad outreach is nonstop. Movement activists are everywhere. They hold mass Purim parties on college campuses. They light huge outdoor Chanukah menorahs in hundreds of cities around the world, and stream the major lightings live on the Internet. They run around in "mitzvah tanks," asking Jewish men to put on phylacteries and Jewish women to light Sabbath candles. They build mikvahs in New Mexico, they teach lunchtime Torah classes on Wall Street, at Microsoft headquarters, and at the National Institutes of Health. They set up *sukkahs* in Brazil and hold Passover Seders for 1,500 backpackers in Katmandu. They run drug rehab centers and soup kitchens. They teach Kabbalah to Hollywood celebrities. They sponsor huge advertising campaigns to promote observance of Jewish holidays, including a notice for Shabbat candlelighting times that had run at the bottom of page 1 of the Friday *New York Times* for so many years that it was included in the paper's satirical millennial issue dated 1,000 years in the future. "We couldn't imagine a world without it," one *Times* editor quipped.

These black-hatted, long-bearded men and their modestly dressed, bewigged wives move into your town without notice and, before you know it, they're koshering your home, teaching you Bible, giving your kid a bar mitzvah, and running daily prayer services—most of it for free.

Chabadniks have set up shop in Los Angeles and Long Island, but also in Omaha, Des Moines, Salt Lake City, El Paso, Little Rock, Anchorage, and—since the summer of 2001—even in Peoria. Nearly 1 million children attend Chabad schools, summer camps, and special events every year. Chabad penetration of the Jewish world is so complete that movement officials in Brooklyn claim their holiday programming efforts reach 10 million Jews a year, nearly three-quarters of the world Jewish population.

But that isn't enough. Chabad's goal is to reach every Jew in the world. Chabad avidly courts the support of the rich, the famous, and the powerful, and has been very successful at attracting celebrities, business tycoons, and world leaders to its cause. Bob Dylan studied with Chabad rabbis in Minneapolis and sponsored a $100,000 building project in a nearby city. Jon Voight headlines the annual Chabad telethon in Los Angeles, a star-studded fundraiser that attracts a long list of glitterati, Jewish and non, from Whoopi Goldberg to Al Gore. Former U.S. President Jimmy Carter helped to light the movement's national menorah in 1979, and Russian President Vladimir Putin did the same two decades later in Moscow. Connecticut Senator Joseph Lieberman and Nobel laureate Elie Wiesel deliver keynote addresses at Chabad banquets; Herman Wouk and the late Chaim Potok were also great admirers. Yitzhak Rabin, Benjamin Netanyahu, Robert F. Kennedy, and Rudolph Giuliani are just some of the politicians who have visited the Rebbe in Crown Heights. Chabad shlichim have opened Congress, and the Rebbe has appeared on the cover of the *New York Times Magazine*. How have these Hasidim managed to convince the world's political leaders and cultural icons that theirs is a movement of import?

In the decade after Schneerson's death, Chabad's infrastructure grew faster than during his lifetime. Between 1994 and 2002, more than 610 new emissary couples took up their postings and more than 705 new Chabad institutions were opened, including 450 new facilities purchased or built from scratch, bringing the total number of institutions worldwide—synagogues, schools, camps, and community centers—to 2,766. In the year 2000, 51 new Chabad facilities were established in California alone.

Annual operating costs of Chabad's empire today approach $1 billion. And that budget doesn't include construction costs for new buildings, which have been going up at an astonishing rate since Schneerson's passing: a $10 million synagogue in Bal Harbour, Florida; $25 million for a Chabad complex in San Diego; $20 million for a Jewish Children's Museum in Crown Heights; plus a $1 million Chabad center in Las Vegas, $2 million for American Friends of Lubavitch headquarters in Washington, D.C., $5 million for a day school in Pittsburgh, and $3 million for a community center in Montreal.

Chabad building projects around the world have kept pace with those of North America: a $15 million girls' school outside Paris; a $14 million community center in Buenos Aires; plus soup kitchens in Brazil, synagogues in Germany, schools in Latvia and Lithuania, and orphanages in Ukraine.

Chabad's expansion into the former Soviet Union alone is phenomenal. In 1994 the movement maintained emissaries in just eight cities in Russia. By January 2002, Chabad had full-time emissaries placed in 61 cities across Russia, Ukraine, Moldova, the Baltics, and Central Asia, with 13,000 children studying in their day schools and thousands more attending their kindergartens and summer camps. In the spring of 2000, Chabad headquarters announced a $30 million commitment to build ten new Jewish community centers in the former Soviet Union that year, an ambitious undertaking capped by the September 2000 opening of a $12 million Chabad center in Moscow, the first significant Jewish building project in the country since the 1917 revolution.

It's easier to count buildings and bank accounts than believers. No one knows exactly how big Chabad is in terms of actual Lubavitcher Hasidim. There's no membership roster, no official census. Many reporters use the figure of 200,000 Lubavitchers worldwide, but that's little more than a guesstimate.

Numbers don't tell the whole story. Chabad is of interest not because of those relatively few Jews who lead Hasidic lives, but because of the success with which these Lubavitchers have made their mark in the non-Hasidic public arena. "You can't measure their influence by the number of guys they have in black hats," points out Samuel Heilman, sociology and Jewish studies professor at City University of New York and author of *Defenders of the Faith: Inside Ultra-Orthodox Jewry.* "Each outpost has relatively few card-carrying Chabadniks. Chabad's influence is measured in the number of Jews they've had an impact on, and that is far in excess of their actual number."

One telling indicator is the number of Chabad rabbis filling leadership positions within the mainstream Jewish communities of many countries. At least half the pulpit rabbis in England, Italy, and Australia, and almost all in South Africa and Holland, are Lubavitchers, and Chabad exerts considerable influence in the Jewish communities of France and Germany. Chabad rabbis control *kashrut* (kosher food) supervision for several key cities around the world, and a Chabad rabbi heads the rabbinical council in Montreal. In the former Soviet Union, Chabad has emerged as the mainstream denomination in what is now the world's third-largest Jewish community. It is the leading force in the newly created Federation of Jewish Communities of the CIS, an umbrella group representing 392 Jewish communities with a $20 million annual budget that is twenty times the money spent by the Reform movement, the next-largest denomination in the region. In the year 2000, Chabad rabbis elected their head Moscow shliach, Berel Lazar, as Russia's new chief rabbi, pushing aside the existing chief rabbi in a stunning power play publicly backed by President Putin.

Chabad does not wield anywhere near the same Jewish institutional muscle in the United States. But the past decade has witnessed a sharp increase in the number of Lubavitchers teaching in non-Lubavitch Jewish schools and filling pulpit positions in non-Lubavitch synagogues in this country. And in the fast-growing Jewish communities of Florida and California in particular, where Chabad Houses have been opening with great alacrity, Chabad is very often the only Orthodox presence in a given town or city. It is becoming the face of Jewish Orthodoxy for the Jewish and the general public.

What is the key to the movement's success? Chabad has money, sure, most of it donated by non-Orthodox Jews. Chabad has a formidable infrastructure. It has an elegant and fascinating theology, an interpretation of reality based on the Kabbalah, or Jewish mysticism, that many Jews find intellectually and spiritually compelling. Lubavitchers are adaptable—more than any other Hasidic group, Chabad has been able and willing to use the political and technological tools of twentieth-century America to promote its cause.

But above all, the reason for Chabad's continued vitality and phenomenal growth can be found in that Brooklyn Marriott ballroom: the shlichim—thousands of smart, idealistic young men and women filled with zeal, energy, and love of the Jewish people, young Hasidim in their early twenties who are willing to leave their comfortable homes and families and move to Shanghai or Zaire, where they dedicate their lives to running Chabad operations they more often than not build themselves from the ground up. And they do it, they say, because the Rebbe wants them to.

"We're carrying on the Rebbe's revolution," says one Lubavitch woman in her early twenties, who moved from Brooklyn with her new husband to establish a Chabad operation in Russia's Far East.

That "revolution" began in 1950, even before Schneerson took over Chabad's helm from his father-in-law, the sixth Lubavitcher Rebbe. One of his first actions was to send a shliach couple that year from Brooklyn to Morocco, beginning the worldwide outreach campaign for which Chabad is now known. By 1995, the first anniversary of Schneerson's death, two or three Lubavitcher couples were being sent out from Brooklyn every week, ready to teach Torah and bring Jews back to Judaism.

And they don't go for a year or two, but for the rest of their lives. These young, newly married Chabad couples leave home with one-way tickets and—if they're lucky—a year's salary. After that, most are expected to make their own way financially, by charging for certain services, such as day school or summer camps, by drumming up donors, and by taking related jobs in the local Jewish community. Chabad headquarters in Brooklyn will supply them with resource materials, adjudicate disputes, and set the general course of the movement's work internationally, but the individual shliach couple is pretty much on its own, with only pluck and willpower to sustain it. Chabad is thus a highly centralized, yet profoundly decentralized movement.

Chabad shlichim are not prisoners, of course. If a shliach doesn't work out, he can move to another city. But leaving the field entirely is almost unheard of. "They don't go thinking, Let's try this for a year or two; they go knowing that's where they'll spend their lives," says Rabbi Zalman Shmotkin, director of the Lubavitch News Service in New York. "On what? On a dollar and a dream."

"Chabad has the biggest army of people in the Jewish world ready to live on the edge of poverty," says historian Arthur Hertzberg, author of numerous books on Zionism and Jewish history. Hertzberg wasn't always a fan of Chabad. When messianic hopes began to swirl around the dying Rebbe in the early 1990s, Hertzberg told the *New York Times* that Chabad resembled the followers of Shabtai Tzvi, the notorious seventeenth-century false Messiah. But his personal encounters with Chabad shlichim since the

Rebbe's death have changed his thinking. His daughter, a member of a Conservative congregation in Fresno, California, sent her children to the local Chabad school, a fact Hertzberg relates with pride.

"Those thirty-five hundred shlichim are the most holy group in the Jewish world today," he declares. "They are every day engaged in *kiddush Hashem* [sanctification of God's name]. Everywhere I go, I bump into one of these young couples working their heads off. They live on nothing, and they stay with it. I can disagree with their theology, but I can only admire them."

Not everyone likes Chabad. The movement's highly public, in-your-face brand of Judaism makes it off-putting to some American Jews, as does the way shlichim seem to steamroll into town, setting up shop with great fanfare in communities where the Jewish population has maintained a more circumspect profile. Chabad's refusal to recognize non-Orthodox Jewish denominations puts the group at odds with the majority of rabbis working in this country, and with most national Jewish organizations. Chabad has been taken to court many times, for everything from zoning violations to public menorahs—most of the time by other Jews. Chabad is criticized both for being too religious and for pushing the outreach envelope too far. Sometimes the same people who reject Chabad's advocacy of a Torah-true lifestyle also criticize the lax dress codes at Chabad services or accuse Chabad-run schools of providing a watered-down Jewish education.

Chabad's right-wing stance on Israel, its interference in Israeli elections, and its support in this country both for a "moment of silence" in public schools and federal funding for parochial schools places the movement on the far right edge of the American Jewish dialogue. But unlike other Hasidic groups, they are still very much a part of that dialogue. Other Jewish leaders say that, like it or not, Chabad's impact on the American Jewish scene has been far-reaching.

"They have made an enormous contribution," says Dr. Norman Lamm, president of the Orthodox movement's Yeshiva University and a critic of Chabad on several fronts. "Wherever you go, you find Chabad Houses. These people are enormously dedicated, driven by great idealism and great commitment to their cause. We have a lot to be grateful to them for."

"They were pioneers in Jewish outreach, which is now universally accepted," says Malcolm Hoenlein, executive vice chairman of the Conference of Presidents of Major American Jewish Organizations. "Each stream [of Judaism] translates it in their own way, but clearly Chabad set the stage by being the first to engage in it in a systematic way. That doesn't mean you have to agree with everything they say, or their particular philosophy. But they definitely have had an impact."

Lubavitch Hasidism is a branch of the general Hasidic movement that emerged in the mid-eighteenth century in the forests of Poland, a charismatic, mystical burst of religious fervor that swept through the millions of impoverished, poorly educated Jewish masses of Eastern Europe and the Russian Empire like spiritual wildfire.

The founder of Hasidism was Rabbi Israel ben Eliezer, or the Baal Shem Tov, the Master of the Good Name. Born around 1700 on the Polish border, this self-taught children's teacher became known first as a wandering healer and miracle worker, and then as the proponent of a new approach to Jewish practice. The Baal Shem Tov, or Besht, countered the prevailing Judaism of his day, which had become the exclusive property of an elite enclave of talmudic scholars, and taught that even the simplest peasant who knows not a word of the Law can approach God directly through heartfelt prayer and an outpouring of his soul. The Besht brought Jewish mysticism back to the people, declaring that every Jew, not just the learned, could drink of its heady waters. He broke down the barriers between the secular and the spiritual, investing the most mundane activities with divine import, and declared that religious devotion was more pleasing to God than rote adherence to ritual. "I have come into this world to show man how to live by three precepts," he said. "Love of God, love of Israel, and love of the Torah."

The Besht's message was revolutionary. His followers broke with certain Jewish norms, adopting specific dress and customs and making ritual modifications, all of which horrified the Jewish establishment. Prizing attachment to God, or *devekut,* as the spiritual precondition for divine worship, early Hasidim worked themselves into ecstatic states during prayer, leading some of the more extreme sects to turn somersaults in the synagogues, or dance under the stars in white robes. By the early nineteenth century most of the more excessive physical practices had been reined in, but the theological underpinnings remained.

Lawrence Schiffman, chairman of the Department of Hebrew and Judaic Studies at New York University, describes the Hasidic approach to God as one of "meaningful joy, a joy that recognizes the world as saturated with the Divine." The character of Tevye from *Fiddler on the Roof*—the simple milkman who argues with God—epitomizes this new Hasid, who by the early nineteenth century had become the dominant figure among Eastern European Jewry.

When the Baal Shem Tov died in 1760, he was succeeded by Rabbi Dov Ber, the Maggid, or "preacher," of Mezritch. The Maggid systematized his master's teachings, laying the groundwork for the perpetuation of his revolution. Upon the Maggid's death in 1773 the Hasidic movement split into many small courts throughout Eastern Europe, each led by its own Hasidic teacher, or rebbe. One of those rebbes was Schneur Zalman, the founder of Lubavitch Hasidism. Schneur Zalman, or the Alter Rebbe, was born in 1745 in White Russia. His innovation was to apply his rigorous Lithuanian method of Talmud study to Hasidism's mystical teachings and emphasis on joyful devotion to God. The movement he founded is known by two names: Lubavitch, after the White Russian town where four of its rebbes were based, and Chabad, an acronym of the Hebrew words *chochmah* (wisdom), *binah* (comprehension), and *da'at* (knowledge).

Whereas some Hasidic rebbes were known for their piety, some for their miracle-making, and others for their exuberance, Schneur Zalman was known for his intellect. By the age of thirteen, so the story goes, he had mastered the entire Talmud with all its commentaries and would spend entire nights delving into the mysteries of Kabbalah. He studied with the Maggid for three years and was encouraged by him to rewrite the *Shulchan Aruch,* or Code of Jewish Law. That was the first of many influential writings, the most notable of which was the *Tanya,* published in 1796, a mystical theology and systematic approach to individual moral and spiritual development and to the concept of Divine Immanence that has become the seminal text of Chabad Hasidism.

Schneerson wrote in his preface to the first English-language edition of the *Tanya* that Chabad Hasidus is a comprehensive world outlook wherein the Jew acts as a link between God and creation, concerned not so much with getting to heaven himself as with bringing heaven down to earth by revealing God's purpose in the details of everyday life.

The Jew is a creature of heaven and of earth, of a heavenly Divine soul which is truly a part of Godliness clothed in an earthly vessel . . . whose purpose is to realize the transcendence and unity of his nature and of the world in which he lives within the absolute unity of God. The realization of this purpose entails a two-way correlation: one in the direction from above downward to earth; the other, from the earth upward. In fulfillment of the first, man draws holiness from the Divinely given Torah and commandments, to permeate therewith every phase of his daily life and his environment; in fulfillment of the second, man draws upon all the resources at his disposal, both created and man-made, as vehicles for his personal ascendancy and, with him, that of the surrounding world.*

This worldview devolves from the Hasidic concept of creation, based on the teachings of the sixteenth-century Kabbalist master Isaac Luria. According to this scenario, before the universe came into existence, God's infinite light filled all. In order to make room for the world to be created, God withheld some of His light, leaving behind a vacuum. When God's creative light reentered that vacuum, everything except God was shattered, scattering sparks of divine light throughout the universe. Those sparks became trapped in physical shells—the animate and inanimate objects that make up our world. The world yearns to return to its original state of light, while nevertheless remaining a physical world. That ongoing tension lies at the root of the world's troubles. It is the duty of the Jews to try to awaken the dormant sparks of light dwelling in the souls of every human being, as part of the process of restoring harmony to the universe.

This entire process is governed by Divine Providence. The Baal Shem Tov taught that God actively supervises everything that happens in the world at every moment. Thus not only does everything happen for a reason, but every action one does is significant because it is part of a divine plan.

For thousands of years—since the beginning of creation—a piece of the world has been waiting for your soul to purify and

---

*In Schneur Zalman of Liadi, *Tanya,* English translation (Brooklyn, N.Y.: Kehot Publication Society, 1962), p vii.

repair it. And your soul, from the time it was first emanated and conceived, waited above to descend to this world and carry out that mission. And your footsteps were guided to reach that place. And you are there now.*

From the beginning, Lubavitchers embraced the ideal of *ahavat Yisrael,* or "love of all Jews." A person's love for his or her fellow Jew must be intrinsic, a love that transcends logic. *Ahavat Yisrael* demands self-sacrifice and constant exertion: One must cherish the other even more than oneself, and without discrimination. All Jews must be loved equally, no matter their level of learning or observance. The Alter Rebbe was once asked by his followers which worship of God is greater: love of God or love of the Jewish people? He replied by quoting Malachi, chapter 1, verse 2: "I have loved you, says the Lord." It follows from that, the Alter Rebbe concluded, that love of the Jewish people is greater, "for you love whom your beloved loves."

Hasidism posits that Jews have a special relationship with each other hearkening back to creation. All of Israel is one body and one soul. When a Jew sins, the entire Jewish body is affected. When a Jew does a *mitzvah,* obeying even one of God's commandments, the merit is enjoyed by all.

This theological understanding gives physical urgency to Lubavitch outreach. Hasidism in general demands that its followers disseminate Torah knowledge among the Jewish people. Chabad takes that requirement a step further by stating that there is nothing more important than this outreach mission.

Chabad-Lubavitch stresses an ancient Torah concept, namely that all Jews are responsible for one another. No Jew is an island of virtue surrounded by a sea of Jewish indifference. The founder of Chabad went so far as to say that a Jew who helps another Jew to regain his Jewishness will find his own heart and mind purified and refined a thousandfold. In helping others the Jew helps himself also.†

---

*Tzvi Freeman, *Bringing Heaven Down to Earth: 365 Meditations of the Rebbe* (Vancouver, B.C.: Class One Press, 1996), p. 34.

†Zalman Posner, *Think Jewish* (Nashville, Tenn.: Kesher Press, 1979), p. 94.

The fifth Lubavitcher Rebbe, Sholom Dov Ber Schneersohn, described the Hasid's role as that of a lamplighter who must carry God's fire on a pole and light all the "lamps," or souls, on his route. Even if the lamp is in the middle of an ocean, Sholom Dov Ber said, the Hasid must jump into the sea and light that lamp. In 1961, Menachem Mendel Schneerson embellished on the metaphor:

> A hassid is he who puts his personal affairs aside and goes around lighting up the souls of Jews with the light of Torah and mitzvot. Jewish souls are in readiness to be lit. Sometimes they are around the corner. Sometimes they are in a wilderness or at sea. But there must be someone who disregards personal comforts and conveniences and goes out to put a light to these lamps. That is the function of a true hassid.*

Chabad teaches that helping another Jew is the purest way of expressing one's love of God. Teaching a Jew about Judaism is one form of help, but even the most material sustenance may serve the holiest purpose. A person may be brought into the world and given seventy years of life just so he or she can help one other person, as Rabbi Schneerson wrote to a Jewish leader in New York in the 1970s:

> Love of one's fellow Jew is not necessarily expressed in an attempt to save the whole Jewish people, but in helping even a single individual. When a poor woman gave birth at the far end of town, Rabbi Schneur Zalman . . . took off his tallit and tefillin and went to her dingy hut to light the fire and prepare some food for her. The Alter Rebbe saw no contradiction in interrupting his prayer to God in order to help a woman in need. On the contrary, such help is the best expression of being attached to God. So how can you— and I say this with all due respect to you—sit by idly in this city, surrounded by thousands upon thousands of fellow Jews who are starving for guidance and direction towards the right path in life, the way of the Torah? . . . Surely you should wish to dedicate all your energies and capacities to this life-saving work.

---

*In Jacob Immanuel Schochet, *Chassidic Dimensions,* vol. 3 of *The Mystical Dimension* (Brooklyn: Kehot Publication Society, 1990), p. 198.

Chabad Hasidus teaches that studying Torah and doing good deeds, which is really actualizing the lessons of Torah, are both part of the ideal Jewish life. But doing good deeds takes precedence, for only through action can the Hasid make manifest the godly spark inherent in every aspect of mundane reality. The entire universe is interconnected, and every deed, good or bad, has cosmic repercussions. The Hasid thus lives with a heightened sense of individual responsibility, aware at all times of the ripple effect of his or her every action. Schneerson would often warn his followers against spending too much time with their books, in the rarefied spheres of private contemplation. In his private meetings and his letters to them, he would always ask, What are you *doing* to change the world? How many children have you taught today? How have you publicized God's message to others today?

While most Hasidim restrict their personal dealings to Jews, and some even to Jews within their own ultra-Orthodox communities, Lubavitchers have never been insular. Their first interest is in kindling the sparks within Jewish souls, but since the early 1980s they have widened their appeal to include non-Jews, whom they urge to remain within their own religions while obeying the seven laws God gave to Noah—no idolatry, no blasphemy, no sexual perversion, no murder, no theft, no cruelty to animals, and the creation of courts of justice. This is crucial because only when *all* God's divine sparks are released and reunited with the Divine Oneness will God's purpose be achieved. "Our job is to make a dwelling place for God in the lower world," says Rabbi Sholtiel Lebovic, a Crown Heights Lubavitcher who runs a nonprofit home-kashering business. "We try to make the world a more and more godly place, until the coming of Moshiach [the Messiah]."

Despite certain ritual and philosophic differences between Hasidism and "normative" observant Judaism, Hasidic Jews remain very much within the Orthodox fold. They obey the same Torah and keep the same laws. They say the same prayer upon wakening, thanking God for restoring their souls to their bodies, and they go to sleep with the same Shema Yisrael on their lips.

Yet Hasidim are considered a sect within a sect because their dress, customs, and adherence to Torah law hearken back to an earlier era when European Jews lived apart from the gentile world. They keep kosher, but maintain a more stringent form of *kashrut,* with each Hasidic sect supervising the production of its own kosher food. As do many ultra-Orthodox,

Lubavitchers drink only *chalav Yisrael,* milk that has been watched by a Jew from the time it leaves the cow until it is bottled. That custom stems from a time when farmers added pig's milk if their cows weren't producing well, a practice that would be impossible in today's corporate dairies.

Hasidim study Torah, Talmud, and the works of medieval scholars such as Maimonides like other Orthodox Jews, but they add the writings of their own rebbes, which become part of their movement's sacred canon. All Orthodox maintain a certain degree of separation between the sexes, but Hasidim separate girls and boys from an early age. Many Hasidic groups still have arranged marriages. Lubavitchers do not, although like many ultra-Orthodox Jews, they date only for purposes of marriage, meeting eligible singles suggested to them by parents, siblings, or matchmakers.

Along with other strictly Orthodox Jews, Chabad Hasidim maintain a literal approach to the Bible. Noah, Moses, Sarah, and Abraham are not metaphors for correct behavior, or even shadowy historical figures, but real, larger-than-life ancestors, directed by God to set the Jewish people on its path. Lubavitchers believe that all human knowledge can be derived from Torah, including science. The world in the year 2001 was indeed 5762 years old, dinosaur bones and Big Bang theory notwithstanding. The same all-powerful God who created the universe and keeps it in continual motion doesn't have to follow the rules of Carbon-14 dating.

Lubavitchers don't recognize the labels Reform, Conservative, or Orthodox. To them, all Jews are one. The downside of that understanding is that they do not recognize non-Orthodox Jewish denominations; to Lubavitch, there is only one legitimate "variety" of Judaism, and that is the version known as Orthodox. But Chabadniks open their arms to non-Orthodox Jews on an individual basis. To them, all Jews share the same God-given soul and are authentically, intrinsically, unavoidably Jewish, no matter what their beliefs or ritual practice. Thus a Chabad shliach may refuse to enter a Reform synagogue presided over by a Reform rabbi, but will welcome into his shul any member of that congregation, including the rabbi, as his or her fellow Jew in good standing.

The Rebbe taught his followers never to embarrass another Jew for knowing little about Judaism, but to teach what they know in a humble and friendly fashion. Non-observant Jews with little formal background who attend Chabad classes and services often point to this immediate, unconditional acceptance as very different from what they have encountered in other Orthodox settings. Chabad shlichim like to play up this aspect of their outreach, setting themselves apart from the "stuffy" world of mainstream Orthodoxy.

Hasidic Jews set out for America in the 1880s as part of the great Jewish emigration that brought 2.5 million European Jews to the New World between 1881 and 1925. But the largest number of Hasidim arrived right before, during, and immediately after the Second World War, when several of the great Hasidic rebbes moved their courts from Eastern Europe to New York to escape from, or as survivors of, the Nazi onslaught.

Unlike earlier waves of Jewish immigrants, these ultra-Orthodox arrivals didn't want to blend into the dominant American culture. They wanted to re-create in the streets of Brooklyn the world they had left behind. Jerome Mintz, in his authoritative sociohistorical study *Hasidic People,** observes that "members of courts that had once stretched from Bratislava to Odessa were now located a few streets from each other" in Williamsburg, Crown Heights, and Borough Park.

In 1940, on a sparkling morning in March, Rabbi Yosef Yitzchak Schneersohn, the sixth Lubavitcher Rebbe, sailed into New York harbor to set up the court of Chabad-Lubavitch in America. When he arrived, there were perhaps several dozen Lubavitch families in New York and equally small Lubavitch communities in a handful of cities such as Detroit, Pittsburgh, and Montreal. After the sixth Rebbe's arrival, America's Lubavitcher population began to swell, enriched by a high birth rate (Hasidim don't use birth control, and families of ten, twelve and even fourteen children are not unusual) and by the movement's energetic creation of *ba'alei teshuva,* or newly religious Jews.

Crown Heights was a Jewish, but not a specifically Lubavitch, neighborhood until the late 1960s, when increasing crime led to a white flight that emptied its blocks of virtually all other Jews. The seventh Lubavitcher Rebbe was the only Jewish leader who exhorted his followers to remain in the neighborhood. "They sustained a community when all the other Jews left and ran," notes Malcolm Hoenlein with frank admiration. "That's a courageous thing to do."

Today, Crown Heights's white population is almost entirely Luba-

*Jerome R. Mintz, *Hasidic People: A Place in the New World* (Cambridge: Harvard University Press, 1992), p. 30.

vitch. The community weathered a housing shortage, economic down-
turns, and deteriorating race relations, including three days of angry riots
in 1991 sparked when an African-American child was struck and killed
by a car in the Rebbe's convoy. Even the Rebbe's death in 1994 did not
decrease its numbers, estimated by the 2000 U.S. Census at about 11,000
individuals, a 17 percent increase in ten years. Outside of Crown Heights,
Lubavitch communities of several hundred families each exist in Los
Angeles, Miami, Pittsburgh, Detroit, Montreal, Toronto, and Chicago, with
smaller communities in a handful of other cities. Combined with the
shlichim and their families, who live in non-Lubavitch communities, one
can assume a Lubavitch population of around 30,000 in this country, and
probably another 80,000 to 100,000 around the world.

Crown Heights is still the emotional and administrative heart of the
Chabad world, but as more and more shlichim have "gone out" since
Schneerson's death, a growing rift has emerged between the major
Lubavitch communities and the shlichim. That is, in turn, causing subtle
changes within the movement. New York University Professor Lawrence
Schiffman suggests that Chabad has been undergoing a transformation
from a group of Hasidim centered around a charismatic rebbe—the
traditional Hasidic model—to a synagogue movement based on a philosophy and liturgy, more like than unlike other mainstream Jewish denominations.

"When the Rebbe became Rebbe, you had a group of Hasidim
focused on their leader," Schiffman says. "Even when they did outreach in
those days, it was a temporary foray into a satellite community. Everybody knew they were Lubavitch. Today the dominant group no longer
lives in Crown Heights—they're out running the institutions."

Chabad's growth and outreach success is directly related to the startling rise of American Orthodoxy during the second half of the twentieth
century. In *Jew vs. Jew,** Columbia University journalism professor Samuel
Freedman writes that in 1930 only a third of American Jews belonged to
a synagogue, only "a fraction" owned a Kiddush cup or bought kosher
meat, and few mikvahs existed outside New York City. At the end of
World War I, there were just five Jewish day schools for a population of
3.5 million American Jews. Through the 1960s, Jewish writers and soci-

---

*Samuel G. Freedman, *Jew vs. Jew: The Struggle for the Soul of American Jewry* (New York: Simon
& Schuster, 2000), p. 34.

ologists confidently predicted that Orthodox Judaism would not last out the century. But beginning in the early 1970s, America's Orthodox community began reasserting itself with striking and unexpected vigor. Day schools proliferated, synagogues opened, more self-professed secular Jews began attending Torah classes, studying Talmud, and even keeping kosher. The entire American Jewish community made a slow but decided swing toward greater Jewish observance. Within the Orthodox world, young modern Orthodox men and women began adopting ultra-Orthodox practices, like avoiding movies and observing the laws of *negiah,* which prohibit touching anyone of the opposite sex, with the exception of one's spouse and immediate family members. The Reform and Conservative movements opened their own day schools, expanded their adult education programs, and began talking more about God.

To what extent Chabad contributed to this Orthodox revival, versus riding to success on its wave, is an open question. But Chabad has certainly capitalized on it. As interest in religion intensified, Chabad shlichim found themselves well placed as the first, and sometimes only, traditional Jewish presence in many American communities. Many American Jews who do not consider themselves observant nevertheless harbor a deep, sometimes inchoate feeling that their Chabad shliach and his family represent a more "authentic" form of Judaism than the liberal variety they grew up with and may still practice.

The arrival of large numbers of Hasidic Jews in the mid twentieth century had a certain trickle-down effect on Jewish practice among the greater American Jewish community, but it had immediate impact on those Orthodox Jews already in America. In the early twentieth century it was common for Orthodox Jewish men to shave off their beards and start speaking English upon landing at Ellis Island. But as waves of Hasidim moved to New York after World War II, codes of modesty long ignored in the New World became re-enforced. Married women once again donned wigs and/or head coverings. Men let their beards grow, according to the biblical prohibition on trimming one's facial hair. Long frock coats and fur hats for men, ankle-length skirts and blouses that covered the neck and arms for women, once again distinguished Hasidic Jews from their less observant brethren.

Among today's Hasidim, Lubavitchers sport the most modern dress. Lubavitch men wear ordinary black suits, white shirts, ties, and black fedoras. Lubavitch women don't bare their legs, but they don't wear heavy, seamed stockings, either.

This more relaxed dress code indicates Chabad's desire to bridge the gap between the observant and non-observant worlds. Here are Jews who live according to the strictest interpretation of Jewish law, who adhere to rigid lifestyle constraints, who don't watch TV or go to the movies or read popular literature, who have little or no secular education, who hang on their Rebbe's every word, but who—alone among Hasidim— nevertheless have made it their mission to engage the modern world.

So much about Lubavitchers appears to be contradictory. They scorn popular media, but they maintain the world's first and largest Jewish Web site, which gets millions of hits a year. They won't shake hands with members of the opposite sex, but they move in the highest government circles. They avoid college, because Schneerson—who himself studied at the Sorbonne and the University of Berlin—decided that America's college campuses would have a detrimental effect on his followers. Yet they jet all over the world on a moment's notice and live in the most exotic, un-Jewish locales. They are zealous about their own *kashrut,* but they open their arms to Jews who eat pork and drive on Shabbat.

The Chabad shliach is nonjudgmental and welcoming toward other Jews, while maintaining his own "authentic" credentials through strict adherence to Jewish law. This combination of operational flexibility and personal scrupulousness can be disarmingly compelling. Rabbi David Eliezrie, Chabad emissary to Yorba Linda, California, described a secular American Jewish family's first contact with Chabad emissaries in a 1993 article in *Moment* magazine: "Suddenly they had a guy living next door that looked like their great-grandfather. But this hassid spoke English and he knew the score of last night's Mets game."

There is no school for Chabad shlichim. All the men have rabbinical ordination, but neither they nor their young wives are taught how to be emissaries in any formal way. Still, they don't go into the field unprepared. All shlichim have spent a great part of their teenage years working as camp counselors or Hebrew school teachers in Chabad institutions, often in foreign countries. Young Lubavitch men spend their summer and winter breaks traveling in pairs on the Chabad circuit, staying with shliach families along the way and doing outreach work. The older girls may spend a year or more helping shlichim in a Chabad House far from home.

After years of approaching Jews on the street or leading impromptu Torah classes in far-flung locales, a young Chabadnik has a pretty good idea of whether he or she is ready to commit to a lifetime of similar work.

Still, no amount of practice in the field can give a person the key tools for effective Chabad outreach: a ready smile and personal charm. To be a shliach, you have to have the right stuff. Rabbi Manis Friedman, educational director of the Bais Chana women's institute in Minneapolis, tells the story of a young hopeful who approached the late Rabbi Chaim Mordechai Hodakov, Schneerson's right-hand man, to apply for a shliach position. Rabbi Hodakov asked the young man whether he was a good organizer. The man said no. Did he speak the language of the country he was asking to be sent to? Again, no. Could he keep accounts, did he know how to fundraise, did he have any particular skills at all? The answer to all these questions was a shame-faced no. In that case, Rabbi Hodakov told him, you'll be a fine shliach, because you're not going to offer a service— you're going to offer yourself. "Being a shliach means that you have surrendered, permanently, your personal identity," says Friedman. "You are no longer a private citizen; you belong to the Jewish people."

The first big jump in Chabad's outreach campaign came in the mid-1960s, shortly after President John F. Kennedy established the Peace Corps. It's not a coincidence, Chabad officials say. Both projects were drawing on the same idealism, the same urge among a generation of young people to be of public service. The Rebbe gave further urgency to shlichus as the movement's main priority in 1972, when he spoke at a gathering convened to celebrate his seventieth birthday. Instead of retiring, Schneerson challenged his followers to establish 71 new institutions in the coming year, "and then 200, and then 400, and so on, and so on." They did, and more. People now in their twenties and thirties who grew up in Chabad were raised with the ideal of shlichus. "Growing up in Chabad today, you know that the greatest thing you can do is be a shliach," says Shmotkin. "Those who don't have what it takes wish they did."

Despite the personal hardships involved in taking up a faraway emissary assignment, it's also true that being a Chabad shliach has certain advantages for these Hasidic youths. It gives them prestige within their community, and the opportunity to get out into the world and interact with people most Hasidim don't get to know. "There are different levels as to why a person would want to do this," says Rabbi Yitzchok Loewenthal, who was twenty-four when he opened Denmark's first Chabad center in 1996. "The deepest level is wanting to help Jews. On a more simplistic level, it's exciting work. It's multifaceted. You are dealing with people, presenting Judaism to a place where it doesn't exist."

"I find it very challenging and exciting," says Rabbi Levi Wolff, a young New Jersey Chabadnik sent off to Perth, Australia, in 1997. "I wake up every morning ready to conquer. When people ask what I do, I say I'm in marketing. I market Judaism. I can't imagine enjoying anything more."

Both critics and friends of Chabad agree that the movement's ability to attract so many non-observant, well-educated American Jews is due largely to the personalities of the shlichim themselves: their sincerity, their intelligence, their warmth. "They're not in it for the money," says Sam Heilman. "They feel they are doing God's work, and that makes them different from Orthodox Jews. Most Orthodox are ready to look down their noses at the rest of the world. Chabad Jews are ready to look out for the rest of the world."

Rabbi Eric Yoffie, president of the Union of American Hebrew Congregations, chastised his own Reform movement at a national convention in 1999 for not having the same passion and deep commitment to outreach as Chabad. "Many, many Jews will tell you that a Chabad rabbi was the first one to care, to really care, about their spiritual lives," he said. Why, he asked, can't Reform Jews, whose spiritual message is more appropriate to contemporary American life, muster up the same enthusiasm?

Although the shlichim are volunteers and, to a certain extent, self-selecting, those who succeed at it share the same characteristics. If they don't have those qualities, they're not given the best postings, or any at all. People like them. "They have this Teflon quality," says Columbia University journalism professor Ari Goldman, who covered Chabad in the late 1980s and early 1990s as the *New York Times* religion reporter. "It's hard to get criticism to stick to them. Most Jews have a warm spot in their hearts for them."

Harvard Law Professor Alan Dershowitz, who serves as faculty advisor to his campus Chabad House, notes that even Jews who claim they don't like Chabad will heap praises on their local Chabad shliach, as if the two are unrelated. "I've met Chabad rabbis all over the world, and these guys know how to create poster children for Judaism," Dershowitz states.

Certainly, Chabad's growth during the past three decades has had much to do with being in the right place at the right time. Their spiritual teachings and public demonstrations rang true with an entire generation of young Americans who responded in a positive fashion to the same in-your-face expressions of Jewish pride that so embarrassed their parents' generation. "Chabad does things no one else has the gall to do," says Beth Preminger, a recent graduate of Harvard University who says that although she ate at her campus Hillel House for four years straight, it was the Chabad activities she attended. "Hillel has a huge, $8 million building, but there are tons of kids who are too intimidated to walk into it," she says. "But when you go to Chabad for Shabbat dinner, it's very *heimish* [homelike]. You get a spiritual feeling. They welcome everyone, but they still have a definite direction to offer."

In a world plagued by moral relativism, many American Jews respond to the certainty of the Chabad vision. "There's a universal human element here," postulates Manis Friedman. "We live in a society wracked by doubt. At times we celebrate that—it feels sophisticated to doubt. On the other hand, it's demoralizing. When people see a shliach, the first thing they see is the absence of doubt. The shliach does not live in two worlds—people find that endlessly appealing, as well as frightening."

Rabbi Moshe Feller says that when he took up his Chabad emissary position in Minneapolis in 1958, God talk was not yet a regular compo-nent of the American Jewish dialogue. He remembers a meeting he had with a Conservative rabbi who took issue with Feller's claim that the Reform and Conservative schools of that day were not doing a good job of instilling Jewish identity in children. "He asked me, 'Rabbi Feller, how can you be so sure there is a God?' I said, 'Rabbi, if that's how you feel, why are you in the rabbinate?' For us Hasidim our relationship with God is a daily reality. Our job as shlichim is to exude total commitment and sureness about Torah and *mitzvot*. This is the success of Lubavitch—our sincerity, not our knowledge of English grammar and literature."

Jews who greet a new shliach couple in their community with hostil-ity might imagine the new arrivals are seasoned missionaries, backed by a well-funded religious organization. They forget, or don't wish to acknow-ledge, that the shlichim are real people—very young people, often newly-weds—who have left their homes and familiar lifestyle to live in a strange new place, with no friends or family, feeling bewildered, alone, and a lit-tle like animals in a zoo. Will they be accepted? Will their children find friends? Will people think they're touched in the head?

Rabbi Berel Levertov, who opened the Chabad center in Santa Fe,

New Mexico, in 1996 when he was twenty-seven, says that small Jewish community reacted with suspicion when he first arrived. "Orthodox, black hat, you know," he notes, with a wry smile. He tried to dispel the awkwardness by inviting Jews to his Shabbat table. Many refused. "Some people feel that traditional Judaism is not for them. But deep down there's a yearning for just that. Slowly, slowly, people are turning around and becoming more comfortable with us."

Much of the hostility toward Chabad derives from the belief that the movement's real agenda is to convert the rest of the Jewish world to their way of life. "Nothing could be further from the truth," insists Rabbi Yehuda Krinsky, secretary of Chabad's three major institutions and the man regarded as the movement's administrative head. Chabad's mission, shlichim say, is to teach other Jews about Judaism in the hopes that this will awaken their dormant Jewish consciousness and lead them naturally to start doing mitzvahs. According to Chabad teaching, each time a Jew performs a mitzvah the world comes one step closer to the Messianic Age.

"We're not trying to get people to live like us," says Rabbi Loewenthal. "I don't tell people to dress in black coats, or do this or that. I don't see myself here to win adherents to Lubavitch. That's not what the Rebbe taught. People should take steps toward their Judaism at their own speed. Each step has value, and not just as a means to an end."

Disingenuous? A bit, perhaps. As Krinsky admits: "I don't want to say a Jew's level of observance is irrelevant, God forbid. But I believe that once the connection is made, those not yet observant will eventually realize the beauty of a Torah-true life."

Chabad's expansion into the larger American—and world—Jewish scene will continue, at least for the foreseeable future. Their schools continue to turn out hundreds of new graduates every year who are eager, and able, to continue their Rebbe's revolution. Schneerson's death has affected the movement and its followers deeply, but their enthusiasm for the mission he gave them continues unabated. "It's a phenomenon that can't be explained," says Moshe Kotlarsky. "The Rebbe's teachings are so ingrained in the people that you find more every day willing to go on shlichus to farther places, with less grandiose expectations than ever before. One guy just called me. He wants to go to Cyprus. Imagine, he's willing to leave Crown Heights and go spend the rest of his life in Cyprus."

In 1999, Chabad's Jewish Educational Media released a video that celebrated the 312 shliach couples who took up new postings that year. The video opens with shots of airplanes zooming down runways, of families saying good-bye in crowded terminals, of taxis picking up piles of labeled boxes on Crown Heights street corners. The image conveyed is of boundless energy, of unstoppable forward motion: We're coming, and we're coming fast. And the comments made by the young shlichim themselves, all in their early to mid-twenties, are telling.

"We grew up seeing the great expansion of shlichus, of people going out to all these different places, and it gave us the tremendous inspiration to give over our lives for other people," says newly ordained Sholom Ber Rodal, on his way to establish a Chabad center in California. One newly married shlicha, standing outside her Brooklyn home surrounded by suitcases, notes, "It's much easier to stay here in Crown Heights and have a very good life, surrounded by all the *Yiddishkeit* [Judaism], but we want to bring other people closer to *Yiddishkeit*. That's how we were raised."

These young shlichim talk about their fears as well. Rabbi Shmuel Zajac, on his way to a lifetime posting in Wellington, New Zealand, admits that the hardest part of the upcoming move is knowing that he and his new wife are further splitting up two families already torn apart physically by decades on shlichus. "My parents are in Brazil, and my wife's parents are in London," he says, adding quickly, "But we have their support to do the Rebbe's work." Mendel Zarchi, on his way to establish a new Chabad center in Puerto Rico with his wife Rochel, remarks candidly: "You ask if, on my own, do I have the strength to undertake this trip? The answer is, I don't know. But the Rebbe is with us, giving us the strength to go forward."

One after another, these smiling couples pick up their bags, their babies, and their Jewish books, and head out to strange new cities they will soon call home. They may not know the language. They may be moving halfway around the world from parents and siblings. But as Mendy Vogel says, on his way to Dallas, Texas, with his new wife Sarah, "The reward is awesome. Knowing that you are changing people's lives forever."

WE'VE GOT BOCA COVERED!:
Chabad Hits South Florida

If Chabad goes where the Jews are, then Chabad had to go to South Florida. Home to 700,000 Jews, most of them retired transplants from "up north," this seventy-mile, three-county coastal stretch from Miami to Palm Beach is the second largest Jewish community in the nation after New York City. One out of four people in Palm Beach County is Jewish. In south Palm Beach County—Boca Raton and neighboring Delray Beach—it's one out of two. Most of these Jews arrived over the past twenty years, as Florida's Jewish population began a steady shift northward from crime-plagued Miami. In 1970, Boca Raton had one synagogue. By 2000, it had seventeen. South Florida's Jews are an affluent community, a community that gives to Jewish causes. And despite the stereotypes, it is an increasingly young community. Much of the new Jewish growth is pre-retirement, including single professionals and young families who have followed their retired parents south. In 1979, when Boca's Hillel Day School opened its doors, administrators were hard pressed to sign up thirty-three students. In 1999, the school had to cut off enrollment at seven hundred. The overflow headed for the Donna Klein Jewish Academy, the Torah Academy of Boca Raton, the Yeshiva High

School, the Reform day school at Temple Beth El, or the new Conservative-affiliated Solomon Schechter school.

Or they headed to Chabad. In 1960, Florida became one of the first places outside the New York metropolitan area to receive a Chabad shliach when the Lubavitcher Rebbe sent Rabbi Avrohom Korf to Miami. By 2001 the state boasted sixty-seven Chabad centers, most of them concentrated in South Florida. And those Chabad operations attracted big donors, who funded spectacular building projects. In 1994, the $10 million Shul of Bal Harbour opened north of Miami Beach. In 1999 a $4 million Chabad synagogue went up in Boca Raton. Two years later a $3.5 million Chabad center broke ground up the road in Boynton Beach. In contrast to its niche status in some other regions with large Jewish populations, Chabad has become an integral part of the Jewish community in South Florida. Its shuls, summer camps, adult Torah classes, and holiday activities are listed in all the mainstream Jewish publications; its supporters number among the community's most socially prominent and philanthropic.

In Boca Raton, three of the city's seventeen synagogues are run by Chabad, under the supervision of Rabbis Zalman Bukiet and Moshe Denburg. They met in yeshiva in Crown Heights in the mid-eighties, and headed out on shlichus together in 1989 when they were both twenty-six. They've stuck together ever since, Denburg heading up the spanking new Morris and Anita Kaufman Chabad Center in central Boca, while Bukiet runs the Jeff Wellman Chabad Center less than three miles away in West Boca. The two rabbis maintain one bank account. They even put their desks next to each other in the same room. In 1999, as their operation blossomed, they brought in a third Chabad shliach, Rabbi Ruvi New, to direct Chabad activities in East Boca.

"We've got Boca covered!" booms Bukiet, throwing his arms out wide and grinning broadly as he ushers a visitor into his West Boca center on Kimberly Boulevard, inside the Boca Hamptons Shopping Plaza. "We could have ten Chabad Houses here," he declares. "Eighty percent of the Jews are unaffiliated. We could reach them all."

When Moshe Denburg arrived in Boca in 1989, the city was not yet at the top of the American Jewish radar. But he'd had his "eye on Boca" for a while. He'd spent time in South Florida as a yeshiva student, and his brother Yossi was already the Chabad shliach in nearby Coral Springs. An opportunity came up when Anita Kaufman, a major Chabad donor from Long Island, announced she was building a second home in Boca and was willing to support a Chabad rabbi there. Denburg seized upon that open-ing, and when Boca's Century Village retirement community announced it was looking for a part-time rabbi, he grabbed that job for his old yeshiva buddy Bukiet.

Denburg initially held prayer services and ran Chabad business from a 1,100-square-ft. rented apartment he shared with his wife and two chil-dren. A folding screen used to separate hospital beds served as his make-shift *mechitza*. He held Rosh Hashanah services that first year in his kitchen. In 1991 the two rabbis moved Denburg's "synagogue" into a pub-lic school music room. For the next two years the rabbis had to move all the music equipment out every Friday afternoon to make room for Shab-bat services, and then haul it back in again on Saturday night.

By 1993, the two shlichim had built up enough of a following to each rent his own space. By the end of that year their operations had grown so much that they were ready to build a Chabad center that would make a major statement in the community. Denburg appealed to Elliot Loewen-stern, a local man who had donated a Torah scroll to his shul, and asked him to be on Chabad's building committee. "He asked who else was on the committee, and I said, 'You're it.'" Loewenstern ended up giving a substantial amount for the synagogue land, and Anita Kaufman donated $1 million for the 24,000-square-foot building itself. Inside, the Dora and Jacob C. Cohen Synagogue, named after a prominent New York—and Miami-based philanthropic couple, was built with money from the Cohens' grandchildren, Boca residents Arthur and Ellen Turkish.

Few of Chabad's biggest donors would call themselves Orthodox, in Boca Raton or anywhere else. So why do these people give such large sums to a movement that represents a brand of Judaism they don't prac-tice? In Arthur Turkish's case it was to honor his grandfather, an obser-vant Jew who immigrated from Poland to New York in 1900 and became a real estate mogul. In later life, Turkish says, his grandfather became "close to the Rebbe" and began giving large sums to Chabad. When Cohen died, Turkish was left the sole trustee of his charitable trust, and decided to spend the money for causes his grandfather would have favored. "I consider myself Conservative, but through my grandfather I developed an affinity for the people who are the real foundation of Judaism," he says. "Chabad doesn't get distracted, it doesn't get lost. They will always be there." Turkish has now switched his synagogue member-ship from his former Conservative congregation to Chabad, out of "love for their dedication," a dedication he says he doesn't have, and doesn't feel pressured to have.

Meeting Anita Kaufman, one would not think "Chabad." She dresses in leather pants and high heels, gives a lot of money to the Federation and Hadassah, belongs to B'nai B'rith, the Anti-Defamation League, and the American Israel Public Affairs Committee, and is the founding partner of a New York-based venture capital fund. But inside her magnificent Italianate home in Boca's exclusive Polo Club community, ten feet away from a painting of a nude woman, in between the bonsai trees and Oriental vases, hangs a large portrait of the Lubavitcher Rebbe. "We all respected Schneerson," she says. "Of course, some called him an evangelist, but he had influence all over the world." Kaufman works hard to dispel anti-Hasidic sentiment among her Jewish friends, taking them to Denburg's *shul* with her, introducing them to the two young Chabad rabbis. Kaufman says the Jews who come to Boca's Chabad center are the same kind of people who show up for Chabad in Long Island. "The big heavy-hitters who give money aren't Orthodox, but they remember from their parents' time," she says. "They won't go to an Orthodox shul, but they feel comfortable at Chabad. Many of their kids have drifted away from Judaism, and they blame themselves. I said to a friend the other day, 'It's not you and me that will keep Judaism alive, it's Chabad and Orthodoxy.'"

To that end, Bukiet, Denburg, and New run an impressive array of programs out of their three Chabad centers. First was a Hebrew school, begun with thirteen children in 1989. Today, forty to fifty children come to Bukiet's building for Tuesday and Thursday afternoon classes, and more than ninety children are enrolled in the Sunday classes at Denburg's Chabad center. Three hundred children attend Boca's Gan Israel Chabad summer camp, and there is a thriving teen program, run by a fourth shliach brought down from New York as Boca's youth director. Bukiet, Denburg, and New have three hundred dues-paying members between their three congregations, but Bukiet insists "we don't push membership," relying instead on voluntary contributions from people who appreciate the work they do. So far, that method has worked, Bukiet says.

They have built their clientele the same way every other Chabad shliach does—by offering programs people want at little or no cost. When Chabad came to Boca, other synagogues were offering Hebrew school classes, but they all required that families join their congregations first, a heavy financial commitment that not all Jewish parents were able, or willing, to make. "You have single moms, whatever," Denburg points out. "So we found our niche—no synagogue membership, just a flat fee for classes."

One salient feature of the South Florida Jewish community, and Boca in particular, is that everyone seems to get along. Chabad runs joint programs with the Jewish Federation of South Palm Beach County, such as an Israeli Prayer Day that drew thousands of people in the fall of 2000. "We take our travellng matzah factory to every synagogue school," Bukiet says, "including the Reform. We are very much a part of this community."

Attorney Stephen Melcer, former head of the local Jewish Community Relations Council, has been involved in Boca's Jewish life since 1980. He attributes the good relations that prevail to the fact that this is a relatively new Jewish community, with no old axes to grind, and he points to the flexible personalities of the rabbis who live and work there. "The rabbis put community rather than their differences first," he says. Bukiet agrees: "In New York it's a turf war. Here there are so many Jews, and the Conservative and Reform synagogues are so strong, that they don't see us as a threat. And I'm not here to be a threat. I do programs in their synagogues, and they know there are certain lines I won't cross. It's not personal."

Chabad in Boca has a particularly close relationship with Orthodox Rabbi Kenneth Brander of the Boca Raton Synagogue. Denburg coteaches a class with him on "Torah giants of the twentieth century," and the men put up flyers advertising each other's programs. When the Boca Raton Synagogue built its mikvah, it shelled out an additional $30,000 to build an underground cistern so that Chabad women could use it, too. The president of Brander's Yeshiva High School is a member of Denburg's synagogue. Many children who attend Yeshiva High School are Lubavitchers, and the school serves *chalav Yisrael* in its cafeteria. "Often the Orthodox establishment and Chabad are at odds with each other," Brander notes. "That's a horrendous situation, and it's never happened here."

But Brander stops short of delivering a blanket endorsement of Lubavitcher Hasidism. He, like Melcer, attributes Chabad's appeal in Boca to the personalities of the shlichim rather than to the movement's intrinsic message. "There's a certain selflessness with which they embrace people, a lack of judgment that makes people feel comfortable." And although he says that this welcoming attitude "is the ultimate," and adds that "it's something we are also trying to create," and although the Boca Raton Synagogue now sponsors a *kollel,* or postordination institute for young rabbis, as well as a beginners' *minyan* (prayer quorum) to attract the newly observant, Brander insists that he is "not trying to emulate Chabad." The Orthodox movement is responding to its own internal dynamics, he says, making its own changes without outside influence. In fact, he adds, Chabad's biggest shortcoming stems from its successful outreach. Once Jews become observant through Chabad, he says, they are no longer satisfied with the less rigorous Jewish education offered by the Chabad rabbis and their wives, or the more simple services of the Chabad learners' congregations. They want standard Orthodoxy—like what he offers. "Families may become observant through Chabad, but after a few years they come to us," he states. "Rabbi Denburg jokes that we should put him in our outreach budget because he brings so many people to our congregation."

Relationships between Chabad and the Orthodox community may be cozier than usual in Boca Raton, but the cooperation is more one-way when it comes to the city's Reform and Conservative congregations. Bukiet may be happy to send his matzah bakery and shofar factory to Reform and Conservative classrooms, but neither he nor Denburg—nor any other Chabad rabbi—would invite a non-Orthodox rabbi to address his own congregation or teach in his school. "That's a problem," Bukiet admits, his brow tightening into a rare furrow. "But it's better to bring up things that unite us, not divide us."

One thing that did divide Jewish leaders in South Palm Beach County was Chabad's refusal to sit on the local rabbinical council, which consists of rabbis from all Jewish movements. That so angered Reform Rabbi Bruce Warshal, former executive director of the Boca Federation and now publisher of South Florida's *Jewish Journal,* that he blocked a funding request from Moshe's brother Yossi, who wanted Federation money for his Chabad school in Margate. "If a rabbi runs a day school and will not sit on the rabbinical council because he does not recognize me as a Reform rabbi, he does not deserve public money," Warshal states. Warshal and Denburg finally came to a compromise. Denburg agreed to sign new Federation bylaws and the rift was healed. But Chabad still doesn't sit on the council.

Getting past people's prejudices against Hasidism, and Orthodox Judaism in general, is still a challenge, Bukiet says. Like other Chabad *shlichim* working in largely non-observant communities, Bukiet and Denburg are more tolerant of ritual lapses than they might be in Crown

Heights. Recognizing that most of the women who attend his services come from egalitarian congregations, Bukiet keeps his *mechitza* low. During Torah services, he sends the Torah over to the women's side for them to touch and kiss, acting more like a modern Orthodox than a Hasidic rabbi. His wife gives talks on the weekly Torah portion—not from the pulpit, which would be forbidden in an Orthodox *shul,* but during the Kiddush after the service, which is still not customary. "Guys visit from Brooklyn and ask, how can I do that? But I don't do anything against the law. I may push the envelope to get people over their hang-ups." Even with the concessions he does make, Bukiet realizes that some Jews simply won't pray in a gender-separated synagogue. "I was brought up that way, so to me it's normal," he says. "They weren't, and I respect that."

Basically, Bukiet says, he and his fellow shlichim spend a lot of time undoing the damage caused by a typical American Jewish upbringing. "Everybody I meet has had something negative happen to them once in synagogue, or with a rabbi, and they didn't go back for twenty-five years," he relates. "People left Judaism because of the stuffiness, the coldness, the attitude that Judaism is a business. It's a shame. We need to create a bridge for Jews to come back to Judaism, by showing them the joy in it. Sometimes, when you bring a Jew into an Orthodox synagogue, he gets embarrassed. He doesn't know what to do. I want to bring him in and make him feel like a million dollars."

No question, Bukiet says, it's hard to get someone in the door the first time. "But once they're in, they see the great atmosphere, the warmth, the excitement, the camaraderie. They meet me, and they see I'm normal. That's a big part of my job—showing people you can be religious and not go crazy. You don't have to wear a black hat and live in Brooklyn. Chabad is like the Florida lottery—we don't want to change your life, just how you live it."

At 8:30 A.M. one morning in March, Rabbi Sholom Lipskar is already teaching his second lesson of the day. He is sitting with a congregant in his private office at the Shul of Bal Harbour, the elegant new Chabad center he directs just north of Miami Beach. The two men are talking about nothing. Well, not nothing exactly—nothingness. The nature of God. The aspects of the soul. The unity of all existence. The kind of thing two middle-aged guys might tend to talk about on a blazing-hot, blue-skied

Tuesday morning in Miami. "Space, like time, has its own substance," Lipskar begins, leafing through the *Tanya* to the chapter they are discussing. "When we talk about 'nothing,' we mean a great oneness. When we talk about Hashem [God], we say *echad*, he is one." But that "one" encompasses all of existence, Lipskar explains.

"Physicality has a perception of its own independence. But a part of the soul recognizes its connectedness, that everything you see is God. There is nothing outside God." According to this philosophy, every Jewish soul has the constant, if unspoken, desire to do Jewish deeds, even if the Jewish person is completely unaware of it. "Where does that desire come from?" Lipskar asks. Why does a non-observant Jewish man agree to wrap phylacteries around his arm when a Chabad yeshiva student approaches him in the street, or—he nods at the forty-something man sitting in front of him—begin studying Jewish mysticism in his middle years? "The soul feels that deep connection to its essence. To Hashem."

Lipskar has a full day ahead of him. At 10:30, he has a private meeting with a troubled congregant. At 10:45, he takes fifteen minutes to make a small dent in the huge pile of papers on his desk. "Faye, we got the tefillin for that bar mitzvah boy, didn't we?" he asks his secretary, crumpling a pink note in his hand. At 11:00, another Chabad rabbi calls to ask how to obtain working papers for a foreign employee. At 11:15 a filmmaker calls to discuss a promotional video. At 11:30 a congregant calls to ask what blessing he should say at the groundbreaking for his new home. At noon there's a funeral, at 12:30 another *Tanya* class, at 2:30 a film interview, at 3:30 a meeting with a computer programmer who's setting up Chabad's new database, at 4:00 Lipskar teaches his fourth lesson of the day, and at 5:00 he officiates at a *bris*. Then dinner, and a 7:30 class to give on the weekly Torah portion.

It's a busy schedule, and the man's already been up for thirty-six hours. He flew to Los Angeles the previous morning to give a talk on Jewish mysticism, and then took the red-eye back to Miami, landing at 5 A.M. and coming straight to the *shul* for morning prayers before launching into his regular workday. At 1 P.M. he pauses in the middle of a Tanya discussion, apologizes, and puts a few eyedrops in his beet-red eyes. "I'm not tired," he insists. "It's just my eyes." A Chabad shliach would never let a small thing like flying back and forth across the continental United States stand between him and doing the Rebbe's work.

Lipskar is one of the luminaries of the middle generation of Chabad shlichim, men and women now in their fifties and early sixties who went out on shlichus in the 1960s and early '70s. This is still the generation in charge of most national Chabad institutions, the main theologians, heads of yeshivas, and the emissaries who head up Chabad in most states and countries. They look behind them for spiritual inspiration to the handful of elderly shlichim still alive who made up the first generation of emissaries sent out by Schneerson in the 1950s. Ahead of them, a much larger body of shlichim in their late twenties and thirties is expanding the field of Chabad operations tenfold.

Russian-born, Toronto-bred Lipskar spent his teenage years in Crown Heights and was sent to Florida by Schneerson in 1969 to teach in Avrohom Korf's Miami Beach yeshiva. At the time, the 250,000 Jews in Miami–Dade County made up 20 percent of the gerneral population, the largest percentage they would ever reach. By the late nineties, those numbers had dropped to 130,000, as the most elderly Jews died off and new arrivals headed north to Broward and Palm Beach counties. Jews had deep roots in Miami, going back to the city's founding in 1896, when most of its merchants were Jewish. But Miami Beach, created in 1913, struggled hard to keep Jews, blacks, and other non-WASPs out. Restrictive property deeds kept Jews south of Fifth Street well into the late 1940s, when Jewish veterans returning from World War II forced the Florida state legislature to overturn anti-Semitic zoning regulations.

The postwar boom swelled Miami's Jewish population from less than 10,000 in 1940 to 140,000 by 1960. But even with the assistance of the legal system, strong anti-Semitic feelings and restrictive property deeds persisted.

In 1981, Sholom Lipskar left his position as principal of Korf's yeshiva in order to start his own congregation eight miles north in Bal Harbour. When he and his wife bought a home in a tony gated community nearby, not only were they the second Jewish family there, but their property deed stated that the home was not to be sold to anyone with more than 25 percent Jewish blood. "When we first came to Bal Harbour, every time we walked down the street, people stopped to look at us," Lipskar relates. "They'd think, what is this guy doing here, in this long black coat? Only because of a sense of self-security, pride in my Jewishness, knowing I was part of a mission, was I able to keep walking down the street without feeling totally inept and offensive." The antipathy toward anything "too Jewish" extended to the Jewish community as well.

"When I listed the Jewish mayor of Bal Harbour as a member of this *shul,* he called to say his pastor at the Church by the Sea was upset, because he's a member there, too," Lipskar says.

Lipskar was invited to Bal Harbour by Montreal businessman Sam Greenberg, who had seen Lipskar conduct services in Miami Beach. For three years Lipskar held services in a card room at the Beau Rivage Motor Inn. Lipskar's wife Chanie would bring in huge pots of her homemade *cholent* to feed the worshipers, keeping the traditional Eastern European Sabbath stew warm on the room's radiator. It was months before they gathered a *minyan,* and a year before Lipskar drew a salary. "I'd go around the building, promising people anything, just so they'd come to services," Greenberg says.

Greenberg took flak from the local Jewish community for sponsoring the young Hasidic couple. "People said I was debasing the value of the community," he recalls. "How could I bring these black coats into the neighborhood?" According to Greenberg, some of the biggest complainers later became major donors to Chabad.

The congregation grew, until weekly services overflowed the small card room. Soon the city of Bal Harbour, which had formerly excluded Jews, was witnessing daily *minyans* at the Beau Rivage, an annual Chanukah menorah in the town square, Passover Seders in the hotel's dining room, Purim parties in the hotel's shopping arcade, and a *sukkah* on its ocean-front sun deck. When the hotel was slated for demolition, Lipskar moved his congregation, now known as "the Shul," to a room at the Sheraton Bal Harbour. When his rapidly expanding membership threatened to swamp that space as well, he moved his operation to a third rented location in a former shoe store, while plans were made to build a permanent home.

In 1994, on the site of the former Sea Patio Hotel on Collins Avenue, the $10 million Shul of Bal Harbour opened its doors. It was a stunning achievement, a massive three-story structure faced entirely in Jerusalem stone, based on the architecture of three Polish synagogues that had been destroyed by the Nazis. The Shul could never have been built if the local Jewish community did not include a critical mass of wealthy Jews who were willing to give serious money to build an Orthodox synagogue, and who were also willing to show up regularly for services. The main services are no longer a "beginners' *minyan*" like that which obtains in most Chabad Houses, where a Chabad rabbi stands in front of a somewhat shy group of newcomers, prompting them gently through the prayer service.

This is a vibrant, knowledgeable Orthodox congregation. Israeli prime ministers have spoken from the Shul's pulpit. Vice-presidential candidate Senator Joe Lieberman spoke there on the Saturday before the 2000 presidential elections.

More than 1,000 people come through the Shul's front door every week. The domed sanctuary holds more than the congregation's 400 dues-paying members and is packed on Shabbat. The women's section is not partitioned off, but raised above and around the central floor, affording the women a clear view of the entire service. Everything about the building is elegant, even regal. The mikvah, the library that holds Lipskar's popular Tuesday evening Torah portion class, the auditorium that hosts bar mitzvahs and wedding receptions, even the bathrooms, are beautifully designed and graciously appointed. That's very much on purpose. The Lubavitcher Rebbe told his shlichim that aesthetics are key to attracting American Jews. If shlichim are going to construct a synagogue, a *mikvah,* a school, it should be the most beautiful one they can afford.

In a community like Bal Harbour, home to an affluent, urbane Jewish community, the Shul couldn't be a little Brooklyn *shteibel.* "This is a big enough place to have the impact necessary in a large community," Lipskar says. "It's a challenge to each Jew that drives past—it reminds him of his Jewishness. If we'd stayed in our small storefront, we would not be able to reach the tens of thousands of people we expect to reach."

The congregation has come a long way from the days when Sam Greenberg had to bribe worshipers with coffee and cake. More than twenty-five classes a week are offered in Torah, *Tanya,* Hebrew, and Kabbalah. Hundreds of people show up. Classes are also offered in Spanish, and the Shul has a separate Sephardic *minyan* for the area's growing South American population. Much like Manhattan's modern Orthodox Lincoln Square Synagogue, or the Conservative B'nai Jeshurun, the Shul of Bal Harbour is known for its *shidduchim,* or matchmaking. It holds Singles' Shabbatons, or weekend-long events, and Friday night services for singles. The congregation reaches out to the elderly and to the Russian community, handing out thousands of menorahs at Chanukah and boxes of matzah at Passover.

Bal Harbour resident David Wolf, thirty-five, says what he likes best about the Shul is Lipskar's monthly "*nachas* report," when the rabbi announces all the congregation's good news from the previous four weeks. "It's great to be part of a shul where things like that happen," he says. Wolf grew up in a Conservative Miami family and says he became observant "slowly," mainly due to his relationship with Chabad and Rabbi Lipskar, whom he met through his newly observant sister. The first time he went to the Shul, he was stunned when Lipskar gave a sermon about the weekly Torah portion. "I was used to sermons about politics, or jokes, things that have nothing to do with Torah," he says. "I'd never heard a rabbi talk about Torah before. It made me keep coming back." During that same service, Wolf says Lipskar taught him about the Jewish tradition of hospitality. At the end of prayers, Lipskar stood up and asked: Who needs a meal? who can offer a meal? "I'd never seen that," Wolf marvels. "People going to other people's homes for Shabbat, when they didn't know each other."

Wolf started to attend classes at the Shul's downtown Miami branch. From a man who says he "wasn't able to open a prayer book," Wolf now prides himself on knowing how to pray the three daily services, and says it's something he's happy to be able to give his children. "For my personal growth, this has been the greatest thing to happen to me," he says. "My friends tell me I'm crazy, I'm losing my mind, what's happening to me? Meanwhile, I hope some of my 'preaching' rubs off on them."

Lipskar has become a kind of Hasidic superstar among a certain segment of not-yet-but-hopefully-soon-observant Jews. His Tuesday evening Torah class draws between fifty and a hundred people. At one point it drew two-to-three hundred, but that was when it was one of the only classes offered. Also, the class is now taped and sent out weekly to subscribers, and is broadcast live on the Internet.

People start showing up a half-hour before class begins, milling around in the hallways, checking each other out. The class is free, but an elderly Hasidic woman sits in front of the door with a *pushke,* or charity box, asking for $5 donations. "You're in for a real treat," one thirty-something woman whispers to her girlfriend. "He's fantastic."

Rabbi Lipskar stands in front of the room, leaning casually on the podium. He's wearing a gray suit, a red-blue-and-yellow-striped tie, and a simple black yarmulke. Aside from the fact that he's better dressed than anyone else in the room, there's nothing about his appearance that suggests he comes from a different world than the one his audience belongs to. The Torah portion for tonight is *V'yechi,* the final chapter in Genesis, which describes Jacob's death in the land of Egypt. "The Torah says that Jacob *lived* in Egypt," he begins. "He wasn't just there, he really *lived* there. The years he was in Egypt—seventeen—have the same numeric value as *tov,* the Hebrew word for 'good.' But how is it possible that Jacob lived his best years in Egypt, in an environment so corrupt, so degraded, that they enslaved the Jewish people?"

Lipskar moves on to a deeper treatment of his twin themes for the evening: freedom versus enslavement, and the individual versus the collective. What does the story of Jacob's death teach about a son's relationship to his father? What does it reveal about a Jew's responsibility to the world? Lipskar speaks softly, conversationally. For three decades he's been presenting the most difficult concepts in Jewish and Hasidic thought to people with little or no background, and he knows how to make it compelling. That's what Chabad is good at, he says. "Chabad takes the most esoteric concepts and puts them into language that anyone can understand. Most Americans don't know Hebrew or Yiddish. When I give my talks, I make sure I translate every single word. When you talk to people in language that is accessible, and the content is Jewishness as it is permeated with the warmth and light of Hasidus, they hear the truth in it."

Lipskar finds that the Jews who show up for his classes today know more Jewish information than those of twenty years ago. "I'm dealing with a more sophisticated group of learners, which means it takes more time to prepare what I'm going to teach," he says. But that's not as significant as the greater spiritual yearning he notices. "There's been an extraordinary change of attitude among so-called nonaffiliated Jews," he says. "Twenty years ago, in order to get someone to wrap tefillin, you had to get into a real dog-and-pony discussion. You had to talk about the intellectual implications, the historical process, you had to prove it: Where does it say it in the text? Is it in the Five Books or is it rabbinic? And it usually came back to a discussion of who created the world or what happened in the Holocaust. Today people are much more receptive. When I put tefillin on someone for the first time and I ask why he never did it before, he says because no one asked him to."

Like every Lubavitcher, Lipskar believes that humankind is on the verge of a great spiritual awakening, predicted by the Rebbe and borne out by the surprising success of Chabad centers around the world. The raw materials are there. The collective will is primed. "All we need is the manpower. We simply don't have enough hands to put tefillin on everyone."

CHAPTER 3

TAKING IT TO THE STREETS:

Mitzvah *Tanks, Tefillin, and Talking to Strangers*

"Excuse me, are you Jewish?" Sixteen-year-old Mendel Wilhelm stares intently into the face of the man he's stopped on a busy sidewalk in downtown Portland, Oregon. Rebuffed by a polite, if cursory, "No, I'm not," Mendel smiles briefly, turns away, and continues his quick, purposeful march down the street, a short, stolid figure whose white button-down shirt, black suit and hat, and flying *tzitzit*—the ritual fringes worn by Orthodox men— are an incongruous sight on this blazing-hot July day in the Pacific Northwest.

It's Friday afternoon, which to a Lubavitch kid means it's time for *mivtzoim,* or "campaigning." Lubavitch schools typically end for the week by noon Friday, releasing students for an afternoon of street outreach. Beginning right after their bar mitzvah, Lubavitch boys tramp through city streets and office buildings every Friday afternoon, looking for Jewish men they can persuade to put on tefillin, or phylacteries, the pair of small leather boxes and straps containing phrases from Torah that observant Jewish men place on their heads and wrap around their left arms during morning prayers. Lubavitch girls stand on street corners or in shopping malls handing out Shabbat candles to Jewish women, along with instructions in how to light them correctly. This early training in street outreach is just as central to Lubavitch educational goals as is learning Torah, Talmud, and the teachings of the Rebbe. Just about every Lubavitch kid today says he or she plans on becoming a shliach, and by the time these young people finish high school, they will have had years of practical experience in the kind of outreach skills they'll need to run their own Chabad Houses.

Mendel comes from a venerable Crown Heights Lubavitch family. During the school year he studies in Brooklyn. This July he chose to join two dozen other students his age at a six-week summer yeshiva program run by Rabbi Moshe Wilhelm, his uncle and the Chabad director in Portland. It's rare to find a Lubavitch boy Mendel's age who just sits home all summer. If they have any expectation of getting a good shliach position in the future, they'll spend their summer breaks working as counselors at Chabad camps, helping out shlichim in outposts, or augmenting their studies in a summer yeshiva program.

The boys in the Portland program bunk down in cots Rabbi Wilhelm and his wife set up in their three-room schoolhouse, which during the academic year functions as a Jewish day school. The yeshiva classes are held in a kind of semipermanent tent attached to the Chabad House, where the boys sit for hours on end, cooled by electric fans as they pore over pages of Talmud and Maimonides. Their teachers are three young rabbinical students, including twenty-year-old Motti Wilhelm, Rabbi Wilhelm's eldest son, who has been returning home each summer from his studies in Crown Heights to help run the school. The boys' day starts at 6:50 A.M. with a trip to the therapy pool at the local Jewish Community Center, which also happens to be a kosher *mikvah,* or ritual bath. (Although mikvahs are mainly used by observant women, who visit them monthly after menstruation ceases, many Hasidic men immerse daily before morning prayers.) Then it's back to the Chabad House for an hour of Hasidic study, an hour of prayer, a quick breakfast, two hours of Talmud, lunch break, more Talmud, a little exercise, dinner, and then more study. "We give them two hours a day outside, playing baseball or basketball, but it's really hard to drag them away from their books," says Rabbi Wilhelm.

Four evenings a week, as a further exercise in community outreach, the yeshiva invites men and women from the local Jewish community to drop by and study with the boys for free. Each boy sits down with two or three adults, some of them old enough to be his grandparents, and takes them painstakingly through the Hebrew text, explaining the Jewish concepts and throwing in the Rebbe's commentaries. The boys prepare the evening's text ahead of time with their teachers, so they know how to convey the information concisely, with the right Hasidic twist.

"It feels great," insists one local woman in her sixties, who has been coming to the study sessions all summer. She says she doesn't feel awkward learning about Judaism from a fifteen-year-old boy. "They're very bright." Another local man, who has been coming to Chabad activities in Portland for more than a year, says that the boys' evening tutorials confirmed what he'd already come to expect from Chabad. "These people really care, and they know how to explain things, no matter how little knowledge we have. They bring us to a place where we can enjoy our religion, and they ask for nothing in return. The rabbi hasn't asked me for a cent. I haven't run into that in any other Jewish organization."

This Friday, classes are over by noon and the boys are wolfing down a hot lunch of meatballs and noodle kugel, getting ready to head downtown with their tefillin bags. The boys will be taking the bus to Pioneer Courthouse Square, a renovated public plaza in the heart of Portland that is filled on a typical Friday afternoon with chess players, street musicians, lunching secretaries, punk skateboarders, and homeless teenagers. It's their last week in the city, and the pressure is on to see how many Jewish men they can persuade to put on tefillin. Some of the boys have been keeping count over the summer, and it's a matter of pride if they can claim more than one or two success stories each week. Street outreach comes more easily to some boys than to others, but they all have to do it. It's part of growing up Lubavitch.

But how do you do it? Do you just walk up to every man in the street, and ask if he's Jewish? Not really, explains Motti Wilhelm, who at age twenty has been doing this kind of street outreach for more than ten years. "You look at the guy first," he says. "Someone who's obviously not Jewish, maybe you won't ask. If he's Chinese or Japanese, for example, he's probably not Jewish. After a while, you begin to know the look." After the initial visual screening, Motti says, there's a second clue. Most non-Jews, asked whether they're Jewish, will say no and continue walking. "The guy who says, 'Why do you want to know?' is probably Jewish."

Other boys use similar spotting tactics. One student says that on Purim he goes to college campuses and stands outside the student union, wishing everyone who passes a happy holiday. "If the guy looks blank, I say, 'Have a nice day.' If he reacts in any way, then I jump!" Chabad's Friday afternoon tefillin campaigns have been going on since June 1967, when the Rebbe first asked Jewish men all over the world to pray daily with tefillin in order to protect Israel during the Six-Day War. It was the first of ten major "mitzvah campaigns" proclaimed by Schneerson between 1967 and 1976 that marked Chabad's massive outreach push into the ranks of the Jewish unaffiliated.

In the 1950s and early '60s Schneerson had sponsored outreach campaigns to promote observance of Jewish holidays. The "mitzvah campaigns" were different; they focused on an individual's private Jewish observance. Schneerson chose mitzvahs that were central to Jewish life and easy to perform, and asked his followers to embark on a mass public relations campaign to encourage non-observant Jews to adopt them. The campaigns included lighting Shabbat candles, putting up mezuzahs, studying Torah, keeping kosher, giving charity, filling one's home with Jewish books, keeping the laws of family purity, loving one's fellow Jews, and giving children a Jewish education. Schneerson's enthusiasm for launching these campaigns was fueled by his desire to revitalize a world Jewish community decimated by the Holocaust, an inferno he, his wife, and father-in-law narrowly escaped. Many shlichim see it as their responsibility to wrap tefillin around the arms of the same number of Jewish men as were murdered by the Nazis.

As each new mitzvah campaign was announced, Lubavitchers hit the streets to spread their Rebbe's word, repeating Schneerson's exhortation to the non-observant: Even if you are not committed to a Torah lifestyle, do one mitzvah today. Critics from the Orthodox world looked askance at the Rebbe's campaigns, believing that it cheapened religious practice to encourage non-observant Jews to perform isolated rituals without adopting the total lifestyle. What good is putting tefillin on a man who will then go and eat a cheeseburger? Doesn't one cancel out the other? To these critics Lubavitchers respond that each mitzvah, in and of itself, is a deed of cosmic significance that activates a person's preexisting connection to God. It is a holy act, worth doing for any reason. Not only that, but one person performing one mitzvah could be the key event that tips the scales of universal goodness and ushers in the Messianic Age.

This theological underpinning gives particular urgency to Chabad street outreach and makes it easier to understand why Lubavitchers rarely take no for an answer. They say they prefer a negative reaction to none at all, because it indicates that the Jewish spark hidden deep in the unobservant person's soul is itching to get out. In *The Mystical Dimension,** Chabad theologian and philosophy professor Jacob Immanuel Schochet writes: "One must speak with fellow-Jews about Torah and mitzvot, and, if unsuccessful, speak again. Even if someone should react antagonistically, do not be discouraged. On the contrary: his antagonism only proves that he is affected."

Street outreach must be conducted "with vigor," Schochet advises, but also gently, with a pleasant smile. Chabad philosophy teaches that a Jew naturally wants to do mitzvahs, even though he may object on the surface. If he continues to object, it's because the Lubavitcher hasn't made a true soul connection. "When not successful at first, one must realize that the fault lies not with the other, but within yourself," Rabbi Schneerson said many times. "The other is receptive, but because your own words 'do not come from the heart,' that is why 'they do not enter the heart.'"

The tefillin campaign looks different today than when it was first instituted. In the early years, Lubavitchers stood on street corners with tefillin, or drove around in "mitzvah tanks," converted vans or mobile homes that they filled with Jewish and Hasidic materials to hand out to interested passersby. Today most Lubavitch boys have regular Friday afternoon routes they develop or inherit from other boys who have graduated, so that they visit the same men every week. But they still get practice in the old-fashioned techniques on Jewish holidays such as Chanukah and Passover, and on Lubavitch holidays—the Rebbe's birthday or the anniversary of the first Lubavitcher Rebbe's release from czarist prison. On those special days, huge mitzvah-tank campaigns are organized in major cities. On Chanukah one recent year, nearly a hundred specially outfitted cars and vans, with giant menorahs fastened to their roofs, paraded for miles through Brooklyn and across the Brooklyn Bridge into Manhattan.

Rabbi Sholtiel Lebovic, a Crown Heights Lubavitcher in his early thirties, says going out on the streets to convince Jewish men to put on tefillin isn't easy. "It takes a while to warm up. You have to be quick on the draw. You can go a whole day and not get anyone, really sweat it out until

---

*Schochet, *The Mystical Dimension*, p. 208.

you get just one person." For boys with less outgoing personalities, it can be particularly tough. "You don't always feel like going out. But the Rebbe told us that when we're not in the mood, we should focus on the other person's needs, not our own."

Sixteen-year-old Mendel is ready to hit the streets of Portland with his tefillin. "I love it!" he beams. With his pudgy red cheeks, glasses, braces, and not a trace of facial hair, he's a kid who inspires smiles rather than frowns from the people he approaches. Some Chabad boys are gentle, persuading men they stop in quiet, sincere voices. Mendel's approach is pure New York attitude. He tips back his hat, cocks his chin and grins, almost daring them to say no. In Brooklyn he doesn't usually do the kind of "cold calling" he and the other summer students do in Pioneer Courthouse Square. He has a regular route that he covers each Friday, a list of one hundred stores along a twenty-block stretch of Kings Highway that takes him five or six hours by foot. His weekly visits to the men who work there are expected, if not always welcomed. But he does enough mitzvah-tank work on Jewish holidays to know that he's facing an easier crowd here in Portland.

"When you go around in the mitzvah tank in New York, most of the people screaming at you are Jews," he says. "Old guys in yarmulkes, walking with their wives, screaming how we're an embarrassment to the Jews. Here they just look at you like you fell off the moon. Or they come up to you and ask, 'Are you Amish or Jewish?'" Jews in New York are more reticent about putting on tefillin in public, Mendel says, because they know a lot of people passing by will know what they're doing. In Portland it's more of an exotic whim, like trying out a hula hoop. "If they don't want to do it, it's usually because they're not interested, not because they're afraid someone will see them." Mendel claims he never gets into arguments on the street, even if he's tempted by the Jews for Jesus crowd. "You're not going to change anyone's mind by arguing with them on a street corner."

It's one-fifteen, and the day is slipping by. Motti stands up and claps his hands for attention. "OK, guys, let's go! It's very hot today, so drink plenty of water." The boys grab their black hats and coats, which they don't wear during class but always don when going out in public, and head for the bus stop. The bus pulls up, and the driver doesn't blink when twenty-two Hasidic boys in full regalia troop past her and take their seats. The passengers, for their part, look too stunned to speak.

When a Lubavitcher is in outreach mode, there's no stopping him.

Twenty-year-old Gershon Avtzon, also from Crown Heights, is sitting next to a clean-cut young man with short blond hair, dressed in a white T-shirt and jeans. Within sixty seconds, Gershon has learned that the fellow is not Jewish, is a youth-group leader and a Bible reader.

"Have you heard of the Noahide Laws?" Gershon asks. In the 1980s the Lubavitcher Rebbe told his followers that although their outreach work should focus on Jews, they also have the responsibility to teach non-Jews the seven laws God gave to Noah, laws of morality that apply to all humanity. The young man says he hasn't heard of the Noahide Laws, so Gershon runs down the list: Don't lie, don't steal, don't murder, etc.

"That sounds like the Ten Commandments," the young man observes. "Well, the Ten Commandments were given to the Jewish people later, on Mt. Sinai. These are for everyone, no discrimination," Gershon explains. "That's cool," the young man comments. Gershon presses on. "Have you heard of Chabad?" He hasn't. "Lubavitch? Hasidim?" The young man brightens. "I read *The Chosen*," he offers. Gershon laughs. "I bet that gave you a bad picture of us." Not at all, the young man insists. It piqued his interest.

The two young men chat quietly until the bus reaches Pioneer Courthouse Square, and the Lubavitch boys pile out. They immediately break off in pairs and fan out in all directions. Some of the duos take up positions at the four corners of the square, strategically poised to hit anyone passing in either direction. Mendel is paired up with his buddy Ari Greenwald of Long Beach, California. The two boys head off to the north. For the next three hours they will walk up and down the same five-block area, trying not to duplicate streets covered by other pairs of yeshiva students.

Mendel is in charge, arms swinging as he strides up the sidewalk. Once in a while, he and Ari confer sotto voce as to the possible Jewish status of an approaching man. "A *Yid?*" one asks, and the other either nods or shrugs. In general, they approach everyone. "Excuse me, are you Jewish?" "Sir, are you Jewish?" Within the first five minutes, they've asked more than two dozen men, without success. Then they come upon an unkempt, portly guy in his mid-thirties wearing jeans, a T-shirt advertising a heavy-metal band, and a blue-and-white baseball cap that reads "Bite Me."

Jewish? Hmmm . . . maybe. Ari asks, halfheartedly, and strikes unexpected pay dirt. "Yeah," the guy mumbles, his pale eyes trying to focus behind thick, round glasses.

"You are?" Ari asks, taken aback for a minute, but motioning to Mendel with one hand as he keeps the guy talking. Mendel charges up and quickly assumes command. "Do you have a minute? Want to put on tefillin?" Mendel is all smiles now. "I wish I had a minute," the guy mumbles, but he doesn't leave. He's still standing there, shifting from foot to foot, waiting for the boys to talk him into it. "Come on, it'll only take a minute, I promise," Mendel urges, as Ari stands to one side, discreetly removing the leather tefillin from their velvet pouch. "All right," the guy agrees, and quick as a wink, Mendel wraps the straps around the man's plump left arm, once, twice, seven times, then does the crisscross across the left hand and an extra twist around the middle finger. As Mendel wraps, he says the appropriate prayers out loud, in Hebrew, word by word, slowly enough so that Mr. Bite Me can repeat each one after him. The man's eyes are shut tightly, and he's shaking slightly as he says the prayers. He needs prompting, but he knows how to pronounce the Hebrew. Clearly, he's had some background. Maybe a day school graduate gone astray? Mendel and Ari exchange quick glances. When it's all over and the man opens his eyes again, he has to blink away a tear.

A live one! This is the kind of encounter a Chabad yeshiva boy dreams of. Mendel starts his follow-up patter: Where are you from? What are you doing for Shabbos? It turns out that the man is from out of town ("That's probably why he agreed to do it so easily," Ari suggests later. "He wasn't afraid anyone he knows would see him.") He's only been in Portland two days, and has no plans for Friday night. Dinner at Chabad House? Sure, why not?

The next hour is less eventful. None of the men Ari and Mendel approach are Jewish—none that admit it, anyway. But almost all are polite, even curious about the well-spoken, strangely dressed young men. Many follow up their "No, I'm not Jewish" with "but thank you anyway." Some offer their own religious or ethnic affiliation: "I'm Catholic," or "I'm Italian." A few are angry. One man who spits out his no thinks for a few seconds before adding, "I'm Muslim," probably hoping for a negative reaction from the boys. They ignore him. Another man, who looks decidedly more Middle Eastern, says he really is Muslim, but, waving his arms back and forth hurriedly, repeats with an anxious smile, "No problem, no problem." "No problem at all," Mendel comforts him, and the two back away from each other courteously.

Pioneer Courthouse Square is filled with young people on this hot afternoon. Pink and green hair, lots of black leather, piercings, and stud collars. One young man with wild, vacant eyes, hugging himself tightly with emaciated arms, is confused by Mendel's question. "Am I Jewish? I don't know."

"Is your mother Jewish?" Mendel asks. The man shakes his head: "I don't know who my parents are." "OK, have a nice day." Mendel hurries away.

The street punks are intrigued by these Lubavitchers, these boys in their oddly formal outfits and their in-your-face questions. It appeals to their sense of the offbeat. Three tattooed teenagers with spiky hair skate up to Mendel and Ari. One says to Mendel, "Hey, what's up, dude?" Mendel asks if he's Jewish. "No, sorry, dude," the kid says. "But hey, you got any change?" "Sorry," Mendel shrugs, smiling. The yeshiva boys don't carry any money with them. All they have is their bus pass home. Mendel follows up; "Do you know about the seven Noahide Laws?" The kid is willing to sit through the speech, so Mendel runs down the list. "That's cool," the kid says, nodding his head.

On one corner of the square, Motti Wilhelm has set up shop with three younger students who still need a little guidance in street outreach. One young man with a backward baseball cap passes the boys, then turns around, points at their outfits and asks, "Hey, you guys Mormon?" "No, we're Jewish," Motti answers. Today, Motti's group is having more success than Mendel and Ari. "I caught three Jews, thank God," one of the boys says with a wide grin. His friend claims five men put on tefillin with him, a personal best for the summer.

Off to the side one of the yeshiva boys is explaining to a curious passerby that they wear the suits and hats "out of respect for God." A neatly dressed man who says he is a direct mail consultant visiting Portland can't resist Motti's friendly pitch. He allows the yeshiva student to roll up his sleeve and wrap the black leather straps around his left arm, as a curious crowd looks on. "Why not?" he explains afterward. "I'm from New York, I've seen these guys all over Midtown. I used to go to the Chabad House in Buffalo when I was in college. But who'd have thought here in Portland?"

One elderly passerby with an Israeli flag sewn to his backpack won't put on tefillin but walks across the street to Nordstrom, buys an iced tea, and brings it back for Motti. Motti thanks him but won't drink it. "I can't be sure it's kosher," he whispers. He waits until the man is long gone before he gives the drink to a homeless person.

Not everyone is happy to see these Chabad students. A teenage girl in low-slung jeans and midriff-baring top, wearing a stud collar and navel ring, brushes past Motti and his cohorts, looks skyward, and exclaims loudly, "Jews, man!" Another young man in a leather jacket elbows past, shouting back over his shoulder, "I'm German," which he clearly isn't.

How does Motti feel when people reject him this way? "Well, if they just walk by and they're not mean about it, that's all right, especially if they're not Jewish. If they are Jewish, and they're open a little bit, I'll talk to them about tefillin, maybe ask them over for Shabbos dinner." No matter what people say to him, no matter the weather, the lack of response, or how many hours he's out there standing in the street, asking the same question over and over again, Motti never looks discouraged. He just keeps smiling. Smiling, asking, and wrapping. "You can't get everybody," he remarks.

Chabad's outreach approach is colored by one central maxim: Make it as easy as possible for a Jew to live more Jewishly. Don't have candles? We'll give you some and tell you the prayers to say when you light them. Don't have a *sukkah*? We'll sell or give you a kit, and even come over to help you set it up. Or we'll bring a mobile *sukkah* past your house, so you can fulfill the mitzvah of blessing the *lulav* and the *etrog* with our careful coaching. We'll create beginner's *minyans*, so you can feel comfortable in synagogue while still observing Jewish law; we'll set up free or low-cost schools for your children to teach them Jewish history and traditions; and we'll help you celebrate life-cycle events and holidays in fun and meaningful ways.

Lubavitchers see themselves as a bridge between the observant and non-observant worlds in American Jewry, extending a welcoming hand to Jews who want to cross over but don't know how, or aren't sure how far they want to go. "There's a fundamental lack of sensitivity within the Orthodox world as to how to deal with the non-Orthodox," says Efraim Mintz, director of placement services and adult education at the Chabad movement's Shlichim Office in Crown Heights. "Some denominations see themselves as God's policemen. We see ourselves as God's salesmen."

In 1990, Lubavitch headquarters embarked on a large-scale advertising campaign designed to encourage Jews to observe Jewish rituals and holidays. It was yet another example of the movement's willingness to seize the tools of the modern world to promote its traditional message. The years 1990 to 1994 were ones of great media outreach. Chabad-sponsored billboards began to appear beside major highways near dozens of American cities, urging Jews to observe the Sabbath or to light Chanukah candles. The *New York Times,* where Schneerson had begun running Purim ads as early as the 1950s, was utilized for a barrage of full-page ads urging Jews to celebrate their heritage. Rabbi Yehoshua Metzger, now the head of Chabad's Midtown Manhattan center, directed the movement's subway-poster advertising campaign in the early 1990s, putting up splashy signs in New York City subway cars that read "Don't Pass Over Passover," or "Start the Year Sweet—Celebrate the High Holidays." Each sign included the dates of the relevant holiday, and the local phone number of Chabad headquarters, which one could call for "a free holiday guide."

The public advertising campaigns reached a crescendo around the time of Schneerson's death, and tapered off afterward. Schneerson had been personally involved in the campaigns, and some shlichim say the heart went out of that particular effort with his passing. Today there are few Chabad-sponsored billboards, and the subway campaign has ceased. Metzger says that he paid $25,000 in 1990 to plaster every one of New York's 6,000 subway cars with a Chabad poster, but that same campaign today would cost, he claims, "ten times as much." Movement leaders still turn to the *New York Times* and other major papers to place holiday ads, or ads urging Jewish observance to mark a particular day of significance to the Chabad movement, such as the anniversary of the Rebbe's death. And sporadic newspaper campaigns crop up, such as the Passover campaign conducted in college newspapers from 1994 to 1997 inviting college students to pick up free "Seder-to-go" kits from their local Chabad House. But, says Shlichim Office director Gedalya Shemtov, "You always need to find new opportunities and keep your imagination open."

Most of the mitzvah campaigns have spawned their own nonprofit organizations that have split off from Lubavitch World Headquarters but are still located in Crown Heights and are closely aligned with movement policies. Mivtza Kashrus is a Crown Heights office that helps people kasher their homes. Mivtza Neshek sends out Lubavitch girls to hand out Shabbat candles; it places weekly ads in the *New York Times* to indicate candlelighting times. Mivtza Taharas HaMishpacha distributes information on family purity laws, arranges tours of local mikvahs, and maintains www.mikvah.org, a Web site of mikvah locations, hours, and fees around the world.

Rabbi Sholtiel Lebovic is director of the nonprofit company Go Kosher, which is run out of his Crown Heights home. He grew up in New Jersey, where as a boy he helped his father kasher Jewish homes. Now he runs a home-kashering operation that whips through 1,500 Jewish homes a year in the Greater New York area. In the competitive New York Jewish market he is able to charge for his services; many Chabad shlichim in other cities will kasher a home for free. Some of Lebovic's clients are observant Jews who have moved to a new home and need help making it kosher, but he estimates that 70 percent are non-observant people looking to make that first step toward creating a Jewish home. "There are a host of reasons," he says. "They could be the parents of children who went to Israel, and they want the grandchildren to be comfortable in their homes. They could be becoming observant themselves, or maybe they're not *shomer Shabbat* [Sabbath-observant] but they want to keep kosher."

Lebovic and his crew can usually kasher a home in one session, including taking all the utensils for ritual dunking in a mikvah, blow-torching the oven, cleaning out the refrigerator and kitchen cabinets, and advising the client on what has to be thrown away. "It's not rocket science," he says. "Lots of rabbis do this. But we have the system down. I try to make it as easy as possible. Once someone has committed to eating kosher, it's just a matter of keeping separate parts of the kitchen for milk and meat, and buying kosher food. If they backslide, that's fine. They can call me and I'll walk them through it again."

Many clients, kashering their homes for the first time, get emotional. They ask Lebovic to say a special prayer for their new kitchen. Unfortunately, Judaism doesn't provide a blessing for kashering a home, so Lebovic obliges by saying a psalm or a general blessing—perhaps a She-hechiyanu, the blessing for a new occasion. "I tell them that they should pray for themselves, but they want the rabbi to do it," he says. "I do this day after day, so I've gotten desensitized. I have to remind myself what a big thing it is for these people. It means identity, it means feeling attached to Judaism. I have to remember that."

———

The *halachic* (according to Jewish law) definition of the word *shliach* is "agent," or "emissary," someone who is empowered by another to act in his or her stead. The Bible's first shliach was Abraham's servant Eliezer, sent by the patriarch to secure a wife for his son Isaac. Eliezer was able to contract a marriage in Abraham's name without his employer's physical presence, because he was legally acting as Abraham himself. So, too, do Chabad shlichim believe that when they are working in their official capacities, they are acting in the Rebbe's stead. Not instead of him, but as him, as an extension of the one who sent them. Still, they must use their own intellect, skills, feelings, desires, and personal style to accomplish their mission. If they fail, the responsibility is theirs; if they succeed, the glory is the Rebbe's.

"The Rebbe did not allow his shlichim the luxury of mindless obedience to his dictates," says Yanki Tauber, editor of Chabad's online magazine. "But neither did the Rebbe send his emissaries to tackle their mission on their own. He empowered them to be 'as he himself,' so that a shliach's every deed is imbued with the awareness that he is acting as an extension of the Rebbe's very person."

Chabad shlichim speak of feeling the Rebbe work through them. "I could never have done this on my own," they repeat. "It's the Rebbe, it's not me." Chanie Lipskar, shlicha in Bal Harbour, Florida, tells of when she and her husband met privately with Schneerson before being sent on shlichus to Miami Beach in 1969. Barely nineteen years old, Lipskar had spent her entire life in Crown Heights, and she was afraid she wouldn't be able to reach the secular Jews of South Florida. But, she says, the Rebbe smiled at her and said that wherever she went, he would be with her. To his day, she, and every other Chabad shliach, feels that to be quite literally true.

In order to have someone else working through you, you have to be able to quiet your own ego. Hasidim call that process *bittul,* or self-nullification. It's a key concept in Hasidic life, particularly in prayer, when one nullifies oneself before the Almighty. It's also at work in the daily experience of a Lubavitcher. "I consider myself an ordinary person, so how can I ignite the Jewish spark in another person?" wonders Rabbi Lebovic. "It's the Rebbe working through me."

Rabbi Chaim Nochum Cunin, twenty-nine, runs the live "chat with a rabbi" Web site *www.askmoses.com* and puts out *Farbrengen* magazine from Chabad of the West Coast headquarters, the Los Angeles Chabad center directed by his father. He started the magazine as an outreach project and had it mailed for free inside other Jewish newspapers. A year later the publication had grown so big that he was faced with taking it on full-time, to the exclusion of much of his other outreach work. But was it a valid shlichus? One evening he was dining with a supporter, and the man said he looked depressed. Cunin didn't respond. Chabad shlichim aren't supposed to spread negativity. They aren't supposed to give in to doubts. They have to put their personal egos aside and allow themselves to be vessels for the Rebbe's work.

The dinner-table conversation continued. Cunin's visitor said, "You're worried about the magazine, aren't you?" Cunin admitted that was true. The man then said, in words that could have come from Chaim's father, "It's not your project, it's the Rebbe's project, and it's not yours to stop." He pledged to fund the magazine for the foreseeable future. "For me, that was a flashlight," Cunin says. "These things come along to show us the way and give us strength to continue."

Working on one's ego is part of being a Hasid. Chabad philosophy teaches that one must submerge the baser, more selfish instincts so that the intellect has mastery over emotion, for the intellect recognizes the universal whereas emotions are too often slaves to personal desire. This does not mean suppressing feelings, but using them carefully. "Chabad Hasidus teaches man to harness his heart in the employ of his brain, to change bad character traits, curb animalistic urges, and sharpen good traits," says Zalman Shmotkin. "Nothing we're born with is perfect, and we have only a few short years here on earth to effect real change. Making the choice to thank God for waking us up, exercising control in what and how we eat, or acting ethically in our business dealings—these are the acts and decisions for which God put us here."

Not every young Lubavitcher wants to be a shliach. But few of them will admit it if they don't, even to their friends. One of the most extraordinary aspects of the Chabad phenomenon is how this community of Hasidim has managed to raise an entire generation of young people who want to spend their lives teaching Judaism to the uninitiated, living and working in a world not their own to spread their Rebbe's message. "We grew up with an emphasis placed on this kind of life service," says Yossi Deren, a fourth-generation shliach living and working in Greenwich, Connecticut. "It was our decision one hundred percent [to go into it], but we still grew up with it. Sometimes we fail to realize the greatness of what the Rebbe accomplished when he sent shlichim out to distant communities; not just in terms of outreach and making it a trendy thing, but the Rebbe imbued us with a belief in people and in the immutability of the soul. We heard it growing up like table talk, and we don't stop to think how profound a concept it is. We just look at it as what we do. But the Rebbe's genius was to make it naturally part of our lives."

From an early age Lubavitchers begin practicing the juggling act between personal study and public outreach that will characterize their future adult lives.

Yechezkel Deren (Yossi's brother) is a seventeen-year-old student at the Lubavitch yeshiva high school in Detroit, Michigan. Crown Heights is still Lubavitch Central in terms of movement leadership and sheer numbers of Lubavitch families, but there are also Lubavitch schools in Detroit, Chicago, Miami, Pittsburgh, Los Angeles, Montreal, Toronto, and Morristown, New Jersey—all cities with sizable Lubavitch populations.

Yechezkel is from Stamford, Connecticut, where his parents are long-time shlichim. He went to live in Detroit when he was twelve, although he could easily have stayed at home and commuted to yeshiva in Crown Heights. But this is all part of growing up in a movement whose motto is *ufaratzta,* or "spread out." It's not only the children of shliach families who are sent away to study. It's common for all Lubavitchers, girls as well as boys, to spend several years in schools far from their homes, even in other countries. Some of the boys in Yechezkel's class are from Detroit, but more are like seventeen-year-old Bentzion Groner, whose parents are shlichim in Charlotte, North Carolina. Bentzion was also sent away at twelve to Detroit, but he took the further step of spending the year he was fifteen in Israel, at Kfar Chabad. That was his choice, not his parents'. He wanted to see the world.

Bentzion and Yechezkel's school day is typical for a Lubavitch yeshiva *bocher.* Learning begins at 7:30 A.M., with an hour and a half of Hasidus, or Hasidic philosophy. That could mean *Tanya* or a discourse of one of the Lubavitcher Rebbes, each of whom had his own style and emphasis. The fifth Rebbe, for example, who led the Lubavitch movement in the first decades of the twentieth century, was a great codifier of Hasidic thought, Yechezkel says, and is studied as "the Maimonides of Hasidus." But the discourses of the seventh and last rebbe, Menachem Mendel Schneerson, receive the greatest attention. "We're all Hasidim of the Rebbe, and we want to study *our* teacher," Yechezkel explains.

The boys study a specific Hasidic text for several days, working with a partner in what is called *havrutas*. Once they've learned the text on their own, they'll listen to a teacher lecture on it, but the lecture is supplementary. The real education takes place in *havrutas*. To an outsider this method of study can appear chaotic. Each pair works at its own pace; everyone is talking out loud; boys are constantly jumping up to find books or consult with other students; people come and go seemingly at random. But that's how yeshiva students have been learning for centuries.

Those ninety minutes spent learning Hasidic texts first thing in the morning are designed to prepare the boys spiritually for their morning prayers, or davening. Praying isn't something you can just do, Yechezkel says. It's very serious, and the central part of a Hasid's day. Prayer connects the Hasid to God. "You need to prepare yourself for something as great as davening," he explains. Morning prayers last almost an hour, and at 10:30 A.M., the boys eat breakfast. By 11 A.M., they're back at their desks for three hours of intensive Talmud, also studied with a partner. This daily period of Talmud study is called "in-depth." Over the course of a year, they'll only cover ten to fifteen pages of text this way, with related commentaries. Later in the day, they approach Talmud a different way, "in-breadth," making a broad sweep of a page or more. At 2:15, it's time for *mincha,* or afternoon prayers. Then lunch, and at 3:30 more Talmud, or Jewish Law, or a look at the weekly Torah portion. Supper is at 7 P.M., and more Hasidic learning follows at 8 P.M., until *ma'ariv,* or evening prayers, at 9:30.

With such a grueling schedule, it might seem that going out on Friday afternoons to do street outreach would be just another chore. To some, it undoubtedly is. Not to Bentzion and Yechezkel, however. "Every Lubavitcher yeshiva *bocher* jumps at doing *mivtzoim,*" Yechezkel insists. "The Rebbe promised us, if we go on the streets and do another Jew a favor, our studies will become a thousand times easier to accomplish."

At the Detroit yeshiva all the students put down their books at noon on Friday and hit the streets. They have regular routes: The younger boys visit private homes, while the older ones go to businesses. Yechezkel has a route of twenty-five offices that he inherited from a boy who graduated. Bentzion developed his own route, which took some doing. He explains how he went about it: "You go to an office and ask to see the list of names of people working there. Then you stand by the elevator and ask people if they're Jewish. Once you find one Jew, you're in. Sometimes security throws you out. But we learn in Chabad not to be stopped by anything." The trick, Bentzion says, is not to push too quickly. The first time a Jewish man lets him into his office, he'll ask the man to put on tefillin. The second week, he'll do the same. Only by the third visit will he ask the man whether any other Jews work in the building.

Yechezkel says he doesn't put tefillin on most of the men on his route. Getting a busy executive to put down his work and let a teenager wrap up his arm and put a black box on his forehead isn't an easy task. But he stocks up on Hasidic literature before he goes out and makes sure to leave something at every office he visits. Yechezkel has one company president on his route who always lets him in even though he refuses to put on tefillin. Maybe, Yechezkel muses, the man simply enjoys the weekly banter with a yeshiva student.

"It was hard to find common ground with him," Yechezkel relates. "He'd say, 'You've done this since birth, it's not possible for someone who's not Orthodox from birth to change.' He said he didn't want to be hypocritical, that he didn't believe in it, so why should he do it? I told him it's not hypocritical. In Judaism it's not all or nothing. This is another brick added to the Bais Hamikdash (the Temple in Jerusalem), and it's good for your soul. I told him that his soul really wants to put on tefillin. I said, 'You know you're a Jew, right?' He said, yes, and I asked why. He said he goes to shul on Yom Kippur, he won't eat ham, and his parents were Jewish. I said, 'So you know you're Jewish; why not put on tefillin, just because you're a Jew?' He said, 'Your argument may be good, but I'm still not doing it.' I didn't want to noodge him too much. It was creating a little bit of an edgy atmosphere. We're taught that we shouldn't be too far ahead of the person."

Don't these boys feel awkward trying to lecture men twice their age about Jewish practice? No, they say, that's not how they look at it. "It's just a nice word on Torah, a Torah thought," Bentzion says. "It's not like I'm trying to 'teach' him."

Again, not surprisingly, plenty of businessmen aren't happy to see those black hats in their waiting rooms. One man on Yechezkel's route heard he was there and shouted at his secretary, "What am I running here, a circus?" Getting thrown out of an office embarrasses some boys, Yechezkel says. "But the truth is, most of us get a kick out of it. The worst thing is getting the cold shoulder, no response at all. If someone throws you out, you know he has strong feelings. Maybe they're negative now, but they could become positive. So you come back, week after week. It's a challenge!"

Street *mivtzoim* is a constant test from the Rebbe, the boys say. "It's uncomfortable in the beginning, sure," Yechezkel admits. "But you have to realize, that's what *ahavas Yisrael* [love of your fellow Jews] is about." Shneuer Kesselman, a twenty-two-year-old rabbinic student at the Detroit yeshiva, says the rejection doesn't get any easier with the years. Lubavitch boys may look like professionals, with their black hats and suits, but underneath it they're just ordinary American teenagers. "It's the emotional part that's tough," he says. "You go out there with a goal you want to accomplish, and you get so many nos. You expect them, but it still hurts."

No one likes to have a door slammed in his face. But when a Lubavitcher holds out tefillin to a Jewish man who walks right by him, or a pair of candlesticks to a woman who shakes her head, the sense of rejection goes deeper than personal discomfort. The Lubavitcher feels he is disappointing his Rebbe. Even youths too young to have known the Rebbe feel that he is watching them, approving or disapproving, every minute of their lives.

Binyamin Wolff is twenty-three, and a rabbinic student at the Detroit yeshiva. He says he's jealous of older shlichim who not only have many personal memories of the Rebbe, but who received actual instructions from him and were able to meet with him in person, or at least receive written answers to their letters. "When we go out today, we know the Rebbe is backing us and wants us to do this. He's watching us. But the older shlichim were literally educated into the work. The Rebbe told them what to do and what not to do. We have the same young strength they had. But they were taken by the hand, step by step."

Binyamin and his friend Shneuer both met the Rebbe briefly as children and young teenagers. Binyamin, who grew up in Morristown, New Jersey, went to *farbrengens* (Lubavitch gatherings) at 770 and he vividly remembers hearing the Rebbe speak. That helps him, he says, relate to Schneerson on a personal level. "At our *farbrengens* today, we try to think back to when we saw the Rebbe. This is something the younger boys in the yeshiva don't have."

From a young age Lubavitchers feel that they represent the Rebbe, their parents, and their community whenever they go out in the public sphere. That's how Bina Lewis, Rochel Goldstein, and Faige Kasowitz feel. The young women, all nineteen, are spending what would be their first year of post–high school seminary studies doing shlichus work in Anchorage, Alaska, helping Esty and Yossi Greenberg, directors of Alaska's Chabad House. The girls found their positions through a free job-placement service run by the Shlichim Office. Faige says the list of shlichim looking for seminary girls to help them out that year was three pages long, single-spaced. "I said, there's no way I'm going to Alaska, it's too far away and too cold. But some girls who were there last year called and told me how great it was." Bina and Rochel had other plans for the year. They were headed to a new Chabad school in Connecticut. When funding for that project fell through, they found themselves scrambling for another open-ing at the last minute. They, too, rejected the idea of Alaska at first. "It was mentioned to us, but we said right away, we're not going. Then Esty called and said we had to come. She can be very persistent."

Halfway through their year in the frozen North, all three young women say they love it. They've been sledding, skiing, bungee-jumping, and ski-flying, and spent Thanksgiving weekend in a snowbound moun-tain cabin without electricity or running water. They work out every night at a local health club, and usually jump in the Greenbergs' hot tub afterward. Not only is it fun to do these things, they say it's a kick to be able to dispel common stereotypes about Hasidim. "People can't believe we wear modern clothes, and we're still Lubavitch," Faige says. "We told some people that we go skiing in long skirts, and they can't believe it."

"It just shows them we can have a good time and still live up to our standards," Bina adds. "They expect extremes from us, and they're shocked that we're normal."

These young women were twelve when the Rebbe died, old enough, they say, to understand what was happening and to appreciate the signifi-cance of what they were losing. All three remember meeting the Rebbe personally, and they say those memories sustain them on a daily basis. When the conversation switches from skiing in long skirts to spreading the Rebbe's message, the giggles cease and their faces grow very serious. "Our job is to bring what the Rebbe taught to other people," Bina says. Faige adds, "I take it as a privilege and an honor to be able to spread the Rebbe's word."

Like the students in the Detroit yeshiva, Bina, Rochel, and Faige grow wistful when they reflect on what it must have been like for new shlichim when Schneerson was still alive. They all plan to become shlichim them-selves and don't doubt that choice for a minute, but they say they feel an emptiness in their hearts when they think about making life decisions without Schneerson's personal guidance. "I'm sure it's harder today," Faige says. "You hear stories about the Rebbe writing back to shlichim, sending them personal letters. I write to the Rebbe's grave of course, but it's different. He doesn't write back."

CHAPTER 4

THE REBBE:

The Enigma of
Menachem Mendel Schneerson

Inside the Lubavitch section of the Old Montefiore Cemetery in Queens, New York, stands a stark, twenty-foot-square granite mausoleum. A simple door leads to a dark, candlelit foyer. Shelves along the walls of the foyer hold tattered books of psalms and prayer, printed in several languages. The foyer has two exits—one for men and one for women—leading out to a central pebble-lined square, open to the skies. And in that square, next to the grave of his father-in-law, the sixth Lubavitcher Rebbe, lie the earthly remains of the seventh and last Lubavitcher Rebbe, Menachem Mendel Schneerson.

When the Rebbe died on June 12, 1994, at the age of ninety-two, his funeral made headlines around the world. The passing of this head of an ultra-Orthodox Brooklyn sect was extensively covered in the *New York Times*. CNN broadcast the funeral procession live, showing thousands of black-hatted mourners crowding the length of Eastern Parkway, crying, screaming, leaning in to touch the simple pine casket of their beloved leader as it passed before them. Since the day of his burial, in death even more than in life, the Rebbe has never been alone. Just as thousands of visitors used to file past him every Sunday at his Crown Heights headquarters, asking for his advice and blessings, his followers, along with the merely curious, now flock to his grave site to seek his protection, beseech his favor, and just be, they say, in the presence of holiness.

Hasidic philosophy teaches that the soul of a departed person hovers near its grave, pending the Messiah's arrival and subsequent ingathering of the resurrected dead to Israel. That is even more true in the case of a *tzaddik*, or "holy one," whose soul, according to Jewish mystical tradition, maintains a particularly close physical relationship to the dead body it once inhabited. The Hasid's desire to be physically near his rebbe persists after death, requiring frequent pilgrimages to the graves of departed *tzaddikim*.

For weeks after Schneerson's death thousands of mourners passed by the newly dug grave every day. Dozens of yeshiva boys stayed round-the-clock, catching a few hours' sleep by leaning against the granite walls or sinking down onto the hard earth, unwilling to leave their rebbe's presence for the briefest moment. Hasidim flew in from around the world to stand by the grave reciting psalms and pouring out their hearts. Some of them, especially from Israel, bought one-way tickets the day of the funeral, convinced that they would soon return to the Holy Land together with the Messiah. Clearly, they believed, the end of days had arrived.

The numbers of visitors tapered off by the end of that first summer, but eight years later hundreds of people still stop by every day, summer and winter, spring and fall. Before Jewish holidays the cemetery is as crowded as it was on the day Schneerson was interred. Chabad officials and shlichim, who used to visit the Rebbe in his office to deliver their reports, now make the same pilgrimage to his grave. They stand at the grave, with heads bowed, delivering their good news and waiting for their leader's blessing. More than 40,000 Chabad Hasidim showed up in June 2001 for the Rebbe's *yahrzeit*, the seventh anniversary of his passing, standing in line for hours to enter the mausoleum and spend a brief moment or two in his presence.

"You feel guided, honored, supported, connected at the *ohel*," says Shternie Notik, a Chabad shlicha in Chicago, using the Hebrew word for "tent" that Hasidim employ to refer to the grave of a rebbe. "I wish it could be another way [than visiting his grave]. But that doesn't change the connection, it doesn't sever or diminish the ties in any way. You leave feeling recharged, empowered. Even today, we get back so much more from the Rebbe than we give."

The Rebbe's grave also attracts many non-Lubavitch visitors. Jew and non-Jew, regulars from Brooklyn and families on their first visit to the United States, the pilgrims arrive. Pregnant women come to pray for healthy babies. Betrothed couples stop by to ask for the Rebbe's blessing on their marriage. Elderly men beseech him for continued health. Young girls come to pray for a husband. They scribble their hopes and dreams on small scraps of paper, which they tear into strips and scatter onto the grave. Those who can't come in person send their entreaties by fax or e-mail, hundreds a day. Those messages, too, are printed, read out loud at the grave site and then torn into tiny pieces that are scattered onto the huge pile of paper that always covers the Rebbe's tomb, a feather-light blanket of sighs and tears.

Who is this man, to inspire such devotion beyond the grave? Who was Menachem Mendel Schneerson, whom his followers called the Moses of his generation, the leader of world Jewry, the man who was, some suggested, the Messiah himself?

The Rebbe's reach was phenomenal, the extent of his teaching and activity breathtaking. A Torah scholar, his commentaries fill more than two hundred published volumes. He labored ceaselessly, whether it was meeting with petitioners in private audiences that often lasted until dawn, or standing for hours every Sunday to pass out blessings and dollar bills to the thousands of people who lined up outside his office, or directing Chabad's worldwide outreach efforts. He held the reins of his movement tightly, exerting his considerable influence on the tiniest detail of every campaign, every published work, anything that carried his name. He would offer practical advice for the most private problems affecting someone's personal life, and the next minute exhort the Jews of Israel not to flee during the Gulf War because Saddam Hussein's Scud missiles would cause no Israeli deaths. He answered thousands of letters a month, offering his carefully considered philosophy and world view to children and world leaders alike. He was deeply committed to preserving the flames of Judaism in the Soviet Union, spiriting clandestine aid to underground Jewish movements in that country for forty years. He created Chabad's worldwide network of shlichim, building on foundations laid by his father-in-law, and personally oversaw its daily operations. He spoke six languages fluently and could get by in several more. He loved children fiercely but had none of his own.

The Rebbe's political clout was felt all the way from Crown Heights, where his headquarters was almost a required campaign stop for New York City political candidates, to Israel, where he influenced key elections despite never having visited the country. In fact, except for frequent trips to his father-in-law's grave in Queens, the Rebbe never left Crown Heights at all during the last thirty years of his life. Presidents, senators, prime ministers, business moguls, and celebrities all came to him, never the other way around.

Schneerson inspired admiration in the most unlikely places. And Chabad headquarters has been assiduous in documenting that praise, on film and in writing.

Every U.S. president from Richard Nixon on has paid homage to Schneerson, signing proclamations in his honor. Several corresponded with him personally. Bill Clinton sent a condolence letter to Lubavitch headquarters the day Schneerson died, calling him "a monumental man," who, "as much as any other individual, was responsible over the last half century for advancing the instruction of ethics and morality to our young people."

Political figures who met Schneerson face-to-face, even if they disagreed with him politically, came away from their meetings deeply moved. "It was the eyes of the rabbi that impressed me, the blue, penetrating eyes that express wisdom, awareness, and deep penetration," said the late Israeli Prime Minister Yitzhak Rabin, whose Labor Party suffered a stunning defeat when the Rebbe's interference scuttled its 1990 coalition-building attempt. But that did not affect Rabin's admiration for the man himself. "I came away with a sense of elation and inspiration, that I've met a leader of the Jewish people."

Former British Prime Minister Margaret Thatcher speaks warmly of the "honor" the world should give Schneerson for "the work he's done, the example he sets, and the inspiration he's given to many, many people." Former New York Senator Alfonse D'Amato and former Speaker of the House Newt Gingrich are among dozens of American politicians who speak of him with awe and fondness. Israeli leaders Zalman Shazar, Menachem Begin, Benjamin Netanyahu, Shimon Peres, and Ariel Sharon all made the trek to Crown Heights at different points in their careers. Begin stopped by on his way to the Camp David peace talks in 1979. Netanyahu visited Schneerson's grave just before Rosh Hashanah 1996, calling him a "great teacher, a great healer, [who] certainly served for me as a source of inspiration."

Connecticut Senator Joseph Lieberman is a frequent keynote speaker at Lubavitch events and a devoted fan of the late Rebbe's work in support of education and Jewish outreach. "I have the most precious memory of when I was fortunate enough to be in the presence of the Rebbe, to listen to him teach, to ask his counsel, to benefit from his guidance," Lieberman said at a Chabad dinner in Washington, D.C. "The Rebbe has been an extraordinarily inspirational leader in taking the traditions of our people, the joys of being Jewish, and communicating it in a very modern context throughout America and the world."

Nobel Laureate Elie Wiesel is another frequent speaker at Chabad events honoring the Rebbe's memory. Wiesel carried on a decades-long correspondence with Schneerson and had several private meetings, or *yechidus,* with him. Like most people who have had private meetings with the Rebbe, Wiesel won't reveal exactly what the Rebbe told him during those meetings, but he speaks often of the impact they exerted on him:

> I know of no one who has left the Rebbe, even after a moment of yechidus, without being deeply affected, if not changed, by their encounter. . . . Time in his presence begins running at a different pace. You feel inspired, you feel self-examined, you are made to wonder about the quest for meaning which ought to be yours. In his presence you come closer in touch with your inner center of gravity. . . . Whenever I would see the Rebbe, he touched the depths in me. That was true of everyone who came to see the Rebbe. Somehow when the person left, he or she felt they had lived deeper and higher, on a higher level.*

The impact of a personal encounter with Schneerson was so great that some people feared it. The late Chaim Potok, who immortalized the Hasidic world of 1940s Brooklyn in *The Chosen,* told Ted Koppel in a 1991 *Nightline* interview that he refused to meet privately with the Rebbe. "There's something about him that is quite literally indescribable, that has to be experienced, which is one of the reasons that I have always hesitated to be in the same room with him," Potok admitted. "I worry about my objectivity being swallowed and overwhelmed by this charismatic man."

---

*From addresses delivered by Elie Wiesel in April 1992 and July 1995 at Chabad events in Washington, D.C.

No one sings the Rebbe's praises more eloquently than Dr. Jonathan Sacks, the chief rabbi of Great Britain, who credits Schneerson with setting him on the rabbinical path. In a memorial lecture delivered soon after Schneerson's death, Rabbi Sacks said:

> Among the very greatest Jewish leaders of the past there were some who transformed communities. There were others who raised up many disciples; there were yet others who left us codes and commentaries which will be studied for all time. But there can have been few in the entire history of one of the oldest peoples in the world who in one lifetime made his influence felt throughout the entire Jewish world. . . . The Rebbe was one of the immortals.

How did Schneerson manage to attract such heavy hitters to his cause, even after his death? That's what fascinated *Moment* magazine editor Hershel Shanks when he was invited to a June 1995 forum in Washington, D.C., where Schneerson was posthumously awarded the Congressional Gold Medal, the first religious leader to receive this highest civilian honor. Shanks says he arrived at the event prepared to be skeptical and came away, instead, deeply affected. Writing later that year in *Moment,* Shanks suggested that "what made the Rebbe so remarkable . . . was not simply his brilliance, his learning, his wisdom, although he apparently had all these, but the force of his personality. He motivated people. He brought out their best. To this task—making Jews better Jews—he devoted his entire self so that all of us would feel we are made in God's image."*

After the Rebbe's death the outpouring of grief, the effusive praise lavished upon him in the world press seemed almost suspect. Eventually, the superlatives began to suffocate each other. Yet the Rebbe was not without critics. He engendered controversy for his opposition to religious pluralism, his aggressive outreach campaigns, and the cult of personality that developed around him during his lifetime and persisted after his death. In an interview in the mid 1990s, Potok spoke of his conflicted feelings: "From the point of view of his personality, he made a fundamental contribution to Judaism. From the point of view of his fundamentalism,

---

*Hershel Shanks, *Moment* magazine, October 1995.

of certain stands he took politically especially vis-à-vis Israel, he almost succeeded in splitting the Jewish people. You have to be very honest about the good and the not-so-good when you come to dealing with a very great man."*

Menachem Mendel Schneerson was born April 18, 1902, in the Ukrainian town of Nikolaev, heir to a distinguished Hasidic ancestry. He was named after his great-great-great-grandfather, the third Lubavitcher Rebbe. His father was a renowned rabbinic leader and Kabbalist, and his mother came from a long line of respected rabbis.

Very little is known about the Rebbe's life before he assumed leadership of the Chabad movement in 1951. As with many world-renowned figures, Schneerson's childhood is shrouded in apocryphal myth. We are told he was a Torah prodigy who had to leave *cheder* by the age of eleven, having already outstripped his teachers. The few tales that are told about the Rebbe's early years emphasize his kindness and his overwhelming concern for other people. When he was three years old, one story goes, hiding from rampaging Cossacks with dozens of other Jews in a basement near his home, he walked around the darkened room soothing screaming infants by giving them candies and placing his hand on their heads. At the age of nine, we are told, he dove into the Black Sea to rescue a drowning boy.

Whether or not these stories are true is perhaps less important than the focus they put on qualities Schneerson later did, in fact, embody. And unlike George Washington, who may or may not have chopped down a cherry tree and then owned up to it, there are thousands of people alive today who can attest to the adult Schneerson's generosity of spirit, concern for humanity, and prodigious Torah knowledge.

In 1923, Schneerson met the sixth Lubavitcher Rebbe, a distant relative, and became active in Lubavitch's underground efforts to preserve Jewish life in the Soviet Union; he remained deeply involved in this work until the collapse of the Soviet Union seventy years later. In 1927, Schneerson followed the sixth rebbe to Latvia, and the following year he married his mentor's second daughter, Chaya Mushka. The couple moved to Berlin, where Schneerson studied philosophy and mathematics at the

---

*Chaim Dalfin, *Conversations with the Rebbe, Menachem Mendel Schneerson: Interviews with Fourteen Leading Figures About the Rebbe* (Los Angeles: JEC Publishing Co., 1996), pp. 160–61.

University of Berlin until Hitler came to power in 1933. They then moved to Paris, where he studied at the Sorbonne and the École Polytechnique. When Germany occupied France in 1940, the Schneersons escaped first to Nice and then, in 1941, to New York, where the sixth Rebbe had moved Chabad headquarters the previous year.

In New York, Schneerson worked briefly at the Brooklyn Navy Yard while simultaneously heading up three new Chabad institutions: *Merkos L'Inyonei Chinuch,* Chabad's educational arm; *Machne Israel,* the movement's social service division; and the Kehot Publication Society. He returned to Europe just once, in 1947, to bring his mother to Brooklyn to live with him. His father died in 1944 after brutal treatment in a Soviet prison, and his brother was murdered by the Nazis. When the sixth Rebbe died in 1950 most Lubavitchers considered Schneerson the heir apparent to the Lubavitch dynasty, but he was reluctant to assume the position. He had not been publicly named by his late father-in-law. Nevertheless, he immediately began functioning as the movement's rebbe, acting as such in all but name until he formally accepted the mantle thrust upon him by his Hasidim in January 1951.

From that day in 1951 until his death forty-three years later Schneerson was constantly in the public eye, but he maintained an unbreachable privacy in his personal life. That life took place largely behind closed doors, in a ten-by-twelve-foot wood-paneled office at 770 Eastern Parkway that became known as "the Rebbe's room." There he would spend his days writing, praying, and studying, and his nights meeting with his followers. Until his last years he would walk home late at night carrying a brown shopping bag filled with letters to answer and papers to edit, which he would bring back to his office early the next morning. He had no confidants except his wife, who died in 1988. None of his followers, even those closest to him, profess to have truly known him.

Yehuda Krinsky worked at the Rebbe's side every day from 1957 until his death. He was the Rebbe's personal driver and spent many long hours alone with him, yet Krinsky insists he didn't know the Rebbe at all. "The more time you spent with him, the more difficult it becomes to describe him," Krinsky says. "The Rebbe had no private life. I don't think there was a moment, from the time he became Rebbe, that his whole life wasn't under public scrutiny. Even when he was home, there were these fellows hanging around the house, looking to see which lights went on, which lights went off, which room he was in now."

The Rebbe was terribly uncomfortable with this kind of adulation. "He'd get so upset when *bocherim* were waiting for him outside 770 to watch him go home," says Zalman Shmotkin. "He'd give us a sharp look, as if to say, Why are you here? Why aren't you learning? More than once he threatened to stop coming to *shul* if people kept looking at him during davening."

The Rebbe listened to the most intimate details of his followers' lives, but offered none about his own, and no one dared ask. He was, Krinsky says, the loneliest man in the world. Chabad Hasidim tell about the time a Hasid came to meet with the Rebbe and the Rebbe put out his hand, but the visitor withdrew, afraid to touch his revered leader. The Rebbe sighed, put his hand down slowly, shook his head, and said quietly, "You, too?"

Lubavitchers attribute to their Rebbe an almost superhuman physical endurance. He developed terrible sciatica in his later years, and walked with a pronounced stoop. He suffered his first major heart attack during Simchat Torah services in 1978, but held in the pain until the end of the service so as not to dampen the evening's joy. Although ill health forced him to restrict his private audiences after 1981, in 1986 he instituted the practice of "Sunday dollars," where he would stand for seven or eight hours once a week in an alcove outside his office, receiving thousands of visitors one by one, speaking to each for a brief moment before handing over a crisp dollar bill, which the recipient was meant to give to charity. He kept up those weekly reception lines until felled by a stroke in March 1992, when he was almost ninety years old. When asked how he found the strength to stand for so many hours, he responded that every human being is a precious jewel, and how could he grow tired counting diamonds?

"His was not the energy of a regular person," says Shmotkin. "There's no question that the Rebbe's rigorous work regimen is a driving force for Lubavitchers. Their own twelve- or fourteen-hour days pale in light of his exertions."

Schneerson's frugality was legendary. At the time of his death his yearly salary was approximately $30,000. Because he never spoke of his own needs and was an intensely private person, his followers hesitated to express their concern for his health and comfort. He spent six hours or more at a time visiting his father-in-law's grave every week, standing stock-still in the rain or snow while he prayed and read letters out loud.

His followers "schemed" to build a booth to protect him from the elements, one Hasid says, but no one dared to mention the idea to the Rebbe. If a thing was a certain way, they felt it was because the Rebbe wished it to be so. His followers' exaggerated belief in the Rebbe's powers to control his physical environment certainly exposed him to more discomfort than he would otherwise have suffered.

The enigma of Schneerson's public persona and private life must be understood within the context of Hasidism itself. Of the many features that set the eighteenth-century movement apart from the prevailing Judaism of its day, one distinguishing characteristic was its creation of the institution of the rebbe, a holy leader whose connection to his followers, his Hasidim, was unbreakable.

What is a Hasidic rebbe? He is first of all a *tzaddik,* a perfectly righteous man. His holiness, piety, and devotion to Jewish Law give him tremendous powers, notably the ability to "move in spheres not understood by ordinary men."* The Rebbe stands between earth and heaven, a pipeline to the Almighty, part of a mighty and mystical chain that stretches back to Moses. Hasidic lore has it that the Baal Shem Tov used to ascend to heaven on Shabbat afternoons, speaking with the heavenly hosts and the Messiah himself.

In times of crisis for the Jewish people, the rebbe-tzaddik can compel God to act. "He is the chosen one who is refused nothing, in heaven or on earth. God is angry? He can make him smile. God is severe? He can induce him to leniency."† This power devolves upon the rebbe not just because of his own personal virtue, but because he does not speak for himself alone. A rebbe is the "root-soul" of his generation, the literal and spiritual embodiment of Moses and inheritor of his great soul, the soul that spoke directly to God. In the rebbe-tzaddik are united the souls of every living Jew, and it is as their physical and spiritual representative that he raises his voice to heaven. Rabbi Moshe New, a Chabad emissary in Montreal, explains that a rebbe is the nerve center of Jews everywhere on earth, even those he has never met. He feels their pain and joy because he is literally connected to them.

This is why Lubavitchers consider Schneerson the leader of world

---

*Mintz, *Hasidic People,* p. 3.

†Elie Wiesel, *Souls on Fire: Portraits and Legends of Hasidic Masters* (New York: Simon & Schuster, 1982), pp. 66–67.

Jewry. It's not hubris, to their way of thinking. It's something ordained by God. "As Jews, we are all one, one great spiritual body," New explains. "The rebbe is the brain, and the brain feels every sensation that occurs anywhere in the body. He is the heartbeat of the Jewish people, that gives them their spiritual energy. Going to the rebbe leaves you with the feeling that there's nothing you can't do, because it's you getting in touch with your own heartbeat, your own center."

A rebbe does not need formal rabbinical ordination to lead his followers. He is born a *tzaddik.* A rebbe-tzaddik can pass that quality, and his title, on to his designated heirs. As Hasidic courts multiplied after the Baal Shem Tov's death, the customs and lifestyles of the Hasidic rebbes began to differ widely. Some, like the Kotzker Rebbe, practiced strict asceticism; the Rizhiner Rebbe flaunted his wealth. Some, like the first Lubavitcher Rebbe, were renowned as Torah scholars. Others, like the Rebbe of Belz, were known primarily as miracle workers. But all continued to exhibit the basic characteristics that became associated with the Hasidic rebbe. One is that a rebbe holds his position at the will of his Hasidim. They choose him to be their rebbe. He is their leader for life, existing on a higher plane and endowed with powers they can only hope to glimpse. But he is also their servant, belonging to them completely. Schneerson's wife expressed this succinctly during a federal trial in New York held to determine ownership of the sixth Rebbe's 40,000-volume library. The wife, daughter, and granddaughter of three Lubavitcher rebbes, she told the court that "the rebbe, and his books, belong to his Hasidim."

A rebbe is responsible for his followers' spiritual and material well-being. He advises them on medical care, marriage plans, career choices, and financial arrangements, as well as more esoteric points of devotion to God. It's an exhausting responsibility, for the rebbe may not refuse to answer his followers' inquiries. In turn, they accept his decisions on their crucial life questions as ordained from above. "His followers owe him blind and unconditional allegiance . . . To question the Rebbe is worse than sin; it is absurd, for it destroys the very relationship that binds you to him."*

The rebbe-tzaddik sets an example for his followers in dress and cus-

---

*Wiesel, *Souls on Fire,* p. 122.

tom as well as spiritual greatness. If he wears long earlocks, or *payes,* and tucks his trousers into white knee socks, so do they. They watch him closely, analyzing his every gesture, adopting many of his personal habits. In emulating his outward appearance, they hope to draw closer to his inner purity, "for all that is attached to the pure is pure" (Bava Kama 92b).

Drawing close to the rebbe—*devekut* in Hebrew—is a central tenet of Hasidism, a vehicle by which one draws closer to God. Hasidim travel long distances in order to visit their rebbe at least once a year, to bring him *kvitelech,* written petitions, and receive his blessing. They crowd in close to their rebbe, eager to be in his physical presence. They pray in huge congregations together with him, they eat at his Shabbos table, eagerly passing around the crumbs from his meal, so all can partake of the rebbe's holy sustenance. The strong collective ethos at the heart of Hasidic life is paralleled in the act of praying, when the Hasid is meant to negate his own self through *bittul,* or "self-nullification," in order to experience spiritual transcendence. "Collective living and praying are indispensable to salvation," writes Elie Wiesel. "Traditional Hasidism had enounced: The self finds fulfillment by losing itself in the collective self."*

Outsiders can glimpse the power of the rebbe-Hasid relationship at a *farbrengen,* a mass gathering where a rebbe expounds on Torah, life, and Hasidic philosophy, punctuated at regular intervals by singing and toasting by his Hasidim. The last Lubavitcher Rebbe's *farbrengens* were legendary. Until his final stroke he would hold them regularly in his *shul* at 770 Eastern Parkway. The Rebbe would deliver his talks while seated at a long table on a raised dais at the front of the room, facing his male followers, who stood before him in the *shul*'s main room. The women listened from their upstairs balcony, leaning forward and peering over each other's shoulders to catch every nuance. Lubavitchers living in Crown Heights used to carry beepers that would alert them if the Rebbe was preparing to deliver a talk, and they would drop whatever they were doing to rush to 770. Chabadniks would fly in from all over the world to be at one of the Rebbe's *farbrengens,* for this was where the magic happened. This was where the Rebbe spoke directly to his Hasidim, inspiring them, guiding them, setting their agenda.

Most powerful of all were those moments of spiritual transcendence

---

*Wiesel, *Souls on Fire,* p. 190.

when Schneerson would pause and indicate, with a nod of his head, that he was about to present a *ma'amar,* a Hasidic discourse. Any Hasidic teacher, even a yeshiva student, can technically hold a *farbrengen.* But only a rebbe can deliver a *ma'amar,* a stream of Torah philosophy believed to be divinely inspired. In *Hasidic People,* Jerome Mintz describes one such scene:

> The ma'amar is more esoteric and deeper in intent than the sicha. Hasidim believe that every ma'amar is like the giving of the Torah at Sinai. The sense of holiness intensifies. The Rebbe ties a handkerchief on his fingers to keep his soul bound on the ground. Everyone in the congregation stands, and they continue to stand for the 20 minutes or the hour that the Rebbe speaks. During this time the Rebbe, however, stays seated, and his eyes remain closed as he speaks. The ma'amar is recited in a different tone of voice than the sicha and a different verbal melody is employed. The ma'amar is similar to davening (prayer), but the text may be academic and intellectual and at the same time deeply personal in discussing the struggle of a soul surviving in the material world. When the Rebbe concludes, there are more songs.*

Chabad shlichim working in the field today have indelible memories of the time they spent in Schneerson's physical presence, the exuberance they experienced in his *farbrengens.* Yossi Greenberg, shliach in Alaska, spent his student years in Crown Heights from 1982 to 1989. He spent almost every Shabbat at 770, and describes the scene of the typical *farbrengen* as "a dramatization of the Talmudic phrase 'a light of God shone above the heads of the scholars.'" Just as Moses' face had an unearthly glow when he descended Mt. Sinai after receiving the Ten Commandments from God's hand, Greenberg says, so did the Rebbe's face shine when he looked down upon his Hasidim. "That shine that came from the Rebbe's face, from his beard, is impossible to explain. In addition, there was the light that came from his eyes, like a laser. When the Rebbe looked at you, it was like a projector beam."

The Hasidim who stood by the hundreds in front of the Rebbe in *shul*

---

*Mintz, *Hasidic People,* pp. 48–49.

would raise their cups of wine to toast him with a *l'chaim,* and when the Rebbe would acknowledge a particular toast by looking that Hasid directly in the eye, Greenberg says the Hasid would lower his gaze, overwhelmed by the Rebbe's penetrating look. "We'd stand on Shabbat sometimes for six or seven hours. We were young kids, eighteen, nineteen years old, each on our own spiritual journey, and the Rebbe knew us through and through. When we saw the Rebbe, we felt that here was a man who lives and feels the truth, a man who is the essence of truth himself. He was the most convincing proof that there is a God."

For Hasidim of his generation and older, Greenberg says, the Rebbe was a personal lodestone, a sage who would take the time to answer the simplest, most personal questions from every individual. "Even when he had thousands of institutions and shlichim, each of us had spiritual crises as students, and the Rebbe would take the time to guide us. He'd write to each of us." Greenberg treasures an answer he received from the Rebbe to one of his pleas for guidance. "He answered me in detail and changed the way I was going. He took his own time to help one young person. Only I know what he wrote. Shlichim won't tell you what the Rebbe said to them. It's very private. Even later, when we no longer were able to go in to him for a personal audience once a year, just standing in front of him, saying *l'chaim* to him, standing in line for dollars—it was such a personal relationship. There was such a feeling that he cared for you. He was watching over each one of us, with such deep personal interest."

Zalman Shmotkin grew up on shlichus in Milwaukee. He remembers his family's infrequent trips to Crown Heights as momentous occasions. Before going into *yechidus* his father would make sure every piece of his clothing was new, in honor of the occasion. "I remember when I was three or four, the Rebbe asked me how many *tzitzit* I had," Shmotkin recalls. "I have this warm feeling of running up the red stairs to the Rebbe's office and then leaving with a feeling of tremendous love. It was more than my *zaide* [grandfather]. I felt, This is my home. I felt safe, secure, loved."

By the time Shmotkin and Greenberg were teenagers, the Rebbe had long since stopped meeting his followers in private audience. "It was a huge issue for me," Shmotkin says. "I felt the love from the Rebbe. I got answers from him, but I would constantly ask myself and God why I couldn't have lived in the 1950s or 1960s, when the Rebbe had more time for *yechidus.* We kids would talk about it all the time. No amount of attention we got from the Rebbe was ever satisfactory. We'd always be hungry for more. It was an indescribable love affair."

By the time he was in his later teens, Shmotkin says he began to focus on what he could do for the Rebbe rather than on what the Rebbe would give him. "We'd try to think up things to please the Rebbe—learning tractates by heart, davening with tremendous feeling. Then we'd write to the Rebbe about it. We were always trying to make the Rebbe happy, but we also knew that nothing we ever did was enough. If you put tefillin on five hundred people one Friday, then how was your davening that morning? How can I do better tomorrow?"

The Rebbe was a constant presence in a Lubavitch student's life, Shmotkin says, acting as a moral compass through adolescent doubt. "For me, grappling with my own internal struggles, the image of the Rebbe pouring out his heart carried me through. He cared so much. To hear the Rebbe talk about the pride of being a Jew, telling us that the world is waiting for us to be what we're supposed to be, was tremendous. The next time you got sidetracked by your petty issues, you'd remember how the Rebbe made you feel that what you do makes a difference in the world."

The care Schneerson took to listen to the people who sought his advice endeared him to them. "The Rebbe could soar to the loftiest heights and never forget for a moment the individual standing before him, or the letter from a widow pouring out her heart to him about her children," says Krinsky.

Lubavitchers look at their rebbe as a constant source of strength that pours out of him into all of them. Rabbi Zalman Posner, Chabad shliach in Nashville, Tennessee, compares a rebbe to a spring that nourishes those who drink from it. "He is a source that never fails. The hassid who maintains a bond with his rebbe is never alone. Though continents and oceans may separate him from his rebbe, he never feels that he has been cut adrift."*

That nourishing power continues after death. "*Tzaddikim* can sometimes prevail in this world even more after their death than in their lifetime, as the confines of the body are removed," says Yehuda Krinsky. "There isn't a shliach in the world who doesn't feel the Rebbe looking over his shoulder."

---

*Zalman Posner, *Think Jewish* (Nashville, Tenn.: Kesher Press, 1979), pp. 27–29.

The Rebbe's followers believed that his spiritual powers literally shone out from his physical body. Some tell tales of standing in the streets of Crown Heights and suddenly feeling their hair stand up. When they turned around, they would find the Rebbe's gaze boring into them, or perhaps even his car simply passing by.

Lubavitchers' intense focus on the personality of their leader led to charges that Chabad was promoting a cult of the Rebbe. Why, critics ask, do Lubavitchers hang his picture everywhere? Why do they continue to ask his advice, now that he's dead?

Some Lubavitchers believe that the Rebbe's prophetic powers extend to the very books that contain his transcribed talks. They write questions for him on a small piece of paper and insert it into one of the Rebbe's books at random, interpreting the Rebbe's "answer" from the words on the page where their note lands. This is not official Chabad practice, and is in fact disdained by a large body of Lubavitchers, but it derives from a central belief common to all Hasidic courts that a rebbe's ability to commune with the heavenly spheres gives him certain otherworldly powers, including the power to work miracles. A rebbe "sees things." He knows things before they happen. His position between this world and the next allows him to draw God's blessings down to earth, through his conscious efforts. He can even invest material objects he touches with those blessings.

Many Chabadniks today attribute miraculous powers to certain ritual objects touched or blessed by Schneerson. Chanie Lipskar still has part of a flask of wine she received from a congregant who went to Crown Heights shortly before the Rebbe's final stroke. The woman, who was childless, had asked Schneerson for a blessing so she would conceive, and the Rebbe gave her the blessing along with some wine he poured from his cup into a container she brought. The congregant gave the wine to Mrs. Lipskar, who has since doled it out to other women looking to get pregnant. She gave some to a woman who was childless after seven years of marriage. The woman drank the wine, gave birth to two sets of twins, and then had a fifth, unintended child after a housekeeper mistakenly gave her a glass of wine from the bottle she'd hidden at the back of her refrigerator. This wine is so potent, Lipskar says, that it has produced at least twenty babies. "The Rebbe is not here physically, but the power of that wine continues," she insists. "Everyone who drinks it says, 'I know I'll get pregnant.'"

The role of rebbe as miracle worker was not as prevalent in the

Lubavitch movement until the ascension of its seventh rebbe. Chabad lore now is chock full of stories of Schneerson predicting the outcomes of medical crises and political events with seemingly pinpoint accuracy. When Jacob Goldstein, a Chabad rabbi who serves as a chaplain in the New York State National Guard, was posted to Israel during the Gulf War in December 1991, he went to the Rebbe for a blessing the night before he shipped out. He told Schneerson that he was taking a *megillah* with him, so he could celebrate Purim, which was less than three months away. "The Rebbe smiled and said back to me, in Yiddish, 'Surely there will be a *megillah* in the desert, but you won't have to read it." The Gulf War ended the day before Purim.

Rabbi Yosef Wineberg of Crown Heights, one of the Rebbe's most senior followers and author of the most popular explanation of the *Tanya,* says that his brother was diagnosed with tuberculosis and told he needed an operation. When he visited the Rebbe, Schneerson told him that the hole in his lung had healed, and the operation was unnecessary, a "diagnosis" confirmed by later doctors' examinations.

One of the best-publicized illustrations of the Rebbe's prescience involved Israeli Prime Minister Ariel Sharon, who was told by the Rebbe during a visit to Brooklyn in the late 1960s that he shouldn't take his scheduled flight home to Israel that night. Sharon heeded the warning, and the plane he was supposed to be on was hijacked to Algeria. People later asked the Rebbe why, if he knew the plane would be hijacked, did he not warn the authorities? Schneerson answered that he didn't know exactly what would happen, he just knew that Sharon shouldn't be on the plane.

Books have been published, chronicling "miracles" wrought by the Rebbe. *Wonders and Miracles: Stories of the Lubavitcher Rebbe* is a two-volume series aimed at younger readers. One story tells of a young girl who has been blinded by a tree branch. She goes to 770, and while she's still outside the synagogue, the Rebbe walks by and wishes her a *refuah shlemah,* or full recovery. Immediately, so the story goes, the girl's glasses break, the swelling in her eye subsides, and by the end of services that day, her sight is restored. In another story a baby girl is badly scalded by a pot of boiling water, and is hooked up to IVs in an intensive care unit. The Rebbe tells her parents to "yell at the doctors," which they do, although not understanding why. It turns out that, due to a clerical error, the baby was receiving the wrong medication, which would have killed her. Today, the book continues, the baby girl is a Lubavitcher mother of fifteen, living in California.

Sometimes the Rebbe's mere blessing is enough to ward off disaster. But in most of the miracle tales, the Rebbe advises people to observe certain mitzvahs in order to effect a solution for their problem. He tells people to check their mezuzahs and tefillin for defects, to eat kosher, to observe Jewish rituals. When order is restored in the religious sphere, so will it be in other aspects of life. A childless couple is told to check the husband's tefillin, where the word "womb" is found to be missing. It's replaced, and they have a baby. Another couple with several retarded children is told to drink only kosher milk, and their next baby is of normal intelligence. A father of a severely ill boy is told to fast on Yom Kippur, and his child recovers.

The stories go on and on. Some Lubavitchers don't like the emphasis put on the Rebbe's miracles. They believe in his powers but say it's not the essence of what he was. Certainly, many of the miracle tales involve the creative interpretation of vague statements made by the Rebbe, statements that might have been taken several ways. But the sheer number of such "miraculous" interventions and predictions suggests to many people, including non-Lubavitchers, that Schneerson had tremendous insight, at the very least, and perhaps something more.

Malcolm Hoenlein, longtime executive vice chairman of the Conference of Presidents of Major American Jewish Organizations, is an observant Jew but not a Hasid. He first met the Rebbe forty years ago, as an eleven-year-old boy on a class trip from Philadelphia. It was right before Simchat Torah, a day when Schneerson would hand out honey cake to visitors. As he went down the line of boys, Schneerson stopped and talked to Hoenlein, asking about his family, his ambitions, and other personal questions, finally giving the boy three extra pieces of cake to take home to his parents and younger brother.

Seven or eight years later, Hoenlein returned to Crown Heights again for Simchat Torah, and the Rebbe remembered every detail of what he'd told him, asking after his parents and little brother. "I was very taken by him," Hoenlein says. "He remembered exactly what I'd told him years before. It was my first exposure to this overwhelming charisma."

The last time Hoenlein visited the Rebbe was in 1991. He was driving through Crown Heights with his son and the young man's bride-to-be and, on a whim, stopped by to get a blessing from the Rebbe. Rabbi Leib

Groner, Schneerson's aide who controlled visitor access, turned to the Rebbe to tell him who the visitors were. "The Rebbe said, 'I know exactly who this is,' and he started talking to me about the work I was doing, things I was involved in. It was incredible, how he would know in such detail about some of those things." Hoenlein's father was very sick at the time, so he asked the Rebbe for a blessing for a *refuah shlema*. Instead, Schneerson turned to him and said that his father "should continue to have *nachas* [happiness] from all the good work you do."

Hoenlein persisted, and asked again for a blessing for his father's recovery. "The Rebbe had been smiling ear to ear. Now he stopped smiling and said, 'Your father should continue to have *nachas* from all the good work you do.' I turned to Rabbi Groner and he just shrugged, so I decided to try one more time. I said, 'Before I leave, Rebbe, I'd like a *bracha*.' He looked at me, this time very straight, and said, 'Your father should continue to have *nachas* from all the good work you do.'"

Hoenlein went home, got his tallis and tefillin and went to the hospital, where his father died that night. Ten years later, he still talks about the incident with wonder. "Did the Rebbe know? Did he not know? I can't tell you."

Schneerson's death in June 1994 ripped through Chabad's gut with razor sharpness, leaving a raw, gaping wound that still bleeds easily. When many Lubavitchers speak about his death, their eyes fill with tears. Most won't even utter the phrase "the Rebbe's death," not because they believe he's still alive—although there are those who do—but because they simply can't bear the pain of acknowledging his absence out loud.

Abba Refson was a twenty-two-year-old yeshiva student when the Rebbe died. He followed the funeral cortege to Schneerson's burial spot in the Old Montefiore Cemetery and never left. Refson spent the first six months living in a mitzvah tank parked on a pathway in the cemetery. "It was more spontaneous than any kind of plan," he says. "I saw people were coming here all the time, nonreligious people, and they needed help, they needed direction." Like most yeshiva students his age, the Leeds-born Refson had always dreamed of going on shlichus. "I never imagined it would be here," he admits.

Refson eventually moved into a small, two-bedroom brick house next to the *ohel*, purchased by a Crown Heights Lubavitcher. The house now serves as a welcome station for the endless stream of visitors. A video of the Rebbe plays continuously on a small TV screen in the front room, where visitors congregate to peruse Chabad literature and catch up with old friends. One bedroom has been converted into a library and synagogue, where classes in Hasidus and prayer services are held. Refson's office is in the second bedroom, which barely has room for his desk, a few cartons of books, and a huge print of the Rebbe against the back wall.

Refson is technically on duty twenty-four hours a day, although he has an assistant who splits the late-night work with him. He's also helped by his wife, a Detroit girl he married six years after he took over the *ohel* shlichus. "I guess she knew what she was getting into," he says with a grin. Daily crowds of 200 to 300 people swell to 800 or 1,000 on Sundays, when Chabad *shlichim* show up with busloads of supporters, on their way to tours of Crown Heights. Three fax machines run continuously, printing out 500 to 600 letters from petitioners every day. Refson's computer receives about 300 e-mailed letters daily as well. Refson and his assistant collect the faxes and e-mails every two hours, take them to the grave, tear them up, and scatter the pieces. They clear away and burn the huge pile of shredded papers two or three times a week.

It's 9:45 A.M. on a bitterly cold Sunday morning in March. A blizzard is brewing in an angry gray sky, but more than fifty people are already waiting their turn to visit the Rebbe. Attached to the back of the house is a thirty-by-one-hundred-foot tent, where visitors sit at long picnic tables writing their letters to the Rebbe. Humming generators power fans that blow hot air over the crowded room. Alongside the steps leading down to the cemetery itself, religious visitors deposit their leather shoes and put on plastic flip-flops, considered more respectful when visiting a *tzaddik*'s grave. Some men step into plastic boxes that are open on the bottom and top, then pull them up around their waists like a kind of square hula hoop. The boxes represent the four walls of a house, and are used to permit *cohanim,* who ordinarily may not step into a cemetery, to visit the Rebbe's grave.

Most visitors are Jewish, Refson believes, but a fair number of non-Jews show up as well, particularly from the surrounding neighborhood, which is largely African-American. "They've heard of the Rebbe, they see this is a holy place, and they want to participate," he says. A few weeks before this March morning, an elderly gentleman from the neighborhood made his first visit. "He was so moved, he brought his whole family the next week." Another African-American man who worked as a janitor for Refson asked whether he could write a letter and take it to the Rebbe. Of course, Refson said, and when the man emerged from the *ohel,* he began pacing back and forth in the tent. Refson asked what was wrong. The man shook his head and said he'd been to many graves, "but there's something strong in there."

Today a young Lubavitcher couple has driven down from Toronto with their three young children. The wife says that when she was a child in the Midwest, she would come to Crown Heights with her parents to get dollars from the Rebbe during his Sunday marathon sessions. It makes her sad to visit the Rebbe's grave, she says, her eyes filling with tears, even though she knows she's not supposed to be sad there. She helps her children write the letters they will take to the grave. Her four-year-old boy asks for *refuah shlema* for his cold. Her six-years-old writes that he "wants Moshiach [the Messiah] now."

Lubavitch couples visit the ohel together when they get engaged to ask for the Rebbe's blessing, just as they used to ask the Rebbe's blessing on their union while he was alive. This Sunday one young couple from Crown Heights has driven out to announce their upcoming nuptials to the Rebbe. "*Now* we're officially engaged," proclaims Zalman, twenty-three, a tall man with reddish-blond hair and a small pointed beard. He and his fiancée, twenty-year-old Miriam, are beaming. Although they grew up around the corner from each other, they didn't meet until set up by matchmakers several weeks ago. This visit is their first formal act together as a couple. "Every time we're about to do something important, we ask the Rebbe's blessing beforehand," Zalman says.

At eleven-thirty, the first bus tour arrives—forty visitors from suburban Connecticut on a day trip to Crown Heights with their Chabad rabbi. One woman in the group describes herself as "close to Chabad," saying she even has a picture of the Rebbe hanging in her living room. This is her first trip to the *ohel,* and she's very excited. Her rabbi has prepared her well for the experience, she says. But later, after she emerges from the mausoleum, her face has lost some of its glow. She admits that she's disappointed.

"It didn't look like what I imagined," she complains. "I thought it would be more open, more grassy. I expected lots of space." But, she says, she appreciates what the site means to Lubavitchers. "It's not the *Kotel* [Jerusalem's Western Wall], but I still felt something."

Everyone comes to the Rebbe's grave with different expectations. Some are merely curious. They stand back from the crowd, watching the crying and praying as if from a distance. Others are heartbroken. They pour out their most intimate secrets in long, scribbled letters, then stand sobbing at the grave.

Not everyone knows why they're there. A young woman in her early twenties is sitting at one of the long picnic tables in the waiting tent, idly chewing her fingernails. She has bright fuchsia hair and her lower lip is double-pierced. She says she hitchhiked down from Montreal the previous week and ended up in Crown Heights at an encounter weekend for Jewish students. She liked the studying but is wary of this visit to the Rebbe's grave. "I'm not sure what I'm doing here," she mutters. "I guess it's like a pilgrimage to any holy place, like going to see the Dalai Lama." She has, she says, very mixed feelings about what she calls "venerating a dead man," and doesn't like the idea of standing next to a grave, talking to a spirit. "It doesn't feel right," she says.

But when she comes out of the *ohel* later, she's very quiet. No, nothing supernatural happened inside. Yes, she still feels uncomfortable with the whole experience. But it wasn't "stupid," as she expected it would be. "The spirit there was very holy," she muses. "Something very holy is in that place."

CHAPTER 5

TORAH AND CHICKEN SOUP:

Chabad on Campus

It's 4 P.M. on a bitterly cold Friday afternoon in December, and Aharon and Rivkah Slonim are putting the finishing touches on dinner for 150. Aharon is tasting the Moroccan-spiced *cholent* bubbling away in two huge stainless-steel cauldrons on the couple's industrial stove, and Rivkah is supervising three of her seven children as they dish five gallons of coleslaw, three enormous mixing bowls' worth of potato salad, and dozens of jars of gefilte fish onto paper serving platters. Nine-year-old Shmulik is carefully ladling matzah ball soup into Styrofoam bowls, while six-year-old Chaya Mushka spoons out generous portions of beet-red *chrein,* or horseradish sauce. Thirteen-year-old Chani is counting trays of roast chicken, to make sure there will be enough left for Saturday lunch. The long folding dinner tables can't be set up yet, because their Chabad House's main reception room has to be used first for Friday night services. Then all the chairs will be cleared away, tables brought in from the next room, tablecloths unfolded, plates, cups, and silverware distributed, and a delicious, four-course dinner will be served to more than 150 hungry college students. For free.

Considering that the guests will be pouring through the door any minute, it's amazing that the kitchen is so calm. But the Slonims, codirectors of the Chabad House at Binghamton University (a division of the State University of New York), have been doing this every week since they arrived as newlyweds in upstate New York in January of 1985. They seemed an unlikely couple then for campus outreach. Except for a couple of summers as a camp counselor in Winnipeg, nineteen-year-old Rivkah had lived her entire life in Crown Heights. Aharon, born and raised in Jerusalem, spoke little English and knew nothing of American popular culture. Neither of them had been to college. But their job was to establish a Chabad House at Binghamton, a state university with 12,500 students, forty percent of whom were Jewish.

None of the students knew the Slonims were coming to town. The local Jewish Federation, financially strapped itself, wished they wouldn't. They had no funding base, just promises of an eighteen-month bare bones salary from the Chabad regional director in Buffalo. And they'd only been to Binghamton once, for three days, six weeks earlier.

"I was so young, so idealistic," Rivkah recalls. "If I had to do it again now, I'd be too filled with fear—fear of acceptance, will we make it financially, am I fit for the job? But when you're twenty, you can conquer the world."

Their first week on campus, the Slonims rented a small apartment and set up a table in the student union, where they handed out Jewish and Hasidic literature, and invited students to drop by for Shabbat dinner. That first Friday night three students showed up. As the semester progressed, the numbers grew to five, then ten, then eighteen or twenty each week. At the end of the school year, forty-five students showed up for a Shabbat weekend "in our little, crummy apartment," Aharon recalls. Five years and two moves later, the Slonims were regularly hosting more than a hundred students every Friday evening, and were raising money to build another building attached to their home, for Chabad activities. By late 2000, they'd outgrown that space as well and were breaking ground on a 2,000-square-foot expansion, set to open in the fall of 2001.

The Slonims' work is never-ending. Along with feeding hundreds of students every Friday night and Saturday afternoon, they hold campuswide celebrations for every Jewish holiday, teach more than a dozen classes a week in Bible, Talmud, Jewish Law and Hasidic philosophy, put out a bimonthly newspaper, bring in lecturers and special programs, run alumni reunion parties, and are available to students for personal counseling. And they still sit at that table in the student union every Monday and Thursday. Plus, there's the constant pressure of fundraising. In Binghamton, Aharon estimates that one-third of his funding comes from the local Jewish community of less than 1,000 families. He raises the rest from his students who have graduated and their parents, whom he solicits twice a year by mail. Still, the Binghamton Chabad House runs on a deficit, and it's one of the biggest, most successful campus Chabad operations in the country.

One reason the Slonims have been so successful is that they're the only show in town. No other Jewish organization has managed to get off the ground, including Hillel, which made several false starts in Binghamton in the 1990s before finally sending a permanent representative in late 2001. Student-led Reform and Conservative groups on campus run Friday night services once a month, but most of those students show up at the Slonims' for dinner afterward. A regional consultant for the United Jewish Communities covering upstate New York says, "We've been trying for years to get Hillel in there," but to no avail. "I attribute that to the charismatic leadership of the Chabad couple," she says.

Rivkah, like any true Chabadnik, dismisses the possibility that she and her husband might be responsible for the success of their Chabad House. It's all "the Rebbe," she insists. "It's the miracle of Chabad, all over the world. Two young kids show up in a neighborhood, they look a little funny, people wonder who they are and what they're doing. But in time, the things that separate us fall away. It's all about the *pintele Yid* (Jewish spark) that's shared by all Jews. That's what the kids feel when they walk through our doors. They're accepted by us. And they learn to accept us in turn."

This Friday night the students start to breeze in by five o'clock, brushing snow off their heads. About forty show up early enough to catch at least part of the prayer service, but most come late, just in time to help move the chairs and tables for the festive dinner. The meal is a long-drawn-out affair lasting many hours, with singing and Torah lessons between every course. Rivkah says that most of their guests are regulars, with thirty to forty first-timers showing up each week. Warren, twenty, is here for the second week in a row, and this time he's dragged his roommate along. Warren grew up in New York, in a secular family with a long history in left-wing politics. "My grandmother was in the Red Army," he states proudly. While studying biology, chemistry, and physics at college, Warren says he "realized there was a God" and decided he wanted to find out more. He began reading the *Zohar* and other kabbalistic books on his own, and last week he discovered the Slonims. He and his roommate are singing all the Hebrew songs with gusto, as if they know them. They don't, but they do know Yiddish. Binghamton has the country's largest undergraduate Yiddish-language program, with more than 150 students, many of whom show up at the Slonims' for language practice as much as anything else.

Carrie and Linda are both juniors, and regulars at Chabad. Carrie writes for the school newspaper and hopes to spend the next year in Jerusalem, "maybe in a yeshiva." Both girls grew up in non-observant homes but are now wearing long skirts, signaling that they are experimenting with greater Jewish observance. Carrie believes that it's students like herself, from secular backgrounds, that are most open to Chabad's message. "The modern Orthodox students are turned off by it," she thinks. "They use their college years to go wild." For her and Linda, the rituals of prayer, *kashrut,* and Shabbat are exotic. They're "turned on," she says, by a world they didn't grow up in.

Linda, who is the Jewish student representative to the campus Intercultural Affairs Council and is running for president of the school's future Hillel group, is also Chabad's "cake lady." Every week she bakes seven or eight sheet cakes in Rivkah's kitchen for the communal Shabbat dinner. Like Carrie, Linda is now more observant than her parents. She brought her mother once to visit the Slonims, but her father, she says, "wouldn't like it." She's talked with Rivkah and Aharon about how to relate to her parents religiously: Should she eat in their house? Should she ask them to observe Shabbat? The Slonims told her never to criticize her parents or confront them with a holier-than-thou attitude. Carrie visited her father recently, and because his home isn't kosher, he'd bought an entire new set of plates so she could eat with him. "I told him, 'Dad, don't worry about it! You're my dad!'"

The kids who come to the Slonims' events regularly are fiercely devoted to them. A commemorative book put out for the couple's fifteenth anniversary on campus is filled with page after page of testimony from past and present students, talking about the deep and lasting impact the Slonims had on them. Very few of the students say they became observant because of their encounter with the Slonims. More talk about feeling "closer" to Judaism, more comfortable with the rituals, more willing to identify with the American Jewish community.

The Slonims are aware that they serve as parent figures for many of the students they attract, particularly those who do become more observant through them. This has sometimes put them in conflict with the students' real parents, who aren't always happy with their newly *frum* (religious) kids. Rivkah relates the story of a young woman who came to one Friday night dinner, plopped down on the Slonims' couch, and announced to Rivkah that she was studying to be a rabbi. "I said, 'That's fantastic, I wish everybody here wanted to become a rabbi.' She told me later that she was blown away by that. She'd told her boyfriend ahead of time she was sure I'd say that I don't believe women should be rabbis, and she'd use that as an excuse to leave without trying us out." The young woman ended up becoming very close to the Slonims, first deciding to become a Conservative rather than a Reform rabbi, and then, as she began to align herself with the Orthodox movement, abandoning that plan altogether to go into Jewish social work.

"Her parents were very upset," Rivkah recalls. "They saw it as a senseless clipping of her wings. She had a beautiful voice, she's articulate, she's brilliant, she would have made a fantastic rabbi or cantor." The parents came to Binghamton to meet with the Slonims and were angry that Rivkah showed up without Aharon. Rivkah found that ironic. "It was almost misogyny, which is what they accuse us of. As if the meeting was no longer important if my husband wasn't there. I thought, 'What am I, chopped liver?'" Since then, parents and daughter reconciled, and the entire family keeps in close touch with the Slonims.

Being a campus shliach is quite different from being a community shliach. While spared a lot of the politicking that plagues Chabad couples in a typical Jewish community, campus shlichim have to play many roles—surrogate parent, teacher, best friend, camp counselor, career advisor, spiritual guide, psychiatrist, on-call chef, and, of course, rabbi. Family privacy is nonexistent. When the first campus Chabad House opened three decades ago, the Rebbe decreed that his campus operations be open twenty-four hours a day. Most Chabad families, like the Slonims, also live in their Chabad Houses, which means that young people are traipsing through their homes at all hours, even after the family has long gone to bed. Rivkah can wake up in the morning and find students crashed out on her couches, or talking together in the library room.

Because their doors are always open, campus shlichim quickly learn that their shlichus is a family affair. The Slonims' children hang out with Binghamton students as much as their parents do, hearing all their troubles, and sometimes, at a very young age, even offering advice. During the Friday evening Shabbat meal, Aharon always gives a *davar Torah,* or explanatory talk, on the weekly Torah portion. The next day during lunch, one by one his children all stand up and give their own remarks on the Torah portion, even three-year-old Yisrael. The children are very aware of their roles as representatives of Chabad.

Interestingly, their exposure to college life hasn't made them question their religious lifestyle. On the contrary, they are sometimes stricter than their parents. One Saturday afternoon Rivkah gives a guest a scrapbook of news clippings, but Chaya Mushka admonishes the guest for looking at it, explaining that it is *muktse*—forbidden on Shabbat. Thirteen-year-old Chani won't do an errand for her mother during services, because it would force her to walk through the men's section of their makeshift synagogue.

Rivkah and Aharon both say their goals have mellowed over the years. Rivkah, who lectures around the country on women's issues in Judaism, says that when she first came to Binghamton she was fired up with the Rebbe's teachings, ready to take on the world. "When you're young, you look at the world in very stark terms, especially if you grow up feeling passionately about something, as we did about Hasidism. In the recesses of your heart you feel that there are those who are [observant], and those who will become. As time elapses, you learn more and more that things are not that simple. You are who you are, and people are who they are. If and when people will take on additional observances is really up to them. The only thing that the Rebbe wanted us to do is to make it possible for them to have the tools they need when they begin to look for themselves."

Aharon adds: "For a student to do even one more mitzvah, to be even a little more involved in Judaism, this is my reward. Of course, I would like more than this. But to each their own."

There are close to 400,000 Jewish college students in the United States, and everyone wants them. Hillel wants them. The Reform and Conservative campus organizations want them. Young Israel wants them, as well as a host of smaller Zionist-oriented and Jewish social-action groups. And

Chabad wants them, too. "This is where people's lives are starting, it's where American Jewish culture is formed," says Rabbi Menachem Schmidt, a Chabad shliach in Philadelphia.

Chabad made its first big push onto America's college campuses in the mid-1960s, when anti-Vietnam demonstrations were beginning, rock music was blaring, and every kind of political, social, and mind-expanding experimentation called out to the country's youth. Schneerson believed that the message of traditional Judaism, carried onto campus by intelligent, sincere young rabbis and their wives, could counter some of the antiestablishment sentiment that was leading Jewish youth astray. For the first few years, Chabad sent single yeshiva students onto college campuses on an ad hoc basis, but the leadership quickly realized that these young emissaries needed the support of marriage and family life. Even so, many Lubavitch parents feared the temptations would be too great for their newly married children.

Those fears were not completely unfounded. Two popular early shlichim—Rabbis Sholomo Carlebach and Zalman Schacter-Shalomi—fell out of grace with the Chabad leadership in the 1950s after blending in too well with the young people they sought to bring back to Judaism. The Chabad leadership felt that, in their attempt to be nonjudgmental, they relaxed their standards too far. Carlebach went on to set up the House of Love and Prayer in Haight-Ashbury, became a noted singer-songwriter, and eventually became the spiritual leader of what came to be known as the Carlebach Shul in Manhattan. Schachter—who added the "Shalomi" to his name in honor of the Camp David peace talks—founded the Jewish Renewal movement.

The first campus Chabad House opened in March 1969 at the University of California, Los Angeles. It was the height of the hippie era, the year of Woodstock, and the Chabad rabbis who ran late-night rap sessions at the UCLA Chabad House had to be up front about drugs, sex, the war, and a host of other real-world problems that many of them had never encountered in their own lives. "It was wild—free love, hippies coming in off the streets," says Rabbi Zalman Bukiet, whose brother-in-law worked at UCLA in those early years.

The UCLA Chabad House was opened by Shlomo Cunin, a young Bronx-born rabbi sent to L.A. by Schneerson in 1965 to establish Chabad's West Coast activities. Rabbi Cunin, who has since built up an enormous operation in California, with almost a hundred Chabad Houses and dozens of educational institutions, had a special fondness for Jews outside the mainstream. "I was very involved with the hippies," he relates. "My name went around, that here's a rabbi that could talk to the hippies. I'd walk in the streets on Shabbos in my *kapote* [frock coat] and tallis. They'd come up to me and say, 'Who are you? What a beautiful coat!' Once I made a couple of friends, they'd come to the house, then they'd bring their friends. They were smart people. We'd talk informally, I'd sing with them, I'd give them straight answers. Even when I differed with them, I did it respectfully. I didn't say, 'You idiot, you don't know what you're saying.' We were just different. This is your opinion, and this is mine."

The hippies were "beautiful people," Cunin insists. Despite the Lubavitchers' embrace of tradition, and the 1960s generation's rejection of it, both groups had in common their critique of the dominant, materialistic American culture. Since the 1950s the Rebbe had inveighed against America's love affair with materialism, predicting a youth rebellion against it. Cunin would find Jewish hippies and runaways in the streets, and invite them home for Shabbos. He'd take them to the local Orthodox *shuls* for prayer services, which did not endear him with the regular worshipers. "The old Eastern European refugees, they'd say, 'Why are you bringing these smelly people into our *shul?*'" He would alternate synagogues, to avoid alienating the same people week after week. But he soon saw that he needed a place just for the young people, so, with Schneerson's blessings, he raised money to open his own on-campus center, which he called a "Chabad House."

In 1972 he opened a second campus Chabad House, at UC-Berkeley, and four months later a third, in San Diego. By the end of 2000, there were Chabad Houses on forty-one U.S. campuses. Each is run by a Lubavitcher couple, and they all feature Shabbat meals, holiday celebrations, and free classes, sometimes for college credit. Big public splashes are de rigueur—outdoor menorah lightings at Chanukah and huge Purim parties that move from dorm to dorm, with much late-night partying and drinking of schnapps, while campus temperance patrols look the other way. Most Chabad Houses also hold prayer services, but on campuses with strong Orthodox minyans, the Chabad rabbi may decide not to run his own. Schneerson directed his emissaries to avoid stepping on the toes of other Jewish groups wherever possible. The essence of the campus Chabad experience is the weekly Friday night dinner, the creation of a warm and loving "home away from home" for Jewish students. That's why it's particularly important that Chabad operations on campus be run by a family, with children, to expose Jewish students from secular backgrounds to religious family life. "I use my children to the nth degree," says one Chabad shlicha who works on a campus in the Northeast. "On Shabbos, I don't hold my baby at all, except when I'm nursing. He sleeps in students' arms the whole time."

In the absence of any central organization to direct them, shlichim from campus Chabad Houses began to meet once a year on their own in the late 1990s, to share information and programming ideas. An unofficial Chabad resource book for new shlichim, *Shlichus: Meeting the Outreach Challenge,* includes a chapter called "The Campus Approach," written primarily by Rabbi Eli Cohen, the Chabad shliach at New York University. He notes that campus work is very important to Chabad, because it touches young people at a point in their lives when they are not yet tied to a particular lifestyle. There is a greater chance that the student will be open to the observant, even the Hasidic, message. But if that doesn't occur, Cohen writes, simply providing students with more Jewish information, dispelling negative images of traditional observance, and turning kids away from drugs or depression is all part of the shliach's work. And today's students who are receiving a positive impression of Lubavitch will be tomorrow's American Jewish leadership.

Successful campus Chabad shlichim are those who know how to talk to kids, and how to give them what they want. Food is a major outreach tool. Rabbi Zalman Deitsch, Chabad shliach at Ohio State University, mans his own kosher hot-dog stand at a busy campus intersection. He also sponsors an annual kosher hot-dog–eating contest between OSU students and the university football team, an event that draws hundreds of spectators and raises awareness of Lou Gehrig's disease, a Chabad charity. Many Chabad shlichim try to run a kosher dining plan. One shliach at an eastern university says that when he started his kosher meal plan, he made it cheaper than the university dining plan, to attract Jewish kids who never even thought of eating kosher. "They only came because it was cheaper than the regular meal plan, but then they started hanging out at the Chabad House and bringing their friends," he says. "It's a great way to get them in there, every day." And, he adds, he knows they're eating one less nonkosher meal.

The 1980s were the years of biggest growth for campus Chabad Houses. Today, Chabad shlichim say privately that attention has shifted away from the college campus and toward community activism, largely because American college students have changed. They're not dropping out or experimenting with different lifestyles as readily as they once did, which means they're less open to exploring radically new spiritual avenues. "Today everyone's in college with their little hand-held Palm Pilots, worried about 'Where will I get my first job? How much will I make?'" says Rabbi Cunin.

Rivkah Slonim sees greater student apathy than when she first arrived in Binghamton in 1985. "There's a rush to get through school and get on with life. When we came, there were students staying here for five years. People were very into social action, a variety of causes. I don't feel a surge of activism like I used to." That means she and her husband have to try harder to interest students in their programs. They reach one-fourth of the Jewish student population, good numbers by most people's estimates, but Rivkah is concerned about the three-quarters they don't reach. "I see huge numbers of Jewish students who are totally disaffected," she says.

Rabbi Eliezer Sneiderman has been the Chabad shliach at the University of Delaware since 1992, and even over the course of one decade, he's noticed that the Jewish sororities and fraternities are pledging significantly fewer students. "I used to be able to knock on the door and get forty or fifty Jewish kids to dinner," he says. "That doesn't happen anymore." Another big change on campus that affects the way Chabad does business, Sneiderman says, is the general ban on alcohol and a resultant drop in student partying. "In the 1970s you could just roll out a keg and attract students. Then it became illegal to serve beer to eighteen-year-olds, and now it's socially unacceptable." In 1994, Sneiderman got permission from campus authorities to serve wine at his Purim and Passover events. "I don't think I'd get that permission today," he remarks.

That's just fine with Richard Joel, president and international director of Hillel, the nation's largest Jewish student organization, with a seventy-five-year history on college campuses. "We have issues with Chabad about drinking on campus," he says. "There's a long tradition of drinking schnapps on Friday night, getting a little tipsy so one can achieve a state of [religious] ecstasy. That's very nice, but it has no place on campus, where a good number of the students are minors."

Hillel, the Foundation for Jewish Campus Life, is Chabad's major rival in the struggle for the hearts and minds of American college students. Hillel acts as an umbrella body for all Jewish organizations on the 110 campuses where it maintains permanent staff. Because it reaches out to all Jewish students, Hillel often finds itself in competition, friendly or otherwise, with Chabad, the only other campus group with the same broad target audience. On paper Hillel treats Chabad like any other campus Jewish group, welcoming it into its fold. Actual relations, however, vary from campus to campus. On some campuses, Hillel and Chabad jockey for position with the school administration, or try to outdo each other by offering bigger, sometimes noticeably similar, Jewish classes and events. Often relations are easier on campuses where Chabad is small and Hillel is well established. On those campuses, the Hillel director and staff tend not to view Chabad as a threat, particularly when the Chabad rabbi himself goes out of his way to be conciliatory. At Ohio State University, Hillel director Joseph Kohane says Chabad is too small to be able to duplicate what Hillel offers. "Their scope is different, there isn't any competition," he says. "They are another Jewish alternative on campus that students might want to check out."

More often than not, relations between Hillel and Chabad on a college campus come down to the personalities of the individual directors involved. And that can change over time. At the University of Pennsylvania, Hillel director Jeremy Brochin describes his relationship with Chabad as "very good." The Chabad rabbi is, he says, "a lovely guy" who, by the way, davens at Hillel, which has a very strong Orthodox minyan. Brochin says that Chabad is small at Penn, with less than two dozen "regulars." It's no threat to Hillel, which Brochin claims draws 1,000 students a week to its activities. "They do their own thing," he says.

Things were very different in 1979, when Rabbi Schmidt opened the first Chabad House at the University of Pennsylvania. "I wouldn't say Hillel gave us a large welcome when we came," he says. "The Hillel director threw me out of the building a couple times." Both Hillel and Chabad at Penn have moved through several directors since, Schmidt notes. But he claims that Hillel at Penn has blocked Chabad efforts to obtain university accreditation for its courses. Students at SUNY-Binghamton and SUNY-Buffalo, both schools with strong Chabad operations, do get credit for many of the classes offered by their Chabad Houses.

Sometimes, Richard Joel says, Hillel staff is "flummoxed" when trying to deal with its local Chabad. That could come as much from a misunderstanding of the Chabad mission as anything else—the welcoming outreach combined with strict personal observance of Halacha. "They're not really interested in coalition building," he says. "It's not their thing. They have their mission, and as long as you don't get into their space, fine." Stepping on toes can be inevitable. "It can be very difficult, if we're trying to do something on a campus, and there's this mitzvah tank that shows up with a guy going up to people and getting in their faces, asking if they put on tefillin today. Students feel threatened. They don't distinguish between Chabad and Hillel, and they think it's a little much."

Rabbi Art Donsky was the Hillel director from 1993 to 1997 for four campuses in Pittsburgh, including the University of Pittsburgh, Carnegie-Mellon, Duquesne, and Chatham College. He says that although the Chabad rabbis on campus expressed the best intentions, "the reality is, they did whatever they could to undermine our efforts." The situation in Pittsburgh is the reverse of campuses with small Chabad operations. The city has a large Lubavitch population of more than a thousand people, with strong ties in the local Jewish community dating back to the 1940s, when the first Chabad day school was founded. "Pittsburgh is an example of where Chabad has been successful in getting into the infrastructure of the mainstream Jewish community," Donsky says. Hillel, on the other hand, didn't acquire its own building until 2000, after years of what Donsky describes as little community support. The result was that Chabad more or less overwhelmed Hillel during Donsky's tenure. "They did the same programs we did, targeting the same kids," he charges.

Some Chabad rabbis pull out the big guns, like the East Coast campus shliach who went to the Rebbe's grave to plead for help in his ongoing struggle with Hillel, which had just moved into a new building across the street from his campus Chabad House. "He davened so hard," his wife recounts. "He said to the Rebbe, 'Please, let them lose a little of the koiches [strength] they have.' And lo and behold, we found out right before school started that the Hillel rabbi left, along with most of their staff. They had to hire all new people."

Chabad has always been completely open about what it's trying to do, Joel says. And he applauds their efforts to expose more Jewish students to Jewish traditions, to encourage mitzvahs and holiday celebrations. "On a basic level, they're trying to share their love of Judaism and their Chabad philosophy in a noncoercive way, with as many people as are interested," he says. There will always be a need for Hillel, too, he believes, because Chabad doesn't meet what he calls "the full range of community needs."

A Chabad shliach won't interfere with Reform or Conservative services on campus, but neither will he help organize them.

Ironically, Chabad doesn't always meet the needs of Orthodox students, either. At Ohio State, Chabad was well entrenched, running its own prayer services, when Hillel director Kohane arrived eight years ago. A group of Orthodox students asked Kohane to organize a modern Orthodox minyan. "Chabad's services are not always the same kind of traditional services these kids are used to," Kohane notes. That's a problem Chabad faces at many campuses. Although its services follow an Orthodox prayer book, and men and women sit separately, it's very much a beginners' service. The prayer book has English translations, and transliterations of the Hebrew, and the rabbi moves slowly through the prayers, explaining as he goes along. An eighteen-year-old modern Orthodox young man, who knows the prayers cold and has to say them three times a day, isn't always interested in taking time to explore the inner meaning of the Shema when he's already late for class.

Despite occasional flare-ups and personality tiffs, Joel has high praise for Chabad's campus operations. "I have a lot of respect for what Chabad does," he says. "Our battle isn't between Orthodox, Conservative, and Reform, but between those who are prepared to own their Jewishness and the clueless." Joel says he is a "big admirer" of the late Rebbe. He admits that he's "stolen programs" for Hillel from Chabad, and has tried to encourage Hillel staffers to emulate the sincerity of Chabad's outreach style. But ultimately, he says, Hillel can't do what Chabad does, because no Jewish organization can match Chabad's personnel pool for training and dedication. Hillel hires professionals, but Chabad grows True Believers. "If you're part of Chabad, and they tell you to go to Pechatch, you go to Pechatch. They are all mission-driven, and prepared to devote their lives to it. [My people] want to go home at the end of the day. It's a different cultural gestalt."

Chabad shlichim are used to making personal sacrifices for the sake of outreach. Eli Cohen and his wife Yehudis live in Crown Heights, but they rent an apartment near the NYU campus in lower Manhattan that they use only on Shabbat. Every Friday afternoon they pile their nine kids in a car and drive to their Manhattan apartment for the weekend, so they can host students for Friday night and Saturday afternoon meals. They found that apartment only two years ago. Before that they went through a few years of apartment-swapping with a Manhattan family that wanted the

Crown Heights "experience" on Shabbat. And for years before that arrangement Eli would bring a couple of his kids with him to NYU every Shabbat and bunk down in empty dorm rooms or in his office, sleeping on couches or even the floor, with his children spread out around him. Sometimes he'd walk to Manhattan, a journey of more than three hours, just to be there for the students. And then he'd walk home. Other campus shlichim have similar stories.

"When you meet a Chabad shliach, you meet a living example of self-sacrifice," says Menachem Schmidt. "To a college kid, who's putting his life in perspective, this is a tremendous lesson in values. Some are ready to embrace this level of religious observance. Others just make the connection, and that's important, too." Schmidt is speaking from personal experience. He was a college sophomore in 1973, a non-observant kid from a Conservative background, when he went to a weekend "Encounter with Chabad" in Crown Heights on the advice of a friend who had become involved with Chabad at Rutgers University. He was so impressed with what he saw that he embarked on his own path toward greater observance, eventually becoming a campus Chabad shliach himself.

Joel wishes he saw more of that dedication among the up-and-coming generation of Jewish professionals. It's not easy, he says, to find Hillel staffers for small schools, or even big universities in rural areas. He's been trying to find a Hillel director for Cornell University, with no luck. "I'm pulling my hair out," he comments. "Maybe I should speak to Chabad about sending someone."

As sprawling, boisterous, and crowded as Friday night dinners are at the Slonims' Chabad House in Binghamton, Shabbat meals at Harvard University's Chabad House are intimate, sedate, even elegant. With 150 to 200 unruly undergraduates piling into their auditorium-cum-synagogue every week, the Slonims have to rely on plastic forks and knives. The young Chabad couple in Cambridge, Massachusetts, can put out their best china and crystal goblets for the 15 to 20 Harvard law and graduate students who gather around their candlelit Shabbat table every Friday evening.

Harvard University seems an unlikely place for the typical campus Chabad success story. It's true that one-quarter of the school's undergraduates and more than one-third of its graduate students are Jewish, but the intellectual brilliance and intense ambition of that student body might not seem fertile soil for the touchy-feely, we-are-all-one approach of the Chabad shliach. But less than three years after their arrival at Harvard, twenty-seven-year-old Rabbi Hirsch Zarchi and his wife Elkie, twenty-four, have insinuated themselves into the university's Jewish life with such quiet finesse that they have built up a rock-solid core of student supporters while completely winning over the campus's Jewish establishment.

"Harvard is not the easiest community in the world—we're all a bunch of prima donnas," says Alan Dershowitz, the feisty First Amendment lawyer and Harvard Law School professor who acts as Chabad's faculty sponsor. Dershowitz decided to sponsor Chabad not just because he believes it serves a need for many students, but because he genuinely likes Chabad's style. "I very much like their proselytizing tactics, as a First Amendment advocate. I think it's great that they get out there and ask people, 'Have you put on tefillin today? Have you done a mitzvah today?'"

Harvard was never high on the Chabad administration's list of target campuses. When Hirsch went to Rabbi Krinsky's office in early 1997 and asked to be sent there with his new wife, he was told that there was no stipend available for Harvard from Chabad headquarters. Krinsky admired his zeal, but felt Hirsch was being a little naïve to think he could tackle such a campus. But Hirsch already knew the place. He'd spent two years as a visiting yeshiva student in Boston and would cross the river each Friday afternoon to Harvard Square to set up his tefillin table. "I'd heard about Harvard, this great institution across the river," he says. "I'd heard there were many Jews there. I knew nothing else about it."

From the first day he showed up at the square, Hirsch says, he got an "incredible response" from passersby, especially the academic community. "I remember having this philosophical discussion with some Ph.D. students about the significance of a commandment, of the Oral versus the Written Law. It was amazing. These were serious students, and they were very comfortable talking to me. I was kind of surprised. Here I was, interacting with sophisticated, secular Jews, and they're turning to me to explain things to them. I wasn't reaching out to them, they were reaching out to me."

Before the Zarchis got to Harvard, they did their homework. First, they made an informal agreement of noncompetition with Harvard Hillel. The campus Hillel House, founded in 1944, is large, well established, and rich, with six or seven different *minyans* every Shabbat, and an $8 million building. It sponsors a strong Orthodox minyan, so Hirsch decided—at least for the first few years— to daven there instead of competing for the same worshipers. Hillel attracts mainly undergraduates who already identify Jewishly, so the Zarchis reached out to Harvard's graduate students. "There's a great deal of loneliness among the graduate students, people floating around in a sea of ideas, highly educated in other areas yet totally ignorant in their Jewishness," says Professor Ruth Wisse, director of the university's Center for Jewish Studies.

"Hillel is wonderful," says Hirsch, "but primarily they're an organization that responds to expressed needs. If a student wants kosher, they create a kosher meal plan. If no one wants weekday services, they don't hold them." Chabad prides itself on meeting needs that a Jewish person doesn't even know he has. "The Jewish community at Harvard is forty-five hundred students. Hillel attracts three-to-four hundred of them. The vast majority are not involved. Those are the ones we have to engage, intrigue, and enrich."

The Zarchis' most powerful outreach tool is Hirsch Zarchi himself. The son of a noted Crown Heights scholar and *mashpiah,* or mentor, Hirsch has inherited his father's penetrating intellect and humble, welcoming demeanor. Sitting at the head of his Shabbat table, he's a slight figure, with merry eyes that turn serious quickly when he's tackling a difficult question. People don't just like Hirsch—they rave about him. "The success of the Harvard Chabad House can be attributed entirely to the personality and energy of Hirsch Zarchi," says Wisse. "Within minutes of meeting him, I knew he was an extremely bright person."

"He's fantastic," Dershowitz agrees. "He respects intellectual life. There have been other rabbis at and around Harvard who have tried to compete with the professors intellectually. That's a recipe for disaster. A rabbi has to bring something the kids don't get in the classroom, and this one does it. Harvard Judaism tends to be very intellectualized. I approve of that myself, but many students get their intellectual quota filled in the classroom. They need something else—spirituality, a closer connection to God. And they find it with Chabad." Dershowitz says there's much about Chabad he doesn't like—the messianism, the excessive focus on the Rebbe. "But there are many positive things about Chabad at Harvard, and for those students who find inspiration in it, I want it to be there."

Not only has Harvard's Chabad House not hurt Hillel; Wisse says it has actually strengthened Hillel by drawing more unaffiliated Jews out of the woodwork. "The paradox of Hillel House is that because it's so successful, it attracts educated Jews who have studied Hebrew all their lives and been to Israel," she says. "The very advanced quality of Harvard Hillel is very threatening to Jews who have no background." Michael Rosenberg, student chair of Harvard Hillel for the 2000–2001 school year, says he loves to go to the Zarchis' for Friday dinner. "I'm egalitarian, but there are times I like to have a nice family-style dinner, and Hillel can't provide that. And everyone who knows Rabbi Zarchi likes him a lot. He's a very outgoing guy, and he's fun to talk to. He's not much older than we are."

One Friday evening at the Zarchis' Shabbat table, Hirsch pauses between the soup and meat course to say a few words on that week's Torah portion, dealing with Abraham's efforts to persuade God to spare Sodom and Gomorrah. He contrasts Abraham's efforts to save an entire city with Noah, who did what God asked and no more. God wants us to care actively about each other, Hirsch concludes. "We all have that obligation," he says quietly.

There are seventeen guests at the table—fourteen law students, two grad students, and an alumnus. The conversation so far has ranged from the legal implications of the 2000 presidential election to the future of the Supreme Court, several novels on the *New York Times*'s recommended list, and a problem in quantum physics. Hirsch holds his own, although he's studied neither physics nor law, and doesn't read novels.

"Coming from Crown Heights, to be able to engage these students so well is amazing," says Beth Preminger, a 1999 Harvard graduate who used to frequent the Zarchis' Shabbat table. Not really, says Menachem Schmidt. People underestimate the effects of a yeshiva education. While the content may be limited to Judaica, the analytic skills and mental rigor demanded of its students leaves them with well-sharpened wits. "A guy like Hirschy Zarchi could talk to anyone about anything," Schmidt says.

Hirsch says he feels absolutely no desire to read the books the students at his table discuss with such interest. If he did, he shrugs, he could pick up the books and read them. There's no law against it. It's just not his thing, and not something he needs in order to reach these young people and inspire them. "I believe that what moves the Jew at Harvard is what moves the Jew in New York or Israel or Bangkok—the warmth, the truth. In Cambridge the difference is there's an intellectual barrier you have to cross first. Once you prove yourself intellectually, they're open to what you have to offer."

Throughout the evening and well past 2 A.M., groups of students come and go. Each one receives a piece of cake, a drink, and a warm welcome from Elkie and Hirsch, who have somehow in the middle of all this commotion managed to put their two small children to bed. Elkie says that since the couple arrived in Cambridge three years earlier they haven't spent one Shabbat meal alone. But she doesn't mind the lack of privacy. It's what she grew up with, as the oldest of a family of twelve living in Crown Heights. "Our house was pretty much Grand Central Station," she remarks. "When I was growing up and the Rebbe was still alive, people would come to Crown Heights more frequently. I think I slept in my own bed no more than three nights a week. I grew up knowing that living means sharing your life with people. Shabbos without guests is not really Shabbos."

The Harvard students who flock to the Zarchis' Chabad House don't feel the Zarchis expect them to become observant Jews. "Hirschy knows most of us in this room will wake up Saturday morning and turn on the TV," says Zena Yostov, a third-year law student who regularly eats Shabbat meals at the Zarchis'. "He still welcomes us. I can't tell you what's deep in his heart, but that's what I feel from him. Sometimes I know he's on the brink of asking me a question, and then I watch him pull away, stop himself."

That self-awareness, that ability to watch themselves even as they're watching others, is a skill drummed into Lubavitch children all through their lives. The patience and quiet persistence that characterizes their outreach is fueled by an undying optimism they also learn from kindergarten on up. Elkie and Hirsch—indeed, most Chabad shlichim—firmly believe that once a Jewish person is presented with the right Jewish information, he or she will respond by reaching out toward greater observance. The need to "do Jewish" is ingrained in the Jewish soul. The possibility that an educated Jew might willfully reject Torah and its teachings is not something they talk about—not to outsiders. "We believe that if they are exposed in a positive, nonjudgmental manner, they will have the knowledge to make choices," Hirsch states. "Right now they're not in a position to choose Judaism. Most of the people who come here barely had a Jewish Sunday school education, and if they did, it was a negative experience."

And even in three years their work has affected people, sometimes in ways neither side realizes. Asked whether her many Friday evenings spent with the Zarchis has influenced her religiously, Yostov answers with a definite no. Then she pauses to reconsider. "Going to them hasn't changed my level of observance, but it's changed my comfort level with Judaism," she reflects. Because she grew up with little Jewish background, she used to feel uncomfortable walking into an unfamiliar synagogue or picking up a prayer book. That's no longer true, she notes. "If I'm able to go to Chabad, I can feel comfortable in a variety of Jewish environments."

That's what the Zarchis want. "These kids are away from home," Hirsch says. "There's nothing specifically Jewish about it. It's a human thing. We create a certain warmth, a feeling of being with family. So they won't say, 'We're going to Chabad,' but, 'We're going to a place that in some way we can call home.'"

CHAPTER 6

NEW KIDS ON THE BLOCK:
Chabad Moves into Your Town

Sholom Ber Tenenbaum unfolds a road map of suburban Chicago and points to the town of Gurnee, Illinois, population 28,000, an hour's drive from the Windy City. "That's where we want to go," he says, his voice shaking with barely contained excitement. "The Chicago Federation thinks there aren't enough Jews there, but we've done our own study, and we found nine hundred fifty Jewish families, plus five hundred next door in Grayslake."

It's April 2001, and Sholom Ber is sitting in the small dining room of the modest one-bedroom Crown Heights apartment he shares with his wife of one year, Feigel. A battered sofa is pushed up against the far wall, and built-in floor-to-ceiling bookcases on two other walls hold the couple's collection of Jewish and Hasidic books, their only visible extravagance.

The Tenenbaums don't want to get too settled into Crown Heights, because since their wedding in late 1999 they've been actively looking to go out on shlichus. Sholom Ber was interested in moving overseas, but Feigel secretly hoped they'd end up living near her parents, who run Chabad of Wisconsin. Feigel's prayers must have found sympathetic ears, because after the couple's pitches for positions in Guadalajara and Finland fell through, they set their sights on Gurnee, a town midway between Milwaukee and Chicago. Founded in 1874, Gurnee was a sleepy little village until 1991, when the newly built Gurnee Mills outlet center drew thousands of young professional families eager to flee Chicago's high rental market. Many of those new arrivals were Jews, who now comprise, by the Tenenbaums' figures, close to 10 percent of the population.

Sholom Ber's road map of Gurnee is covered with dozens of carefully penciled circles, each one representing a Jewish household he's found— the target clientele of the Tenenbaums' future Chabad House. With no synagogue in town, and just a Conservative lay-led congregation that meets at the Woodland Middle School library, the Tenenbaums will have a clear playing field. The only Jewish toes they'll have to worry about stepping on belong to their mentor, the Chabad rabbi in Buffalo Grove, ten miles away. He runs a successful preschool, so they won't set up a competing one. But before they get final permission from Chabad headquarters to move to Gurnee, they have to raise enough money to cover their first year's expenses, about $90,000. That's a growing trend in Chabad. Until quite recently, every new shliach got initial seed money from Chabad headquarters in Brooklyn, usually equal to one or two years' budget. Sholom Ber has given himself four months to accumulate what he needs, figuring he'll raise 90 percent from Lubavitcher families in Crown Heights. He has labored for weeks on his computer to create a glossy fundraising brochure, which outlines his first-year programs and projected personal expenses down to the last meal. Then he'll start working the phones and knocking on doors. He's hoping that two families he knows will give him $4,500 each, and that another two will cough up $3,000. "That's big money for Crown Heights," he says. He'll ask for only $750 or $1,000 from the other potential donors he approaches.

Once established in Gurnee, he'll switch the bulk of his appeal to local Jews who use his services. It's a labor-intensive method of fundraising that every Chabad shliach knows well and, for the most part, dreads. But that's the way the Rebbe wanted it, Sholom Ber explains. "If 770 provided our budget, we wouldn't be forced to make those connections in the local community. And it's a two-way street. When people invest in your programs, they take pride and interest in your success."

There's no master plan for future Chabad Houses hanging on the wall at 770. New Chabad operations are started pretty much on an ad hoc basis. The road to Gurnee was laid in the summer of 1999, when two Lubavitch yeshiva students showed up there as part of Chabad's summer volunteer program, which sends hundreds of pairs of yeshiva boys around the world during their summer vacations to do Jewish outreach in places that do not have permanent Chabad Houses. Along with handing out Jewish literature, speaking in local synagogues or JCCs, and checking *mezuzahs,* these traveling yeshiva *bochers* sniff out neighborhoods that might be able to support a new Chabad House. Binyamin Wolff, then a twenty-one-year-old student at Chabad's Detroit yeshiva, was part of the advance team sent to Gurnee. He and his partner checked into a motel, picked up a local phone book, and started looking for Jewish names. "We sat in the room all day with our cell phones, calling all the Cohens and Goldbergs, seeing who would meet with us. We brought all our own food—tuna fish, bread, dips, instant soup. We only went out to buy coffee." The response they got was not even lukewarm. "Hardly anyone was interested. Sometimes we'd get the answering machine, and we always left a message, 'Hi, we're rabbis here in town,' but no one called back. A lot of names we thought were Jewish turned out not to be." The students managed to make just two appointments. One canceled. The lone Jew who responded positively allowed them to put up a mezuzah on his door.

"We decided the phone calls were too scary," Binyamin continues. "So we decided to go door-to-door. If we're already standing there, maybe they'll let us in." Most people were still reluctant to speak with the unknown young men in the black hats, although some of their children went outside to take a look at the curious vehicle the students were driving, a "sukkah-mobile" they built to attract attention and encourage Jews to observe the Sukkot holiday *mitzvah* of blessing the *lulav* and *etrog.* Eventually, Binyamin and his friend collected fifty Jewish names that were later handed over to the Tenenbaums. It wasn't much, but it was enough to convince Sholom Ber and Feigel to pay a market-research agency to do a Jewish population survey of the town. They had to be sure of a potential donor base, because they were about to make a lifetime commitment to a place they'd never seen. Just before Passover 2001, Sholom Ber went to Gurnee for two days to meet some of the families on Binyamin's list. These weren't people who had promised to give money. Far from it. They were mostly local Jews who simply evinced no hostility to Chabad when Binyamin and his friend contacted them two years earlier. When Sholom Ber rang their doorbells, he didn't even tell them he was considering moving to Gurnee. He just handed them boxes of matzah and wished them a good Passover. "I was very low-key," Sholom Ber says. "I didn't say I was moving to Gurnee, because it wasn't sure yet." Then he and Feigel drove through the town for an hour, Feigel pronounced it "beautiful," and the die was cast.

In August, Sholom Ber flew back to Gurnee to rent a townhouse. He found a place on the east side of the city, not as close to the main Jewish neighborhood as he'd have liked, but he had to strike a balance between proximity and expense. The Tenenbaums are budgeting only $36,000 a year for their own needs, the typical salary of a young shliach couple. On September 6 they packed up the car and drove from Brooklyn to their new home. Their first week in Gurnee they prepared a press release announcing their arrival and sent it to nine hundred Jewish names they pulled out of a purchased mailing list. After kashering their kitchen, the couple sat down to plan their first programs: a Sukkot party in their home and a children's reading hour Feigel hopes to start at a local library or bookstore. Those first steps they make in Gurnee are crucial. They've come to town fired up with enthusiasm for a mission their new Jewish neighbors may find alienating. And this isn't just a "first job," a stepping-stone toward something better. Everything is at stake, Feigel notes. "We're here for our entire lives."

Since the Rebbe's death in 1994, about a hundred newly married Lubavitcher couples have gone out on shlichus each year. Some of them have had experiences similar to the Tenenbaums', who represent the norm in setting up a new Chabad shlichus—lots of elbow grease and creative thinking as a couple builds a Jewish center from the ground up. But Chabad has exploded so rapidly in the 1990s that old operational patterns have expanded and shifted, creating shlichus possibilities that didn't exist before. In the former Soviet Union, for example, there are two major donors who pay the salaries and expenses of shliach couples, relieving them of the constant burden of fundraising that plagues their counterparts in other Chabad Houses. The educational and social service components of Chabad's work in Russia are much more time-consuming than they are in America, and shlichim there face the added personal trials of living the rest of their lives, and raising their children, in, quite literally in some cases, Siberia.

Even in the United States, where Chabad operations in Florida and California are expanding almost as rapidly as in the former Soviet Union, the traditional pattern of a young couple creating a Chabad House from scratch is no longer the only possibility. Many young couples are taking secondary positions at existing Chabad Houses, where ten or twenty years of success have enabled an older shliach to hire a young rabbi and his wife to help out, as directors of a preschool or instructors in an expanding adult education program. The growing fields of Jewish publishing, Internet outreach, and expanding job opportunities within the central Chabad institutions in Crown Heights, Los Angeles, Pittsburgh, Montreal, Detroit, and elsewhere have opened up a wide range of career positions that are still considered shlichus, the Rebbe's work. "That's the wave of the future," says Rabbi Moshe Kotlarsky. "As the world gets smaller, we'll be sending more and more couples as the second, third, even fourth in a city."

Another expanding field for a new Chabad shliach is being hired as the pulpit rabbi for a non-Lubavitch Orthodox congregation. Almost the norm in countries such as England and Australia, the growing American phenomenon of a black-hatted Chabad rabbi leading services at nominally modern Orthodox *shuls* is testimony to increased interest in Orthodoxy, a growing acceptance of Chabad as part of the American Jewish mainstream, and the fact that Chabad rabbis, unlike some of their Orthodox counterparts, will go virtually anywhere.

The most glaring difference between going out on shlichus today versus a generation ago is that the Rebbe is no longer personally directing the operation. Every new shliach couple still visits the Rebbe's grave to get his "permission" and blessings on their posting, but that's nothing more than a formalized ritual capping a process that is already decided. It's a lot different than having the Rebbe ask you, in a personal meeting, to go live your life as his emissary in Nashville or Los Angeles, which is how shlichim were sent out in the 1950s and early '60s. By the 1970s, the Rebbe's personal involvement in determining the placement of every new shliach began to taper off. A potential shliach couple would write to the Rebbe, suggesting one or several positions they were considering, and asking for his approval. Sometimes he would reject their ideas and suggest a different shlichus. Usually, he approved their proposal, or circled one of several suggestions they offered. Young shlichim heading out into the field during the Rebbe's lifetime knew they were doing his personal bidding in a way no young Chabadnik today can feel.

The first Chabad shlichim in this country were sent out in the mid-

1940s by the sixth Lubavitcher Rebbe, Yosef Schneersohn, to open Jewish day schools in Pittsburgh, New England and the New York metropolitan area. In 1948, Schneersohn sent Shmuel Dovid Raichik, a yeshiva student from Warsaw who had helped orchestrate the escape of many Chabadniks from Nazi-occupied Europe, to California as a roving emissary. The diminutive, soft-spoken Raichik spent the 1950s and '60s crisscrossing the country by train and bus, surviving for weeks on crackers and sardines, as he laid the groundwork for the first Chabad Houses throughout the West and Midwest. In 1949 the sixth Rebbe sent Zalman Posner to Nashville, Tennessee, as the pulpit rabbi for an Orthodox congregation, a position he still fills fifty-two years later.

That was the extent of Chabad shlichus in this country when Yosef Schneersohn's son-in-law, Menachem Mendel Schneerson, assumed leadership of the worldwide movement in 1951. The seventh Rebbe continued the policies laid down by his father-in-law (whom he continued to refer to as "the Rebbe" until his own death forty-three years later). But even in his first year of leadership, Menachem Mendel Schneerson set forth a new activist approach that would characterize Lubavitch for the remainder of the century, a tactical shift that would focus the movement's message on non-observant Jews. In a 1951 interview with *Jewish Life* magazine (a publication of the Union of Orthodox Jewish Congregations of America), the new Rebbe stated:

> *Orthodox Jewry up to this point has concentrated upon defensive strategies. We were always worried lest we lose positions and strongholds. But we must take the initiative and wage an offensive. This, of course, takes courage, planning, vision, and the will to carry on despite the odds.*

Even before he officially accepted the mantle of Chabad leadership, the new Rebbe sent out his first shliach to North Africa to establish Chabad schools and welfare services. Attention was focused on expanding operations in Europe, South America, Australia, and Israel through the mid-1960s, while Chabad's growth in North America remained slow. From 1957 to 1965, the number of new Chabad centers in the United States could be counted on one hand: Philadelphia, Minneapolis, Los Angeles, Detroit, and Miami. The pace quickened after the Rebbe proclaimed his first mitzvah campaign in 1967, to include Seattle, Milwaukee, Buffalo, and Kansas City. By the early seventies, Chabad Houses began to mushroom. Each decade since has seen exponential growth in the number and scope of Chabad operations, overseen by an administrative system put in place by the Rebbe early on. The first shliach sent to a state or country becomes the "head" of that region, in charge of hiring all future shlichim in his territory, determining which cities or campuses are ripe for Chabad inroads and, when necessary, disciplining shlichim who run too far afield of Chabad directives.

Rabbi Kotlarsky began working at Chabad headquarters in 1971, a year after his marriage. He now administers the movement's worldwide network of shlichim, including its summer volunteer program, which sent out 260 yeshiva students in 2001, and its Passover Seder project, which recruited and trained 600 volunteer students to run community Seders that same spring. When a Chabad House in Shanghai needs money for a down payment on a new building, or when a regional head is clashing with a younger shliach or with a local Jewish community, Kotlarsky is the one who flies in, writes the check, or picks up the phone to soothe rumpled feathers. With a work force this big, Kotlarksy says, it's to Chabad's credit that he has to deal with only ten to fifteen personnel problems a year. "The Rebbe told us we shouldn't enter into *machlokes* [arguments] when we go into a new city," he says. "Whenever I'd go to a place where we wanted to open a Chabad center, I'd meet with the Federation, the Jewish Community Center, local rabbis, and potential donors. We have warmer responses in some places than others." The Rebbe laid down four main directives for entering a new city, Kotlarsky says: Don't cause friction, make sure you have a financial base for the first year, build a mikvah if none exists, and avoid countries on the verge of revolution.

Young Lubavitch couples setting out today have a wealth of institutional resources to back them up. Shlichim who moved to the Midwest or foreign countries in the 1950s and '60s were pretty much on their own. Their only guidance from headquarters, aside from mimeographed copies of the Rebbe's weekly talks that would arrive irregularly by mail, came during occasional visits to Crown Heights. Phone calls were expensive, and long-distance travel was for extraordinary occasions. One midwestern shliach relates how in the 1960s and 1970s he would call the pay phone next to the synagogue at 770 whenever he knew the Rebbe would be delivering a talk, and would ask whoever picked up the phone to leave it hanging on the wall, so he could catch a few minutes of *Hasidus* before someone else happened by and hung up the receiver. Today shlichim fly in and out of New York on a moment's notice. Some come every month to pray at the Rebbe's grave. Annual conventions—November for the men and February for their wives—give shlichim from around the world a chance to share programs, swap stories, and pick up a morale boost for the coming year.

The biggest material resource for Chabad emissaries is the Shlichim Office in Crown Heights, which opened in 1986 primarily as a job placement service for new shlichim. By the late 1990s the office was placing half of all shlichim in their permanent positions. A sampling of openings from the summer 2000 listings shows the breadth of jobs open to today's shliach: "Large Chabad day school on West Coast seeks technology and information coordinator"; "Large Midwestern Chabad center seeks candidate to found, direct, and expand Jewish community library"; "Well-established Chabad *cheder* in Florida seeks teachers for grades 6–8"; "Chabad center in Germany seeks *shochet* [ritual slaughterer], with possibility for community outreach and teaching position for spouse."

But the Shlichim Office's major role today is providing material resources for use by shlichim in the field. Its thirteen staff members produce and distribute prepackaged professional courses for adults on dozens of Jewish and Hasidic topics, including elaborately produced holiday programs, which it sends out for free or at cost to Chabad centers all over the world. An example is the "*shiurim* series," a box of materials sent to each Chabad House two or three weeks before a Jewish holiday. It contains sample outlines of a three-week course, or *shiur,* on the holiday, pages in English to hand out to students, a sample press release, supplementary teachers' material including biographies of all the personalities associated with the holiday, and answers to typical student questions. The *shiurim* series also provides courses-in-a-kit that are tied to issues rather than holidays, such as "women in Judaism" or "Jewish mysticism."

The Shlichim Office does a good portion of its work before major Jewish holidays. In early December it does bulk buying of Chanukah menorahs, mailing 200,000 menorahs to field shlichim in December 2000 for $1.50 each, less than a third what they would cost in a retail store. In March-April, they send out colorful boxes of matzah for Chabad Houses to give out during Passover programs.

Probably the most popular holiday programs provided by the office are the shofar factories, menorah workshops, and matzah bakeries created for the holidays of Rosh Hashanah, Chanukah, and Passover. Other

Jewish denominations now run similar programs, but Chabad's is the most comprehensive, reaching an estimated 1,500 Jewish schools and synagogues in 2001. Chabad Houses in larger cities might set up one of these programs for three or more weeks, inviting local synagogue religious schools or day school classes to come by for a nominal fee so the children can bake their own matzah, carve their own shofars from real rams' horns, or make clay menorahs that they fill with olive oil they press themselves in a real olive press. In smaller communities the Chabad rabbi might conduct such programs in JCCs or Jewish schools using a "traveling" shofar factory or matzah bakery developed by Chabad headquarters. The local press is invited to these colorful hands-on workshops, and few editors can resist giving prominent placement to such photogenic stories.

The most elaborate program provided by the Shlichim Office is the massive Great Jewish Children's Expo, a traveling exhibition of Jewish history and practice that fills two 48-foot trucks and cost $350,000 to develop. The center charges $10,000 to bring the Expo to a city, which means a Chabad shliach usually enlists the cooperation of local JCCs and Jewish schools to help fund a visit. Since 1993 the Expo has toured more than forty cities, spending up to a week in each place. The main exhibit, which covers Jewish history from Adam and Eve through the creation of the modern state of Israel, takes up more than 5,000 square feet, along with an additional three rooms for Jewish videos, an arts and crafts center, and space for a Jewish-oriented game show, complete with Chabad host and prizes for the winning teams.

All of these material resources, developed in Crown Heights and shipped out to Chabad shlichim working in the field, help make the shliach's job less labor-intensive so he can concentrate on actual outreach work. Gedalya Shemtov, who has directed the center since 1988, remembers sitting in his basement for weeks every spring as a young boy in Detroit, helping his father wrap candies and cookies for hundreds of Purim gift baskets. Now the Shlichim Office provides shlichim with ready-made Purim baskets—in three languages.

Growing up as the son of a shliach, Shemtov naturally assumed that he, too, would spend his life on shlichus at a new Chabad House. But when he wrote to Schneerson to ask for a placement, the Rebbe told him to discuss his options with other shlichim—and they suggested he take over the center. Schneerson was still alive and very much in charge when Shemtov agreed to stay in Crown Heights. He wonders whether he would have done the same today. "Since the Rebbe's passing, there has been a tremendous desire among young people getting married to go out on shlichus. They see it as a way to continue the Rebbe's work. It wasn't that way when I got married."

The Shlichim Office didn't exist in 1968 when Feigel Tenenbaum's parents, Rabbi Yisroel and Devorah Shmotkin, set out from Crown Heights as the Rebbe's shlichim to Wisconsin. When he arrived in Milwaukee, Israeli-born Yisroel spoke almost no English. He only recognized two English letters, *P* and *R,* the telephone exchange in his yeshiva's Brooklyn neighborhood. Once he knew he was going to Wisconsin, he pulled out a *Reader's Digest* article on Israel's recently concluded Six-Day War and worked his way through it with a Yiddish-English dictionary.

Milwaukee already had three Orthodox rabbis and a functioning day school in 1968, and there was no warm welcome for the new couple. "No one rolled out the carpet for us," Yisroel recalls. "Not a red carpet, not even a green one." Because Lubavitch Hasidim have a different standard of *kashrut* than other Orthodox Jews, the Shmotkins had to import and freeze all their kosher food. To obtain *chalav Yisrael* milk, Yisroel would set out for a dairy farm once a week at 2 A.M. with his bucket and hand-held pasteurizer. Many long winter nights he'd drive for hours on snow-covered back roads to put up a mezuzah for a family in northern Wisconsin, while his wife waited nervously at home. But the only hardship he and Devorah really felt, they say, was the loneliness of being so far from their parents, friends, and Brooklyn Lubavitch community.

Devorah Shmotkin says that in those years Chabad didn't have organized campaigns for new shlichim to develop in their communities. The Shmotkins compiled their first mailing lists by collecting bulletins from all the local synagogues, writing down any names that appeared in the articles, and looking them up in the phone book. "The work was different then, more one-to-one," Yisroel says. "I came with such enthusiasm, such energy, and I wanted to give it all to the Jews here."

Milwaukee's Jewish leadership was "apprehensive" about the new couple's intentions, Yisroel says. Nevertheless, he and Devorah ran Shabbat programs and evening sessions in the Reform congregation's summer camp, and every synagogue invited them to teach classes at one time or another. As their support base grew, and some Reform and Conservative congregants began switching their affiliation to Chabad, "we were no longer so 'cute,'" Yisroel notes wryly. That's when the conflicts heated up, and the Shmotkins found themselves facing stiff opposition to their funding requests from the Milwaukee Federation.

Attorney Joe Bernstein, past president of the Jewish Federation of Milwaukee and of the Jewish Family Services' Community Relations Council, is a self-proclaimed non-observant Jew who has supported Chabad in Milwaukee for fifteen years. "When Yisroel came here, he was very young and could barely speak English," Bernstein says. "When I look at his children, it's amazing to see the competence they have, and the respect the community has for them. People don't realize how their father had to crawl and scrape to get there." Shmotkin's sons Mendel and Shmaya, and their wives Devora and Devorah Leah, all in their twenties, run much of Chabad's operation in Milwaukee today. Two other sons work at Chabad headquarters at 770: Zalman directs the Lubavitch News Service and Chabad's on-line Web site, and Eli heads the Jewish Educational Media service, which produces Chabad videos. The younger Shmotkins are much more PR-savvy than their father, modern guys who know how to schmooze with donors and Federation bigwigs. But they started with a leg up, Bernstein says, thanks to their parents' painstaking work. They won't have to face the community antagonism their parents faced, largely because most members of the city's Orthodox congregations today are people who became observant because of the Shmotkins. "Animosities still exist, but the level of hostility is muted," Bernstein says.

When Rabbi Berel Shemtov arrived in Detroit on New Year's Day 1958, neither he nor his wife of one week had ever been there before. The Rebbe said to go be shlichim, so they went. They rented a second-floor apartment for $20 a month, borrowed a typewriter, and set to work. For years they cooked all their food on a hot plate, entertaining guests almost every Shabbat. To a young man born in Russia, whose parents were married in a Siberian labor camp, it must have seemed like luxury. But the elderly widow who lived downstairs couldn't figure them out. She told a friend, who passed the story on to Berel, "They have no furniture, no carpets, but they sing and dance all the time."

Soon after his arrival, Shemtov made his first fundraising call, asking a wealthy Detroit Jew for $10,000. The man told him to leave the city. Today, Detroit's Lubavitch operation is one of the nation's largest. Thirty-five shlichim work under Shemtov's organizational umbrella, which includes a full-time yeshiva, a summer camp that draws five hundred children each year, and a forty-acre campus still in development that will contain the college-accredited Michigan Jewish Institute, a large synagogue, and a $4 million therapy facility for special-needs children. Like the Shmotkin children, Rabbi Shemtov's sons and daughters have followed in his footsteps, all of them shlichim or shlichim-in-training. They deal in a high-tech, high-profile world their parents could hardly have imagined. But at the end of the day, the work still comes down to a pencil, a road map, and a lot of fast talking.

When a Chabad rabbi and his wife move into town, not everyone is happy to see them. Lubavitchers insist they don't come into a town without an invitation, but that invitation could come from one or two local Jews friendly to Chabad. To the Chabadniks their arrival heralds a much-needed injection of *Yiddishkeit* into a community lacking real Jewish spirit. They're only there to help, they argue, by providing Jewish services, mostly for free, in a nonjudgmental atmosphere. Who could object?

Plenty of people. From its earliest days Chabad has made enemies, most of them among the Jewish establishment it consciously set itself up against. In 1772 and again in 1781 the entire Hasidic world was formally excommunicated, by the Vilna Gaon, the leader of the Lithuanian *mitnagdim,* or Orthodox opponents to Hasidism, and the greatest figure in world Jewry of his age. The *mitnagdim* feared that Hasidism's emphasis on mysticism and unbridled passion in religious observance would lead to a disregard for Torah and Jewish Law. They distrusted the Hasidic institution of the all-powerful rebbe, which they called idol worship, and considered many of the movement's ritual innovations heretical. "Every day is for them a holiday," read the Gaon's first excommunication decree. "When they pray they raise such a din that the walls quake. . . . They deviate in their prayers from the text valid for the whole people. . . . They conduct themselves like madmen and explain their behavior by saying that in their thoughts they soar into lofty spheres." The first Chabad Rebbe, Shneur Zalman of Liadi, traveled to Lithuania with another Hasidic rebbe in 1772 to meet with the Gaon, but the two visitors were refused admission. Shneur Zalman was later denounced to Russian authorities by *mitnagdim* on trumped-up charges of treason and was imprisoned in the St. Petersburg Fortress—twice.

By the mid-nineteenth century hassidim and *mitnagdim* reached an uneasy truce, teaming up together to fight the new, common enemy of

Jewish Enlightenment. The enforced brotherhood survived through the early twentieth century as Orthodoxy waned in the New World, but once the forces of traditional observance regained popularity in the postwar American Jewish community, old antagonisms resurfaced. Today, Chabad's most virulent opponents are found both on the left and the right of the Jewish spectrum, from Reform Jews who oppose Chabad's right-wing political stands in Israel and its nonegalitarian prayer services, to Orthodox leaders who, like the Vilna Gaon, find the group's ritual innovations and blind veneration of the Rebbe deeply suspect.

Often the lines of criticism merge. Rabbi Eric Yoffie, president of the Reform movement's Union of American Hebrew Congregations, says he finds Lubavitch "worship" of Schneerson "virtually blasphemous," and notes that "false messianism has always caused dangerous problems for the Jewish people." And the late Rabbi Eliezer Schach, leader of Israel's right-wing United Torah Judaism Knesset bloc and a sworn enemy of Chabad messianism, stepped up his public campaign against Lubavitch after Schneerson intervened in Israel's 1989 election to Schach's political detriment. Schach supporters began posting signs around Jerusalem's religious neighborhoods denouncing Schneerson as a false Messiah and urging Jews to boycott Lubavitch services and institutions.

But that's nothing compared to the treatment meted out to Chabad shliach Avraham Berkowitz, the twenty-six-year-old executive director of the Federation of Jewish Communities of the CIS, soon after he arrived in Moscow from his native Detroit. He was nearly drowned in a *mikvah*.

Tensions were running high among Russian Jews in 1999, when the mainstream Russian Jewish Congress, a post-Soviet Jewish funding organization headed by media baron Vladimir Gusinsky, found itself pitted against the newly created Lubavitch-sponsored Federation of Jewish Communities for leadership of the country's million-strong Jewish community. Also at stake were tens of millions of dollars' worth of Jewish communal assets, old synagogues, and other historic buildings that were being returned to local Jewish communities by the government's property restitution program. Battle lines were drawn in June 2000 when the Federation elected Berel Lazar, head Chabad shliach in Moscow, as Russia's new chief rabbi over the Congress's own long-standing chief rabbi, Adolf Shayevich. Russian President Vladimir Putin came out strongly on Chabad's side in the leadership squabble, cutting the ribbon at the September 2000 opening of Chabad's $12 million Jewish Community Center in Moscow just weeks after Russian authorities issued an order for Gusinsky's arrest on corruption charges.

In December 2000, as Berkowitz was concluding a private discussion in Moscow's Choral Synagogue—a discussion dealing, ironically, with easing tensions between the two groups—he was grabbed by three thugs and dragged downstairs to the synagogue's mikvah. One man stood guard while the other two pushed Berkowitz's head under the water. Thinking fast, the young Chabad rabbi played dead, and his attackers fled. A lackluster police investigation turned up no leads. Sources in the Choral Synagogue told reporters that it might have been congregation members angered by Chabad's attempts to "take over their synagogue." Berkowitz suspected a more organized effort. Whatever the case, it's clear that the near-drowning reflected the lengths to which Chabad's opponents are willing to go. At least in Russia.

Things are a bit different in America. So long as Chabad was small, a cultural curiosity limited mainly to Brooklyn in the 1940s and '50s, it didn't raise too many Jewish hackles. There was even a short honeymoon between Chabad and the greater American Jewish community in the late sixties, when Israel's victory in the June 1967 war gave Jewish pride a collective shot in the arm. "There was a rosy period after the publication of *The Chosen*," says Vivi Deren, shlicha in Stamford, Connecticut. She recalls particularly good relations with the Reform movement in those years. "We taught in their schools. We were the *Fiddler on the Roof* people. As long as we were cute and quaint, it was all right. Then we got bigger, and a memo went around warning that we were weaning their children away from their way of life."

As Chabad became more public in its outreach work and began moving into more Jewish communities, the need grew for some advice to new shlichim on how to temper hostile reactions they might encounter. In 1991, *Shlichus: Meeting the Outreach Challenge,* a collection of essays by Chabad teachers and shlichim edited by Chana Piekarski, was published in Crown Heights. It's the closest thing Chabad has to an operations manual for its emissaries. One volume devotes several chapters to the delicate business of establishing a new Chabad center, all with an eye to placating the local Jewish establishment and garnering good press for Chabad activities. First impressions are crucial, writes Cincinnati Chabad Rabbi Sholom Kalmanson, in a chapter titled "Your Ticket to Blitz Success." The new shliach couple should "utilize every avenue of communication to make [its] presence felt so that everyone knows 'you're here to stay.'" A good first step, Kalmanson writes, is a newspaper ad announcing the couple's arrival in town, preferably signed by local non-Chabad Jewish leaders.

Shlichim are advised to build a *minyan* as quickly as possible, to give themselves "a vehicle for acceptance in the community as a formal pulpit rabbi." They should organize a highly publicized event timed to the first Jewish holiday after their arrival, to give immediate visibility to their activities.

Other chapters in this how-to book deal with communicating effectively through the media ("Hosting a radio talk show is not difficult"), setting up nursery schools (it offers a "solid financial base" and is less threatening to other Jewish schools and congregations than activities targeting their adult members), and making personal connections ("Share in family *simchas,* be there in time of need, call from time to time just to say 'hello.'").

The book's advice doesn't always work. Sometimes it backfires. When a new shliach couple moves to town, the local rabbis, Federation leaders, and principals of Jewish schools often see them as a spiritual— and financial—slap in the face. One Reform rabbi in a small New England town says his congregation, the only *shul* in town, was overwhelmed by the Chabad rabbi who moved there in 1999. "He started to do programming. Somehow he got hold of our mailing list and he flooded our members with mailings. I called and asked him to stop, and he said he got the list from the Federation. He appeared to want to get involved with the Jewish community, but it didn't work out that way. He continues to insult our synagogue and its members. He told the local press that there is no Jewish presence here, and that's why he came. But our congregation has been here for twenty-five years."

When it comes to getting involved in the greater Jewish community, there's often a "damned if you do, damned if you don't" syndrome at work. If a new Chabad rabbi starts making the rounds, getting press coverage, and throwing splashy holiday parties, local Jewish leaders accuse him of being pushy. If he stays more to himself, holding his own events without much fanfare, he's accused of being standoffish. Despite the counsel offered in *Shlichus: Meeting the Outreach Challenge,* many Chabad shlichim don't join their local board of rabbis or attend Federation events, because they would then find themselves interacting with non-

Orthodox rabbis as "colleagues," and because they can rarely eat anything served there. That, needless to say, angers many local Jewish leaders, but some admire the Chabadniks' refusal to relax their standards. They see it as setting the bar for Jewish observance in their community. Gail Sack, an executive board member of the National Council of Jewish Women, was a major force in getting her Hartford, Connecticut, Federation to provide glatt kosher food at its meetings precisely so the Chabad rabbi and his wife could attend. She did it partly for *klal Yisrael,* the good of the greater Jewish community, but also because of her personal appreciation for Chabad's work. The Sacks were longtime members of their local Reform congregation when Gail's husband was diagnosed with cancer some years ago. No one called from their synagogue to see how he was doing. But Rabbi Yosef Gopin, director of West Hartford's Chabad House, a man they'd never met, started visiting their home every day. That human gesture forever endeared Chabad to Gail. She and her husband now support Gopin's center financially, in addition to their Reform congregation. And she doesn't care what anyone says. "Chabad reminds us of what we should be doing, how Jews are supposed to behave," she says. "It's what we teach our children, but we don't do it ourselves."

Howard Gases, executive director of the Jewish Federation of Greater Monmouth County, New Jersey, is another Jewish communal leader who appreciates what Chabad offers. "They have tremendous passion for being Jewish," he says. "When I needed a roof for my *sukkah,* I called Chabad." Gases has been meeting his local shliach once a week to study Hasidus. "Do I think he's trying to turn me into a Chabadnik? I don't think so. Would he be happy if I did more *mitzvot?* Of course. So would any other rabbi." Another Chabad rabbi is about to start teaching classes in Gases's home, for free. "I'd like to know how many other rabbis would run to do that," Gases remarks. Gases has been trying for years to convince his Federation board to fund its local Chabad schools, but he is up against stiff opposition. "People have these misgivings about Chabad," he notes. "They think they're a cult, so they don't want to give funding. And the president of my board just had her home kashered by a Chabad rabbi!"

Like other Orthodox groups, Chabad does not recognize Reform, Conservative, or Reconstructionist Judaism. With few exceptions, they won't enter a non-Orthodox synagogue—certainly not during services— or sit on committees with non-Orthodox rabbis. On a personal level, many Chabad shlichim maintain friendships with Reform and Conservative rabbis, who are always, of course, welcome at Chabad activities in their capacity as Jews. But not in their capacity as rabbis, which makes non-Orthodox Jewish leaders bristle.

Rabbi Arthur Ruberg of Congregation Beth El in Norfolk, Virginia, is one of very few Conservative rabbis to describe his relationship with his local Chabad shliach as "very close." The two men check with each other before scheduling holiday events, and they both support the town's sole Jewish day school, where the Chabad rabbi and his wife teach alongside members of Ruberg's Conservative congregation. When Ruberg's son celebrated his bar mitzvah, the Chabad rabbi canceled his own Shabbat services to stay overnight close to the Conservative synagogue. He wouldn't come to the service itself, but he did stop by the reception afterward to offer congratulations. And when the shliach's son was bar-mitzvahed, he held the next-day party in Ruberg's social hall. Ruberg isn't blind to the convoluted reasoning. "I don't want to be Pollyanna-ish," he says. "Do we share everything? No. There are lines beyond which Chabad will not go and areas where I hold my ground."

Rabbi James Goodman serves as the pulpit rabbi of two Reform congregations in St. Louis, Missouri. In 1989, Goodman's daughter became critically ill with a heart ailment, and the St. Louis Chabad center sent a message to the Rebbe on her behalf. The word came back from Crown Heights that Goodman should perform a certain Jewish ritual before his daughter's surgery. Goodman did so and the girl recovered, but that wasn't what drew Goodman closer to Chabad. "All of a sudden, we felt tied up in this weird network," he explains. "It felt very supportive, in a very undogmatic way. My wife and I are both Reform rabbis, and there was no business about that. We just felt connected."

Goodman still studies with his local Chabad rabbi once a week, and he and his wife run coffeehouses in the Chabad synagogue. He also gives money to Chabad and has become more observant—the Chabad rabbi kashered his kitchen. "But I still work on Shabbos," he notes.

While individual rabbis may work well together, the leadership of the Reform and Conservative movements temper their praise for Chabad's outreach work with serious criticism of Chabad on many other levels.

UAHC head Eric Yoffie has kind words for what he calls Chabad's "good work" and says that the rest of the Jewish world can learn from them. "They focus on the everyday *tachliss* [physical details] of Jewish observances like studying Torah and prayer, the day-to-day elements of Jewish life, and I admire that," he says. "I admire their ability to find young people who go all over the world to bring the message of Judaism where otherwise it would be lost. There's a tremendous sense of mission that exists in Chabad in a way that it doesn't always exist in other movements."

That said, Yoffie finds a certain disingenuousness in Chabad's open-arm policy. Here's a movement touting a strict level of Jewish observance that is so eager to get people in the door, he charges, that it relaxes its standards to a ridiculously low level. "Chabad has in many cases become the voice of Jewish minimalism," he maintains. "If you want to be bar-mitzvahed with us, you have to come to religious school, and not just for a month but for one or two years. And we expect parents to participate. Chabad comes in under the banner of 'we take everybody' and provides an alternative to a more serious, ongoing commitment. People who don't want to join a synagogue, parents who don't want to be involved in any way or who want a bar mitzvah on the cheap, will often turn to Chabad. On balance, it's sort of bizarre, given where they're coming from and given their own fundamentalist approach to Judaism."

Another point of contention between Chabad and the rest of the Jewish world is whether or not Chabad really wants to avoid conflict with existing Jewish institutions. On paper, that's policy. The Rebbe would always counsel shlichim going to a new city to avoid duplicating events and services already offered by other local Jewish groups, for the sake of preserving good community relations. But spurred on by Chabad's phenomenal growth this past decade, many Chabad shlichim are eager to flex their muscles. "It's a whole new institutional dynamic," says Rabbi David Eliezrie, director of the very successful Chabad center in Yorba Linda, California. "When a shliach comes to town, the Federation wants to tell us what to do. But we don't toe their line. The Orthodox rabbi wants to tell us what to do, but we don't toe their line. The Reform rabbi wants to tell us what to do, but we don't toe their line. Today we can get a building built in half or one-third the time we could twenty years ago. We have the credibility."

Other Chabad shlichim are very careful to "get along with the Schwartzes." In 1988, Rabbi Yisrael and Vivi Deren arrived in Stamford, Connecticut, to begin Chabad operations. Stamford already had a strong Orthodox community and the Derens knew they couldn't just steamroll into town. Not only that, but the city's Orthodox shul had suffered a breakaway congregation ten years earlier, and the Derens didn't want to open old wounds by presenting another organizational threat. "They were perfectly happy to have us there, but things would have been very difficult if we'd tried to start our own congregation," Yisrael says.

Although the Derens had hoped to open a women's study institute right away, they spoke to local Jews and learned that what the community wanted was a Jewish nursery school. So that's what they established, in a building they still rent from the Orthodox *shul* next door—the *shul* where, in another instance of careful cooperation, Yisrael holds his weekly Tanya class. Like all Chabad nursery schools, the Stamford school attracts nonaffiliated as well as affiliated Jewish kids. It has proved to be the Derens' most effective way of drawing entire Jewish families into a more Jewish lifestyle. "We measure the success of our nursery school by how many kids move on to regular Jewish day school afterward," Yisrael says.

The fact remains, however, that especially in towns with an active Jewish community, many Jews drawn to Chabad House activities are already members of other congregations, usually Reform or Conservative, but sometimes Orthodox as well. When those Jews sign up their kids for Chabad preschool or for adult Hebrew classes, or start donating regularly to their local Chabad House, that presents a direct financial threat to existing Jewish institutions. Most Chabad congregations don't charge membership dues, and even when they do, the amounts tend to be nominal. And their doors are always open, for free, on Yom Kippur and Rosh Hashanah, the only days of the year many loosely affiliated Jews attend services. In a wealthy suburb, where membership in a Reform or Conservative synagogue easily tops $1,000 a year, plus required building fund contributions, and where High Holiday tickets are either unavailable to nonmembers or cost hundreds of dollars, the Chabad alternative can look pretty attractive. That makes Chabad's critics seethe.

"This is not just in terms of synagogues, but especially in terms of Jewish education," says Allan Nadler, associate professor of Jewish studies at Drew University in New Jersey and a former pulpit rabbi. "Instead of sending their kids to the Hebrew Academy or a Solomon Schechter school, where they'll get an excellent, balanced Jewish education, parents look at Chabad and see they can send their kids there and save five hundred dollars. Parents have a disincentive to send their kids to a top-notch Jewish school because Lubavitch is cheaper." Nadler, a longtime critic of Chabad on many fronts, says the Joseph Kushner Hebrew Academy, an Orthodox day school in his New Jersey town, "loses kids every year to Lubavitch." He claims it's not because the education they get at Chabad is better. In his opinion, Chabad day schools provide a "narrow Jewish education," with little Hebrew or Jewish history, no Zionist history, and an overemphasis on Talmud and Hasidic mysticism. It's just dollars and cents, "so the parents can build another jacuzzi."

Rabbi Jerome Epstein, executive vice president of the United Synagogue of Conservative Judaism, the conservative movement's organizational arm, is also concerned that Chabad's low-cost schools and summer camps may attract parents who aren't aware of what their children are learning there. "If you decide that you want to affiliate with Lubavitch, that's terrific," he says. "But if you were to take my six-year-old and seduce me into bringing her in with a low-cost education, or a college student to come not because of the services but because of a free meal, or a Purim celebration where there's a lot of booze, then I think you're bringing in people under false pretenses." He tells of one five-year-old boy who came home from his Chabad preschool and told his father that if he didn't say the Shema his bones would fall off. "His father went to talk to the teacher, who said, 'Yes, every word of the Shema is connected to a bone in the body, and it is our belief that if you don't—'" Epstein spreads his hands and shrugs. "I don't say all Lubavitchers are this way, and it's one thing to say to a child you have to say the Shema, but to do it with fear? If a teacher believes such a thing, it's going to creep up in all kinds of lessons. I've heard people complain that Chabad rabbis say if you don't check your *mezuzot* something bad will happen. I think some people judge Chabad as authentic without knowing what Chabad really believes."

One could say that it's to Chabad's credit that so many Conservative and Reform Jews are willing to switch their spiritual and financial affiliation to the Hasidic group. A Conservative rabbi just outside New York, who has battled Chabad's efforts to install a public menorah in his town, openly acknowledges that "it's *our* problem when they are able to reach a significant number of our members and get financial support, when we can't get it for our own institutions." Even Epstein maintains that Chabad's success means "we have to do Chabad better than Chabad," a difficult task considering that many of the same characteristics that so annoy Epstein and other non-Orthodox Jewish leaders also give the Chabad movement its strength and its appeal to outsiders. "They're unswerving," Epstein declares. "They have the right answer and they're passionate about it.

Many Conservative rabbis don't exude the same firm conviction. As a Conservative rabbi in a congregation, one looks for ways to make people comfortable. We look for ways to bend. Lubavitch, to its credit and its discredit, says, No, this is what we are, and this is what you have to do."

Ismar Schorsch, chancellor of the Conservative movement's Jewish Theological Seminary in Manhattan, sees it instead as a concerted effort by Lubavitch to tap into already thriving Jewish institutions rather than reaching out to the unaffiliated. "A lot of Chabad 'outreach' is really 'inreach,'" he charges. "They undercut established institutions. When Chabad moves into Great Neck and offers the same service for nothing that Reform and Conservative synagogues already offer, they do no good. They're a discount store. They weaken established synagogues that provide the social capital for the organized Jewish community."

Schorsch didn't bring up Great Neck by accident. In 1994, Chabad moved into this wealthy, heavily Jewish Long Island town, a community that already boasted more than a dozen synagogues of every Jewish denomination, and immediately alienated the local Jewish establishment by getting city approval to place a large Chanukah menorah on the village green. Bad feelings simmered until January 2001, when Chabad announced plans for a multimillion-dollar, four-story, 69,000-square-foot center on Manhasset Bay, right across the street from Temple Emmanuel, Great Neck's largest Reform congregation. Then the anger exploded. That June hundreds of residents packed three public hearings on the issue, arguing that the enormous project would adversely affect the city's environment, aesthetics, and traffic patterns. But their anger had deep religious and sociological undertones, as have similar public arguments in other communities, such as Tenafly, New Jersey, and Rockland County, New York, where Chabad has moved into wealthy, largely non-observant Jewish neighborhoods. A large, successful Chabad House prompts other observant Jews to move into the neighborhood. They open kosher restaurants, buy up available housing, try to get *eruvs* installed around the town's perimeter so they can carry on Shabbat, and generally make, so the argument goes, "normal" Jews feel uncomfortable.

A Reform rabbi in Great Neck, criticizing "the overbearing immensity" of Chabad's building proposal, suggested at one public hearing that Chabad "think through this project in such a way that the town itself is content with it, because we all have to learn to live with one another." As of the summer of 2001, Great Neck's Chabad rabbi, Yoseph Geisinsky, insisted to a *Forward* reporter that he was "not trying to cause frictions" and would change his plans if that would result in communal harmony. But, he warned, if the Jewish community can't promise they will welcome his compromise, he won't make the effort.

It's an attitude problem, says one non-Lubavitch rabbi in Great Neck, who declined to be identified. "Chabad came into our community, a community with many synagogues, including several Orthodox ones, and they came in with the attitude that they were going to show us how to do things right. I admire the Lubavitch movement for many things they do. I stand in awe of them. They bring Jewish life to far-flung communities with real missionary zeal. But in the process they make it clear that they're the only ones doing things right."

"Many of our congregations find it intimidating when Chabad comes in and says, 'We're going to teach you how to observe Shabbat,'" agrees Jerome Epstein. "What gives them the chutzpah to say that? Congregation leaders come to me and say, Chabad wants to come in and provide a Shabbat experience for my congregation, for free. I say, take them up on it, but tell them you want to go to their community as well and teach them how to observe Shabbat. They won't buy that. They're only willing to give, not to take. They have the monopoly on what is right."

UAHC head Yoffie doesn't care for that "holier-than-thou" attitude, but he also claims not to be terribly worried about it. Competition between religious movements is healthy, he feels. "If people aren't happy with synagogue X, they found synagogue Y. I don't spend a lot of time wringing my hands over it." At any rate, he doubts that many Reform parents are sending their children to Chabad schools and summer camps, despite Chabad's claims to the contrary. And even if they are, he believes that the infatuation won't last. "They offer a brand of Judaism that has very limited appeal," he says. "The equality of women is a foundational belief for Reform Jews. If we're losing people who don't believe in that, then they don't belong here."

Yoffie reveals that his own college-age daughter had increased her level of Shabbat observance and started attending services at the Chabad House in Westfield, New Jersey, within walking distance of her home. Yoffie went with her once, but says it's "not my brand of Judaism." And he doesn't think she'll stick with Chabad for long. "She is a very smart, very Jewishly sophisticated young woman who comes to the *shul,* sits in the back, and listens to these thirteen- and fourteen-year-old boys stumble over the Torah portion that she can read better. And she, of course, cannot participate. So apart from the fact that she may be doing all this just to aggravate me, in the final analysis this isn't a Judaism that she, or the majority of American Jews, is going to buy."

If Chabad shlichim bought that argument, they would never be able to move into new towns and set up shop the way they do. But they don't buy it, and that's why they succeed.

Yossi and Maryashie Deren were twenty-three years old in 1996 when they moved to the wealthy Connecticut suburb of Greenwich, a ten-minute drive from Yossi's hometown of Stamford. They started calling the handful of names Yossi's shliach parents had given them as potential contacts and were shocked at the negative responses they got. "Thank God we were so naïve," Yossi says. "If we'd known what we were getting into, we never would have been able to do it. On a college campus, you know exactly what you have to do—bring the kids in and get them involved. But in a community like this, people have their lifestyle figured out."

The 10,000-strong Jewish community of Greenwich looked askance at the new Hasidic couple in their midst. "The Hasids are coming to town—watch out! They thought we wanted to set up a yeshiva, with black hats walking up and down Greenwich Avenue," Yossi relates. Two months after they arrived, the young couple sent out *shalach manos,* Purim gift baskets, to every Jewish family on their list. One person sent it back with a nasty note asking why they bothered, since he wasn't one of their supporters.

Tempers cooled as local Jews met the soft-spoken young rabbi and his wife, who were careful to make social calls on all the local rabbis and heads of Jewish organizations. Maryashie describes how nervous she was on her first visit to one Greenwich woman, whose daughter she now tutors for her bat mitzvah. "I'll never forget walking into that house, a typical Greenwich home," she says. "I remember her walking down the stairs, dressed so well, and I thought, I'll never get through to her. I laugh now to remember how intimidated I was."

"We were nervous, yes, but we were given so much more than we knew," Yossi says. "If we'd been taught about outreach techniques, it wouldn't have worked. We were taught truths—Torah, Jewish soul—we were taught how to smile, to be nice. And people responded."

In four years, the Derens have had a visible impact on the Greenwich Jewish community. Their first year, they held Purim, Lag B'Omer, and

Chanukah parties that drew hundreds of people. Two years later the local Reform congregation organized its first Purim party. The following year, the Jewish Federation held a Chanukah celebration, and the year after that the Conservative synagogue had its first big Lag B'Omer bash. Maryashie feels that although these duplicate parties may be stealing some of Chabad's thunder, increased observance of Jewish holidays will eventually create a bigger pool of committed Jews. And some of those people might even, she adds with a laugh, gravitate to Chabad events.

The Derens now raise virtually all of their annual $250,000 operating budget from local donors, who also contributed $1.5 million in 1999 to purchase the three-story building that serves as the Chabad House and Deren family home.

From the beginning, Yossi made a concerted effort to get along with the local Jewish establishment. Local Conservative and Reform rabbis spoke at the dedication of the Greenwich Chabad House when it opened in September 2000. One of those rabbis often comes to the Derens' Shabbat dinners, his wife attends Maryashie's weekly Torah classes, and the executive director of the local Federation praised Chabad in a talk at a recent General Assembly of United Jewish Communities.

But that doesn't mean everything's rosy. According to a member of Temple Sholom, Greenwich's Conservative *shul,* at a November 1999 board meeting Chabad was discussed as an organizational threat and a challenge to the growth of the temple's membership. The meeting concluded, the member says, with talk of the congregation's need "to move to the right" in order to stop losing members to Chabad.

The Greenwich Jews who come regularly to Chabad activities see it as an antidote to what they describe as the money-driven lifestyle that dominates their community.

"Greenwich is such a WASP town," says Joan Mann, past vice president of Temple Sholom and a former president of the local Federation. "When Chabad first came in, we wondered, What do they want? What will be their turf? I'm not a neophyte. I understand what Chabad is about. But from the beginning, I welcomed them. Their whole approach is so nonthreatening, so inclusive. When I want Jewish education, I go to them." Mann is still a dues-paying member of her Conservative congregation. "It's not one or the other," she points out.

Margye Black, a past president of Temple Sholom's sisterhood, attends Maryashie's Torah class regularly and sends her children to the Derens' summer camp, which she says upset her husband. "My daughter went for one week and started davening at home, and my husband went nuts. He doesn't want them at that camp next year. But they love it so much, and they're almost the only Jewish children in their school. So what do I do? It's a big conflict." Black says she "struggles all the time" with the question of how much of Chabad's teachings she wants her children to absorb. "Maybe they know they can't do the job on me, but they can get my kids," she muses. "My husband says we're being brainwashed, that we don't see the complete picture. I don't know. But what I get from Maryashie's class is invaluable."

Sometimes even the strongest efforts are not enough, as Chabad Rabbi Levi Zirkind and his wife Chani found when they were posted to Fresno, California, in 1990. Fresno is a conservative city of 450,000 in California's Central Valley that is known for its vegetable fields, dairy farms, and a municipal government continually accused of corruption. A couple of thousand Jews live there, but they don't advertise their Jewishness. When the Zirkinds arrived straight from Brooklyn, they stood out like two black thumbs. As per protocol, they made an appointment to meet one of the local rabbis. "When we walked in, Levi tried to give him *sholom aleichem,* but the rabbi wouldn't shake his hand," Chani says, furrowing her brow at the memory. She says the rabbi told them he'd pay to send them and their belongings back to Brooklyn that same day. "This is a Reform town," he informed them. That was the first of many social setbacks. "The Rebbe teaches us *ahavas Yisrael,* love your fellow Jews," Chani says. "So why this malice? And why does it come from the pulpit?"

The Zirkinds had been "invited" to Fresno by a small group of local Jews, but they quickly found there wasn't enough interest from the community to support a full-time Chabad center. Chani runs an afternoon Hebrew school for elementary-age children, and Levi holds Torah classes for adults twice a week—when anyone shows up—and tutors a handful of bar mitzvah boys. To support his family of six, Levi also works as a prison chaplain and as a kosher supervisor for several large food-packaging plants. But the most difficult part of their shlichus was the day in 1999 they sent their seven-year-old son Mendel away to Chabad school in Montreal, where Levi's shliach parents live. "You can deal with the financial pressures, you can deal with the headache," Levi says. "But sending away your child for *chinuch* [education], that's hard." Chani's eyes tear up when she thinks about it. "We know we're doing the right thing, but—" Her voice breaks. "It's the hardest sacrifice a shliach can make."

Elaine Colett is a member of Fresno's Conservative congregation, but she sends her two children to the Zirkinds for Jewish education rather than to her own synagogue's Hebrew school. "I wanted a place with a real spiritual leader," she explains. "When I saw what they offer here, how they make Judaism come alive, I thought, This is what I want for my children." Colett says she considers the Zirkinds her friends. But friendship only goes so far. "Do I want my family to have this lifestyle? No. Do I want my children to marry their children? No. But they are sincere in their beliefs, and this is the best Jewish education available, without question." Colett's neighbors warned her that Chabad was a cult, that the Zirkinds would try to indoctrinate her children. That didn't happen, she says, but the stereotype persists. "The community is very negative, still today."

The Zirkinds believe they can overcome lingering hostility by personal example. They smile, they call people again and again, they refuse to get angry or depressed when turnout for their carefully planned events is less than what they'd hoped for. They remain convinced that they are doing God's—and the Rebbe's—work and seem genuinely perplexed at the lack of interest, at the suspicion they've encountered so many times. "Every Chabad House you go to, you can see that the rabbi and his wife are real people," Chani points out. "When people meet them, the stigma soon falls away. Maybe that's why the Rebbe sent out shlichim— to break down the barrier between Jews that's unfortunately there. But sometimes it gets very lonely."

CHAPTER 7

THE FROZEN CHOSEN:
Looking for Gold in Alaska

At three o'clock on a January afternoon the sun is already setting in Anchorage. Inside the home of Perry Green a *mohel,* one who performs Jewish ritual circumcisions (*bris* or *brit milah*), is about to usher a fourth generation of Alaskan Greens into the Jewish faith. Eight-day-old Jack fidgets in his grandfather's arms, his tiny eyes screwed up tightly against the harsh light of the medical lamp trained upon him.

It's not easy to hold a *bris* in Alaska. The *mohel* had to fly up from Seattle, a four-hour trip. The kosher cold cuts were special-ordered from Brooklyn. The guests had to get off work early so the ceremony could be completed before the Far North sun set in the winter sky. "This is the first command-ment God gave to the Jewish people," intones the *mohel,* as he makes last-minute preparations to an imposing array of medical instruments lined up carefully on a clean towel in front of him. "No matter their level of observance, Jewish parents have done this for four thousand years. Throughout history, this was the mitzvah that was targeted by govern-ments bent on destroying the Jewish people."

Turning to the infant, the *mohel* makes one swift, cutting motion with his hand. The baby lets out a thin wail, drowned in loud shouts of "Mazel tov!" as the crowd breaks into a boisterous session of hand-clapping and singing.

There are just over 3,000 Jews in Alaska, out of a total population of more than 600,000. And they're scattered over a frozen territory as big as one-third of the entire Lower 48 states combined. The state has so few Jews, and they're so hard to get at, that Alaska was not even included in the Council of Jewish Federations' 1990 National Jewish Population Survey. Half the state's Jews—about 1,500 people—live in Anchorage, where they are just outnumbered by the city's 2,000 wild moose.

There have been Jews living in Alaska since the mid-nineteenth century, rough-hewn men and women trading in furs, whale blubber, and dry goods. The first Jews came from Russia and Scandinavia, giving way to American ex-pats following the U.S. purchase of Alaska from Russia in 1867. Their numbers jumped during the Klondike Gold Rush of 1896, although fewer Jews were actual miners than commercial entrepreneurs aiming to relieve the miners of some of their newfound wealth. Few descendants of those nineteenth-century Jewish arrivals still live in the state.

According to a privately funded 1995 survey, just 6 percent of Jews living in Alaska today were born there. Most arrived from the Lower 48 in the last twenty-five years, attracted by the economic boom of the Alaskan oil pipeline. They're professionals and managers rather than fur traders, and, like most other Alaskans, they're overwhelmingly young. Also like other Alaskans, most of them came here to get away— from the rat race, from family, from personal problems. From the past. Tradition doesn't count as much in Alaska as carving out your own fate.

It's not surprising, then, that there isn't much Jewish communal life. The intermarriage rate hits 90 percent in rural areas. In the early years so many Jews married native Inuit that they came up with a name for their children: the "Jewskimos."

If you want to marry Jewish, young Alaskan Jews complain, you have to leave the state. That's what Perry Green's nephew David did in 1996, when he was twenty-three and fresh out of college. He headed for New York, and met his wife Shani at a Simchat Torah party on the Upper West Side. He was lucky she was willing to move to Alaska. "It all happened so fast," Shani says. "If I'd thought about it, I don't know if I would have done it." Another single Jewish man from Fairbanks has run full-page ads for years in the national Jewish press, looking for a bride. He spent three months in Manhattan in 1997, where his exploits on the Jewish singles circuit were chronicled every week in *New York* magazine in a column titled, "Nice Jewish Boy Seeks Hot-blooded Jewish Girl for Love in Colder Climes." Four years later he was still single.

In early 2001, Alaska had just one rabbi. No *mohel,* no Jewish cemetery or Jewish home for the elderly. No Hadassah chapter, JCC, or Federation. No *mikvah,* and just a smattering of kosher packaged products—all fresh kosher meat and dairy has to be imported, and is prohibitively expensive.

A *bris* is a big deal, something that happens only once every year or two. That's why the party at the Greens' home this cold January afternoon is almost self-consciously festive. The Greens are one of Alaska's preeminent Jewish families, for several decades the only observant family in the state. Baby Jack's great-grandfather David, a pioneering fur trader from New York, immigrated to Alaska in 1922, setting up a major fur emporium and kosher home in one shot. His sons Perry and Jerry, now in their sixties, inherited both the fur business and the Jewish commitment. Today they are partners in David Green Furs and cofounders of Anchorage's traditional *minyan,* Shomrei Ohr (Guardians of the Light). Shomrei Ohr functioned as a lay-led congregation through the 1980s, meeting irregularly in Perry Green's home. Their only rabbinical leadership came from visiting Chabad rabbinical students, who would travel through the state every summer as part of the movement's "Peace Corps" program.

The first traveling Chabad students showed up in 1970. In 1990, the Greens appealed to the Chabad rabbi in Seattle, Sholom Ber Levitin, to send them a permanent rabbi. He chose the newly married Greenbergs: twenty-five-year-old Yossi, a Russian-born yeshiva *bocher* living in Crown Heights and facing a brilliant future in the Rebbe's court; and his twenty-one-year-old bride Esty, a smart young woman from the Shemtov family of Detroit. Why them? "No one else would go," Yossi says. "Rabbi Levitin called all his former students, and they said Alaska's too small, it's too far away, there's not enough money there to support a Chabad community." Not that Alaska's so bad, he rushes to add. But for a Lubavitcher couple to live so far from Crown Heights, so far from their families, from any kind of Orthodox life, from the intellectual stimulation and emotional comfort of their close-knit yeshiva world, and to know, above all, that they're going to raise their children in this non-*frum* world, isn't an easy decision.

Still, it was what Yossi wanted—more than Esty, he admits. "We had many other offers, but I felt I had extra energy, the inspiration I got from being close to the Rebbe. I felt I had to pay back what the Rebbe gave me, by giving back to Judaism. I wanted to make an impact, and I felt a remote place would be best." Yossi's dedication runs in the family. One of seventeen children, he has a brother serving on shlichus in Shanghai, two sisters in Odessa, Russia, a sister and a brother in Texas, and another sister in France.

In late 1990, Esty and Yossi came out to Anchorage for a short visit. "We went hiking with the community, and fell in love with the place," Yossi says. They came home, packed up, and by early 1991 had moved to Alaska to set up the state's Chabad Center. When they arrived, there was one other rabbi working in Anchorage, Rabbi Harry Rosenfeld of Beth Sholom, the city's Reform congregation, which had 170 member families. The two men maintained fairly good relations for eight years, until Rosenfeld moved to Buffalo in 1999, leaving Yossi, at least temporarily, as Alaska's sole rabbi. There are Reform congregations in Fairbanks and Juneau, but both are lay-led. Weddings, funerals, *brit milahs* and baby namings, bar and bat mitzvahs, Hebrew school, Shabbat services, holiday celebrations—after Rabbi Rosenfeld's departure, Yossi has to do it all.

The phone starts ringing in the Greenberg home at 7 A.M. and doesn't stop until past midnight. There's always food bubbling on the stove, hot coffee in the massive percolator, and usually a friend or two sitting at the kitchen table, waiting to be fed. By seven-fifteen every morning, Esty is dressed and out the door, headed for the all-day preschool she runs in a rented space a few miles away. She also runs a half-day kindergarten, an afterschool Talmud Torah, a Sunday Hebrew school and summer camp, and she teaches women's classes. Yossi handles the administrative and fundraising duties of the Chabad center, as well as running prayer services, holiday celebrations, and adult classes in Anchorage. Outside Anchorage he ministers to the 1,500 Jews living in the rest of the state, ranging from the 300-strong community in Fairbanks, a twelve-hour drive to the north, to small towns that may have just one or two Jewish families.

On any given day Yossi may hop a small plane or jump into his aging station wagon to head for "the bush," as he calls it, where he performs weddings, teaches bar mitzvah boys, counsels families, puts up mezuzahs, hands out Jewish literature—all for free.

In ten years Chabad operations in Alaska have grown steadily. The preschool is up to twenty children. The Greenbergs had to move it out of their basement in the mid-nineties, when they exceeded the state's home-school limit of twelve pupils. Shabbat services attract thirty to forty worshipers, with holidays drawing more than a hundred to the Greenbergs' basement *shul*. After services the chairs are cleared, the long tables brought out again, and Esty holds a *misibat Shabbat,* or children's gathering, downstairs while Yossi teaches adult education upstairs, at the family's kitchen table. Then everyone is invited for lunch.

The Greenbergs' biggest annual event is Chanukah. Like many Chabad couples on shlichus, they choose Chanukah to make their loudest public splash—a blow-out party in a downtown conference center, complete with public menorah-lighting and partying until the wee hours. Three-to-four hundred people show up, including a good chunk of Beth Sholom's membership, and Chabad's Chanukah celebration is always front-page news in the local papers. Yossi and Esty put a lot of time and money into their events. That's part of what the Rebbe taught, Yossi says: American Jews expect the best, so if you want them to show up, that's what you better give them. "The Rebbe always told us, If what you do isn't perfect, isn't the absolute best, that's how people will view Judaism. We are on stage 24 hours a day. Everything we do is in the public eye."

Board members at Anchorage's Reform congregation say there is little tension between Chabad and their community. "We're on the frontier, we can't be shooting at each other," says Rich Mauer, Beth Sholom president. Mauer says there's an easy give-and-take between the Reform and Chabad communities. He notes that many intermarried families send their children to Chabad's preschool and Talmud Torah, but when it comes time to do a bar or bat mitzvah, the kids of non-Jewish mothers move over to Beth Sholom.

The small size of the Jewish population has something to do with the lack of communal conflict, but, as in many other places, the Greenbergs' personal charm is what really melts the ice. "The rabbi and his wife transcend some of the ritual issues because they're such nice, warm, good people," Mauer says.

Some members of the local Reform community chafe when Chabad is called by the local press to explain an upcoming Jewish holiday, or to comment on current events in Israel. "The only time I feel threatened by Chabad is when reporters go to Rabbi Greenberg instead of coming here, and then present his comments as the face of the Jewish community," says

Anchorage attorney Marla Greenstein, vice president of Beth Sholom. "There are times when his values are in direct conflict with what I believe, but to the outside world, there is just one Jewish community."

"The Greenbergs fit in very well, but do people still say things against them? Sure," says Jerry Green, who davens every Shabbat at the Greenbergs' home. "But they're not trying to make people Orthodox. If they did try, actively, they wouldn't succeed."

Karen Greenberg is a forty-something medical equipment saleswoman from New Jersey who moved to Anchorage in 1997 for a better job. Like most new Jewish arrivals, she was a college graduate, single, and not observant. But she wanted to connect with the local Jewish community. "I called the Reform rabbi. His secretary called back. She sent me a bunch of brochures telling me how much it cost to join. Then I called Rabbi Greenberg. He called back himself, and invited me to dinner. It was an easy choice."

After that first dinner, Karen forgot about the Greenbergs until Rosh Hashana approached. Rabbi Greenberg called her again, asking if she had a place for High Holiday services. "I was so impressed that he would think to welcome me, or even think about me at all. So I went to his home again, and that's when I met all the fun people my age who hang out at Chabad. Before that, going to *shul* on Shabbos was the furthest thing from my mind. Now I was going, little by little. I felt so welcome."

Karen goes to Chabad services and attends Yossi's Tuesday night Torah class, but she is no *ba'al teshuva*. She wears jeans, goes to bars, drives to synagogue on Shabbat—the typical picture of the secular Jew who starts going to Chabad. It hasn't changed her lifestyle. But it's changed something in her psyche. "I had to leave New Jersey and come to Alaska to find my Judaism," she says with a wry smile. She also had to leave New Jersey to start giving real money to Jewish causes. In the past year, she's become part of the Greenbergs' small but loyal group of local donors, a handful of people Yossi has personally nurtured and upon whom he depends to keep his Chabad Center going. "I'd always tried to give *tzedaka* [charity]," Karen says, "but this is the first time I'm giving so much. Don't tell my parents. They think Chabad is a cult."

Karen Greenberg's experience of growing up in the heavily Jewish northeastern United States and avoiding Chabad until she finds herself in the hinterlands is not unusual. Yossi and Esty are constantly hosting Jewish tourists who find them in the phone book, on the Internet, or even through Beth Sholom. Most of them are people who might never have called a Chabad House at home. "We get modern Orthodox Jews who don't feel they 'need' Chabad back in New York, then they come to Alaska and suddenly the only kosher food they can find is at Chabad, the only mikvah is by Chabad," Yossi says.

For a Hasidic family, living in Alaska means that everything is just a little more difficult. The proximity to the Arctic Circle is hard on everyone, but it wreaks particular havoc with the Jewish calendar. In winter Shabbat begins in the early afternoon on Friday, which is trouble enough for a working couple. But in summer, Shabbat can drag on forever. In Anchorage, where the sun sets at eleven-thirty at night, Shabbat doesn't officially end until Sunday morning, when the first stars appear.

When Passover arrives, in early spring, the sun doesn't set until after 11 P.M. But tradition dictates that the four cups of wine required during the Seder be drunk after nightfall. With seventy or eighty guests at their Seder table, the Greenbergs stall as long as they dare, reading more stories from the Passover Haggadah, singing more songs, dragging out a service already notorious for its interminable length, until the sun finally sets and Yossi shouts, "OK, let's drink those four cups now!" Some years, when nightfall is particularly late, the Greenbergs take advantage of a special exemption that permits the Seder to begin early. They do an entire Seder with their guests from the community and then, at midnight, they wake up their own children and do it all again. Exemptions are for the less observant members of their communities, not for their own families.

Shopping for food is another constant headache. One Anchorage supermarket started carrying Empire kosher chickens and an assortment of other kosher products in 2000, but, Esty explains, "We Lubavitchers have a higher standard." She buys her fruit, vegetables, and some canned goods locally, but all the family's meat, bread, and dairy products have to be special-ordered and flown in from the continental United States. "The food comes by freight on Alaska Airlines," Yossi says. "We go to the airport, schlep all the boxes into the car, come back to the garage, unpack all the boxes and put everything in the fridge. It's a three-hour celebration."

OK, so Alaska is far away. OK, so it's lonely. OK, so you have to home-school your children and then send them away to Lubavitch schools, like Mendy, the Greenbergs' eldest son, who was sent to live in Chicago when he was nine. But the hardest part about living in Alaska, Esty says, is flying to Seattle every month to use the mikvah.

There used to be a mikvah in Anchorage. It was built in 1974 at Elmendorf Air Force Base for the wife of an Orthodox Air Force chaplain, the only mikvah ever built by the U.S. military. By the time the Greenbergs arrived, it was in horrible shape, with a bumpy concrete floor and a piece of rusted metal sticking out of the middle that served as an intermittent heating device. "Sometimes we'd come in and the water would be all brown," Esty says. "Sometimes it would overflow and soak the carpet, and be freezing cold. In the winter there would be icicles hanging outside the door. It would be ten below and we'd have to shovel our way in." The fact that tradition requires mikvah use after nightfall made the conditions even more difficult. Yossi says he and his wife never took out-of-town visitors there. "It was an embarrassment to Judaism," he jokes.

But at least it served its purpose. And it allowed the Greenbergs to move to Anchorage. Chabad shlichim aren't permitted to settle in a place that has no mikvah, unless they have funding in hand to build one. Which, of course, the Greenbergs did not. But the Air Force couldn't afford to keep a mikvah in working order forever. In June 1999 the Air Force demolished the nearly unused ritual bath in order to expand the base chapel. Since then, Esty and two or three other local observant women have been making the four-hour flight to Seattle every month, at $450 a pop.

Still, flying to Seattle is better than sharing your mikvah with a moose. One summer night Esty accompanied a woman who is afraid of flying to a nearby lake for her ritual monthly immersion. According to Jewish Law, any fresh body of water can serve as a mikvah, although lakes and oceans are discouraged because Jews are supposed to avoid placing themselves in physical danger. Nevertheless, the two women headed for the lake just before midnight. They waited until the last late-night bathers had gone home, and then surreptitiously prepared to disrobe.

At the critical moment, just as the other woman was about to slip naked into the freezing-cold lake, two baby moose leapt into the water ahead of her. Mama Moose emerged from the trees to stand guard over her frolicking progeny. Esty and her somewhat shaken friend waited until moose bath time was over, then completed their ritual. Needless to say, that was their last trip to the lake.

In the spring of 1999 the Greenbergs embarked on a fundraising campaign to build a new mikvah. It quickly became part of a major building campaign to construct an entire Chabad center, with a synagogue and room for their expanding preschool and kindergarten. The $1.6 million main building, which would contain the new synagogue, schoolrooms, and offices, would have to wait, but the mikvah couldn't. Still, where would they get $250,000 to build it? Local donors and parents of children in the Chabad preschool were already coughing up more than half the $150,000 yearly budget to run current Chabad activities, and had told Yossi repeatedly that they couldn't and wouldn't pay for a new building, not in a city that already had a perfectly good synagogue. And they certainly weren't going to pay $250,000 for a mikvah that few of them used.

Then Chabad philanthropist George Rohr stepped in, with a $60,000 check that arrived by Fed Ex just in time to persuade the Air Force to give the Greenbergs a three-month window before the old mikvah was destroyed. That was the turning point in the building campaign. Soon afterward, a visitor invited Yossi back to his Long Island synagogue to make a fundraising pitch. That netted them another $25,000. Shani Green also helped raise money, sending articles about Alaska's "mikvah crisis" to two New York Jewish papers, the *Jewish Press* and *Jewish Week*. Within days of publication, checks started pouring in, ranging from a bar mitzvah boy who sent $5 to the young Manhattan woman who sends $18 from every paycheck.

It's ironic, Shani says, that she moved to Alaska and found herself raising money for Chabad. Growing up in Brooklyn in a modern Orthodox family, she wanted nothing to do with Hasidim. "I'd see their mitzvah-mobile and I'd say, 'Oh, please!' Then I moved here, and my outlook changed completely. The rabbi and Esty are such selfless, giving people. And because of them, my son will have a Jewish education."

If there's one thing Rabbi Greenberg hates, it's flying. Which is why, when he finds himself on a small commuter plane the morning after the Greens' *bris,* bouncing his way out to the Kenai Peninsula, two hours southwest of Anchorage, he's doing his best to keep a smile on his face. "Oh!" he yelps, clutching the seat in front of him as the plane goes over a particularly bumpy stretch, then giggling nervously as the craft straightens itself out again. "I really hate this," he mumbles. Yossi is headed to Sterling, population 2,000, a forty-minute drive from Kenai Airport. James and Jackie Barsis and their three children, lately of Albuquerque, are the only Jews in town. James is a mechanic. Jackie works at Planned Parenthood. The couple help run a lay-led congregation of eleven families from the surrounding region. One regular worshiper has to drive an hour and a half to get to services, held once a month in a local community center. With only one other Jewish child in the congregation, there is no Hebrew school.

That's why Yossi is flying there. For the past six months he has been helping the Barsises' fourteen-year-old son Josh prepare for his bar mitzvah. Josh attended the Greenbergs' day camp the previous summer and came home raving to his parents about how he had to have a bar mitzvah. Jackie called Yossi, and he said that if Josh promised to study diligently, he'd meet with him once a month to prepare him for the ceremony. They had to start from scratch. Josh didn't even know the Hebrew alphabet. Now he can read simple phrases, if haltingly.

Although their progress is torturously slow, Yossi insists that his bar and bat mitzvah students understand both the words they're saying and the Jewish meaning behind them. Unfortunately, neither Jackie nor James can help their son. They both grew up in Reform households but can't remember much of what they learned as children. When Josh is going over prayers from the Siddur, Jackie can follow along in the English transliteration to check his pronunciation, but that's about it.

"There's no one here to help our kids learn except Chabad," says Jackie. "I don't know all the ins and outs of Lubavitch Judaism, but I really like the rabbi," James says. And both he and Jackie like the fact that Yossi doesn't charge for his bar mitzvah lessons. "Growing up in New Mexico, the synagogues there charge for everything," James continues. "Everything has a dollar amount. I don't think that's the point of religion. It's not what God had in mind." Instead of charging for teaching Josh, Yossi asked Jackie and James to sponsor a guest lecturer he brought into Anchorage last year. That cost $500, which James admits may be more than what he would have paid for the bar mitzvah lessons, but James likes that it was something he could give to the entire community.

The next morning Yossi is on the road again. This time he's driving to Wasilla, an isolated town an hour north of Anchorage in the Mat-Su Valley, to put up a mezuzah on the Mahoy family's new home. As he drives, Yossi talks about his family and the road that led him to Alaska. He was born in Moscow in 1965, the son of a Lubavitcher scholar who spent seven years in a Siberian labor camp after the Second World War. In the late forties Soviet authorities were allowing people with Polish citizenship to leave the USSR. Underground Chabad cells in the Soviet Union forged Polish papers for hundreds of Lubavitcher families caught behind the Iron Curtain. Yossi's father, Moshe, was part of a group of yeshiva students who helped arrange the illegal departures, until, with six friends, he himself approached the Polish border in 1947, where they were arrested.

Brought in for interrogation, Yossi's father insisted he was just going to Poland for a visit. The way Yossi tells it, the Soviet officer slammed his fist down on the desk and shouted, "We know exactly who you are and where you were going—to New York to see the Lubavitcher Rebbe!" All six students received the same sentence: twenty-five years at hard labor.

Moshe was put to work with 1,000 other prisoners building a new electric station in Siberia. About 20 prisoners in the camp were Jewish. As that first summer of incarceration came to an end, the Jews began thinking about the approaching High Holidays. How could they observe Yom Kippur? They had already bribed guards to allow them to hold services in the barracks, but where would they get prayer books?

One day Moshe noticed a civilian engineer walking around the camp, a man hired to help design the new station. Suspecting that the man might be Jewish, Moshe sidled up to him and asked, in Yiddish, *"Kenstu mir efsher helfen?"* (Could you maybe help me?) The man's eyes flickered in recognition, and Moshe asked him to find a Machzor, a High Holiday prayer book, and smuggle it into the camp. A few days later the engineer told Yossi's father that he'd located a book, but it belonged to his girlfriend's father, who needed it for his own Yom Kippur services.

No problem, Moshe said. If the engineer would bring him the book, he'd copy it by hand and return it in time for the holidays. The smuggling operation succeeded, and Moshe spent several hours a day for the next month crouched inside a wooden box he'd built, copying the precious book line by line.

Seven years later, following Stalin's death, the Siberian Gulag began to empty out and Moshe was released. The only thing he took with him was his handwritten Machzor. He returned to Moscow, married, and in 1967 moved with his wife and children, including two-year-old Yossi, to Israel. The Machzor went with them. In 1973, Moshe brought it to

Brooklyn as a gift for the Rebbe. Today that hand-copied holiday prayer book lies under glass in the Rebbe's memorial library on Eastern Parkway, but Yossi has a Xeroxed copy that he brings out for his own High Holiday services in Anchorage, as a tribute to his father's heroism.

With that kind of personal history, it's no wonder that Yossi felt the need to, as he puts it, "do something special" with his life. At seventeen, Yossi left Israel and came to study in Crown Heights, to be close to the Rebbe. He entered Brooklyn's Lubavitcher yeshiva and, like all Chabad rabbinical students, was sent away to another yeshiva for two years, in his case, to Seattle. By the age of twenty he was back in Crown Heights, where he and a friend began working on a fifty-volume set of the Rebbe's talks. He was also part of a select group of men who would memorize the Rebbe's lengthy Shabbat talks and copy them down afterward. That was the only way of preserving Schneerson's public addresses, as no writing or tape-recording is permitted on Shabbat. By the age of twenty-five, Yossi had published his own book, *The Early Years,* a meticulous chronicle of the Rebbe's first year as head of Chabad.

"Maybe you look at me and think, This is a man who belongs at 770 writing books," the soft-spoken Yossi muses. "But the Rebbe wanted us all to go out on shlichus. It's more than a philosophical decision, that the Rebbe gave us a sense of responsibility to the Jewish world. That's true, but it's also a debt that I'm paying back to the Rebbe for the years of richness, of enjoyment, I got at his *farbrengens.* We all feel so fortunate that we knew the Rebbe, and now we feel that we have to pay him back. We can't not do it. I'd feel almost guilty if I weren't a shliach. I don't think I could sleep at night."

Ten years into his shlichus, Yossi says that he still feels the same drive, the same excitement, that he felt when he and Esty first set out. "It's not just that the Rebbe won our hearts and minds. He also gave each one of us a second motor, a millionth of a percent of his sense of commitment and dedication. It's built into us, it's part of our psyche. That's what makes us happy. It's what makes us feel good about what we are doing."

That constant energy combined with the ceaseless smiles is often used against Chabad shlichim as evidence of their fanaticism. "Some people think we're robots, just doing what the Rebbe says without thinking, like soldiers—he commands and we go forward." That's not true at all, he insists. Every young Chabadnik goes through the usual adolescent crises, a period of questioning everything he has been taught. Some leave the fold. Those who remain do so because they have chosen that life, consciously, with all it entails. The trade-off is a surety of purpose that eludes so many people living in today's world of constantly shifting values and expectations. "We feel like we are the only people on earth walking around with a sense of purpose. We feel we know who we are and where we are going."

After an hour's drive through gorgeous mountain passes, Yossi arrives at Karen Mahoy's car wash. Karen moved to Wasilla from Miami seventeen years ago to marry Steve, who is not Jewish. But she tried to make sure her three children got some kind of Jewish education. Before the Greenbergs showed up in 1991, she taught basic Hebrew to a group of local children, most of whom now go to the Chabad summer camp and holiday services in Anchorage. She'd tried taking her family to Anchorage's Reform synagogue, but she says the rabbi gave her non-Jewish husband the cold shoulder. The Greenbergs, by contrast, "are completely welcoming." Karen's fifteen-year-old son Kyle went to the Greenbergs' Sunday school for years, but held his bar mitzvah in Baltimore, at his grandfather's insistence. That's another reason why Yossi is eager to get out to the Mahoys' today. Kyle's bar mitzvah was in a classical Reform synagogue, which means the boy did not put on tefillin to signify his transition from boyhood to maturity. "I'm going to do that with him today," Yossi promises.

Kyle is a lanky teenager wearing a backward red baseball cap and no shoes. He smiles shyly at the rabbi, who jokes about not seeing him lately at services. "Come on, Kyle, let's put on tefillin before sunset," Yossi urges. As he unwraps the set of leather straps he always carries for such occasions, he explains the ritual and its meaning to the boy. "You know what makes a home Jewish? It carries a mezuzah. You know what makes a body Jewish? It carries tefillin. When you put on tefillin, your body becomes a vehicle to carry the Torah's spiritual message."

He shows the straps to Kyle, describes how the Shema prayer is written inside the little black box, and talks him through the prayers a Jew says when he dons the contraption. Wrapping the straps around Kyle's left arm, he quips: "Here you're checking your Jewish blood pressure. You put it next to the heart, and on your head, the two most important parts of the body." Taking Kyle's hand, he explains how to wrap the straps around the fingers three times to create the letter *shin,* for shema, and then seven more times around the arm to make ten, the number of God's aspects, or *sefirot,* according to kabbalistic teaching. Then there's the tefillin for the head, with four chambers representing the four times tefillin is mentioned in the Torah.

After the tefillin-laying, Yossi grabs a hammer and puts up a mezuzah on the family's back door, leading the family in the appropriate Hebrew blessing. Just as with the tefillin-laying, he takes them through the procedure easily, with smiles, never making them feel awkward because they don't know what comes next. As he packs up to leave, he says casually, as if the thought had just occurred to him, "Hey, Kyle, why don't I make a commitment to come out here one Sunday a month and teach you for an hour, at your own level?" The offer means the rabbi will give up an entire day a month to make the long trek out to Wasilla. Kyle hesitates—he works on Sundays, and besides, how far does he want this Judaism thing to go? But the rabbi's smile wins him over. "OK," beams Yossi. "It'll be your spiritual injection for the month."

In the car driving back to Anchorage, Yossi talks about the dilemma he faces with intermarried couples like the Mahoys. "We could ignore them, because the father is not Jewish. And then three Jewish souls are lost forever to Judaism. Or we could embrace them, because they are Jewish kids, and their father is a wonderful human being. We accept the family and help them to raise the children Jewishly. That way, we'll end up with three more committed Jews."

In the Mahoys' case, because Karen is Jewish, Yossi's choice is clear: Her children are Jewish, according to Halacha, traditional Jewish law. He wouldn't be visiting the family and putting tefillin on Kyle if that were not true. Children of mixed marriages where the mother is not Jewish may take part in some Chabad preschools, camps, and holiday celebrations, but they may not participate in Jewish rituals. Yossi won't train them for a bar mitzvah, or call them up to say a blessing over the Torah. The same is true for non-Jewish spouses of Jews. But that's basic Orthodox Judaism, he points out, not simply a Lubavitch invention. In fact, Chabad shlichim are more open to these kinds of mixed families than the general Orthodox world, a bone of contention between the two communities. Chabad's welcome mat is not dependent, as in some Orthodox circles, on a Jew's level of observance, or on whether a man or woman has decided to marry a non-Jew. It is true, however, that shlichim in outlying regions like Alaska are more lenient in this regard. If they weren't, they would alienate local Jewish communities that are, invariably, heavily intermarried.

Just then, half an hour outside Anchorage, the sun breaks through the clouds and glitters brightly off the snow-covered mountains. The car radio says it's 38 degrees outside, unseasonably warm. Winter has been warmer than usual this entire year. The greenhouse effect? Yossi doesn't think so. "When the Rebbe sent us here, he gave us an extra dollar for *tzedaka* and said we should come warm up Alaska. I think, after ten years, that's what we've done."

CHAPTER 8

HOLY DIP:

Mikvah Makes a Comeback

Rabbi Aaron Raskin stares abashedly at the four boys seated across the table from him. A thin, wiry young man who turns a mean handstand at parties, Raskin is a Chabad emissary from Crown Heights whose shlichus hasn't taken him very far from home. He's employed as the pulpit rabbi of Congregation B'nai Avraham in Brooklyn Heights, a once-floundering Orthodox *shul* that needed a dynamic rabbi to boost its membership. Raskin took the job and, like any other Chabad shliach, quickly opened a preschool and built a mikvah. Not only does the mikvah serve women in his own congregation, it has become a major tool for Jewish outreach in a neighborhood that is fast filling up with young Jewish families.

Raskin is not a shy man. He likes to hang around outside the mikvah and drag passersby in to tour the facilities. He also gives regular tours of the mikvah to Reform and Conservative groups from the neighborhood. Most of his visitors are women. That makes sense. Although a mikvah is used in conversion ceremonies and to make cooking utensils kosher, and although Orthodox men may immerse themselves before Shabbat or Jewish holidays, mikvahs are mainly used by observant Jewish women who visit every month after they finish menstruating to prepare themselves for resuming sexual relations with their husbands.

Raskin has his mikvah patter down pretty cold. But here, staring back at him with the carefully cultivated blankness of early adolescence, are four Hebrew school boys, eleven and twelve years old. They showed up for their tour with Rabbi Serge Lippe, spiritual leader of the Reform Brooklyn Heights Synagogue down the block. Lippe is seated next to Raskin on one side of the large oak table, trying gamely to break the ice.

"Do you know what kind of synagogue you're in?" he asks his charges. Two of the boys say, in unison, "Orthodox." What kind of Orthodox? Lippe presses. "Hasidic?" one boy suggests, with a sideways glance at Raskin's straggly beard, black yarmulke, and signature Lubavitch suit and tie. No, not really, Lippe continues. Although Raskin is a Chabad rabbi, the synagogue he serves is modern Orthodox.

"Like Joe Lieberman!" another boy chimes in happily. "And what are we?" Lippe prompts. "Reform," the group intones. Lippe smiles and turns to Raskin. "They're all yours, Rabbi."

"So, ah, what do they know about mikvah?" Raskin asks in an offhand tone. "Not much," Lippe responds, his mouth twitching slightly.

Raskin takes a deep breath. What should he say? Should he begin his talk with the mystical elements of mikvah? How regular observance enhances a couple's married life by restoring sexual desire after niddah, a ritual period of enforced physical abstinence? Or perhaps he should focus on the details of how an observant Jewish woman checks her body to determine when seven blood-free days have passed, so she can immerse in the spiritually cleansing waters?

Maybe this isn't what the Rebbe meant by outreach. Then again, maybe it is.

In the Jewish world, few rituals have sunk so low and then soared so high again as the mikvah. It's one of the oldest Jewish traditions. The Israelites at Mount Sinai were said to have purified themselves in a mikvah before receiving the Torah. In Jerusalem, archeologists have discovered stone mikvahs from the Second Temple period. They were used by Jews to remove impurities before entering the sacred Temple grounds. Even today, tradition teaches, a mikvah is the most important building in any Jewish community. A congregation is required to mortgage its synagogue, even sell off its Torah scrolls, in order to raise money for a mikvah.

Taharat mishpacha, or "family purity," is one of the three commandments observed specifically by Jewish women, along with lighting Shabbat candles and removing a portion of dough from the Sabbath bread
before baking. It is arguably the most important of the three. You can live
without bread, and Shabbat arrives whether you light candles or not, but
without a mikvah, observant Jews can't have sex. That renders all questions about Jewish continuity moot.

In times of oppression, observant Jewish women have gone to extraordinary lengths to fulfill their monthly mikvah obligations. Lubavitcher girls
are told bedtime tales of their predecessors in Stalinist Russia who would
go out onto the frozen lakes at midnight and dig holes in the ice with pick-
axes in order to immerse themselves in a body of pure water.

Nevertheless, as religious observance plummeted this past century,
mikvah use declined and mikvahs themselves fell into disuse and closed
down. In the early years of the twentieth century, New York's Lower East
Side was dotted with mikvahs to serve the legions of Jewish immigrants
pouring in from Eastern Europe. By 1960, there were just two left, and
they were, according to observant women who lived in the neighborhood, run-down and ill kept. If that was the situation in New York, Jews
in the rest of the country turned their back even more resolutely on what
was viewed as an antiquated relic of a misogynist culture. Many Jewish
women, asked today about mikvah, wrinkle their noses in disgust. Thirty,
even twenty, years ago the mikvah represented, to non-observant as well
as some observant Jews, all that was wrong with traditional Old World
Judaism. Many Orthodox women who maintained the practice did so
almost furtively.

By the end of the twentieth century, however, mikvah use was on the
upswing. It even became strangely hip. Articles by non-observant Jewish
writers began popping up, describing their first mikvah visits in glowing,
often mystical terms.

Jewish film festivals in New York, Washington, and San Francisco
have scheduled evenings of "mikvah movies," black-and-white avant-
garde works by young, secular women filmmakers. Jewish women who
observe few or no other Torah commandments are reinventing mikvah
use to mark milestones in their lives such as divorce or menopause, or as
a healing ritual after rape or breast surgery. In the 1990s at least ten Conservative synagogues and several Reform temples in North America built
their own mikvahs.

Ironically, the women's movement of the 1970s was one of the first catalysts in the revival of the mikvah. On one hand, Jewish feminist thinkers launched a vitriolic attack against a ritual that seemed to imply a woman's body is dirty, in need of monthly cleansing after menstruation. On the other hand, many women's groups saw in mikvah a tool for feminine empowerment. Looking outside the dominant paradigms of Western culture for rituals that spoke their language, women's groups mined traditions such as Wicca and Celtic druidism in search of intrinsic feminist messages. For many of these spiritual seekers, mikvah struck a chord. While belonging to what they saw as a patriarchal religion, mikvah is nevertheless a ritual for women only, supervised by women only.

When a woman goes to the mikvah, she enters a completely female world. First, she scrubs and soaks her body for at least half an hour, in private, and then she calls the *shomeret,* or "mikvah lady." The *shomeret* examines her for absolute cleanliness, and then escorts her to the ritual bath, watches while she dunks herself completely beneath the water's surface, and finally pronounces her ritually purified. Every step of the process is conducted and controlled by women.

The laws of mikvah give the Jewish woman control over a couple's sexual relations, which become governed by the rhythms of her body rather than by her husband's sexual desire. They state that marriage does not give a man access to his wife's body at any time or place he chooses. This, too, is seen by many women as a profoundly feminist message.

The 1970s and '80s were years of growing popular interest in health, nutrition, and alternative healing techniques. Spa treatments, hot tubs, and massage therapy gained mainstream acceptance. A Jewish ritual involving spiritual cleansing in water, accompanied by prayer, no longer seemed outlandish or old-fashioned to a population entranced with water- and body-centered practices.

Still, Jewish feminists weren't throwing themselves into the waters right away. Most of the glowing writings and lectures supporting mikvah came from within the Lubavitch community itself, specifically from highly educated women, many of them feminists who became *ba'alei teshuva,* or returnees to the faith. They became the major spokeswomen for family purity, speaking to their non-observant sisters in language the secular world understood.

None of this, however, had reached critical mass in the spring of 1975 when Schneerson, during a *farbrengen* before a major Jewish holiday, spoke enthusiastically about making mikvah use a new Chabad mitzvah campaign. To the shock of the Lubavitchers sitting in the crowded *shul* at 770, Schneerson urged his shlichim to encourage regular practice of family purity as part of their general outreach efforts to non-observant Jews.

The Rebbe's words fell like a bombshell on his followers. Crown Heights resident Bronya Shaffer, a popular speaker on Chabad's mikvah lecturing circuit for the past twenty-five years, recalls that the speech "sent shock waves through the entire Orthodox community." Talk about mikvah? To outsiders? "People flipped out. The words *taharat mishpacha* were not spoken in *frum* families."

During her decades of lecturing on mikvah to Jewish women's groups, Shaffer has seen a steady change in popular attitudes toward the practice. "You can follow it in Jewish women's writings. The anger of early feminism has abated, and the younger women have grown up with the fruits of feminist labor without having to fight the battles themselves." At the same time, she says, more mikvah-observant women have moved into the business world, taking up careers that bring them into daily contact with non-observant Jews. "The convergence of all this in the past generation has changed people's attitudes. Spirituality isn't seen as hokey anymore. As all kinds of weird stuff became OK, so did mikvah, and not just for observant women."

After their initial shock at Schneerson's 1975 talk on family purity, Chabad shlichim picked themselves up and forged ahead on their Rebbe's latest mission: publicizing mikvah use among the general Jewish population. Within weeks Chabad adult education programs were including sessions on mikvah. Chabad centers around the world launched capital campaigns to build mikvahs. And not just any mikvah, but the best, the most beautiful, most expensive they could manage. Schneerson spoke often about the importance of aesthetic construction. New Chabad mikvahs have marble-lined walls, crystal-blue water, oversized private bathtubs, and an abundance of potted ferns, and the splashy brochures advertising them tout their resemblance to the country's top spa resorts.

No self-respecting shliach would think of stinting on his mikvah. It's the first, and invariably most expensive, part of any new Chabad operation, one that often puts the shliach at odds with his local donors, few of whom use a mikvah themselves or see much need for one in their town. This makes perfect sense in the Chabad framework, where mikvahs serve more than a strictly utilitarian function. They're making a statement, and making it loudly: We're here, we're religious, and we're part of your world.

One rainy February morning Raskin is giving a visiting group of Chabad women emissaries a tour of his mikvah. The women gasp as they walk in off the noisy Brooklyn street, into a darkly lovely foyer decorated in Early California Gold Rush: mahogany-paneled walls, heavy velvet curtains tied back with tasseled cord, and discreet lighting provided by ornate wall sconces. "When it comes to decoration, don't worry about the money," Raskin counsels his visitors, most of whom are just about to build mikvahs in their own communities. "The difference between top-of-the-line tile and next-best is nothing. It'll come back to you in *brachot* [blessings]." He points to the walls, surfaced with expensive, imported salmon-colored Jerusalem stone. "I had a guy come in here and say he'd give me tile for free. But it was cheap tile. You walk in here, and you see class."

Raskin's mikvah is a place you'd love to go for a quiet few hours of introspection and bathing, especially if you're a young married mother with children. That's precisely his goal. He could have saved $30,000 by utilizing existing water pipes behind the congregation's sanctuary instead of constructing everything from scratch, but then a woman visitor would have to walk through the synagogue, past the main sanctuary, to get there. Every man praying would know that she'd just finished menstruating, and would be going home soon to have sex with her husband. "She'd never come back," Raskin says. "Our objective as Chabadniks is to get people to go to mikvah, without breaking Halacha. You have to start slowly, like with the *aleph-beis*." So the entrance is private. The space is beautiful. And potentially embarrassing questions are kept to a minimum.

Questions like: Are you married? Is your husband Jewish? If the answer to either question is no, a woman is not permitted to use the mikvah. That's standard Orthodox Judaism—only married Jewish women are commanded to use the mikvah, therefore the "magic" works only for them. Any woman can dunk, but without that wedding ring, no spiritual cleansing takes place. In many mikvahs, the mikvah lady on duty will ask those questions of any woman she doesn't know, to keep the operation kosher. With Chabad, however, *delicatesse* prevails. "The first time a woman shows up at our mikvah, we don't ask questions," Raskin claims. "On the way out the mikvah lady will ask, So where do you live? Who's your husband? But only afterwards. If you ask before, she won't even come in."

It's a far cry, if only a few subway stops away, from Raskin's upscale spa-in-a-brownstone to the strictly utilitarian central mikvah of the Crown Heights Lubavitch community. The Crown Heights mikvah is scrupulously clean, but there are no bells and whistles. No dark wood paneling, no plush carpeting or psychedelic domed ceilings. But then, the Crown Heights mikvah doesn't have to worry about drumming up business. Its clients aren't coming in looking for a tranquil, spiritually uplifting experience. They come because mikvah observance is a commandment from God.

Within the Lubavitch community, mikvah is used as a kind of sex-ed tool, in classes that teach young brides-to-be about their future sex lives. Bronya Shaffer, who teaches many such classes, says that these young women are already committed to observing this mitzvah, and most of their questions have to do with the details of correct practice. "It's a mitzvah from Torah, so we do it. Period."

When she talks to non-observant women, though, Shaffer admits, "I'll use whatever is of interest to women today to get them to want to do it." What's a hot buzz word today? "Intimacy," she says. So most of her talks to general audiences focus on how regular mikvah use restores intimacy to a marriage; how it preserves a woman's own privacy, creating individual intimacy; how it can bring a woman into closer, more intimate connection with God.

"Mikvah is all about boundaries," she says. "I always talk about the basic prohibition against sexual intercourse during *niddah* [the state of ritual impurity that begins at the onset of menstruation and ends seven days after its cessation, upon immersion in the mikvah]. Depending on who I'm talking to, I go through the whole progression of [prohibited] behaviors: sleeping in the same bed, hugging and kissing, passing food. Then, if it seems too weird to them, I'll stop. There's a sensibility to where someone's at." In the modern world, Shaffer explains, people touch hands casually without thinking that it might lead to sexual intimacy. The Talmud, however, sees a direct link between the two. "The Gemara says that sexual intercourse is prohibited during *niddah*. But then it lists all the other activities that are prohibited because they might lead to sexual intercourse—any physical intimacy, even if it's not sexual. Even touching fingertips. I talk about these as boundaries, and we discuss how creating clear boundaries is a necessary part of real intimacy." Usually at this point, Shaffer says, she'll launch into a discussion about codependence and how mikvah use can restore wholeness to a woman's personality.

"You can't be intimate with someone if you're not whole yourself," she states. "The need to recognize where I end and my husband begins is essential to developing intimacy. Mikvah helps define that."

Shaffer also likes to talk about the power of touch, and how it can create a false sense of closeness between husband and wife. When you're both tired at the end of a long day, and you crawl into bed exhausted, the easiest way to connect with each other is to reach out and touch your spouse. "It feels good. We're connected. But when that goes on and on, you can wake up one morning after twelve years of marriage and say, Who is this person lying next to me? If the only part of myself I've given to my husband is my body, I've alienated myself from him." Observing the laws of family purity forces a couple to develop real communication skills, she points out. When you can't touch physically, "kissing" with a look, or talking through a problem instead of drowning it in a hug, brings a couple closer.

This is the kind of talk Shaffer directs at her groups of non-observant women, but she touches on the same themes with her Lubavitcher brides-to-be. They live in the modern world, exposed to many of the same stimuli as their secular peers, and have emotional needs and practical questions that weren't as present a generation ago. "My mother still has a hard time when I mention mikvah in front of my children," Shaffer says. "And because of my Hasidic background, I very much want to shield my children, not from sex, but from its vulgarization. It's just too precious, and too private. Still, it's hard to get to age nineteen in New York City and be utterly clueless. Kids talk. They overhear things, on the bus, on billboards, in magazines."

So while Shaffer outlines the basic facts of married life to her young Lubavitcher brides, she adds in a lot more. "Of course, I focus on the laws, but I also teach them how to use the tools of this mitzvah to relate to their husbands better. Sensibilities have changed. 'Relationship' is something I never heard my parents talk about. Even with me and my husband, it was years into our marriage before we talked about it."

By the way, Shaffer mentions, these young brides' future grooms are being inducted into the mysteries of married life in parallel classes taught by Chabad rabbis. They learn the same laws of family purity as their wives, but they also learn how to please their wives sexually, something the Torah commands them to do.

Rivkah Slonim also lectures widely on the subject of mikvah. (Her book, *Total Immersion: A Mikvah Anthology,* is one of the best sources for a wide range of traditional interpretations of the mikvah.) But she takes a different tack: She has no patience for brochures and lectures that try to lure women into mikvah observance by playing up the ritual's mystical and romantic aspects. Yes, she says, mikvah has the power to improve your marriage. Yes, it's wonderful to take a few hours out of your busy day and focus only on yourself, in quiet, beautiful surroundings. Yes, the actual moment of immersion can be tremendously uplifting. But that's not why you do it, she says, and it's deceptive to present the ritual as anything other than what it is.

"We keep it because it's a divine commandment," she declares. "Enough of the posturings! What upsets me more than anything is the way mikvah is packaged. Because people thought mikvahs were dirty and unattractive, our brochures talk about how clean they are, how beautiful, like a spa. Because it's called irrelevant, we say how it will enhance your marriage. Because they say it's misogynist, we say how it's mystical, how it's about female empowerment. Mikvah is a *hok,* the kind of commandment that defies understanding. We have no idea why God doesn't want us to eat pig, or wear a garment of linen and wool. Mikvah is the same." And precisely because there's no rational explanation for such laws, because they reside in the sphere beyond human intellect, they have the power to draw a soul closer to God.

Slonim is running through her mikvah spiel for a group of largely non-observant Jewish women from around the country who are visiting Crown Heights with their Chabad shlichot. The shlichot are attending their own annual convention in the Oholei Torah boys' school on Eastern Parkway, while these VIP visitors, women active in Chabad congregations, are being escorted around Brooklyn to the principal Lubavitcher sites: the Rebbe's grave, the Rebbe's room, the Rebbe's library. Now they're seated on folding chairs in a small lecture room on the top floor of the community's central mikvah. They're a middle-ground audience: Chabad has already hooked them in, as donors or almost-observant Jews or both, so they're open to the message; but, unlike women who grew up observant, they still need to be persuaded that this particular mitzvah is worth the effort.

That's Slonim's forte. An outgoing and energetic woman with a freckled face and eyes that squint almost shut when she laughs, which is often,

Slonim's most striking physical feature is her short, spiky, frosted blond-tipped *sheitel*. That *sheitel* says a lot. In a world of shoulder-length bobs for the young wives and bouffant curls for the elderly, Slonim's punk-rock 'do hints to non-observant women they can be Lubavitch without sacrificing their individuality.

Slonim spends about an hour running through the details of mikvah observance and why it should be practiced. She moves back and forth between street humor and the deepest Hasidic mysticism, weaving a compelling rationale for what she tells the group is something she "cares deeply and passionately about," a mitzvah that is "the nexus of our intimate lives." Mikvah is, she says, "one of the most basic commandments, right up there with Shabbat and *kashrut,* yet people think it's some kind of custom for the black-hat fanatics, the overweight woman with her wig on askew."

Far from that, she continues. It's about the very essence of the individual's relationship with God, a way that a woman can connect with the Almighty in private, wordlessly, intimately. "I can't explain why that transformation takes place. Why a woman who walks in in a state of *niddah* walks out able to be united with her husband. When a woman walks down these steps into the mikvah, that submerging of the self into the waters is letting go of the 'my.' My intellect. My intuition. In that moment of self-negation, that letting go of the self, at that moment, the purity sets in." But that doesn't mean this spiritual revelation happens every time a woman visits the mikvah. "People can tell you how wonderful your mikvah experience will be, but for every woman who feels renewed, rejuvenated, spiritual, there are ten women who just feel cold." That's why, she tells her visitors, you can't adopt the practice because it feels good. If you do, what will happen to your observance if the good feeling deserts you one month?

"I heard that mikvah makes sex better," one of the women says. That's true, Slonim responds. The fact that every physical contact between husband and wife is prohibited for at least two weeks of the month, down to touching hands and sitting on the same couch, means that when physical relations are resumed the night after a woman goes to the mikvah, they are, in Slonim's words, "explosive."

"I'm constantly amazed when people tell me they can't remember the last time they were together," she says. "With *niddah,* you're constantly thinking about when you'll be together again. The couple is constantly communicating about this, in private ways. Sexuality is at the forefront, all the time." When you are forced to express your love for your husband in words, rather than with a quick pat or a kiss, "it fosters a deeper kind of intimacy." But, she says, her face crinkling into a huge smile, "I won't promise you that mikvah will send your sex life through the roof!"

Slonim and Shaffer are highly articulate women and gifted public speakers. But every Chabad rabbi and rebbetzin in the field is expected to teach local women about mikvah use, a task many of them find daunting. "It's a very delicate thing for a young shlicha to start talking to other women about mikvah, about what goes on in their intimate lives, behind closed doors," says Kraindy Klein. "She's just getting used to her own intimate life." Klein is one of a small group of Lubavitcher women who run Mivtza Taharas Hamishpacha (aka JEWELS), Chabad's outreach and resource center for family purity issues. Their small, upstairs office on Kingston Avenue in the heart of Crown Heights is a clearinghouse for speakers, tapes, books, classes, and walking tours designed to spread the Rebbe's mikvah message. When the office first opened in 1975 to draw attention to the Rebbe's newest campaign, it focused on older, post-menopausal women. That was a strategic move. According to Jewish tradition, a woman's last visit to the mikvah may take place any time after menopause, even years later, and will bring blessings down upon her children and grandchildren even if they themselves don't observe mikvah laws. In 1975 it was easier to get that older generation of Jewish women into the mikvah. They remembered the custom from their childhood, often sentimentally.

Over the years, as mikvah use has increased, the office has greatly expanded its services. Staffers maintain a Web site—www.mikvah.org—which lists mikvahs around the world, along with their fees and hours of operation. Not only are new mikvahs being added to the site weekly, speakers' bureau director Chana Seligson says she gets more and more requests for information from Reform and Conservative congregations. "Sexuality is out there. It's plastered on billboards, everywhere. People are interested in mikvah because they're interested in sexuality. This [campaign] is an attempt to approach it in a spiritual, meaningful way."

Devorah Leah Rosenfeld, a popular speaker on the JEWELS circuit, says she isn't surprised at the surge of interest in mivkah use among non-observant women. "It's a very private, easy way to start keeping more

Judaism," she says. "Keeping kosher can send a family into a whole hulla-baloo. Keeping mikvah is a way to keep one basic tenet of Judaism with nobody looking over your shoulder." Taking teenaged girls on mikvah tours may make some people uncomfortable, but Rosenfeld thinks it's important. "If these kids are marching in and out of the mikvah when they're thirteen, it won't be so scary to them when they get older."

CHAPTER 9

SHOW ME THE MONEY:
Raising Funds and Influencing People

When rabbis and Jewish leaders from outside Lubavitch look at the success of Chabad's schools, camps, adult classes, and other outreach programs, many of them say that if they had the same money, they could do just as well. People imagine there's a bottomless pot of gold at Lubavitch World Headquarters that the shliach can tap into whenever he wants. "People think we just call up 770 when we need money," says Yossi Greenberg in Alaska. "Not only that, but when we fundraise, they think we're sending that money *back* to 770."

In fact, each Chabad center must support itself. Shlichim in the field are responsible for their own fundraising, and they must find the money they need not only for their own operation, but also to raise their children, pay their mortgage, and put food on their table. Fortunately, shlichim take few family vacations.

Because Chabad fundraising is so decentralized, and the money raised by local shlichim is plowed right back into ongoing projects without central accounting of its passage, it's impossible to know exactly how much money Chabad raises each year. The movement's worldwide operating budget for 2002 approached $1 billion, but that does not include capital building funds or monies for special projects. It's just the tip of the Luba-vitch iceberg.

It's clear that Chabad raises a lot of money. But you'd never know it by looking at 770 itself. The headquarters of this international organization that raises almost a billion dollars a year is literally falling down. Anyone who suspects that the movement might be siphoning off money for itself only has to climb the dank, dingy staircases in this building, look at the paint peeling off the walls, the electrical wires hanging from holes in the ceiling, the broken chairs and old boxes littering the hallways, and the general shabbiness of the entire place to know that this is not where the money is going. Schneerson never permitted his aides to "waste money" on his headquarters. Give it to my shlichim, he ordered. Movement officials have continued this conscious neglect since his death, although some of the younger rabbis working in the building chafe at its condition. You can't bring visitors into the place, they grumble.

The same financial neglect applies to shlichim's homes. Shlichim in the field may sink millions into their Chabad centers, synagogues, and mikvahs—responding to Schneerson's request that buildings destined for public use be as aesthetically pleasing as possible—but their own homes are modest, again patterned after their Rebbe's lack of personal ostenta-tion. This is particularly striking in the homes of the oldest, most power-ful shlichim—like the Fellers in Minneapolis, the Shemtovs in Detroit, the Shmotkins in Milwaukee, the Derens in Stamford, the Cunins in Los Angeles—but the same aesthetic carries through to their children's homes. These people don't redo their bathrooms. Their kitchen fixtures and appliances have seen better days. They've raised ten, twelve, or more children three or four to a bedroom, where mattresses tend to sag and wallpaper is often mismatched or peeling. The only nod to spending comes in the living room, invariably the largest, most opulently decorated room in the house, because that's where guests are brought. Shlichim's living rooms are all furnished in similar fashion—floor-to-ceiling book-cases filled with Bibles, Talmuds, books of biblical commentary and Jew-ish Law, *Tanya,* and volumes of the Rebbes' teachings. There are lots of chairs and couches for reading and talking, and a long dining room table holding silver candlesticks and other Jewish ritual objects. The only pic-tures are family photographs and Jewish-themed prints or paintings, including at least one large, centrally positioned portrait of the Rebbe.

Shlichim do not spend money on themselves because they are personal emissaries of the Rebbe, and everything they do, including the way they live, reflects on their movement and its teachings. "They're the monks of the Jewish community," remarks Rabbi Ismar Schorsch, chancellor of the Jewish Theological Seminary. "They're prepared to live on Grub Street. That's what monks do."

While shliach couples share equal responsibility in running their Chabad centers, just about every couple assigns major fundraising responsibility to the husband. It's the part of their job shlichim say they dread above all else, and it doesn't get any easier with time. Aharon Slonim, shliach in Binghamton, New York, for more than fifteen years, says he still gets a queasy feeling in the pit of his stomach when he has to pick up the phone to ask a donor for money. When he gets a rejection, he feels, he says, "sick for days."

They don't teach fundraising in Lubavitch yeshivas. "You learn fast when you don't have food on the table," remarks Detroit shliach Levi Shemtov. In fifty years just a handful of Chabad centers have collapsed due to financial difficulties. The rest somehow make it.

If there's a key to Chabad fundraising, it could probably be described as bulldozer belief. "They are the best salespeople I know," says Rabbi Jerome Epstein, of the United Synagogue of Conservative Judaism. "They don't understand the word 'no.' 'No' to them translates as 'maybe,' or 'come back tomorrow, I'm not ready yet.'" The Chabad shliach believes that his mission is sacred, and if he pursues his work wholeheartedly, the money will be found to keep it going. He approaches each potential donor with an optimism that is infectious. When the shliach asks for money, he doesn't apologize. He's not asking the donor to assume an onerous burden, but is rather presenting him or her with the opportunity to be part of a wonderful mitzvah, the continuation of the Jewish people.

"They are fabulous fundraisers," acknowledges Dr. Norman Lamm, president of Yeshiva University and a very successful fundraiser himself. "And they've latched onto some very wealthy people."

Most shlichim have a wide pool of small donors, but all of them have cultivated one or more financial anchors, the big donors who give the big money. Without those big donors, Chabad could not do its outreach work. Its operating style requires making Judaism available for free, or close to it, for people who would not go out of their way to seek it out. The thinking is that once people begin to appreciate what Chabad does, they'll give money. Wealthier Jews are expected to give more, but again, not because they "should," but because they "get to." You're rich, so you get to play a bigger role in the bringing of Moshiach.

Chabad's ostensible target audience is the majority of American Jews who are not affiliated with Jewish life, but in fact many of those who end up at their services and in their schools are members of Reform, Conservative, and Reconstructionist congregations. Every dollar these people give to Chabad might have gone to their own movements, and that angers many non-Chabad rabbis. *Forward* editor J. J. Goldberg points up the irony of Reform Jews in America who give money to an organization that works against their movement's political and religious interests in Israel. "When non-Orthodox Jews give Chabad money, it indirectly funds their campaign in Israel for no territorial compromise [with the Palestinians] and no recognition of Reform Judaism," he notes.

Schorsch suspects that a large source of Chabad's revenue comes from Conservative Jews. "Conservative Jews believe in *klal Yisrael* [the Jewish community], so on principle they support every worthy cause in the Jewish community," he says. "I've heard it said that seventy percent of Chabad's revenue comes from Conservative Jews. That's pure guesstimate, but it's plausible." Schorsch won't go on record opposing such donations, although he's spoken out against Chabad fundraising among Conservative Jews in other forums. But it concerns him. "From a sociological perspective, I think it's grand," he insists. "I applaud the ecumenism of Conservative Jews. But what does it mean denominationally? It means I have to wait in line with others before contributions come my way."

Other Jewish leaders believe that Chabad fundraising helps all Jewish causes, because it brings people who may never have given charity into the general Jewish donor pool. "I think most rabbis and synagogues would agree with me," says Jacob Solomon, executive director of the Greater Miami Jewish Federation. "The more people give, they more they give in general."

What constitutes a "big donor" varies from place to place. Someone who gives $5,000 a year is at the top of Yossi Greenberg's list in Alaska but would hardly rate a blip on L.A.'s financial radar. Chabad's two largest donors are international business mogul Lev Levaiev, a Russian-born diamond tycoon who mainly supports, to an annual eight-figure tune, Chabad operations in the former Soviet Union, and George Rohr, a New York-based money manager who funds new Chabad centers around the world and rivals Levaiev in the former Soviet Union.

But Levaiev does not fund projects within the United States, and Rohr does so only selectively. Most Chabad shlichim working in major American cities have their own million-dollar donors. Some are national figures, like cosmetics tycoon Ronald Lauder, former chairman of the Conference of Presidents of Major American Jewish Organizations and long-time supporter of Israel's Likud Party; Revlon billionaire Ronald Perelman, who flies Crown Heights yeshiva students to his island estate on Fridays to ensure a Shabbos minyan; real estate mogul Sheldon Adelson, developer of the $1.5 billion Venetian Hotel in Las Vegas; the list goes on.

Each of these donors has a personal reason for donating to Chabad. For Lauder it was visiting a Chabad school for Soviet refugee children in Vienna in 1986, when he was the newly-appointed U.S. Ambassador to Austria. Speaking at a Chabad dinner in Washington, D.C., in July 2001, Lauder said that when he saw those Russian-speaking refugee children he was hooked. A visit to the Rebbe in Crown Heights a few weeks after the Vienna experience—arranged by the Vienna Chabad rabbi—cemented his commitment. "The Rebbe knew what I was going to do," Lauder related at a Chabad dinner in D.C. "The Rebbe always knew what I was going to do, a year or two before I did it." Soon after his meeting with Schneerson, Lauder set up a network of Jewish summer camps in Eastern Europe. By the late 1990s, 7,500 children were spending summers at those camps each year, all on Lauder's dime. Lauder credits Schneerson with encouraging him to get involved in Jewish organizational life. "The Rebbe changed my life," he declared.

When the Rebbe was alive, shlichim would honor their biggest donors by bringing them to Crown Heights for personal meetings with Schneerson or, later, to pass by the Rebbe on Sunday to receive the dollar they were then supposed to give to charity. Now these supporters spend two days in Brooklyn at the shlichim's annual convention, where they take part in a concurrent "lay leaders" convention. They learn Torah from movement leaders, and are regaled by speakers who tell them—quite correctly— how esssential they are to the movement's continued success. They join the shlichim for the convention's gala closing banquet, glimpsing for one evening the joy and passion that animate the Hasidim whose work they support.

"There's big money in this room," whispers shliach David Eliezrie, pointing out some of the more well known Jewish leaders dancing the *hora* at the movement's November 2000 convention. "There's Mike

Abidor, he chaired the [United Jewish Communities] General Assembly this year. He davens in the Chabad *shul* in Riverdale. And there's Michael Steinhardt, one of the founders of Birthright Israel. This is the first year he's come."

Some big donors are what Eliezrie calls "outside givers," those who give money to Chabad but don't take part in its activities. Most of the lay leaders, however are "inside givers," wealthy men and women who give money to several Jewish causes in addition to Chabad. "The guy who built the JCC in Orange County is a major donor to Chabad," Eliezrie confides. "Why are people giving us money? Because they come to our classes. They give us money because we are serving them."

Montreal textiles attorney Michael Chernak came to the November 2000 convention with his Chabad rabbi, Moshe New. His first contact with Chabad was in 1992, when a friend invited him to Shavuot services at New's Chabad House. "I'd been to Conservative, Reform, Orthodox, Reconstructionist, but I never found what I was looking for," he says. "I was tired of hearing rabbis talk about politics. I worked in politics, I didn't want to hear it from a rabbi. We walked in, and Rabbi New was there talking about Torah. It was a combination of spiritual and academic, the first time ever I sat in *shul* and really learned something. I felt I was back in university. I had no clue about the davening—I went back for the rabbi's speeches." Chernak's initial attraction to Chabad was intellectual, but he soon found himself spending every Shabbat at New's Chabad House, where he now acts as the cantor, prepares the kiddush, and sets the table for *se'udat shlishit,* the Saturday afternoon festive meal. He also gives money, "not a lot," he demurs. But he gives, steadily, mainly because of his admiration for his shliach. "Rabbi New can speak to a Ph.D. or to someone with a high school education, and he speaks to each one at his own level," he says. "It doesn't matter how wealthy you are, or how much money you give. Everyone is made welcome."

Many of the lay leaders at this convention say that their Chabad shliach touched an emotional chord they didn't even know they had, awakening a side of themselves they'd kept hidden in their lives as successful, professional American Jewish men. Dr. Richard DuBou is a plastic surgeon from Louisville, Kentucky who became close to Avraham Litvin, his local shliach, when the two men served together in 1991 on the board of Louisville's Jewish day school.

"He was the only one who laughed at my jokes," DuBou maintains.

"We're both New Yorkers, and we hit it off. He's a very vibrant, charismatic guy." It took two years before Litvin followed up on the connection, when he invited DuBou over for dinner and asked him to buy a $500 piece of equipment for the Chabad House. DuBou acquiesced, and thought no more about it. Then in 1996 he was diagnosed with a dangerous bone disease. He went for advice to his Conservative rabbi and to Litvin, who is the pulpit rabbi of Louisville's Orthodox congregation. Litvin told him to put on tefillin daily and write a letter to the Rebbe's grave.

DuBou took his advice, put on tefillin every day, and watched incredulously as his disease melted away. He stops short of seeing a direct connection between his prayers and his recovery. The man's a physician, after all. "What am I going to say, superstitious stuff?" he bristles. "Still, a little divine intervention never hurts." DuBou has since dropped out of his Conservative synagogue and in 1999 was elected president of Litvin's congregation, where he's begun studying *Tanya*. He says he doesn't understand the animosity many of his Jewish friends have toward Chabad. "People get upset when they talk about the Rebbe and the coming of Moshiach, but they're doing great work, especially in Russia. They're not crazies, like the other Hasidim. I've never heard my Chabad rabbi say a bad word about anybody else, and that's incredible. In Orthodoxy when I was growing up, [Judaism] was a religion of nos. In Chabad it's a religion of yeses. Chabad rabbis laugh a lot. They really have a ball."

Chabad shlichim court business leaders for their money and prestige, but they also have been very successful at attracting politicians and Hollywood celebrities, some of whom turn into donors but most of whom contribute by lending the movement a certain social cachet. If Bill Clinton carries vintage Chabad books back from Moscow on Air Force One for personal delivery to the Rebbe, if Al Gore stumps for the cause and Joe Lieberman appears in Chabad videos, that's called having friends in high places. Lieberman, by the way, is one of the few political supporters who is also a donor—before his election to the U.S. Senate, he was a Chabad lay leader in Stamford, Connecticut.

But why does actor Jon Voight, who's not even Jewish, headline West Coast Chabad's annual TV telethon? Why have Whoopi Goldberg, Carroll O'Connor, Elliot Gould, Anthony Hopkins, and Michael York lent their efforts to the show? Why does Gail Papp, widow of the late theater producer Joseph Papp, sponsor annual fundraising dinners at the New

York Hilton to raise money for a Ukrainian orphanage and medical clinic run by Chabad's Tzivos Hashem children's organization? And why are Tony Randall, Meryl Streep, Liza Minnelli, and James Earl Jones up on the platform next to her?

Each celebrity has his or her individual reason for helping Chabad's fundraising effort. Some like the nonsectarian nature of Chabad's social service work—its drug rehab clinics, its soup kitchens. Some like the way Chabad conjures up their own Jewish memories from childhood. Some are doing a favor for a friend. Some are there because the others are there; success begets success.

Bob Dylan is one of the biggest names associated with Chabad, although his connection has waxed and waned over the years. Born Robert Zimmerman in the small Minnesota town of Hibbing, Dylan was allegedly bar-mitzvahed by a rabbi in a black hat and white beard who showed up in his town one winter night, taught him his Haftorah portion, and disappeared soon afterward. In the early 1980s, Chabad "rescued" Dylan from a brief flirtation with Christianity, and for several years he studied with Minneapolis shlichim Manis Friedman and Moshe Feller, whom he also visited for Shabbat dinners. Manis Friedman is still refered to as "Bob Dylan's rabbi," and a glowing blurb from Dylan appears on the front cover of Friedman's book on marital intimacy, *Doesn't Anyone Blush Anymore?* Dylan made surprise appearances at the 1988 and 1989 telethons, once playing "Hava Nagilah" on the harmonica with his religious son-in-law, and he's been sighted almost every year at Chabad High Holiday services, most recently in Encino, California in 2001, where he was honored with an *aliya* to the Torah on Yom Kippur morning. He came to the Rebbe for Sunday dollars more than half a dozen times, and word has it that he gave $100,000 for a Chabad building in Minnesota named after his father, but the notoriously reclusive star won't give interviews on this or any other subject touching on his current religious affiliation.

Most Jews who give money to Chabad are, like Bob Dylan, not Jewishly observant, although like Dylan they usually have Jewish memories from their childhood. Some become more observant as they continue to take part in Chabad activities. Others do not. They give to Chabad for a variety of reasons. Some, particularly the older generation, give partly out of a sense of guilt—these Hasidim are leading the kind of Jewish lives they themselves "should" lead, but know they won't. It's an easy way to soothe one's conscience without having to change the way one lives. People like the attention the Chabad rabbi and his wife bestow on them. They like the one-on-one classes, the personal touch. "There's a boutique quality to some of these rabbis, a 'personal rabbi' mentality," Jacob Solomon notes.

Many non-observant Jews feel nostalgic when they look at their shliach and his family. They may remember Passover Seders at their grandparents' home, or recall seeing faded photographs of long-bearded immigrant ancestors, and they want to recapture that sense of warmth and family connection. They feel these Lubavitchers have tapped into something that has eluded them. Some donors talk about this with great wistfulness. In our rush-rush world of failed marriages, crushed hopes, and materialist excess, they yearn for the more essential, close-knit, coherent lifestyle Chabad seems to represent. Wouldn't life be simpler, they wonder, if I could only believe? Wouldn't it have more meaning if I could live, as Elie Wiesel put it, at that "higher, deeper level" all the time?

That's how Yehuda Krinsky understands Chabad's appeal to non-observant Jews. "They realize the authenticity of their shliach, and of Lubavitch in general," he suggests. "Words that come from the heart penetrate the heart, and with our shlichim, their words come from the depths of the soul. People see that, and that's why they're so well received across the board." Every Jew, when pushed, wants to pass on a Jewish heritage to his or her children, Krinsky says. "They look at their own children and grandchildren, and they're frightened by what they see. Nobody wants to feel that the whole chain of Jewish lineage is going to end. Some people don't care, but most do, deep down. And people have means. If I have fifteen million dollars, why shouldn't I give the shliach twenty-five thousand?"

Many Jews like Chabad's spirituality, particularly those who remember the 1960s and their own spiritual searchings outside Judaism. Others respond to the learnedness of their Chabad rabbi, and appreciate the intellectual rigors of studying *Tanya* or Talmud with a teacher who does not berate them for their lack of Hebrew. Others still, especially parents of young children, are attracted by Chabad's educational offerings for children. Remembering their own less-than-riveting Hebrew School experiences, they are thrilled, if somewhat taken aback, when their children can't wait to go to *shul.*

Todd Lappin is a fundraising consultant for Chabad in Milwaukee, where he also sits on the board of the city's Jewish Federation. He had no contact with Chabad in 1991, when he was diagnosed with lymphoma. He wasn't terribly worried at first, he says. Rabbi Yosef Samuels, one of the city's Chabad shlichim, stopped by to see him. "It was very nice, but it had no meaning for me," Lappin recalls. Then just before he was scheduled to start chemotherapy, a tumor was found on his kidney. That changed his perspective. "Instead of being cocky and arrogant, I accepted all prayers. Now the rabbi became a constant visitor." The affected kidney was removed and Lappin looked forward to recovering from surgery before beginning chemo for the lymphoma. The day before his first chemo treatment a CAT scan showed that the lymphoma had mysteriously disappeared. "To this day the doctors don't know what happened," Lappin says.

That "miracle" didn't transform Lappin's life. He rebuffed Samuels's invitation to visit the Rebbe's grave and says he is no more observant than before the disease struck. But the circumstances of his recovery, and the personal friendship he developed with Samuels along the way, served to broaden his outlook on his own Jewish identity. In 1998, Yisroel Shmotkin, Chabad's regional head for Wisconsin, asked Lappin if he'd help out with Chabad fundraising. Lappin asked for a tour of Chabad outreach programs and was impressed with the Shmotkins' successful nursery school, which has since spun off as an independent nonprofit corporation, and with the Living Legacy Jewish holiday programs run by Yisroel's son Shmaya, which Chabad has taken to every Jewish school in the city. Lappin liked the fact that the Shmotkins reached out to all Jews, without demanding that they become more observant, and he agreed to come on board as a fundraising consultant.

Milwaukee real estate developer Armin Nankin is one of the Shmotkins' largest donors. He also gives money to the Jewish Theological Seminary, and to Milwaukee's non-Chabad Orthodox yeshiva, each of which he says serves a community need. Like many longtime donors, Nankin feels a deep longing for the spiritual life of a Chabadnik, but knows he won't give up the trappings of the modern secular world. "We aspire to be like them, we want to live that life. It's the way it should be. But we can't drag ourselves away from the TV. We're here on earth only a short time. Most of what we do is a waste. Lubavitchers don't waste their time. Each minute is devoted to something meaningful. Who wouldn't want to emulate that?"

If his own attraction to Chabad is deeply felt, he knows that those he solicits on Chabad's behalf give for other reasons. "I'd say most of the friends I solicit are ambivalent. Some want nothing to do with Chabad. They give money only because I ask them to."

Many older men who give substantial sums of money to Chabad share Nankin's feeling that Chabad represents something the world has lost. Chicago attorney Shaul Bellows, head of the First Health Care nursing homes group, is the first-generation American-born son of Eastern European immigrants and a nephew of author Saul Bellow. He gives to Chabad's Chicago office of F.R.E.E., the Friends of Refugees from Eastern Europe, because the Russian-speaking Jews learning English and celebrating Jewish holidays there today remind him of the Holocaust survivors his grandparents helped bring to America fifty years ago.

"It was heartwarming to be at Grandma Fannie's High Holiday table in the late nineteen-forties," Bellows recalls. "I'd see this sea of immigrant humanity, not speaking English, happy, appreciative, creating a new life. When I peeked inside [the F.R.E.E. center], I saw the same humanity, exactly the same picture. My father would often say there's nothing that separates us as American citizens from those refugees other than seventy years, and we have a responsibility to reach out and do what we can. Chabad makes it easy, meaningful, and substantive, and I feel uplifted to be able to help."

Bellows's initial attraction to Chabad's humanitarian work moved to a deeper level after he went to Crown Heights to meet Schneerson in 1987. "When you are in the presence of the Rebbe, you had the impression he only had eyes and ears for you," he relates, echoing the words of other first-time visitors. "He focused on you in such a way that it blocked out everything else in the room. The electricity, the spiritual and physical aura of the Rebbe was so intense, it was as if time and space were suspended." Bellows says he never expected to be so moved. "I'm not given to great outward emotional expression," he remarks. "I certainly didn't expect the deep feeling of awe and reverence. I was taken with his ability to immediately connect with a fellow human being, to be so insightful after a few minutes of conversation about the feelings and needs of that person. I felt it had to be a God-given gift."

It's the same pattern repeated with other key donors of a certain age. They came to Chabad for one reason or another and became irrevocably hooked—and financially committed—once they met the Rebbe. With

Schneerson gone, Chabad has lost not only its spiritual guide and its charismatic leader, but its major fundraising tool.

"I wonder sometimes how much the loss of the Rebbe has meant," muses Avraham Berkowitz, executive director of the Federation of Jewish Communities of the CIS. "As many and as great fundraisers as there will always be, the Rebbe is the heart and soul of Lubavitch." Berkowitz notes that George Rohr, who funds much of the work Berkowitz does in the former Soviet Union, speaks of the Rebbe's personal impact on him when he addresses Chabad groups. "I believe that the reason why he gives so freely every year is because he had direct contact with the Rebbe. I always wonder, will another Rohr family appear in the future? If I'm going to fundraise for my projects, I'm only going to get a certain amount of money. I will only always be a little splash of water. The Rebbe was the ocean."

What constitutes power in the post-Schneerson Lubavitch world? If geographic coverage is the criterion, then in terms of sheer miles and numbers of people affected, the most powerful Chabad shliach is Rabbi Berel Lazar of Moscow, head of Chabad activities in the former Soviet Union and newly declared chief rabbi of Russia. In the coming decade he will probably further cement his position as the voice of Jewish Russia, the world's third-largest Jewish community.

If political influence is the determining factor, then the father-son team of Avraham and Levi Shemtov would probably take the title, through their positions as head of Chabad's Washington, D.C., office and directors of the American Friends of Lubavitch, a prestigious supporters' group of political and business leaders.

If institutional control is key, then Yehuda Krinsky and, again, Avraham Shemtov lead the pack. They hold influential positions in Chabad's national organizations, they have great personal prestige devolving from years of working closely with Schneerson, and they are the men most often quoted as speaking in Chabad's name.

But if money is power, then Chabad's sixty-two-year-old West Coast director Rabbi Boruch Shlomo Cunin has few peers. In 2001 not only did he raise his own $10 million operating budget and another $5 million for capital expenses, he controlled more than a hundred Chabad centers and twenty-eight schools or social service institutions in California and

Nevada, choosing new shlichim for his territory and determining which projects were created where. That level of financial independence gives a shliach a certain amount of operational leverage. Cunin has his fingers in many pies, jetting back and forth to New York, Moscow, and Washington on high-level Chabad business, having his picture taken with just as many presidents and world leaders as Krinsky and the elder Shemtov.

Cunin is a whirlwind of a man, a brash, blustery guy who hugs his (male) friends, laughs loudly, talks at the top of his lungs, and isn't ashamed of tears. He loves to talk about his boyhood in the Bronx, where, he says, he learned to defend his Jewish identity with his fists. "I'm an American boy, and I can hit a baseball," he says. The son and grandson of Lubavitchers, Cunin was sent out on errands by the Rebbe as a young teen, and was thrilled when Schneerson posted him to California in 1965 with the order, as Cunin tells it, to "take the West Coast." L.A.'s big, largely unaffiliated, and wealthy Jewish community was laid out before him like a glittering jewel, if he had the moxie to grab hold of it. And he did. His slap-on-the-back style of conducting business was perfect for the place. "I would not have been as successful in Minnesota," he deadpans.

When it comes to confronting Hollywood celebrities, business tycoons, or Jewish organizational heads, Cunin is fearless. He marches into their offices, states his position in unequivocal terms, and waits out the opposition. He's weathered lawsuits, badgered politicians, and has been rumored to tear up checks in a donor's face if he thinks the amount is too small. He expands Chabad's West Coast operations at a startling rate. In June 2001, after returning from a visit to Crown Heights on the seventh anniversary of Schneerson's death, Cunin announced he was opening seven new Chabad centers that same week. Five had no office space. Two had no shlichim. But when Cunin wants to open, Cunin opens.

"He's unstoppable," remarks Los Angeles County board of supervisors member Zev Yaroslavsky, who has known Cunin since the late 1960s. "If you're in a war, you want him in your bunker."

Cunin's fundraising skills became clear early on when he decided to purchase a building in 1969 for his burgeoning Chabad operation at UCLA. He and his assistant, Rabbi Avraham Levitansky, went out to look for a suitable building to buy, undeterred by the fact that they had no money. They were driving a broken-down truck filled with empty soda bottles left over from a Hebrew school party. When they came to the

UCLA campus, they saw a man pounding nails on a building that had a large "For Sale" sign. "We didn't want him to see us, he'd see we have no money," Cunin relates. "So we memorized the number on the sign and quick went in front of Safeway to a pay phone to call. But we have no coins. Between us, we don't have ten cents. But God gives us wisdom. Levitansky remembered the bottles, five cents apiece."

The two Lubavitchers ran into the Safeway, cashed in their soda bottles, and called the phone number. They reached a recording that gave enough information for Cunin to calculate the building's purchase price at $2.5 million. "So we go to Marv Goldsmith's house, he's a real estate man, and I say, 'Goldsmith, this is going to cost two and a half million dollars.' Goldsmith says, 'Are you crazy?' He gets out his calculator and says it'll cost two hundred fifty thousand. So I made a mistake with a zero. He says, 'You madman, where are you going to find two hundred fifty thousand dollars? You don't have twenty-five cents to your name.' I say, 'We already found two and a quarter million dollars right in your house, what's the problem with the rest?'"

Now that the price had been whittled down, Cunin had to negotiate with the building's owners. He called Allan Lazaroff, president of L.A.'s newly created Friends of Lubavitch. "I said, 'Al, we have to go negotiate for this piece of property.' Al said, 'I'm not giving you money.' I said, 'Al, who's talking about money?'" In the elevator on their way to the meeting with the building's owner, Lazaroff asked Cunin how much money he had. Cunin admitted he had nothing. "Lazaroff was furious. Smoke was pouring out of his ears. We go into the meeting and I say to the owners, 'We're a Jewish organization, you should give us the building for nothing.'" Not surprisingly, the building's owners refused. They suggested monthly payments of $2,000 instead. "I said, 'Well, a thousand a month I could cough up.' Lazaroff went crazy, he knew this deal was never going to happen. I said, 'Tell you what, why don't you sell it to me for a hundred twenty-five thousand dollars cash, with a thirty-day escrow. It'll be off your hands.'" The owners went into a huddle, and then asked Cunin how much he could put down. He said he had $50,000—a complete fabrication.

"Lazaroff turns around, and the smoke is now pouring out of both ears, the eyes and the nose. I say, 'I need two weeks, I have to clear contingencies, I haven't talked to the Rebbe yet.' So they say, 'How much are you putting down for the deposit?' I say five thousand dollars. They start drawing up the papers, and ask for the check. I say, 'Check? Mr. Lazaroff, could you please write out a check for five thousand dollars?'" By this time, Cunin says, Lazaroff had softened. "He'd seen a young kid just pull off this business deal, and he didn't want to see it evaporate. He wrote out the check. I kissed him and said, 'Mazel tov.'

"Then we get to the elevator. We're alone. He turns around and says, 'How could you have no money coming up in the elevator, and then you suddenly have fifty thousand dollars? Where did that $50,000 come from?' I said, 'From you!' And he just lost it. He threw his arms around me and said, 'OK, you have the fifty thousand dollars. Now where are we finding the rest of the money?' And that's how we built our first Chabad House."

From the beginning Cunin had a checkered relationship with Los Angeles's Jewish establishment. Soon after he arrived, he tried to organize Jewish classes for religious-release hour, a program that took children out of the public schools for an hour a week to receive instruction in their faith. Chabad headquarters was very active in this program in New York City at the time. L.A.'s religious liaison committee told him he needed approval from the Jewish Federation Council, and when Cunin went to meet with council heads, they told him that the city's Jewish community opposed mixing religion with public school education.

Cunin had his own answer. "I told them, Let's get the record straight. You may be big guys here, but on me, you got nothing. My boss is God. Moses who tells me what to do is the Rebbe. I'm a train coming down the track, and you can either get on board, step out of the way, or be run over. Gentlemen, this meeting is closed. I am starting a release program. It's been approved by the Supreme Court, and I advise you to get out of the way."

Following this auspicious initial meeting with the Jewish establishment, Cunin learned he needed credentials to run the release-hour program. Clearly, the city's board of rabbis wouldn't back him up, so he resuscitated a defunct organization, the Los Angeles Orthodox Rabbinate, had letterhead printed up, wrote his own letter of accreditation, and persuaded almost two dozen local rabbis to sign it by telling them that the others had already signed. The audacious ploy worked. Now he needed space for his weekly classes. Again, no synagogue would give him a room, so he decided to buy a trailer and construct a classroom on wheels.

"I went down to El Marti and saw a trailer that would be great. The guy wanted twenty-five thousand dollars or some ridiculous amount. I didn't have a penny, I was making seventy-five dollars a week." Somehow Cunin convinced the dealer to drop the price to $5,000, put off the first payment for thirty days, and let him drive the trailer away with no money down. "I'd never driven such a thing before. I pull up to the house, blocking the whole street, people are honking. Just then my wife's water breaks. She's giving birth to Chani, our first. I have to get her to the hospital, this trailer is blocking the whole street, and then someone knocks on the door. It's an old guy, he needs a place to stay for the night. I said, 'My wife is giving birth, but you're welcome to stay.' My wife has the baby, she gets an infection, the old guy sleeps on the couch, and in the morning we find out, excuse me for saying, that he's irrigated the cushions. Never mind, my world is coming to an end anyway, with the trailer and the school and fighting the *meshugoyim* [crazy people], and I'm all alone and I have no money." Over a cup of coffee Cunin poured out his tale of woe to his elderly visitor, concluding with the $5,000 he owed on the trailer. "So the guy says, 'Do me a favor and come with me to the bank, I have to do some business.'" Cunin followed the old man to the bank, where he handed the young rabbi a cashier's check for $5,000.

Communal relations weren't helped when, later that year, Cunin convinced another dealer to give him a small open-roofed trailer to use as a mobile *sukkah*. "I saw a trailer going by on Fairfax Boulevard. with a sandwich board advertising something, and I said, 'What a great idea!' So I followed the trailer to a parking lot where I see a half-dozen of these dilapidated vehicles. I go inside and there's a little *Yiddel* [Jewish man] behind the counter. I say, 'Are these trailers for rent?' He said, 'For a price anything's for rent.' But he wouldn't pay for the liability insurance, so I said, 'OK, sell me the trailer.' He said, 'It's not for sale.' I said, 'That's good because I have no money, so give it to me.' And he gave me the trailer." After Sukkot, Cunin hooked up the trailer to the back of his Chevy Nova, along with two large bullhorns, and drove the contraption to Federation headquarters. He started circling the building, shouting, "Give your child a free Jewish education! Call Chabad!" through the bullhorns. "It was beautiful," he recalls.

Cunin rarely hesitated to sweep past people who stood in the way of his plans to expand Chabad's West Coast operations. He clashed repeatedly with Jewish organizations and the ACLU over public menorah lightings in several municipalities, and in 1989 he became embroiled in a messy law-suit over ownership of the Bayit, a Jewish student cooperative at UCLA that Cunin took over for Chabad activities, using what his opponents alleged were duplicitous tactics. A settlement was reached in 1995 and the Bayit returned to student hands, but rancor remained. "I can't go into the terms of the agreement, but Chabad came out nicely," says Los Angeles journalist and researcher Avi Davis, president of the Bayit's current board.

Cunin's "act first, finance later" style of conducting business helped land him $18 million in debt by the mid-1980s. A $21 million estate fortuitously left to him by an elderly local woman saved the day. The woman hardly knew Cunin, but he had stopped by one day when she was going through a painful divorce, and he stayed to listen to her. That windfall, combined with two other $10 million donations, enabled Cunin to spread a little wealth around to other Chabad Houses in similar financial trouble. He's never come close to collapse since, but he keeps dozens of index cards, each documenting what he owed to a particular bank or individual in the 1980s, still tacked up on the inside of his office door. He now controls more than $35 million worth of assets, but whenever he's feeling cocky, he just takes a look at the door. "I flew too high," he confesses.

In thirty-five years Cunin has developed many friends in City Hall, including Yaroslavsky, whom he supported in his initial campaign for City Council in 1975 and followed all the way to county government nineteen years later. But in a town where non-Jews in government are loath to say no to a funding request from a Jewish constituent, Yaroslavsky insists that Cunin "has never played the Jewish card." He received first city, and now county, funding for his drug rehab clinic because, Yaroslavsky says, in a field crowded with charlatans and dollar-skimmers, Cunin and Chabad standout for their altruism and honesty. "This is work most people don't want to touch, and Cunin has always delivered."

Cunin has also over the years amassed quite a collection of Hollywood supporters, including film producer Jerry Weintraub. Weintraub is a major philanthropist whose name is linked to more than thirty charities, Jewish and not, including UCLA's Jane and Jerry Weintraub Center for Reconstructive Bio-Technology, built in 1997. His personal friendship with the elder George Bush, with whom he summers in Kennebunkport, has earned him the moniker "Hollywood liaison to the White House."

Weintraub first met Cunin in 1980. "I came to the office one day and there was a rabbi sitting in my waiting room. It's not uncommon. I'm involved with a lot of philanthropy, and rabbis have always come to me for money." Weintraub walked right past Cunin, entered his inner office, and asked his secretary what the bearded guy wanted. "She said he wants to see you. I said, I have no time to see him, just give him a check for ten thousand dollars. That's what I used to give to rabbis. I said, Give it to him and get him out of here." But Cunin turned down the check. He wanted to see Weintraub, nothing less. "I let him in. A rabbi who turns down ten thousand dollars, I had to let him in." Cunin told Weintraub that the Rebbe had sent him personally to get the producer involved in Chabad. But Weintraub said he had too much on his plate, and for the next few years he continued to send money to Cunin while declining to become further involved.

Some years later Weintraub was on his way to Moscow with philanthropist Armand Hammer to meet with former Soviet prime minister Mikhail Gorbachev. "We were trying to do something on Jewish immigration, and other things for the president which I won't discuss," Weintraub recounts. The night before his flight he was restless. He got up at 3 A.M. and turned on the television, "an obscure satellite channel that I never watched." On the screen was the Lubavitcher Rebbe, speaking live from 770. "The Rebbe makes this whole speech, and suddenly he says, 'There's a man listening to me tonight who's on his way to Russia.' There's no way he could have known I was watching this. I woke up my wife and said, 'You have to watch this!' The Rebbe said, 'When this man goes to Russia, he thinks he's working on helping the Jewish people get out of Russia, but that's not the purpose of his trip. That will take care of itself. He has much more important things to do there, and that's what he should concentrate on. He'll go, have success, and come back and have more success here.' I was totally blown away. So was my wife."

The weirdness continued. When he returned from Russia, Weintraub became ill and was rushed to the hospital for an emergency operation on a Sunday afternoon. "Just as they're pushing me into the operating room, Shlomo Cunin is standing there. He puts a dollar bill in my hand and says, 'This is from the Rebbe.' There's no way Cunin could have known I was at that hospital. I said to myself, If I get out of this operation, they've got me. Two coincidences were too much."

Weintraub indeed recovered and became a major feather in Cunin's cap, helping him restructure his crippling debt and cohosting his annual telethon. A fellow Bronx native, Weintraub says he likes Cunin's style. "Most of the Jews out here, the Beverly Hills crowd, they don't like Hasidic Jews. They're afraid of them, or embarrassed by them, for whatever reason. I think they're great. There are a lot of things they believe that I don't, a lot of things they do that I don't. I don't keep a kosher home, I don't go to *shul* on Friday or Saturday, I don't say prayers every morning. But they never force me to do anything and I never force them to do anything, so we get along great."

As with so many other longtime donors, it was a personal meeting with Schneerson that cemented the connection. "When I looked into the Rebbe's eyes and he looked into my eyes, and he took my hand and I held up the Torah with him and prayed with him at 770, I was in the presence of something that I could never explain." When his parents were ill, he took his father to see the Rebbe. "When he went in to meet the Rebbe, he could hardly walk. The Rebbe took his hand and said, 'You're going to be fine. You're not sick and your wife is not sick.' My father bounced out of there. My mother got better. The Rebbe gave his blessing and she was fine." Weintraub acknowledges that these sound like crazy stories. But, he insists, they happened. "I don't like to talk about the supernatural. I don't know if the Rebbe was the Moshiach or not. I only know that he had powers beyond the powers of anybody I ever met."

Even today Weintraub says that he turns to the Rebbe when he needs help. "I talk to him. I do it out loud. I don't go to psychiatrists, I handle my own problems, except when I need to talk to him. When I have a real bad problem, I close the door and I talk to him about it. And he gives me answers."

On August 26, 2001, Weintraub is standing on a sound stage off Sunset Boulevard, trying to whip up enthusiasm from a studio audience filled with two hundred Lubavitchers. "OK, people, we need you to clap," he admonishes. The stage lights dim to blue, Camera One wheels in, and a spotlight is trained on a young boy wearing sidecurls and knee pants— Anatevka, circa 1905. The boy raises a fiddle to his chin and begins playing a klezmer tune. A second young man, also in stylized Hasidic garb, emerges from the wings and begins a slow-motion Eastern European dance. The music gets louder, the pace quickens, the dancer's pirouettes follow closer upon each other, and then the stage explodes in a shower of

lights and electric guitars as a dozen Lubavitch yeshiva students leap forward, twisting, turning, doing handstands and cartwheels in a frenzied
circle. Cymbals clash and a booming voice rings out: "To Life! *L'chaim!*"

This is the twenty-first annual Chabad telethon, Cunin's fundraising
masterpiece, a bizarre cultural phenomenon that could only happen in
America—a televised fundraiser for a Hasidic group, a group whose
members don't even watch TV, that has Hollywood celebrities of all faiths
and none publicly extolling the virtues of "doing mitzvahs" and "bringing
Moshiach." Chabad's first telethon in 1980 was born of tragedy: a fire,
still unsolved, that destroyed the organization's West Coast headquarters
and killed three young people asleep inside the building. Carroll O'Connor and Jan Murray cohosted that first event, which raised $1 million
toward rebuilding. O'Connor pledged $5,000 on his own. Twenty years
later Cunin's annual telethon was raising close to $6 million a year, half
his operating budget, and had become the single most graphic demon-
stration of this Hasidic group's ability to rope in big-name celebrities.
Elliot Gould and James Caan have been fixtures from the beginning,
joined over the years by a long list of glitterati who show up each year to
sing, dance, and appeal for funds to help Chabad's drug rehab clinic and
other social service programs. Sid Caesar, Bob Hope, Michael Douglas,
Whoopi Goldberg, Shelley Winters, Tony Danza, Regis Philbin, Steve
Allen, Edward James Olmos, Shirley Jones, Anthony Hopkins, and Michael
York are part of the odd collection of stars who have lent their efforts to
the cause.

The show has become so hip that it has engendered a rash of telethon-
watching parties in certain L.A. circles, where folks gather in living rooms
to see which stars will show up next to kick up their heels with Cunin.
One year the cast of *Friends* filmed a special segment for the telethon,
lauding Chabad's work and asking viewers to send money. It was a return
favor for Cunin's permission to rebroadcast an earlier *Friends* episode that
showed several *Friends* regulars watching actual telethon footage. Rabbi
Cunin's sons wrote the script for the special segment, which was rewritten by the show's creative team. "We're funny, but they're funnier,"
admits twenty-seven-year-old Chaim Cunin.

The Chabad telethon lasts for seven hours and features a montage of
celebrity tributes interspersed with musical entertainment. It's broadcast
nationwide, and since 2000 has been streamed live on the Internet, where
viewers can chat live with some of the celebrities. Volunteers in the stu-

dio and at toll-free numbers around the country take phone-in pledges, which are broadcast in a running stream across the bottom of the television screen: *Cantor and Mrs. Baruch Cohen, $1,800 . . . Mr. and Mrs. Gary Finder, $1,800 . . . Dr. Barbar Kreitzer, $5,000 . . . Mr. and Mrs. John Kuzmersky, $3,000.* Every hour on the hour, the amount raised so far is flashed on a big board and Cunin joins the celebrities onstage for a celebratory *hora.* If you're not looking closely, you might miss the fact that somehow in the midst of all the hubbub, Hasidic norms of modesty are respected. Both male and female celebrities speak, but only men are permitted to sing and dance. When a group of college students, recently returned from a Chabad-led trip to Israel, make a special presentation, the young men are invited to join the dancing while the women are quietly led offstage.

Backstage in the VIP waiting room, Elliot Gould is sipping coffee, waiting for his scheduled slot. Gould has appeared on every telethon since the first. "We can't do enough," he says. "They need all the support we can generate. I've visited the drug center, and it's not about drugs, it's about a value system. Rabbi Cunin invests all of his energy in this work, and I follow him."

Meanwhile on stage, Michael York is looking natty in a tan suit and black yarmulke as he puts his arm around the shoulders of a homeless man Chabad has been helping. "The streets of this, the richest city in the world, are filled with starving and homeless men, women, and children," he pleads in his on-air pitch. "It doesn't matter what color you are or what religion, Chabad will be there to provide for your needs. Go to your phones now and call." Afterward, York says that he has no particular ties to Chabad, but he's always willing to fundraise for drug rehab and homeless programs. "If I'm able to help out, why not? I'm just glad I was free and able to be here," he says. Later, while chatting with viewers on the Internet, York fields a question from a woman who wants to know how much money he's donating to Chabad. "I'm giving time," York types back, "—and love."

Of all the celebrities who lend their name to the Chabad telethon, none is more personally committed to the cause than Jon Voight. The Academy Award–winning star of *Midnight Cowboy* has been a guest on Cunin's telethons since the late 1980s, along with hosting several other Chabad fundraising efforts, notably the Israel-based Children of Chernobyl rescue program. He's become a friend of the Cunin family, studies Torah, and reads Hasidus, having, by his own admission, a bookcase filled with the writings of Elie Wiesel and the Lubavitcher Rebbe. He stops by Chabad centers whenever he's filming on location. "I call up the local Chabad rabbi and say, 'Let's have a *farbrengen!*' The nice thing about having a little celebrity is you can give people some support in their work."

Voight first met Rabbi Cunin in the mid-eighties as a return favor for a friend who wanted him to appear on the telethon. Voight stopped by Cunin's drug rehab clinic and was impressed to see the rabbi sitting at a table in the cafeteria, his coat off and his shirtsleeves rolled up, arm-wrestling the addicts. "These were weight lifters, real characters. They were all lined up, and one after another, he's putting them down. Some-one told him I was there, so he put on his coat, grabbed me, and gave me a hug. I thought, This is my kind of guy."

Voight's heart was completely won over when he visited Cunin in his office. "The modesty of it struck me. You could tell that whatever money they raise goes to helping other people. I was there for half a minute when a couple came in with a child. They said they were in need. The rabbi said, 'What do you need?' They said, 'We don't have money for fur-niture. We need a couch.' He looks over, sees a couch in the lobby and says, 'Is this a nice couch?' I said I had a truck downstairs, so the two of us are carrying this couch, we're in the elevator with this thing and we get it in the truck. When Rabbi Cunin tells the story, he says how remarkable it was that I helped. But of course the real story was his response, which was immediate. That doesn't mean anybody can come in here and take the furniture, but it was something remarkable to observe."

Like many other stars who stump for Chabad, Voight is not Jewish. He had a strict Catholic upbringing, but his observance level declined when he came to Hollywood. "I made mistakes in my early life," he admits. When he met Cunin, he was already engaged in what he calls "a spritual seeking" among many religions. He reads voraciously and likes what he's found in Judaism, although he has no intention of converting. Even more than Judaism's intellectual heritage, Voight says he appreciates the value Judaism places on doing good deeds. "It's not how much you know, although learning is certainly a great aspect of it, but what you do," he says. "I think that is certainly portrayed by Chabad. And that's why I help them. Rabbi Cunin has exhibited tremendous energy for helping people, in every gesture, and all in good cheer."

It's the morning after the telethon, and Cunin is in his office before 8 A.M. He should be exhausted. As he does every year before the telethon, he flew to New York Thursday night, spent Friday until sundown at the Rebbe's grave, flew back to Los Angeles Saturday night, and then danced for seven hours on television on Sunday. But he's still ready to rock 'n' roll, and he has a lot of follow-up calls to make, to remind donors to send in pledges they made in the heat of the moment the previous evening.

"This is our major presence for the year," he notes. "All our major gifts tie back to the telethon. You know that twenty-one-million-dollar gift? She was a telethon watcher." The nonsectarian nature of Chabad's rehab clinic, nursery school, and other social programs is "very important for public relations," he adds. "People see we are in this community, not preaching down to them from the [Beverly] Hills. The telethon knocks down preconceived ideas about Hasidim, so when we come to someone they say, Oh, yes, you're the people with the drug center, you're the people with the nursery school. They don't say, Oh, you're the guys in the black hats with the collection box."

By 9 A.M., Cunin's son Chaim wanders in, bleary-eyed, carrying a bag of fresh bagels. He's followed by another young rabbi, the Chabad shliach in Reno, Nevada, a city also under Cunin's purview. The visitor shows Cunin his donor sheet. "I'm trying to up this guy's twenty-five thousand dollars to forty thousand," he remarks. "Then I could clean off my credit cards." Cunin rebukes him gently: "Why not use it to pay off your second mortgage?" The young shliach reminds Cunin that the increased donation would pay off Reno's new mikvah, which he was able to build for half price thanks to "connections." Cunin cautions. "Be careful not to push the guy too much. You don't want to lose the twenty-five thousand dollars."

The phone rings, and Cunin takes the call. It's a woman whose son, a young actor, has a drug problem. They were at the telethon last night, and are now staying in a local hotel while she tries to convince her son to enter Chabad's rehab program. "We need to get him into treatment as soon as possible," Cunin tells her. "I hate to be so frank, but we have to take a tough stance." Cunin says he'll send over "a couple guys" from the rehab center to help move the mother into an apartment. "Don't worry, we'll take care of the rent until you're on your feet," he tells her. "You will not be on the street, I'll see to that. Put the boy on the phone." Cunin listens to the young man's excuses for a while, then begins rolling his eyes and humming "Home on the Range."

"Listen, my friend, I wrote all the songs in the book," he says sternly.

"You're a successful actor, but if you're not willing to make an appointment at the center and get off the range, I can't do more for you. Here, talk to Meir." Cunin hands the phone to Meir Cohen, a gray-bearded Israeli rabbi who flies in once a month to do counseling at the clinic. Cohen listens to the young man for a minute, then puts his hand over the receiver and whispers to Cunin, "He says he doesn't want to go in. He sees his psychiatrist every day, and that's enough."

"*Bubbe meises* [old wives' tales], the psychiatrist," Cunin grumbles. "His mother says he won't eat. Get him into the program or he'll be deader than a doornail."

The actor and his mother finally hang up, and the phone rings again. This time it's an elderly man from the Fairfax district, L.A.'s old Jewish neighborhood. The man is on speaker phone. He talks with a heavy Yiddish accent. "I can't give you money, rabbi, because my wife and I live on Social Security, but I have six trees I raised that I'd like to give you," he says. "They're each worth thirty dollars, so that's a hundred eighty dollars." Cunin passes his hands over his eyes, which are suddenly wet. For one moment all bluster is gone.

"Those trees are worth more to me than a hundred eighty thousand dollars," he tells the caller in a soft voice. "I'll plant them by the new girls' school we're building so the *kinderlach* [children] can see how trees grow. And I want you at the planting ceremony."

Hanging up, Cunin sighs and looks at the picture of Schneerson hanging on the wall behind his desk. "The Rebbe was like a gigantic generator," he begins. "All of us, the shlichim, strove to be good receptacles at the end of the power grid. The Rebbe set up all these people in all these places, like in a military machine. We are the Rebbe's generals, doing what we have to do, caring for the spiritual needs of the people under us as well as catering to their physical needs.

"Then the Rebbe left us. He left us with a phenomenal yearning that doesn't let us stop for a second, a yearning and a love that drives us. Another building, another human being, another good deed. The Rebbe said, Do what you can to bring Moshiach, so you do more and more. A girls' school in the morning. A drug facility. Poor people. Do what you can to bring Moshiach. Not think what you can. Not verbiage of what you can. *Do* what you can."

And he picks up the phone again.

CHAPTER 10

FRIENDS IN HIGH PLACES:
Washington, D.C.

Rabbi Levi Shemtov is striding full speed down the fourth-floor hallway of the Hart Senate Office Building in Washington, D.C., a big smile plastered on his face. "Hello, Senator," he says, turning quickly to catch a backhanded wave from a midwestern legislator.

It's early May 2001, and Shemtov is excited because he's just spent a half-hour with Senator Joseph Lieberman, who agreed to be honored at the annual dinner of American Friends of Lubavitch scheduled for the coming fall. It's one of his biggest events of the year, a D.C. fundraiser that draws several hundred political and business figures, and Shemtov is pleased that the former vice-presidential candidate is his headliner. "He wanted to do it last year but couldn't because he was raising money for his own campaign, so he figured he would make it up this year," Shemtov confides.

Two young congressional aides walk past. "Hey, Rabbi," one shouts. Shemtov smiles even more broadly and grabs a fast shake as he heads toward the elevator. The doors open, and a three-man cleaning crew steps out. They see Shemtov and their faces brighten. "Hi, Rabbi," says a young African-American man pushing a cart filled with Lysol, mops, and scouring powder. Shemtov grabs his arm for a two-handed pump.

It's not enough that Chabad's man in D.C. knows the name and phone number of just about every congressman, senator, and foreign ambassador in the nation's capital—he also knows their legislative assistants, their secretaries, and the people who clean their offices. "You have to do a lot of schmoozing," he says. "That's the nature of the industry in this city."

Chabad has sent emissaries to the far reaches of the Jewish world—to Shanghai, São Paulo, and Khabarovsk. But one of its most significant accomplishments has been its ability to penetrate the halls of power right here in the United States, taking its message of *ahavat Yisrael* all the way to the nation's capital. Levi Shemtov was just twenty-five in 1993 when he took over Chabad's capital beat from his father, Rabbi Avraham Shemtov, who had been shuttling down to D.C. from his Philadelphia office on a regular basis since the 1970s. The younger Shemtov learned the ropes fast.

D.C. is a shlichus unlike any other. Levi's official title is Washington director of American Friends of Lubavitch, a prestigious supporters' organization created by his father in 1975 and chaired by Revlon magnate Ronald Perelman. But his placement in Washington puts him in position to broker key deals for Chabad all over the world.

Like other Chabad emissaries, Shemtov is a teacher, bringing Torah and *Yiddishkeit* to the Jews in his region. It just happens that his clientele includes White House staffers, members of Congress, and foreign diplomats. He puts up a public menorah like any other shliach, but his is across the lawn from the White House. His Purim party is on Capitol Hill, and his lunch 'n' learn sessions are in the Capitol basement.

Because this is Washington, Shemtov's mandate extends way beyond the usual limits of Chabad outreach. He's a teacher and a chaplain, but he also functions as a lobbyist-without-portfolio, found on any given day rushing from office to office, button-holing senators on issues of concern to Chabad headquarters, arranging meetings between legislators and the Chabad shlichim from their districts, advising non-Jewish staffers on Jewish protocol. He also serves as an ad hoc diplomat. He's on a first-name basis with dozens of ambassadors and State Department officials, stepping in to help Chabad shlichim abroad regain control of a Jewish building, get permission for a new Jewish school, or just renew their visas in a hurry. He lunches with prime ministers, he flies to Buenos Aires, Moscow, and other world capitals, and he navigates political jungles with firm good humor. He has a knack for bringing people together, always making sure to seat ambassadors next to the Chabad shlichim working in their countries, so they can develop relationships. Shabbat meals at the Shemtov home draw a powerful and eclectic crowd, from international Jewish business moguls to embassy officials to yeshiva students on holiday. At the September 1999 opening of Chabad's new D.C. headquarters, Joe Lieberman said to him, "As I watch you negotiate the various politicians, my gratitude is that you didn't move to Connecticut and decide to go into politics."

Other lobbyists and heads of Jewish organizations gaze enviously at Shemtov's access to the people that matter in Washington. How does this rabbi get into the White House so often? Why do hundreds of power players—senators, representatives, foreign ambassadors, and the intellectual elite—show up for Chabad dinners, luncheons, and even breakfasts, where they listen for hours to speeches lauding the legacy of the Lubavitcher Rebbe?

"He's put Chabad on the map in D.C.," says Thomas Kahn, staff director of the House Budget Committee and a regular at Shemtov's holiday parties on the Hill. "This is a city with long knives and long memories. He has amazing rapport with a wide range of political leaders, and I can't think of a single person who has anything but nice things to say about him."

Kahn credits Shemtov with influencing his own increased Jewish observance. More important, Kahn says that his contact with Chabad has made him sensitive to the needs of the Orthodox. Kahn was on the executive committee of D.C.'s Jewish Community Center when it was debating whether to go to the trouble of getting kosher certification for its new restaurant. "Levi convinced me how important it was to have a kosher restaurant that could be used by the entire Jewish community. If I didn't know him, it might not have happened."

Rabbi David Saperstein heads the Reform movement's Religious Action Center in Washington, where he often finds himself lobbying at cross-purposes with Chabad. He says that Shemtov's rabbinical title helps him. "There is in Congress still enormously high regard for religion and representatives of religious groups," he says. "Doors are open to them. Conversations take place that otherwise would not." Politicians like to be associated with religious figures, Saperstein says. "It helps that Levi's *kippa* and beard fit their image of what a religious person should look like," he notes.

Shemtov is well known in Congress because he has made a concerted effort to spend time there. "He has an ongoing presence on the Hill like no other Jewish organization has, and the lobbyist who is there all the time develops relationships others do not," Saperstein says. "He's open, warm, engaging. He's willing to appear with representatives from the different Jewish streams so he doesn't alienate members of Congress who identify with them. He's the kind of Orthodox presence they like." And, Saperstein adds, "people appreciate" the religious service he provides, a rare touch of the spiritual in days filled with the mundane and the contentious.

White House spokesman Ari Fleischer is a regular at Chabad events in D.C. He merited a wink in the gossip columns in the fall of 2001 when he skipped a meeting on rescuing the airline industry to attend Shemtov's Rosh Hashanah services. Fleischer met Shemtov in 1993, when he was working for New Mexico Senator Pete Domenici and Shemtov was making the rounds of legislative offices, looking for Jewish staffers. "He saw my name and took a chance that I might be Jewish," says Fleischer, who grew up in a Reform household in Westchester, New York.

Fleischer helped Shemtov organize High Holiday services on the Hill that year in a rented hotel room. The two developed a close friendship, and Fleischer became president of the Capitol Jewish Forum, a support group for Jewish legislators and congressional staffers Shemtov created in 1998. "When I moved to Washington, away from my family, I practiced my religion on an occasional basis," Fleischer says. "The rabbi's presence helped me to practice it on a much more regular basis, and that's uplifting. As a man, as a person, he has a wonderful touch, a way of reaching out to people who are not like him. He does so gently, he does so effectively. He's come to Washington to help bring the Jewish religion closer to Jews, but he doesn't do it from the point of view of a zealot."

On this particular day in May, Shemtov is wearing all his hats. After 6 A.M. prayers, he heads downstairs from the apartment he shares with his wife and four children on the top floor of American Friends of Lubavitch headquarters on Embassy Row. First on the agenda is a phone call from the Lithuanian ambassador, who is canceling a lunch date. Would the rabbi meet him the next morning for breakfast instead? "Mr. Ambassador, for you I'll change what I have scheduled," Shemtov promises. Hanging up, he explains that Chabad owns a historic synagogue building in downtown Vilnius but wants to give it to the government in exchange for a municipal building the Chabad shliach is now renting for his day school. Shemtov is flying to Vilnius in a week to negotiate with the president of Lithuania, and the ambassador has agreed to help.

"I'm not coming empty-handed," he adds. To sweeten the deal, Shemtov has secured private funding to renovate a rural cemetery in Lithuania, along with an endorsement from the U.S. Commission for the Preservation of America's Heritage Abroad, a group that supports Jewish restoration projects in Eastern Europe.

Shemtov has a few more calls to make before leaving his office. President Bush is going to China soon and Shemtov wants him to visit the synagogue in Shanghai, which the Chinese government nationalized and has begun allowing Chabad to use occasionally for holiday services. He also has to talk to the Chabad shlichim in Brazil and Argentina about a cooperative project he's trying to put together with the Inter-American Development Bank. The bank is planning an antipoverty program for Latin America, and Shemtov thinks Chabad humanitarian projects in South America should be included. He wants the shlichim in the region to come up with a pilot project to present to the bank's organizing committee. "I had dinner with the bank's president, and he said if I can raise part of the money for the project, they'll kick in the rest. Maybe they'll even give scholarships so more kids can stay in school, their parents can go to work, and the family can rise above the poverty line."

Here Shemtov is building on an existing relationship. The IDB cohosted his last Chanukah party for the international community. The previous year Chabad held its December bash at the International Monetary Fund. "When people get an invitation to an American Friends of Lubavitch Chanukah party at the IMF building, it's pretty impressive," he notes.

What's interesting in all these foreign transactions is that *Levi* is flying to Lithuania to negotiate the property switch, and *Levi* is going to the Ukraine to help dedicate a new yeshiva, and *Levi* is heading to Bratislava to convince the Slovakian Education Ministry to give school credit to Jewish children studying in a religious school across the border in Austria. All of these places have their own Chabad shlichim. Why do they need a fixer to fly in from D.C.? Again, it's the power of personal relationships. Shemtov has the ears of people who matter in the capital of the world's last remaining superpower, and it's sometimes easier to work through a country's top ambassador abroad than it is to attempt a frontal assault on the presidential palace. He's parlayed his D.C. connections into negotiations with a dozen heads of state. "Trying to navigate each country's political shtick isn't easy," he says. "If I write a book someday, I'll call it *Dancing in a Straitjacket*."

Levi Shemtov holds no public office. He's not an ambassador, or even an official lobbyist. So why do people listen to him? "It's a fascinating phenomenon," says Kahn. "He'll meet with the ambassador to Uzbekistan in the morning about the return of a synagogue building, and a senator in the afternoon about the kosher food in the Senate dining room." The rabbi's ability to get things done is due largely to the power of his personality, Kahn says, but is also testimony to Chabad's worldwide presence. The Uzbek ambassador meets with him not just because of his Washington connections, but because Chabad is the dominant Jewish presence in Tashkent.

The same equation obtains at home. Elected officials know that Shemtov represents a group that is active in their home districts, a group that attracts political and financial heavy hitters. Some politicians, like former Republican Speaker of the House Newt Gingrich, seem to have real admiration for Schneerson and Chabad's work. Others may be motivated more by the easy political mileage gained from attending a few Chabad dinner events. "We're not just a 'Hasidic group from Brooklyn,' we're a Hasidic group active in forty-four states," Shemtov says. "We're not a political organization, but we have many supporters with political clout."

Chabad is widely perceived in Washington as representing the interests of Jews in general, rather than a narrow Lubavitch agenda. In contrast to Israel, where the group has been involved in actual electoral politicking, Chabad maintains a low political profile in the United States, outside of New York City issues that affect Crown Heights. Chabad "lobbying" in D.C. is limited to issues such as funding for parochial schools and advocacy of a "moment of silence" in public schools. On both issues the group's positions are based on the Lubavitcher Rebbe's support for an educational system that inculcates values as well as imparts knowledge.

Gingrich spoke to that point in 1995 at an all-day event in Washington at which the Rebbe was posthumously awarded the Congressional Gold Medal. Not only did Rabbi Schneerson live the ideals he preached, Gingrich said to the gathering, but those he touched—like Levi Shemtov—do the same. Their idealism makes them stand out from the usual crowd of paid petitioners, Gingrich said. "If you're in our business and you're approached every day by dozens of high-paid lobbyists with their explanations of temporary measures that will enrich this or that group, and then someone walks up to you with integrity and authenticity and sincerity and doesn't ask you to help them increase their profit margin but instead says, for the good of the world, that this is something noble and idealistic that should be recognized, then whether you're a conservative Republican or liberal Democrat, you'll find it a positive thing."

By noon Shemtov is helping to lay out trays of smoked salmon, tuna fish, carrot sticks, and sliced fruit in a basement room of the Capitol, preparing for his weekly lunch 'n' learn session with congressional staffers. Today's topic is politics from a Torah point of view. He will be referring mainly to Pirke Avot, a book of ethical teachings traditionally studied between Passover and the fall holidays. "The Mishnah gives contradictory advice," he tells the seventeen staffers who show up for the class. "One *mishnah* tells us to '*abhor* taking high office and do not seek intimacy with the ruling power.' Another says simply to '*be wary* of people in high office.' How should we reconcile the two?"

The solution, he suggests, is to evaluate each government on its merits. In the Soviet Union, where the ruling regime enacted laws that prevented Jews from living Jewishly, it was correct to avoid entering the political fray. "When you have a government like the American government that serves people so they can live freely, you *should* be involved in it," he says. "Even so, you should be careful. People in power might not have the ethics of Pirke Avot."

Shemtov's goal, clearly, is to help these young bureaucrats infuse their work practices with Jewish values. The group takes the challenge seriously—this is a rare chance for many of them to explore their own moral codes. One young man has a question: "Israel had an intimate relationship with the South African government under apartheid. Doesn't that go against your rule?" Yes, Shemtov admits. "The government of Israel has dealt with very unsavory regimes, because it's had to. And the government of Israel, like any government, can't always do the preferred thing."

But Shemtov's focus, he reminds the group, is on individual behavior, not government actions. He explains the Hasidic concept of "loving one's fellow" and suggests how it could be applied in their daily life. "Imagine what the Hill would be like if more people had this attitude," he points out. Everyone chuckles. "It's difficult to go up to two people who aren't getting along and try to make peace between them. But that's what God wants."

Now Shemtov turns the discussion to a comparison between Hillel and Shammai, the two great rabbinical opponents of the mishnaic period. Shammai, who interpreted Torah law narrowly, only saw what was in front of him, Shemtov explains; Hillel, whose legal rulings were more magnanimous, accentuated the positive, the potential for good. That, too, could be a tool for political behavior. "If we realize that a divine eye is watching what we say and do, maybe we will be more careful in our actions, more truthful," he advises.

"Or at least get our story straight earlier," one young man quips.

After class, Shemtov has a meeting with Horace Cooper, director of coalitions for House Majority Leader Richard Armey. "There are important votes scheduled for Yom Kippur and Rosh Hashanah, and a couple of Congress members asked me to get the dates changed," Shemtov says. Why him? He's a nonpartisan outsider, he explains, and can appeal to the majority leader on the basis of religious sensitivity.

The dates were changed. And a Jewish calendar—a gift from Chabad—now hangs in Armey's office.

After his meeting with Cooper, Shemtov has a closed-door consultation with a congressional chief of staff who is considering conversion to Judaism. Chabad usually shies away from converting people, but Shemtov is where Capitol Hill and the White House turn when they have Jewish questions. By four-thirty he's back in his Embassy Row office; outside, a taxi is waiting to drive him to a meeting of the mayor's advisory council. D.C.'s mayor, Anthony Williams, is a friend of Chabad's, honored one year by American Friends of Lubavitch, and Shemtov knows he'll be defending the man this afternoon to a group of Jewish leaders who think he's not moving fast enough to fund a new Jewish school. "They blast him for permitting Farrakhan rallies, which doesn't help," Shemtov says, noting that the mayor himself does not attend those rallies.

At seven-thirty, he's scheduled to escort Israeli Chief Rabbi Meir Lau to a fundraising dinner for an Israeli medical association. "I was supposed to take a five P.M. flight to Europe, but I'll have to take the last flight out later tonight instead," he says, jumping into the cab.

Wherever Jews have lived as a minority, they have sought the protection of the ruling king, czar, or sultan. Chabad in America is no different. The group made its first appeal to Washington in 1927, asking then President

Hoover to pressure the Soviet government to release Yosef Yitzchak Schneersohn, the sixth Rebbe, who was in prison facing execution in Moscow. The White House contacted Soviet leaders, and the death sentence was commuted to exile.

When Menachem Mendel Schneerson took over Chabad's helm in 1951, he turned his attention to creating an ongoing Lubavitch presence in the nation's capital. Representatives were sent to Washington for specific meetings or ceremonies through the 1950s, and in 1960, Schneerson sent Avraham Shemtov, his Philadelphia shliach, to take part in a White House conference on education.

Promoting government support for a values-centered public education system was very high on Schneerson's personal agenda. America's leaders had the responsibility, Schneerson said and wrote on numerous occasions, to stem the rising tide of juvenile delinquency and the collapse of families and neighborhoods by inculcating values of fellowship, democracy, and individual morality in the nation's children. If parents weren't doing it at home, then it was up to the schools.

Avraham Shemtov went back to D.C. in 1970 for the next White House education conference, and by the late 1970s he was pushing the Rebbe's first Washington campaign—the creation of a department of education, separate from the existing Department of Health, Education, and Welfare. Shemtov was later appointed to an intergovernmental advisory committee on education—the only religious figure on the committee—and spent hectic months lobbying for congressional support for a Cabinet-level department of education. President Carter supported the idea, and Schneerson wrote to him to express his hopes that other nations would follow the U.S. lead.

In 1978, Carter declared the first "Education Day USA" in Schneerson's honor. It has since become an annual event, signed into effect every year by the president. The 1978 proclamation scrolls are on prominent display at the Rebbe's library at Chabad headquarters in Brooklyn. When the new Department of Education was created in 1980, Avraham Shemtov was a guest of honor at the inauguration ceremony. In 1997, at a tribute commemorating the third anniversary of the Lubavitcher Rebbe's death, U.S. Secretary of Education Richard Riley thanked Schneerson for his early and concerted support for the department's creation. "His voice, so respected and beloved, helped to make it happen," Riley said, adding, "So I owe my job to him."

The same impetus animated Schneerson's support for nondenomina-
tional prayer in school, which he later amended to support for a "moment
of silence," a proposal still being considered by the U.S. Supreme Court
in 2002. A federally mandated moment of silence, Shemtov explains, will
force parents to take responsibility for their children's spiritual life, for
certainly the child will come home and ask his or her parents what to say
to fill those sixty seconds.

Chabad threw its first big Washington bash in 1977, to celebrate the
Rebbe's seventy-fifth birthday. On that day Senator Hubert Humphrey
and Representative Tip O'Neill hosted 66 senators and 134 representatives at Washington's first governmental glatt kosher reception. The
event, reported on widely in the national press, began a tradition of near-
yearly events organized by Chabad in D.C. that regularly bring together a
wide range of the nation's political leaders.

Through the Shemtovs, Chabad has maintained personal relationships
with every U.S. president since Gerald Ford. Ford came to Philadelphia
in 1975 to attend the founding ceremony of American Friends of Lubavitch. That marked the first time an American president showed up at a
Chabad event. Ford was, the elder Shemtov says, "traditionally inclined,"
and "very responsive" to Chabad's message of the need to teach ethical
behavior.

Shemtov was introduced to Jimmy Carter through domestic policy
czar Stuart Eizenstat, who later served as deputy treasury secretary in the
Clinton administration. On his way to his first meeting with Eizenstat,
Shemtov was asked by a security guard at the White House gate if he
knew where he was going. "I said yes. When I got to Eizenstat's office, I
said, wouldn't it be wonderful if my boss, who knows where he's going,
and your boss, who has the tools to get there, could work together?"
Eizenstat was later instrumental in getting permission for Shemtov to
erect the first national menorah in Lafayette Park in December 1979.

Chabad's closest presidential relationship, Shemtov says, was with
Ronald Reagan, who corresponded personally with Schneerson. The two
men exchanged letters for years, and Chabad delegations were both the
first visitors to the White House when Reagan was elected and his last
visitors on his final day in office.

Even with presidents, however, Schneerson didn't alter his modus
operandi. In 1979, Shemtov put in a request to the White House to meet
with President Carter on the Rebbe's birthday. "I got a call from the pres-

ident's secretary, excited, and she said, Rabbi, I have an appointment set for you and Rabbi Schneerson tomorrow with the president at eleven o'clock. I said, there must be some mistake. Rabbi Schneerson does not leave his office. The appointment I sought was for a representative of Rabbi Schneerson." The secretary was taken aback. Who refuses a meeting with the president? A few minutes she called back to tell Shemtov that the president would call instead, to wish Schneerson a happy birthday by phone.

Shemtov hesitated, and then told the secretary that he'd have to check the Rebbe's schedule. "She said, 'What? There's somebody in the world who won't take a call from the president of the United States?' I told her it's not a question of him taking or not taking the call, but he might not be [in his office]. On this day he meditates all day in prayer at the resting place of his father-in-law." It was, Shemtov recalls, a "sticky moment." When he checked the Rebbe's schedule, it turned out that Schneerson would, indeed, be out of the office all day and unable to speak to the president. "I called her back, and she said the president understands."

At times, the D.C. shlichim have weighed in on issues of concern to Israel. In the 1980s, during a *shmitta* year (every seventh year, Jewish farmers in Israel must let their land lie fallow) Chabad helped push through a U.S. Department of Agriculture arrangement to help Israeli farmers sell to Arab countries produce that they would otherwise have to give away. When the deal—which involved using the United States government as a middleman—looked as if it wouldn't go through, Shemtov sat down with the chief of staff of the Senate Agriculture Committee and showed him the Bible portion explaining the concept of a sabbatical year. The legislation was eventually passed, and Shemtov says its supporters were shocked. "Jewish lobbyists couldn't accomplish it," he notes. "This was a big savings for Israel."

The bulk of Chabad's work in Washington is not so particularistic. Shemtov remembers seeing New Jersey Senator Frank Lautenberg one day in the early 1980s in the Senate lobby. Lautenberg, a staunch supporter of Soviet Jewry and of increased U.S. aid to Israel, stopped to greet Shemtov. "He said, Rabbi, what issue are you here on, Soviet Jewry or Israel? I said, I'm here on every issue." There is no such thing, Shemtov emphasizes, as an issue that does not concern the Jewish people—that's what the Rebbe taught.

Avraham Shemtov still heads Chabad delegations to the White House three or four times a year, working in tandem with his son to promulgate the Rebbe's message in the nation's capital. Like his son, the elder Shemtov is usually considered a lobbyist, but that's not a label he favors. He prefers to call himself a messenger, sent to Washington not only to see what he can get for Chabad, but to remind the nation's political leaders of the ethical ramifications of their actions. During his years in Washington, he has spent long hours discussing ethics and morality with administration and congressional officials. He typically starts business meetings with a lesson from the week's Torah portion.

Chabad has developed powerful political relationships, Shemtov believes, because politicians are touched by the shlichim's concern not for their vote so much as for their soul, their *neshama*. "The Rebbe identified a vein, a live nerve which I don't believe was properly identified before. People think of Washington as politics, that the only way you can get through is if you have the numbers, if you have the dollars. Not so. Every single one of these people has their personal, individual moments. They are very important, they're answerable to their electorate, but at the same time they still have a *neshama*. That *neshama* may be even more activated in Washington than elsewhere because in Washington that fellow sits down and remembers that a stroke of his pen can mean so much. It can save so many lives. That reminds him of how important every human being is. The Rebbe believed that, and when I spoke to someone, I was his messenger."

Chabad's interest in Washington has to do, certainly, with what government can do for Chabad and the Jewish people. But Lubavitchers also view the nation's leaders as potential mechanisms for promoting ethical behavior and publicizing the Chabad message.

Even a president can be a tool for Jewish outreach. In 1984, Minnesota shliach Moshe Feller accompanied Avraham Shemtov to the Oval Office, where President Reagan was signing the proclamation for that year's Education Day USA. After signing the document Reagan stood up and pointed to the black skullcap on Feller's head.

"Rabbi, you call that a *kippee*, don't you?" Reagan asked. "It's a *kippa*, Mr. President," Feller responded, and went on to explain that Jewish men cover their heads as a sign of respect for God. The president liked the explanation. "I got a letter today from a rabbi talking about a kippa," Reagan continued. "I'm speaking to twelve thousand people tonight, and I'm going to throw away my speech and read the letter instead." So not only did Feller have the privilege of explaining what a yarmulke is to the president of the United States, he managed to have God talk inserted into a major speech before the American people.

Chabad is sometimes taken to task for its pursuit of celebrity endorsements, for the pleasure shlichim express when a governor or a prime minister lights a Chabad menorah, or when a senator praises the Rebbe in a public forum. To a certain extent, Levi Shemtov says, personal pride is at play. "It's a validation, sure," he admits. "When a prominent public figure participates in one of our events, it's a brighter star in our constellation."

But more important is the publicity such figures attract. "If there are people who can be used as examples, who are in positions of power, what better way to spread the message?" asks Feller.

One of the Minnesota shliach's first brushes with celebrity power came in 1965, when Los Angeles Dodgers pitcher Sandy Koufax announced he wouldn't pitch the opening game of the World Series in Minneapolis because it was scheduled for Yom Kippur. Not since Hank Greenberg's Rosh Hashanah boycott three decades earlier had American Jewish boys felt such pride.

Feller, then a young rabbi and a big baseball fan, felt he had to do something to capitalize on the gesture. If Sandy Koufax, the most famous Jewish player in the world, says he's not pitching on Yom Kippur, God's telling me something, he remembers saying to himself. "I had to project his *Yiddishkeit*. I decided to do it through tefillin." Feller ordered a pair of tefillin (and, remembering that Koufax was a southpaw, made sure to specify that it had to be a set for a lefty), and the day after Yom Kippur he went to the downtown hotel where Koufax was staying. How would he get to the athlete? Try playing the religious card, he thought. "I went to the front desk and said, 'I'm Rabbi Feller here to see Mr. Koufax.' They assumed I was his rabbi, and immediately they were reverent."

The desk clerk gave Koufax's phone number to Feller, and the rabbi dialed the room. Koufax picked up. "I said, 'I'm an emissary of the Lubavitcher Rebbe. You've done more for Jewish awareness than anyone, and I want to give you a pair of tefillin.'" Koufax invited Feller up to his room, where Feller says the great pitcher was "a little taken aback" by the young rabbi's knowledge of competitive sports. Feller presented the tefillin to

Koufax, who said, "Rabbi, everyone made a big deal about me not pitching on Yom Kippur, but I didn't pitch on Rosh Hashanah, either."

Thirty-five years later Feller recounts the story with obvious relish. "I put tefillin on everybody. So why not Sandy Koufax? If we can use someone in the public light to popularize mitzvahs, why not?"

And if you can get a vice president, and then a president, personally to carry your holy books from Russia to the United States for you, so much the better.

Although Chabad's official business in Washington has been carried on since 1960 by the Shemtov father and son team, in the decentralized world of Lubavitch activism, several Chabad shlichim have developed their own Washington ties. One of them is Shlomo Cunin, who in 1988 became involved in a high-level diplomatic effort to secure the release from Russia of 12,000 historic books and manuscripts belonging to the Lubavitch movement. The library had been left behind in Russia in 1917 when the fifth Rebbe fled from the advancing German army. After the Bolshevik government came to power, the irreplaceable collection of Judaica was sent to the newly nationalized Lenin Library in Moscow. The Soviet government ignored seventy years of appeals by three Lubavitcher rebbes to release the books, but in the late 1980s, Prime Minister Mikhail Gorbachev indicated that he might be ready to deal.

Cunin, part of a three-rabbi team sent to Moscow by the Rebbe in 1988 to locate the books in the Lenin Library, took on the task of securing their release with single-minded passion. Schneerson sent him back to Moscow in 1991, where he remained for three years trying to drum up support for the books' transfer to the United States. Quickly realizing that he needed the backing of the American government, Cunin sent his six teen-age sons to Washington, where the yeshiva boys spent three weeks knocking on Senate and State Department doors, looking for letters of support to send to Gorbachev.

Levi Cunin was nineteen and studying in Crown Heights when his father called from Moscow to tell him that he and his brothers should leave their studies and drive to D.C. the next morning. "It was something, to walk out of a yeshiva environment one day, from studying two pages of Talmud and a couple of pages of the Code of Jewish Law, into the arena of Washington, D.C. There was no guide book to tell us how to go about doing what we were about to do."

"At yeshiva they don't put too much emphasis on who runs things and what's the difference between the Congress and the Senate," adds Levi's brother Yossi, who was seventeen.

The boys rented a minivan and drove from Brooklyn to Washington. They parked outside the FBI building and, armed with lists of names of senators, started knocking on doors. Unaware of correct protocol, they got more done through sheer chutzpah than if they had gone through the right channels.

Tzemach Cunin, fifteen at the time, remembers that he and his brothers tramped into Massachusetts Senator Edward Kennedy's office that first morning without an appointment. "My father said he wanted us to go see Senator Kennedy, so we walked in and said we'd like to see the senator. His staff just looked at us."

The first morning was filled with wasted efforts. Chaim Cunin, then sixteen, spent an hour pouring out his case to a woman in Senator Lautenberg's office before discovering she was just a secretary. Two of the other brothers wasted an equal amount of time outlining the history of the Lubavitch library in Russia to a staffer in an office of the Environmental Protection Agency.

"It took a while before we got any idea of what was going on in Washington," admits Levi. "But sometimes you get more accomplished when you're naïve."

By the end of that first day, the Cunin boys figured out that it would be easier to buttonhole senators in the hallways than try to get through their front-office staff. But how would the boys recognize any of them? "The magic moment was when we got hold of that little book with the pictures of all the senators in it," says Levi. "That was for us like the Bible was to Moses—a revelation." The boys befriended the Capitol police, who allowed them to ride back and forth on the underground subway that links government offices on the Hill. They sat in the front cars, where the police would seat senators, and learned to make their case during those five-minute private rides. Once, Chaim was sitting in the front car of one subway with California Senator Alan Cranston, when he passed a train going in the opposite direction and saw one of his brothers sitting in that front car with Senator Richard Shelby of Alabama. "There we both were, both sitting in the front seat with a senator, having our respective meetings," Chaim recalls. "The senators caught each other's eyes, and we all started laughing."

Not every impromptu meeting went as well. One afternoon the six boys showed up at the White House gates and asked the security guard to let them in to see the president. They'd brought along *shalach manos* for the president, an enormous Purim basket filled with candies and other bonbons. The guard was, Chaim remembers, "very nice," but explained to the boys that this was not how one got in to see the nation's leader. "He gave us the phone numbers we had to call and sent us on our way," Chaim says.

By the end of five days, the Cunin boys had secured letters of support from seventy senators. They spent another two weeks in Washington, by the end of which time most of the nation's elected representatives knew about these yeshiva boys and the books they were trying to get out of Russia. Senators Lieberman, Lautenberg, and Kennedy were early supporters of their campaign, along with then Senate Majority Leader George Mitchell and then Senate Minority Leader Bob Dole. By the end of 1991, Al Gore was firmly behind the Cunin effort, cosponsoring legislation with Lieberman calling on the Russian government to release the Lubavitch library. In May of 1992 the entire United States Senate signed a letter to President Boris Yeltsin urging him to make good on his pledge to release the books. A similar letter was signed by 135 members of the House of Representatives.

By the summer of 1992, world leaders were appealing directly to Yeltsin to send the books to Lubavitch headquarters in Brooklyn. During the Bush-Yeltsin summit that June, President Bush and Secretary of State James Baker pressed the Russian leader to hand over the library. Senator Dole raised the issue again with Yeltsin during the latter's visit to Kansas.

When Gore and Clinton swept into the White House that November, Gore promised that he'd move the book campaign forward. He made good on his pledge in December of 1993, when he flew back from a special trip to Moscow cradling in his arms a hundred-year-old leatherbound, gold-embossed *Tanya,* a particularly precious volume from the collection, which had been presented to him in a special goodwill ceremony at the Russian State Library.

When President Clinton went to Moscow for a summit meeting the following month, he sent word ahead to Yeltsin's office that he would like to leave with some of the Lubavitchers' books. The Russian State Library agreed to release seven more books, but only as an interlibrary loan to the Library of Congress. The loan papers weren't signed by the time Clinton had to leave Russia for a meeting in Switzerland, so the books were flown to Zurich by chartered plane, where they met up with the president and flew back with him to Washington on Air Force One. Three weeks later the Cunin boys and their father took part in an emotional ceremony at the Library of Congress, where the books were formally handed over to the Librarian of Congress, Dr. James Billington, who had been helping Chaim Cunin arrange the D.C. end of the deal while Cunin senior was handling the book transfer in Moscow.

As of early 2002, American presidents and senators continue to pressure the Russian government, but since Clinton brought back those seven books on the presidential plane, nothing more of the Lubavitch library has been released by the Russian State Library. What's remarkable about the story of Cunin and the Rebbe's books is not so much what it accomplished—only 8 out of 12,000 books and manuscripts have been released—but that six yeshiva boys in Washington were able to attract such overwhelming, bipartisan support for what is really quite an arcane issue within the complex web of U.S.-Russian diplomatic relations. It's not something that earned its backers very much political capital. The senators, representatives, State Department officials, and presidents who met with the Cunins and backed their efforts so strenuously did so in large measure from the heart.

"Looking back, I think they listened to us because we were so real," Levi muses. "There's an old saying in the Talmud: When something comes from the heart, it enters the heart."

"Besides," adds Yossi Cunin, "have you ever seen all six of us together?"

CHAPTER II

LONESOME COWBOYS:

Salt Lake City, Portland, and a Seder in Bangkok

Salt Lake City, Utah, might not appear to offer the most fertile soil for the Chabad message. World headquarters of the Church of Jesus Christ of Latter-day Saints, it's the capital of a state with 1.6 million Mormons and just 4,000 Jews. But when Chabad Rabbi Binyomin "Benny" Zippel and his wife Sharonne rode into town in 1992 to set up Utah's first Chabad center, they found a city—and church—leadership that greeted them as brothers.

"We consider ourselves of the tribes of Israel," says Elder Jeffrey Holland, a member of the Quorum of the 12 Apostles, the body that, under a three-man First Presidency, leads the worldwide Mormon church. "There's a very long and very close theological and personal tie to Judaism."

Mormons believe they are descended from the lost biblical tribe of Ephraim. They are, they say, the people of the New Covenant, entrusted with building a new Jerusalem in the American West. They consider Jews the people of the Old Covenant, whose divinely ordained mission it is to rebuild Jerusalem in the Jewish homeland of Israel. Biblical references abound in Utah, which Mormons call "Zion." A "Jordan River" runs around Salt Lake City. The church's central building is called the Temple, and its Assembly Hall boasts a large Star of David, a conscious representation of the ingathering of the Jewish people in Israel, which the church supports as a necessary precursor to the End of Days.

From the day in 1847 when Mormon leader Brigham Young herded his cattle, his oxen, and his beleaguered followers to the mountain-ringed valley near Utah's Great Salt Lake in search of a safe place to practice his new religion, relations between the state's Mormon majority and its few Jews have been mostly cordial. A wrinkle developed in 1995, when it was discovered that overzealous church officials had performed postmortem baptisms on nearly 400,000 long-dead Jews, many of them Holocaust victims, working off lists of names they took from immigration records, Jewish encyclopedias, and the church's own genealogical database. The church has since then agreed not to baptize dead Jews unless a living family member requests it and—since 1959—*living* Jews have, at least, not been singled out for proselytizing.

When the Zippels showed up in Salt Lake City, the city's Mormons were entranced with this young family that, like them, dressed in modest garb, preached the Bible, and obviously scorned birth control. A church that sends out its own young men for two years of missionary work before marriage has, Holland notes, a special "understanding and sympathy" for the lifelong mission of Chabad emissaries. Sharonne's Mormon obstetrician refuses payment for delivering "the rabbi's babies," and Benny is inundated with requests to speak to Mormon groups. "I talk about Avraham, Isaac, Jacob, Sarah, Rivka, Rachel, and Leah—they love that stuff," he says. "But it's getting to be too much. I've started to tell them I charge, just so they won't ask me all the time."

Soon after he arrived, Zippel was invited to meet with LDS President Gordon Hinckley, the church's worldwide leader. Hinckley told the rabbi that he believed strongly in the rights of Jews to practice their religion and pledged his help if Zippel should ever need it.

Zippel needed that help right away. An Italian citizen married to a Canadian, Zippel had to apply for a green card in order to stay in Utah. His initial request was denied, sending him into a panic. Then he remembered Hinckley's offer. "I called and he said, 'No big deal, Rabbi.' Two hours later I got a call from an attorney with one of the top law firms in Salt Lake City, the firm that handles the LDS church's legal work." The lawyer resubmitted Zippel's paperwork to the INS and, not surprisingly, this time the rabbi got his green card.

The 3,000 Jews who live in Salt Lake City keep a low profile. Most of them know each other and try to get along. Zippel's relationship with Utah's Jewish Federation, rocky at first, improved after he agreed to sit on its board of directors. Now the Federation gives him an annual $4,400 grant for his Hebrew school, after years of telling him not to bother applying. Federation executive director Teresa Bruce, who attends Zippel's weekly Torah class for women, says the Chabad rabbi has "done so much for this community" with his "joyful and spiritual" approach to Judaism. "If that's what Chabad is evolving into across the nation, it's a good thing," she says. "I don't agree with his philosophy one hundred percent, but I don't agree with Reform or Conservative one hundred percent either."

Rabbi Fred Wenger is the spiritual leader of Salt Lake City's Kol Ami congregation, a combined Conservative-Reform group with about four hundred family members. Wenger says he and Zippel, the only two rabbis in the city, "work smoothly together and have a real friendship." The rabbis run joint programs so long as there's no ritual component. They hold an annual Holocaust Remembrance Day event at the State Capitol, but are careful to call it a commemoration rather than a service. Zippel used to teach in Kol Ami's Hebrew school, but asked not to be listed as faculty.

Wenger acknowledges that he's lost some congregation members to Chabad, but doubts that the number is large. And in Utah, where less than 10 percent of the Jewish population is affiliated with any synagogue, anyone who spreads more *Yiddishkeit* is all right in Wenger's book. "If I'm committed to a liberal Judaism that is inclusive, then I can't be doctrinaire about who we bring into it," he says. "You have to take the parts of Chabad that are good for you and ignore the rest. I have no doubt that the children and grandchildren of some of the people who've moved to Chabad will move away from it. In a community like this, people will always come and go."

Jews began arriving in Utah in the mid-nineteenth century, mostly merchants and Gold Rush followers looking to build new lives far from the ties of family and religion. "You need a sense of adventure to live in Utah," notes Eileen Stone, author of *A Homeland in the West: Utah Jews Remember.* "You have to make it on your own, which is what the early Jews here did, and still do."

Benny Zippel fits right in. He, too, is an iconoclast, a *ba'al teshuva* from an Italian family of businessmen. He has a B.A. in modern languages and serves as a volunteer sheriff's chaplain, on call for emergencies, which endears him to the community. He's not a shy man. He jokes, he sings, he wildly overestimates the number of people who show up for his services—not unusual among Chabad shlichim—and he's persistent. Once you get on his mailing list, you're stuck there for life.

Zippel also does outreach in Idaho, Wyoming, and Montana, states without permanent Chabad centers. Most of his work in those states is carried out via the U.S. Postal Service and the Internet. He has offered to run prayer services or classes in any of their towns, but no one has yet invited him in.

Utah's Jews respond well to Zippel's overtures. At the November 2000 Chabad convention in Crown Heights, Michael Wolf, a Salt Lake City businessman, spoke about his first meeting with Zippel. "When he came to town, I shook my head," Wolf related. "How would an Orthodox Jew make it in Salt Lake City?" Zippel showed up in Wolf's office one day and asked whether he'd ever put on tefillin. He said he hadn't, so Zippel told him to roll up his sleeve immediately. "I guess I was moved by it, because I called him the next week and asked him to come put tefillin on me again. That's how it began. Then we started a men's group. I invited guys like me, businessmen raised in Salt Lake City, men who couldn't give a diddle about Judaism. He touched a spark in them."

Living in Utah has been harder on Sharonne than on Benny. She home schools the couple's five children, a choice she would not have made voluntarily. In the absence of any Jewish school in the state, she says she has no option. At nine and a half their oldest son, Avremi, has moved beyond her scope in his Jewish studies, so he learns with a second young Chabad rabbi the Zippels brought out to Salt Lake to help with Chabad House programming. Soon the Zippels will have to send him away to a full-time Chabad school.

Like other Chabad families living outside Lubavitcher communities, the Zippels are limited in their social interactions. Neither they nor their children eat at other people's homes, or at community weddings or bar mitzvahs—unless Sharonne does the catering. Sharonne misses being near her family in Toronto, and she fears her children are missing out by not having other Lubavitcher friends who live close enough to visit. "In Toronto, my kids fall over themselves when they see other kids with *kip-pas*," she comments.

Avremi says the only way he can keep in touch with his close friends, other Lubavitch boys he meets at camps set up for the children of isolated shlichim, is by e-mail. But he says he doesn't mind. He feels special, knowing that he and his family are unique in Utah. "The kids in my bunk at camp always ask how I survive here in Utah without kosher pizza and ice cream. They ask if I feel weird walking around with a yarmulke and *tzitzit.* But living in Salt Lake City isn't bad. The Mormons have a lot of respect for religion. I miss the restaurants and the candy shops, but there's a trade-off. I like home schooling, and I like that my Jewish friends here ask me about holidays and stuff. I'm proud to be a shliach of the Rebbe. If you think you can't survive without pizza, I say you are quite mistaken."

Living in out-of-the-way places, without Lubavitch—or even other Orthodox—neighbors, seems to be more difficult for Chabad women than for their husbands. It could be that the women are simply more open about discussing it. But the burdens of cooking every meal, hosting constant visitors, directing summer camps and schools as well as home-schooling the couple's own eight, ten, or more children, fall more heavily on the shlicha than on the shliach.

And no matter how long a Chabad couple lives in a community, there is always a lingering barrier between them and the rest of the local Jewish population. The Lubavitchers' strict observance of *kashrut,* their avoidance of TV, movies, concerts, and mixed-sex dancing, and other lifestyle choices preclude a lot of casual socializing. The shliach's mission-driven existence has a lot to do with it as well. Chabad shlichim are always onstage, constantly aware of themselves as representatives of a movement, a rebbe, and a way of life that holds them to a "higher standard."

These topics are high on the agenda at the annual convention of Chabad shlichot, held every February in Crown Heights. "How do you relate to your women supporters?" began one presenter at the 2001 convention, speaking to a roomful of shlichot who, like her, lived in outlying Jewish communities. "If they want to go shopping or to a movie with you, say no. You're still their rebbetzin, and you can't lower your standards. They don't need another best friend, they need a role model."

This shlicha, a longtime emissary in a small Canadian city, was speaking at a workshop called "The Many Dimensions of the Shlicha's Life." For almost four hours emissary after emissary took to the microphone to express recurring feelings of inadequacy and self-doubt, and to share tips for improving self-esteem in the face of preschools on the brink of financial collapse and Torah classes in which your students have college degrees and you don't.

"We are dealing with women who are very well educated, who dress well, who look well, who take care of themselves," said one shlicha, an American Lubavitcher living and working in South America. "If we haven't figured out very clearly who we are, we can be very challenged by them. We look at these career women in our communities, and we can feel like a pile of mush."

It takes constant reminding, by oneself and one's friends and family, that the Chabad shlicha is doing her rebbe's work. "If you want to get closer to the women in your community, you have to have self-esteem," the first presenter continued. "We have to constantly take out our ticket and know we're riding first-class. The Rebbe gave us that ticket, the Rebbe's serving the drinks, and the Rebbe made sure we have extra seating room."

Representing the Rebbe's message means that a shlicha always has to look her best. "If you look shlumpy and unkempt and unhappy, why would anyone want to be *frum* for that?" the shlicha declared. "We always have to be happy. We always have to present ourselves well. We are selling this amazing first-class ticket, and we have to look great to do it. Part of it's physical and part of it comes from the inside, from our pride, from feeling so connected."

One shlicha at the workshop complained about feeling embarrassed at Jewish social events in her midwestern city where her dark stockings, long-sleeved dress, and wig stood out in a sea of glamorous women. One day she was taking her children to the zoo, and on an impulse she put a baseball cap on her little boy to cover his yarmulke. "Why do we have to make a spectacle of ourselves all the time?" she charged. "But then I remembered that every time we go out and we look like a Jew, we make an impression. We may not always know the effect it has on a Jewish person who sees us out walking with our sweet little boys in their yarmulkes and *tzitzit*. But I think I've turned on more people to *Yiddishkeit* just by walking back and forth to *shul* on Shabbat than anything else."

Living on shlichus, a Chabad couple's children face temptations they'd rarely face if they were brought up in a Lubavitch neighborhood. Like their parents, Lubavitch children don't eat in non-Lubavitch homes, they don't go to movies or play video games, they don't attend theater or listen to rock music, and they don't participate in mixed-gender play after the age of three. These restrictions can put a serious crimp in a child's social life. One shlicha at the 2001 convention told the story of her six-year-old son who wanted to go ice skating with a local Jewish group on a Saturday night.

"He called home to ask for permission, and my heart went out to him," the woman related. "My husband and I felt it was inappropriate, but he's only six. My twelve-year-old son was listening in, and he took the phone. He said, 'Levi, you're a shliach. How would the Rebbe feel if he saw you ice skating? The music isn't Jewish, there are girls everywhere. It'll be hard for you right now not to go, but when you come home, I promise we'll do something special, just the two of us.' He hung up, and I cried. Who calmed down my six-year-old? Not me or my husband, but my twelve-year-old son."

Devorah Wilhelm has been a Chabad shlicha in Portland, Oregon, since 1983. When her oldest son, Motti, turned nine, she sent him away to a Chabad school in Los Angeles. He lived with her parents, but she still felt guilty. "Sometimes we don't feel we're always there for our children," she muses. But she clearly underestimated the extent to which her son feels committed to the mission she and her husband have chosen, a mission Motti never asked to be a part of but which is nevertheless now part of his blood.

For the past three summers Motti, now twenty, has returned home to Portland to teach in his father's summer yeshiva, instead of going off with Chabad to Russia or Africa on a more glamorous summer "Peace Corps" assignment. And once, upon returning home from a successful Lag B'Omer program run jointly with the Portland Jewish Federation, Devorah heard the phone ringing as she and her husband walked in the door. "I knew it was Motti," she recounts. "He said he'd been davening all morning that there shouldn't be rain, so our program would be a success. How many other twenty-year-old kids are so involved in their parents' lives?

"Sending away your children is a very big struggle. It was harder with my older children—no kosher food, no other Orthodox kids for them to play with. It's easier now with my younger children, because there are more *frum* families they can visit, but I believe the older ones have benefited from these challenges. Family life is more closely knit on shlichus. Children learn to care for each other."

The Wilhelms' years in Portland have not been easy. The city's Reform and Conservative congregations each have close to 1,000 family members, but after seventeen years, the Wilhelms still only have forty-five children in their day school, and Devorah's husband, Moshe, struggles every year to make his budget. "This isn't a town that welcomes Orthodoxy," notes Priscilla Kostiner, president of the city's Jewish Federation.

Devorah says she's often felt discouraged. "In Russia, [shlichim] open a school and have five hundred children. In middle America we don't see success that quickly." For several years, when enrollment in her school was dangerously low, Devorah called 770 to ask whether she should close it. She was always told to keep it going.

"I have this dream of going to the [convention], where other shlichim say they have five hundred kids in their school, seven hundred people in their congregation, and I stand up and say, at least our school exists. Is it where I want it to be? No. Will it be? I don't know. I hope so. It's a struggle. I hope there will come a time when I don't have a stomach ache wondering if I will have enough kids in this or that class next year. But if you really believe in what you're doing, like I really believe that Portland needs a community day school that teaches Torah values, you keep going, even when the community isn't behind you. You go back and study what the Rebbe wrote to people, and you ask for his blessings."

Rabbi Yosef Chaim Kantor leans forward in his chair, his sleeves rolled up against the 98-degree heat outside. It's April in Bangkok, and the full blazing heat of a Thai summer has the city in its grip. Despite the antiquated air conditioner blasting away over his shoulder, beads of sweat stand out in his red beard and his shirt collar is dripping.

It's Friday afternoon, two days before Passover 2001, and Kantor is fielding calls from Chabad yeshiva students who will be running huge communal Seders for thousands of Israeli backpackers in six separate locations throughout Thailand and Nepal. The phone rings. It's his distribution manager, calling from the Bangkok airport with last-minute requests.

"How many Haggadot do they need in Chiang Mai?" Kantor shouts into the receiver. "Two hundred fifty? Send another hundred fifty to Koh Samui. Do they have enough yarmulkes? What about lettuce? We'll send another two hundred head to each of them tomorrow."

The rabbi hangs up the phone and sighs. Just four hours until Shabbat begins, and another crisis has struck. Two hundred of the four hundred chickens he's readied for the Seder meal were refrigerated improperly and have spoiled, so he has to slaughter another two hundred birds right away. Not only is Kantor the ritual slaughterer for all of Thailand, he might be the only one in the entire Far East. "It's not the most pleasant part of my job," he admits. "But when it gets tough, I just think of the Jews who come to me for kosher meat. I know that if I don't have it, they go down the street [to a nonkosher butcher]. So it's a big mitzvah."

This is Kantor's eighth year as the Rebbe's shliach in Thailand, and every year his Seders get bigger. The logistics are staggering. All the fruit and vegetables have been bought in local markets: 1,000 heads of lettuce, 2,000 eggs, dozens of barrels of potatoes, tomatoes, onions, and eggplants. Everything else has been shipped in from Israel: more than 700 pounds of matzah, 700 bottles of kosher wine, 1,300 pieces of gefilte fish, dozens of bottles of kosher-for-Passover cooking oil and spices. And all of these supplies have to be carted, dragged, and flown to their final destinations by a handful of Lubavitch yeshiva students who have come in from New York and Jerusalem to help out for the holiday.

Of all the holiday programs run out of Lubavitch World Headquarters in New York, Passover is the biggest. In 2001, Chabad rabbis and students conducted almost 9,000 public Seders in 23 time zones around the world, serving half a million dinner guests.

Many of the Seders Chabad runs are held in communities where Chabad maintains permanent shlichim. But some are organized in obscure regions of Africa, Asia, Central and South America, and even North America, run by yeshiva students who fly in, locate a place to hold a festive meal, cook all the food, find the local Jews, convince them to show up, lead the Seder, clean up, and fly out. In the former Soviet Union alone, a quarter of a million local Jews took part in nearly six hundred Chabad Seders in April 2001, a mammoth operation underwritten by Lubavitch headquarters and three major donors. Some of those post-Soviet Seders hosted more than 1,000 guests. Others were more intimate, with 100 or 200 invitees. Most of the guests paid nothing.

In the Far East, Chabad's Seders are legendary. They're different than the Seders in Russia or Africa because their clientele—twenty-something Israeli backpackers, fresh out of the army and on the road for a year or more—are as transient as the yeshiva students who fly in to serve them.

By the mid-1980s Chabad headquarters became aware of this critical mass of young Israeli travelers, and they were determined to bring the holidays to them. In 1988, Chabad's first Seder in the Far East was held in Katmandu, Nepal. A couple of Lubavitch yeshiva students flew in from Australia with kosher wine and boxes of matzah to set up an impromptu meal on the Israeli embassy lawn. Seventy-five tourists showed up for that first, unadvertised Chabad Passover celebration. Within a few years, the Katmandu Seder had become the largest in the world, drawing close to 2,000 travelers every year, mainly by word of mouth. Bangkok was second, followed by Chiang Mai, the Thai islands, and then Singapore, Japan, Hong Kong and, by 2000, Vietnam.

Brooklyn-born Kantor was hired in 1993 as the pulpit rabbi for Bangkok's two struggling Jewish congregations, but the two-to-three hundred Jews who live permanently in Bangkok, hardly noticeable among the city's 10 million Buddhist majority, don't provide much fodder for Chabad outreach. Far richer yields were promised by the nearly 100,000 young Israeli travelers who troop through Thailand every year. Clad in tie-dyed shirts and sprouting fresh tattoos and piercings, they trek through the northern hill-tribe villages, smoke dope in the guest houses of Chiang Mai and Kanchanaburi, dance all night at full-moon parties in the southern islands of Koh Samui and Koh Phang Gan. And eventually they all pass through Bangkok, where they follow the hordes of other impecunious travelers to the $4-a-night hostels on Khao San Road.

Khao San, the major thoroughfare in Bangkok's Banglamphu district, hasn't changed much since the 1970s. Barely two blocks long, it's packed with cheap massage parlors and coffee shops that sell hash along with the scrambled eggs. The same glum street vendors peddle the same tired merchandise they've had on hand for decades: rock 'n' roll T-shirts, cotton draw-string pants, wooden bowls, brass elephants. The smells of curry and red-hot chili peppers only partially mask the pungent odors of human and animal refuse, and it's all accompanied by the constant pounding of techno music that blares out from every window and store-front. In deference to the large number of Israeli tourists, many of the café menus and hotel signs are in Hebrew. Restaurants sell hummus and pita to Israeli youths tired of pad thai and fried rice. The Internet cafés advertise cheap calls to Tel Aviv.

This was the neighborhood on which then twenty-four-year-old Yosef Kantor and his wife, Nechama, set their sights soon after their arrival.

The young wanderers of Banglamphu were open to all kinds of spiritual searchings in their journeys through the Far East—why not Judaism? In the fall of 1993, Kantor rented a building off Khao San Road and started bringing in Chabad yeshiva students to offer Jewish services, lectures, and free Shabbat meals. On Friday afternoons the young Lubavitchers would drive up and down the street in a small truck, blasting out Hasidic music through loudspeakers and inviting the bleary-eyed backpackers sipping espresso in outdoor cafés to "come on by for Shabbat!" Young secular Israelis who would not be caught dead at a Chabad House in Tel Aviv found the *Yiddishkeit* less threatening, even a welcome taste of home, after months on the road. They showed up for dinner, they ate the brisket, and they sang the Shabbat songs, songs they often surprised themselves by remembering.

"It's nice to feel the Shabbat spirit after traveling so long in Asia," said Eric Grossman, a young man from a Tel Aviv suburb who dragged his friends to Kantor's Shabbat dinner one Friday in early 1995. Grossman freely admitted that he hadn't been to a synagogue since his bar mitzvah ten years earlier. "In Israel, they force Judaism on you. I don't go for that studying all the time, that looking in the Talmud for all your answers. But this," he nodded toward the brightly lit dinner table, "this is great."

By Passover 1995 the Bangkok Chabad scene was so big that Kantor brought in a second, Israeli-born Chabad couple to help him run the show on a permanent basis. Rabbi Nechemya Wilhelm and his wife, Nechamie, moved into a small apartment on top of the rented Chabad House, where they still live with their four young children, right in the heart of the sex and drugs of Khao San Road. Massage parlors offering "full body rubs with oil" run twenty-four-hour-a-day businesses next door and across the street. Drunk and stoned youths stumble into the Chabad House at all hours of the night. It's an odd place to bring up Hasidic children.

"My children are more protected here than anywhere else," insists Rabbi Wilhelm, who, twenty-two years old when he arrived in Bangkok, was younger than many of the backpackers he served. In addition to running Shabbat and holiday services, Wilhelm acts as an ad hoc social worker and drug counselor, and is often called upon by the local police and Israeli embassy to deal with young travelers strung out on dope or psychedelic mushrooms. As a private citizen, he has more "freedom of movement," says one Israeli embassy official. He has flown in psychologists from Israel. He convinced a Thai police boat to go out in a typhoon to pick up a disturbed Israeli woman stranded on an island. He shelled out $5,000 bail for a pair of young Israelis arrested on marijuana charges.

"I never encountered this in the Hasidic world where I grew up," Wilhelm admits. "But when I bring home someone in trouble, my kids are right there to see it. They help out, they bring glasses of water, they watch while I take care of the person. They're not frightened. They see that this is another Jew. I explain to them that this is what can happen when you grow up with no religious background."

The Chabad operation on Khao San Road grew much faster than Kantor's two community-based congregations and the kindergarten class he and his wife opened in 1998. By 2001 only fourteen local children were enrolled in the class, eleven of them the sons and daughters of the Chabad shlichim. Kantor doesn't think he'll extend his school into the older grades—there isn't the clientele.

But the Israeli backpackers continue to arrive, crowding into Rabbi Wilhelm's Shabbat dinners, coming back for his drop-in Torah classes. In the main tourist season, upward of two-to-three hundred people show up for a single meal. In the spring of 2001, Kantor signed a thirty-year lease on a larger building down the block from the old Chabad House in Banglamphu. By March a construction crew has ripped out the building's guts and was starting work on a synagogue, kosher restaurant, dining hall, and new quarters for the Wilhelms' growing family. Passover is around the corner, Wilhelm is expecting six hundred guests or more for the Seder, and two days before the holiday the building still has no floor, walls, or electricity. The second-floor room where the Seder is to be held is filled with dust and has no lights, stairs or—worst of all—air-conditioning. Wilhelm is getting a little nervous.

Still, a Lubavitcher has to believe in Divine Providence. "There will be a miracle, you'll see," he promises with complete confidence, as a dozen Thai workmen rush past him with plastering trowels and stacks of nail-studded boards. "This place will be ready in time."

In the taxi on the way to slaughtering his Passover chickens on Friday afternoon, Rabbi Kantor reflects on the mission that has brought him, his wife, and family to Thailand, to the steaming and alien city where they expect to spend the rest of their lives. "Frankly, I thought I'd end up in Long Island or New Jersey," he says. "Maybe the Midwest. Never a place like this."

But in 1990, just before Rosh Hashanah, the larger of Bangkok's two congregations sent a desperate plea to Chabad headquarters. "We hadn't had a rabbi in years, and the ones we brought in on a temporary basis were a bunch of no-goodniks," says a local woman. "We're a small Orthodox congregation; we couldn't afford a full-time rabbi. We knew the only place we could turn was Chabad." Still, the woman says, the congregation hesitated. "Some people were nervous about bringing in Chabad. In some communities they move in very strongly, and once they're in, they stay." Bangkok's Jews keep a low profile, living on what they describe as the edge of simmering anti-Semitism. Chabad's public demonstrations of Jewish identity would have to be toned down, she explains. This woman refuses to have her name printed; after thirty years in Bangkok, her next-door neighbors still don't know that she and her husband are Jewish.

Newly ordained Rabbi Levi Shemtov ran High Holidays in Bangkok in 1990 and 1991, but then accepted his permanent posting to Washington, D.C. When Rosh Hashanah 1992 rolled around, he suggested Bangkok to his friend Kantor, just married and looking for a job. Kantor asked the Rebbe, and Schneerson's reply was unequivocal: Go. "Our families were not excited about us moving here," Kantor admits. "My mother was apprehensive, and Nechama's parents were aghast. We're all prepared for spiritual wilderness on shlichus. The physical distance was what bothered us—Bangkok is so far away. But when you get an answer from the Rebbe, you go."

Being a pulpit rabbi put Kantor in the middle of community politics he'd prefer to have avoided. "You're expected to do many things as a pulpit rabbi," he says. "When we ran out of Diet Coke in the kosher shop downstairs, people got angry." Kantor supplements the small stipend he receives from Bangkok's two congregations by overseeing *kashrut* certification for several local food-processing plants and for El Al flights in and out of Thailand. That's not really what he was trained to do in yeshiva, he notes. "A lot of the work here centers around food. Sometimes I think, I didn't come here to be a caterer. But the Baal Shem Tov said if you can do a favor for another Jew, great. If it helps him spiritually, even better.

"Do I feel like this is my home? No. It will always be a struggle. But the Rebbe is gone, and there's no one to tell me to leave. So I'm content to stay."

Kantor's wife Nechama is less sanguine about her life in the Thai capital. Born and raised in Canada, Nechama spent years in Los Angeles before marrying Yosef Chaim and uprooting her entire life. "I'm still not used to the smells," she admits. "I walk to school with my girls every morning, and we pass all the food stalls along the road. I don't think I'll ever get used to it." Sometimes when she's out walking with her children, the Thai people stare and point at her large family, even coming over to touch the children's red hair. Once when she was in her eighth month of pregnancy, she was in a department store and all the saleswomen ran over to whisper and count her five children, point at her bulging belly, and collapse in giggles. "So I counted them back, all seven of them staring at us," Nechama recollects. "It was very embarrassing."

The Kantors have an eight-year-old daughter, and they've already started talking with her about going away to a Lubavitch school in Australia or America. But Nechama doesn't like to think about it. "Will I send her away? I can only hope that Moshiach will come before that. One day at a time, that's all I can say."

Back in the Chabad House on Khao San Road, half a dozen Israeli travelers have shown up to help prepare food for the Seder. Shabbat is just hours away, and Passover begins at sundown Saturday, the moment Shabbat ends, meaning that all the food for Shabbat and the first two days of Passover has to be readied on Friday. "My mother would die if she saw me here," says twenty-two-year-old Idan Ben-Horin, a soft-spoken former Israeli army medic from Ra'anana who is busily chopping carrots into an enormous tin cauldron. Ben-Horin heard about the Chabad Seder a few months earlier, on his first stopover in Bangkok. He went on to Burma but hurried back to the Thai capital this week. He's gotten caught up in the excitement of holiday preparations and has spent all day peeling potatoes, cleaning dusty chairs, and carting buckets of food from the old Chabad House kitchen to the new dining hall down the block.

Standing next to Ben-Horin, her hands covered in flying potato peels, is twenty-seven-year-old Orly Goreshnick from Ramat Hasharon, a tall young woman with short red curly hair and a pierced nose. She says that like the other Israelis helping the Wilhelms get ready for Passover she had no contact with Chabad back in Israel, where she and her family are strongly secular. A few months earlier Goreshnick was traveling through Nepal with two girlfriends, and she surprised herself by suggesting they stop in at a Chabad House for Shabbat. "In Israel I'd never go to Chabad, but here I feel more open to it," she says. Already looking for spiritual enlightenment, the young Israeli woman discovered something precious in the mystical teachings she found among the Hasidim in Nepal and

India. It has changed her attitude toward religious Jews, she says with a quiet smile.

"I still have a problem with the ultra-Orthodox, but Chabad is more liberal," she says. "I spent ten days with Chabad in India. They looked me right in the eye, not like the other *haredim* [ultra-Orthodox]." When she gets back to Israel, she plans to spend time at Chabad's adult outreach program in Safed—just to learn more, she insists. She's not going to become "religious." But if she does—well, she shrugs, and smiles shyly.

Twenty-two-year-old Lubavitcher Dovid Hadad is coordinating the Israeli kitchen volunteers that Friday afternoon. Hadad is from Kfar Chabad, a large Lubavitch community outside Tel Aviv. He's been in Thailand for five months, as part of a year off between completion of yeshiva studies and the beginning of an intensive nine-month study period leading to rabbinical ordination. He helps run services, teaches classes offered for free to the travelers, rounds up men for *minyans* three times a day, and lends a hand wherever needed. "Bangkok stinks, but the work with the Israelis is great," he says, glancing away for a moment from the piles of peeled eggplant he's checking for bugs which, if not removed, would render the vegetable nonkosher.

Before arriving in Bangkok, Hadad spent a year studying in Brooklyn, then six months helping out at a Chabad House in Chile and three months doing outreach in Peru. Small and dark, with a quick smile, the young Lubavitcher is popular with the travelers, many of whom hail him by name as they walk into the Chabad House to check the bulletin board for notes from their friends or to pick up mail the rabbi holds for them. Hadad dispenses free travel advice, counseling one group of young Israelis headed for a three-day Jeep trip up north to buy travel insurance. "Otherwise you could get stuck for a lot of money," he points out.

Hadad says he much prefers the outreach work he does outside Israel. "People are more open when they're traveling," he notes. "There's so much to do in a place like Bangkok. The work is every day, and you can see the fruits of what you do." Hadad says he has years before he has to decide on a permanent placement, but he's used the past year on the road to help him make that choice. "If I had to decide now, I'd choose a place like this. I hate Bangkok, but I don't look at the city, I look at the work. Really, I could live anywhere."

Upstairs, the Wilhelms take a ten-minute break in their frenetic holiday preparations. Both were up until 4 A.M. the previous night and have had less than three hours of sleep. Nechemya was running vans of food and supplies back and forth all night between Kantor's storage space in the eastern part of the city and the new Chabad House. Nechamie was chopping tomatoes and cleaning chickens at her kitchen sink, preparing three days' worth of meals for her own family. She also has to prepare all the food for two complete Seders that her husband and his yeshiva-student helpers will eat back at her house each night after the public Seders, where they will be too busy running the show to fulfill their own ritual obligations. There's another reason for the second Seder—Lubavitchers maintain a level of stringency in their own Passover observance they wouldn't impose on their guests.

Nechamie is shocked at the suggestion that she might be lonely in Bangkok. "Never!" she insists. "There are so many Israelis coming through all the time." But her interactions with the young backpackers take place only on a superficial level. To them she will always be the rebbetzin, as her twenty-seven-year-old husband will always be the rabbi. "I have to be the perfect woman," she comments. "They look to me as a role model. Even if I'm not, I have to fake it. I miss having a best friend. My husband has to be my mother, father, best girlfriend, everyone."

Nechamie was raised on shlichus in Kiryat Gat, an impoverished development town in the south of Israel. Growing up with eleven sisters and brothers, all of whom are either emissaries or dreaming of it as their future, Nechamie says that she hopes to go to the next shlichot convention in Crown Heights so she can see her newly married sister, who just took up a posting with her husband in Moscow. "I haven't seen her for a year," she says. For the rest of her life, Nechamie will see her shliach siblings only at conventions or family occasions—weddings, bar mitzvahs, or, God forbid, funerals. Still, she says that living in Bangkok is much easier for her than Kiryat Gat was for her American-born mother.

Maybe it's easier because she keeps the city so much at a distance. Like many Chabad shlichim in isolated outposts, the Wilhelms are strangely dissociated from the country in which they live. In six years they've taken only two trips outside Bangkok—one to Chiang Mai for a bris, and one three-day vacation on the island of Koh Samui. That's typical of Chabad shlichim. For all their frequent-flyer miles and their postings in far-off lands, Lubavitchers seem to float untouched through the exotic locales in which they live and work, part of and yet apart from the foreign cultures whose languages they learn but whose ways they refuse

Rabbi Menachem Mendel Schneerson, the seventh Lubavitcher rebbe, in a photo taken at the 1954 wedding of one of his students.

The Rebbe waves to children as they march past him in a Lag B'Omer parade in Crown Heights, Brooklyn, in 1983.

Schneerson salutes a boy wearing a "general's cap" that marks him as a member of Tzivos Hashem, Chabad's children's organization. The boy has just received a small cup with wine that was poured from the Rebbe's cup.

The Rebbe presides over a *farbrengen* at 770 Eastern Parkway in the early 1970s.

Rabbi Menachem Shmuel Dovid Raichik puts tefillin on a man he's just met on an airplane. This is a common Chabad outreach practice, for which the late California shliach was legendary.
(Photo: Raichik Family Archives / Chabad-Lubavitch Media Center)

Rabbi Hirsch Zarchi, the Chabad shliach in Cambridge, Massachusetts, addresses the crowd at a menorah-lighting ceremony in Harvard Yard. Facing him is Professor Alan Dershowitz, Chabad's faculty sponsor at Harvard. In the coat and scarf is former Dean of Students Archie Epps III.
(Photo: Harvard Chabad / Chabad-Lubavitch Media Center)

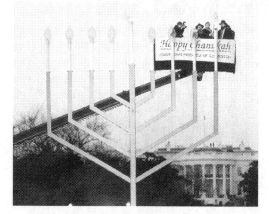

United States Deputy Secretary of Defense Paul Wolfowitz helps Chabad Rabbis Avraham Shemtov and Levi Shemtov light the National Chanukah Menorah on the Ellipse near the White House on December 9, 2001.
(Photo: Rick Bowmer / Associated Press)

Rabbinical students Hirsch
Minkowitz (left) and Reuvain Mintz
(right) with a "customer" in Osaka,
Japan. Minkowitz and Mintz, then
on their Far East post-seminary
"tour," are now full-time shlichim in
Georgia and California, respectively.
(Photo: Chabad-Lubavitch Media Center)

Rabbinical students Eliezer
Zaklikofsky (center), now
a shliach in New Jersey, and
Levi Wolff (far left), now
shliach in Australia, lead
Chabad's 1996 outdoor
Seder in Nepal, which hosted
more than 1,000 guests—
most of them Israeli tourists.

Chabad Rabbi Zalman
Grossbaum teaches children
at the Joseph Kushner Hebrew
Academy in Livingston, New
Jersey, to look for the reflection
of the flame in their fingernails
as they light the Havdalah candle
that marks the end of Shabbat.
The class is part of Chabad's
traveling Living Legacy program.

A Chabad shlicha (in long skirt) gives Shabbat candles and instructions for lighting them to two young women on a college campus in Milwaukee. *(Photo: Mel Askotzky)*

Ronald Perelman, Chabad donor and Chairman of the Board of Revlon, Inc., inscribes the last letter of a Torah scroll at the Beth Rivkah Lubavitch girls' school in Crown Heights in February 1999, under the watchful eyes of Rabbis Avraham Shemtov (left) and Moshe Klein. *(Photo: David Karp/Associated Press)*

Meryl Streep and Tzivos Hashem executive director Rabbi Yerachmiel Benjaminson at the inaugural dinner of the Joseph Papp Children's Humanitarian Fund in Manhattan in May 2000.
(Photo: Pace International Photography, New York City / Cedarhurst)

Elie Wiesel and Senator Joseph Lieberman greet each other after their keynote speeches at the 1997 Chabad banquet in Washington, D.C. Rabbi Avraham Shemtov, national director of American Friends of Lubavitch, stands in the center. *(Photo: American Friends of Lubavitch)*

Jon Voight (second from left) hams it up on stage at the 1995 Chabad telethon, flanked by (from left to right) Rabbi Shlomo Cunin, head of Chabad West Coast, Robert Eglund, and Jan Murray.

Russian President Vladimir Putin (left) sits with Moscow Chabad shliach and Russia's Chief Rabbi Berel Lazar at a March 2002 meeting celebrating Passover and the one hundredth anniversary of the Rebbe's birth.

Former New York City Mayor Rudolph Giuliani visits the Rebbe at 770 in August 1991. *(Photo: Chaim Boruch Halberstam)*

A delegation of shlichim present newly elected President Bill Clinton with a dollar from the Rebbe, which Clinton drops into a *pushke*, or charity box.

(Photo: The White House / Chabad-Lubavitch Media Center)

Flanked by Chabad shlichim from around the world, President George W. Bush signs the Education Day Proclamation in March 2002. This presidential proclamation has been signed annually in the Rebbe's honor since 1978.

(Photo: The White House / Chabad-Lubavitch Media Center)

to adopt. A Lubavitch home will always look the same, no matter where in the world it is located. The same books are on the bookshelf, the same matzah-ball soup is on the stove, the same Rebbe's portrait hangs on the living room wall. And no matter where they're brought up, almost every Lubavitcher—except the native Israelis—speaks fluent English with the same American accent, a tribute to the movement's persistent homogeneity.

At seven-thirty on Saturday evening, the first night of Passover, hundreds of young Israelis are tramping up the stairs in the new Chabad House off Khao San Road. Somehow, Rabbi Wilhelm's miracle has happened. In twenty-four hours, the walls have been painted, the floor laid, and lights installed in the ceiling. The air-conditioning units put in place just hours earlier are cranking away for all they're worth, but they'll give out in an hour or so, spitting out warmed-over air in fits and spurts throughout the evening.

The Seder is called for seven-thirty, but an hour later guests are still arriving. Some have made the effort to find that one unwrinkled shirt lurking at the bottom of their backpack, but most look like they've stepped right off the beach. An already festive holiday atmosphere is heightened by dozens of impromptu reunions, as young Israelis throw their arms around friends they haven't seen since the army—or since India. Dovid Hadad and two other visiting yeshiva students take tickets at the top of the stairs, but less than half the guests have bothered to buy them. People are used to Chabad providing things for free. The yeshiva boys just smile and let everyone in, too polite to mention that the $11 tickets, all sold before the holiday weekend, cover just one-third of the evening's expense. Rabbi Kantor estimates that the three Seders he's holding this year in Thailand will cost him $50,000 above and beyond what he takes in from ticket sales. And it's the only event he charges for all year.

Inside the crowded dining hall, Rabbi Wilhelm and his team have run out of chairs. People are lining the walls, fanning themselves with paper plates and extra Haggadot. "Friends, please don't take pictures," Rabbi Wilhelm begs, as cameras flash left and right in violation of the Jewish holiday.

Finally, the reading begins. Young Israelis who boast of never going to synagogue, of never getting through the entire Haggadah at their family Seders, are gamely shouting out the Passover story in unison as Rabbi Wilhelm leaps from table to table, whipping up enthusiasm.

"If I get to your table and you don't know where we are in the story, you lose!" he shouts, to great laughter.

The first two cups of wine are poured and drunk, the Seder plate is displayed, Hillel's matzah-and-horseradish sandwich is constructed and devoured, and by ten-thirty the festive meal is finally underway. In a nod to the Israeli guests, eggplant and shredded carrot salads are on the table, but the rest of the meal is pure Eastern Europe. Gefilte fish is followed by matzah-ball soup, then on to boiled beef and root vegetables. Thailand shows up only at the dessert course—fresh papaya and pineapple chunks.

"Tonight, we're all one family," Wilhelm shouts again, to a roar of applause. By eleven-thirty the final two cups of wine have been downed, and Wilhelm leaps onto his chair to lead a rousing version of "*Echad, Mi Yodea?* [Who Knows One?]" After the first four verses he exhorts all six hundred guests to stand up and continue singing. Two verses later he encourages them to stand on their chairs. "Let's get higher!" he shouts. The singing grows rowdier and rowdier, so he hesitates on the verge of inviting them all to stand on the heavily laden tables. No, maybe this is enough for one night. "We're high enough physically, how about reaching inside to grow higher spiritually?" he suggests.

Sometime after midnight the Seder is over and the crowd spills noisily out into the late-night Bangkok street. Saturday night is in full swing. Susie's Bar beckons around the corner, the massage girls are parading across the street, and the street vendors are loudly hawking their wares. Many of the Seder guests will head back to their hotels, but just as many are off to the cafés and dancing clubs of Khao San Road. Rabbi Wilhelm and Rabbi Kantor must know that. They've given up comfortable lives in New York and Kfar Chabad for no other reason than to bring *Yiddishkeit* to young Israelis traveling through Thailand. So don't they find the partying, especially right after a Passover Seder, a little disheartening? Maybe, but they can't allow themselves to dwell on it.

"We're not trying to create *ba'alei teshuva* here," insists Wilhelm. "Just getting them to feel a little *Yiddishkeit,* that's already a lot."

Two nights later the Wilhelms, Kantors, and some of the visiting yeshiva students are sitting around the Kantors' dining room table recovering from the holiday. They pick at bowls of fried potatoes, green salad, and cold cuts, as Rabbi Kantor waits for calls to come in from the field reporting back from the Seders in Koh Samui, Chiang Mai, and Nepal. Refrigeration is a problem everywhere. He already knows that the soup in Koh Samui spoiled and had to be prepared again at the last minute. Now he hears of an even bigger screw-up in Nepal, where a well-intentioned hotel employee unplugged all the refrigerators every night to save money, not realizing that a Passover meal for 1,500 people was rotting away inside. "So they ate pickles and salad instead," Kantor relates.

At 11 P.M., the front door bursts open and nineteen-year-old Levi Touger strides into the room. He's come straight from Chiang Mai, where he and a couple of other yeshiva students ran a Seder for 230 tourists. "It was trippy," he says, with a beatific smile. "One long trip straight up. Unbelievable!"

Like Hadad, Touger is in Bangkok for half a year. At nineteen he's already a rabbi, unusual in Chabad circles. "Talent," he explains with a wide grin, leaning back in his chair with his arms behind his head. Touger is from an American Lubavitcher family living in Jerusalem, and unlike the soft-spoken Hadad, he oozes Brooklyn spunk. "I flew into Chiang Mai Friday afternoon with all the lettuce. Got there two hours before the Big Bang. We had an amazing Shabbos. The energy, you're not gonna get that in any club. You have to join the Chabad Club for that."

The yeshiva boys at the Kantors' table are bursting with adrenaline. They're young, away from home, doing the Rebbe's work, seeing amazing sights, and it's all pretty heady stuff. The enormous Seders are over, they're no longer on stage, and they're letting off steam with a barrage of playful shoving and jokes. Touger is regaling the table with tidbits from the Chiang Mai Seder.

"The meat was so white that the Americans thought it was *chazir* [pork]," he reports. "They said, you guys eat this stuff? I said, sure!"

"Hey, you should go into politics," one of the students shouts at Touger. "Nah, it's all about show business, man," Touger retorts, leaning back even further in his chair.

"How about used cars?" another *bocher* jibes. Touger just smiles.

Some of the Lubavitch boys in Bangkok are on formal half-year shlichus. Some have just flown in for a few weeks to help out, like seventeen-year-old David Drizin of Crown Heights. He usually spends Passover with his family in a hotel in Miami Beach, but this year he set out for the Far East with a couple of buddies to do the Chabad House holiday circuit. "I heard the Seder in Bangkok was amazing, and I had to see it," he says. Did it live up to his hopes? "Oh, yeah!" he says emphatically.

Drizin worked hard the past week. It's a taste of the shliach life he plans to embark on one day. His father is a businessman in Brooklyn, but he hopes for a shlichus "someplace warm" like Singapore, or maybe Miami. "Anyplace but New York," he says. Only three of his classmates might choose to stay in New York, he says. The rest are all headed out. But, he muses, maybe their children or grandchildren will one day return to Crown Heights, which might seem as exotic to them as shlichus in Thailand now seems to him.

Nineteen-year-old Shaya Boas is in Bangkok for the month, taking a break from a year-long prerabbinical course in Crown Heights. His parents paid his way there and, like the other *bocherim,* he's helping out for free. "My dad called to ask if I was having fun. I said, it's not fun exactly, it's hard work, but I'm doing something useful. I feel good. There's a limit to how much fun you can have, and then you want to *do* something."

Boas wants to do the same thing next Passover, maybe in a different place in the Far East. "I hear they're going to open Cambodia next year," he says hopefully. Like his friends, he's taking as much advantage as he can of his temporary freedom. Soon enough he'll be married, starting a family, and tied to a Chabad House of his own.

"I love being nineteen," he confides. "You have no commitments yet, you can just travel all over. My grandmother says this is the best year of my life and I should enjoy it."

CHAPTER 12

FROM GRANOLA TO GOD:
The Ba'alei Teshuvah

Ilana Jablonski is sitting at a Seder table in Bangkok nervously patting the long, dark blond hair on her new *sheitel,* the wig many Orthodox and all Chabad women wear to cover their own hair. "It's the first week I'm wearing it," she whispers. "The humidity here makes it look awful!" Ilana and her husband Yossi are *ba'alei teshuva,* or "returnees to the faith," formerly non-observant Jews who now keep kosher, observe Shabbat, and follow the other basic tenets of Orthodox Judaism. Ten years ago they were living hand-to-mouth in Bangkok's Banglamphu youth hostel district, selling homemade jewelry on the streets. Today they live with their two young children in an Orthodox neighborhood in Melbourne, Australia, where Ilana is a family physician and Yossi works as a goldsmith. For the past three years they have been coming back to Bangkok every Passover to help Rabbi Kantor and his wife run their communal Seders. Yossi wears the black hat and white shirt of a Chabadnik; Ilana has on a long, flowing dress and her new wig.

"Yossi has wanted me to cover my hair for a while," Ilana says. "He never pushed, though. He said, 'Do it when you're ready.'"

The Jablonskis' path to their observant lifestyle was gradual. It began in 1991 in Bangkok when they went to a Chabad-sponsored Rosh Hashanah dinner, not because they were looking for religion, but because the meal was held in an air-conditioned hotel. "We were poor, we couldn't afford air-conditioning," Yossi says. "We said to each other, 'Don't tell anyone we're going, they'll think we're crazy.'" Two years later they met the Kantors and a spark was lit. "The way they prayed was so inspiring," Yossi recalls. "I saw these two people, so innocent. This was a big push for us."

Yossi and Ilana stayed in Thailand for another few years, following the backpacker circuit to a southern Thai island filled with bungalow villages, then on to Nepal, Japan, and India, still making and selling jewelry, but now reading about Judaism as well. In Japan they decided to stop working on Friday nights, traditionally the biggest night for street sellers. Instead of suffering financially, they sold all their stock in two months. Yossi took it as a sign. "If you look after Shabbat, Shabbat will look after you."

In 1994 the couple returned to Ilana's native Australia and began to live as observant Jews. "We moved very slowly," Yossi says. "I was in my thirties, I wasn't going to change overnight." Even when they started keeping Shabbat, the Jablonskis drew the line at identifying themselves as Lubavitchers. "We said, 'We'll never be like those penguins,'" Yossi laughs, referring to the outfit he now wears. "We only saw the costumes, not the ideas behind them."

Ilana's parents weren't happy with the changes they saw in her, particularly when she announced that she could no longer eat in their nonkosher house. "My mother thinks I'm nuts," Ilana says bluntly. "She said, 'Do what you want, but don't cover your hair. And if you do, for God's sake don't wear one of those horrible *sheitels.*'" Relations have improved "a bit" between them, "but it's still hard," Ilana admits. And she won't budge on the *sheitel* issue. "You have to stick to your principles," she states. Patting her head again, she sighs. "It feels hot. But I'm very proud to be wearing it. It goes beyond modesty. There's a deep kabbalistic meaning to a woman covering her head. It brings *brachos* [blessings] down from Hashem directly, on my entire family. A lot of *brachos.*"

When people hear the word "Chabad," many of them think *ba'al teshuva.* Ask an American Jew what he or she fears most about the group, and you'll probably hear, "They want to make everyone just like them." On a literal level, shlichim say, that's absurd. But on a deeper level, behind the low-key outreach and the nonjudgmental acceptance of Jews who don't observe Jewish traditions, is a fervent hope that at least some of the message is getting through. The purpose of Chabad outreach, after all, is to rekindle Jewish souls and put them in touch with what the Lubavitchers believe is every Jew's natural instinct, which is to live observant Jewish lives. If a Jew does one mitzvah, that's great. If he does many, that's even better. If he adopts an observant lifestyle, and is therefore in a position to do mitzvahs every day, that's best of all. Chabad shlichim may say they don't want everyone to be observant, but they all keep count of the "frummies" they've nurtured and sent on to Crown Heights for further education. Each one is another notch in Chabad's spiritual belt, a concrete validation of the movement's values and lifestyle.

Hasidism itself can be looked at as a sort of *ba'al teshuva* movement, sweeping through the *shtetls* of Russia and Poland two hundred years ago to reinvigorate Jewish life. *Teshuva* means "to return," and Chabad *Hasidus* teaches that every Jew should strive to be a *ba'al teshuva,* pushing his or her Jewish practice to ever higher levels. The history of Lubavitch in America is that of a small postwar Brooklyn community that grew by attracting other Jews to its way of life. What was different about the early converts to Lubavitch religious practice is that virtually all came from observant households. They were making the switch from one kind of Orthodoxy to another, Hasidic variant. Chabad's real *ba'al teshuva* phenomenon took off only in the 1960s, when Menachem Mendel Schneerson's determined outreach campaign directed at Reform, Conservative, and unaffiliated Jews began to draw into Chabad large numbers of young people with little or no Jewish background.

Beginning in the late 1960s, Chabad set up an entire adult educational system to accommodate this sudden influx of newly Orthodox Jews. First came Hadar Hatorah in Crown Heights, the first *ba'al teshuva* yeshiva. In the early 1970s, Machon Chana in Crown Heights opened for women and Tiferes Bachurim, opened for men in Morristown, New Jersey. Other institutions followed.

The heyday of the *ba'al teshuva* explosion was the 1970s, a decade of spiritual experimentation that sent tens of thousands of young Jews to ashrams, churches, and Buddhist temples. Some of those religious adventurers ended up turning back to their own Jewish roots, and Chabad was there to welcome them. In tune with the radical times, those who returned to Judaism in the 1970s and early '80s generally did so with ferocious single-mindedness. They tended to go all the way very quickly, donning black hats or long-sleeved dresses as soon as they started eating kosher, coming to live in Crown Heights and, when they arrived there, requesting *shidduchim,* or arranged marriages.

In those years, when Chabad was setting up its first campus Chabad Houses, the target audience was what shlichim called the "lost generation," the baby boomers who had to be saved from drugs, sex, and radical lifestyles. Rabbi Shlomo Cunin tells the story of one such *ba'al teshuva* who came to his UCLA Chabad House soon after it opened in 1969.

"She was a gal called Francine, and she was living with her boyfriend. She'd show up here with her long hair, a big cape, and this gigantic dog. We had a women's weekend once, very intense. On Saturday night, she said, 'Rabbi, what I hear from you is so beautiful, I'd really like to become part of it. But I'm living with a man. You view me as dirty, don't you? You view me as nothing, don't you?' I said, 'Why are you making up how I view you? Why don't you ask me?' So she asked, 'OK, how do you view me?' And I said, 'As a beautiful Jewish soul that has just begun to breathe.' She was stunned. 'You have to get more oxygen to your soul. Do you think you could begin by lighting Shabbat candles, after we talk about what it means?' She asked if she could light the candles in the home where she sleeps with this man, and I said, 'Absolutely.' Today she lives in Jerusalem with thirteen kids and a wig that comes down over her nose."

Physical clues, indistinguishable to outsiders, set these early *ba'alei teshuva* apart from the "FFB," or "*frum*-from-birth" segment of the local Lubavitch community. They were still single at ages when their FFB counterparts had long been married. Their clothes were slightly different, their Hebrew more hesitant, and their Yiddish nonexistent. Intellectually, some of the newly religious women put their college education to use, editing and writing for Lubavitch publications, where they would argue against the feminist movement and radical politics from the perspective of former insiders. Social acceptance in the Lubavitch community came more slowly. Following an initial open-arms welcome, the newly religious arrivals in Crown Heights found themselves in the position of anyone moving into what is essentially a small-town community. It takes time, and a light touch, to insinuate yourself into your neighbors' good graces.

Marriage was a way to integrate, but in those early years most BTs married within their own group. It was difficult to find a *shidduch* for a *ba'al teshuva* from within the more prestigious Lubavitch families, although there were exceptions. But as the critical mass of *ba'alei teshuva* grew, and they began filling more and more positions in the Lubavitch infrastructure, the distinctions between the newly religious and the born-religious began to fade. Twenty years ago it was rare to find a Chabad shliach who wasn't a born-and-bred Lubavitcher. Today it's common to find shlichim whose parents were *ba'alei teshuva* and who have grandparents, aunts, uncles, and cousins who are not observant. Whereas many *ba'alei teshuva* prefer to keep quiet about their own non-observant past, their FFB children rarely feel the same reticence.

Rabbi Avraham Berkowitz, a Chabad shliach in Moscow, grew up in Detroit with parents who became religious in the early 1970s, just before he was born. He's proud that his mother still works as a novelist and computer engineer for Ford, and that he's been exposed to things other Lubavitchers had to learn about from afar. "My grandparents are very secular," he says. "My grandfather in Bel Air prefers that I don't wear a yarmulke in his house, so I wear a baseball cap. I learned to respect them as secular Jews. They don't keep kosher or Shabbos, but these are my grandparents. I never looked at them as people I had to teach about Judaism. I look at them as Jews, whose practice is different than mine. I think it's helped me understand secular Jews, the people I meet in my work now. I'm able to show them my tradition without imposing on them, and the results are much greater."

Ba'alei teshuva who marry each other and then become Chabad shlichim are a more rare phenomenon. Yosef and Hinda Langer, Chabad shlichim in San Francisco who became religious in the early 1970s, were probably the first such couple. Not only did they become observant very quickly, but within five years of their first encounter with Chabad, they were working as official representatives of the movement. That's faster than it would happen today.

If there is such a thing as a typical Chabad shliach, Yosef Langer is not it. His business card shows him, black hat, white beard and all, astride his "mitzvah bike," a refurbished meter maid's motorcycle on which he tools around the city. "I'm trying to take the Rebbe's message to the streets," he says. "People are afraid of anything too Jewish, you have to garb it in a different costume." The mitzvah bike "puts a smile on people's faces," he says. "It's my shtick." Yosef calls himself the rock 'n' soul rabbi, and says he aims his message at the new generation of music fans, the inheritors of the hippie movement he once was part of. He was not a Deadhead in the sixties, but he started hanging out at Grateful Dead concerts in the early eighties, spreading the Lubavitch word. He would hand out two-for-one Grateful Dead concert tickets at his Chabad House. Anything to get the kids in the door.

In 1997, Langer drove to the Woodstock anniversary concert in an RV loaded with a hundred challahs and sheet cakes, arriving just in time to welcome in the Shabbat with hundreds of curious young rock 'n' rollers. "It was awesome," he recalls. "We were giving challah away, touching souls." Concertgoers gawked at the sight of this rabbi with the long white beard and "Grateful Yid" T-shirt running around giving *l'chaims* to stoned fans. At one point, singer-composer Wyclef Jean of the Fugees came backstage with his entire family to get a *bracha* from the rabbi. "I do my work and have a good time doing it. There's nothing in Judaism that says you can't have a good time."

Yosef was born Gary Langer, a "nice Jewish boy from Oakland." After what he calls a "conveyor-belt bar mitzvah," Yosef says he "ran in the other direction, getting pretty dinged up in the sixties." In 1969, he left college during his last semester, did a stint as a merchant seaman, and then joined a church in Oakland to study metaphysics. One day someone in the church asked him to explain the infinity of the *aleph-bet,* or Hebrew alphabet, which has certain mystical powers according to Kabbalah. Not knowing the answer, he turned to his grandparents' rabbi, who sent him to a Lubavitcher scholar nearby. "I rode my bike to his house, in my Afro and tie-dyed shirt, knocked on his door, and asked him to teach me the infinity of the *aleph-bet.* He said that my question was typical of the American push-button spirituality. The way of Judaism is to take one step, and then another."

Yosef studied the Hebrew alphabet with his new teacher for six weeks and was then invited down to the newly organized UCLA Chabad House. He spent three months there, studying Judaism and working in the kitchen, and says the experience "blew my mind." Things were just getting rolling at UCLA, a place that would soon begin churning out *ba'alei teshuva,* and the young rabbis there were charismatic and filled with energy. "There was Cunin and Schwartzie [Shlomo Schwartz] and [Avraham] Levitansky and [Yerachmiel] Stillman—it was so fun being around those guys. There was so much camaraderie. It was so real, so down-to-earth, yet with the deepest *Hasidus.*" Twelve weeks later, in December 1970, he left for Crown Heights carrying his first pair of *tzitzit,* a present from Rabbi Schwartz. Yosef taught Schwartzie to make guacamole in exchange. "They sent me off to New York with a carrot juicer, my pay for working in the kitchen. It was the first carrot juicer in Crown Heights. People got on my case about it. They called it idolatry, all this emphasis on natural food."

In early 1971, Yosef met Hinda, a newly religious former college student and single mother who had just arrived in Crown Heights from the State University of New York, Binghamton. Hinda was, she says, a "Hebrew school drop-out," who walked out of her Conservative *shul* in Flatbush, New York, on Yom Kippur when she was fourteen. While still a teenager, she joined the Students for a Democratic Society and other radical political groups, and worked for third-party mayoral candidates in Brooklyn. "I wanted to be the female Lawrence Ferlinghetti," she says. "I carried around a copy of 'Howl' in my pocket." In 1966 she started college in Binghamton, abandoning politics for writing, spiritual exploration, and marijuana. She began meditating and doing yoga, and at eighteen married her boyfriend, dropped out of school, and got pregnant. Then she met Meir Abehsera, a *ba'al teshuva* who taught macrobiotics at a Binghamton health food restaurant. Hinda was trying to get off drugs. She responded both to Meir's healthy lifestyle and the warmth she found at his family's Shabbat table.

"It seemed so authentic. I'd been asking two questions in my meditation: Why was I born Jewish, and would I be shown my Master in this life? I decided that I'd never know what it meant to be Jewish if I didn't try." Hinda began keeping Shabbat and in March of 1971, went with several other SUNY-Binghamton students on a group trip to Crown Heights. Some of those SUNY drop-outs are still living as Lubavitchers in Crown Heights today, she notes. On that first trip the group met the Lubavitcher Rebbe. For Hinda that was it. "When I saw the Rebbe, I knew that this was my Master in this lifetime."

A month later the now-divorced Hinda moved to Crown Heights with her infant son. She was an unusual *ba'al teshuva,* and not just because she was a single mother. Her macrobiotic diet raised eyebrows among the Hasidim. "One woman invited me for Shabbos. I didn't eat white bread or mayonnaise or chicken. She thought I was nuts." But Hinda felt immediately drawn to Lubavitch and says she didn't find the religious transition bumpy at all. "I used to be in women's consciousness-raising groups, and what I saw in Chabad was strong women. Everything I'd been involved in before—the politics, the spiritual stuff—it all came together for me in Torah, which was the whole picture. I didn't have conflicts becoming *frum*. Things that were true called out to me from within."

The Langers married soon after they met, and in 1975 they were sent as assistant shlichim to the Chabad House in Berkeley, California, the first *ba'al teshuva* couple assigned to such a position. By 1979, Yosef was in charge of the entire Bay Area Chabad, including new centers in San Francisco and Marin County. In 1985 the couple moved into the San Francisco Chabad House, which they still oversee. Being *ba'alei teshuva* has definitely affected their shlichus. They had to try harder to learn prayers and customs other Lubavitchers grow up with. They had to get used to having people traipse through their house at all hours of the day and night, again something that born Lubavitchers are used to. On the other hand, they were intimately familiar with many of the real-life problems that showed up on their doorstep. "I was around all that sex and drugs in college," says Hinda. "But the shlichim who are not *ba'alei teshuva,* how do they deal with it?"

Because they didn't have a family support network to fall back upon when times were rough, Hinda and Yosef say they have relied more heavily on the Rebbe, even today. "It's impossible to put into words how I feel the Rebbe's constant presence," Hinda says. "Maybe I feel it more because I'm a *ba'al teshuva.* Some of the shlichim, when they have questions, they call their parents. For me, the Rebbe is my *kesher* [connection] for what is and isn't appropriate, not my parents. They gave me my integrity, but not my Judaism."

In a conference room at the historic Archer House inn in Northfield, Minnesota, two dozen women in long skirts are listening to Rabbi Manis Friedman talk about shaking hands with men. "It's nothing, right?" he says. "Nothing erotic or sensual about it, it's just a handshake, right? So what happens if someone shakes your hand, and holds on to it a second or two too long? You freak out."

Sexual energy always exists between men and women, Friedman says. That's the way God created us. So synagogues that don't separate men from women on the grounds that you're not supposed to notice the gender of the person sitting next to you are striving for the impossible. "You're either in a congregation of *tzaddikim,* or of the living dead. Either way, why would you want to belong?" Physical contact between the sexes is powerful stuff, he continues. It needs to be contained through modest dress and behavior, not only to prevent sinning, but also to heighten legitimate sexuality. "If shaking hands with a man means nothing, if walking around naked means nothing, then what's left? That's the tragedy. The man who's had dozens of women by the time he's thirty—that's tragic. The man who gets excited when a woman even brushes past him—that man is still alive."

It's Day Four of a week-long summer session at Bais Chana, Chabad's Minneapolis-based program for women who are moving toward greater religious observance—a crash course in Hasidic Judaism for *ba'alei teshuva*. Friedman, Bais Chana's educational director and keynote lecturer, is holding forth on his favorite topic: intimacy and relationships. Friedman knows how to work a crowd and how to present Lubavitch philosophy to the outside world. A popular speaker on the national Jewish circuit, author of dozens of books and tapes aimed at the newly and the not-yet religious, Friedman has been with Bais Chana since it opened its doors in 1971. He's Chabad's *ba'al teshuva* rabbi, having shepherded more than 10,000 girls and women through Bais Chana's doors these past thirty years, together with Bais Chana cofounders and Chabad's Midwest directors, Rabbi Moshe and Mindy Feller.

"When we first came to Minneapolis, people said, Who needs them?" Moshe Feller says. "But when we started schlepping their kids back from Hare Krishna and Christianity, they saw what we could do."

In its first decade Bais Chana, named after the Rebbe's mother, drew mostly college-age women from non-observant homes. "They were more combative, more confrontational," recalls Rabbi Feller. By the early 1990s, attendance was down, reflecting a more conservative, less fragmented society. In the late nineties, enrollment was on the rise again. "When there's turbulence in the country, that's when the youth are looking for spirituality, and Chabad Houses send us more girls," says Mrs. Feller. "In more complacent times, we get more older women, more married women."

Bais Chana turned out a lot of full-fledged *ba'alei teshuva* in those early years. One was Hinda Leah Sharfstein, who dropped out of her freshman year of college in 1980 to attend the school. Today she lives in Crown Heights and is the program's executive director and founder of its alumni association, Bais Chana Women International. The women who attend Bais Chana programs are "a reflection of the times," she says. In 1980 "cultural mores had broken down, and people were left to grapple with what remained." The women who showed up in the nineties seemed more Jewishly savvy, Sharfstein says. "I've noticed over the years that people have a greater spiritual vocabulary. You can talk about 'God creating every moment,' and people get it, without explanations."

The changes at Bais Chana are similar to those observed throughout the Chabad movement. Shlichim around the country report that *ba'alei teshuva* of the twenty-first century aren't the same as those of the 1970s or '80s. "Chabad today is more about working with families," says Rabbi Zalman Bukiet, Chabad emissary in Boca Raton. "It's different work than on campus in the sixties and seventies, when we worked with guys rolling in off the streets in their dungarees. Today we're in residential areas, dealing with family problems, relationships. People who come to Chabad Houses today want to learn slowly. They're not teenagers going wild."

This particular Bais Chana session is a one-week course called "The Soul of Torah/The Nature of the Soul." It's the last of three week-long women-only sessions this summer and will be followed by a couples' program, something Bais Chana added a few years ago. Like every Bais Chana course, "The Soul of Torah" has participants in the classroom from 8 A.M. until well past 2 A.M. A typical day begins with breakfast, then morning prayers, followed by two classes on *Tanya* and prayer that last until 1 P.M., when lunch is served. Morning classes always run over schedule, so there's never time for the planned after-lunch break. The afternoon is filled with classes on marriage and relationships, and a talk on female modesty. Sometime around 9 P.M., the long day concludes with a final marathon session led by Rabbi Friedman. His evening talks are loosely based on *Tanya,* but the discussion invariably breaks down quickly into a question-and-answer free-for-all between Friedman and the women who have come to learn from him.

By 9 P.M., Friedman is seated at a desk in the front of the classroom, his hands folded in front of him, an expression of mock severity on his face. Then, slowly, he starts to smile. The smile widens, a growing crescent moon peeking out from the long gray-and-white beard that wafts down to the top of his desk. For a full minute he says nothing, just sits and smiles wordlessly at the crowd, which itself falls silent. What is he thinking? What mystical secrets is he about to reveal? Then he begins to speak, softly, slowly, pausing to listen to his own words between sentences, making sure that they convey just what he wants to say. Friedman is a compelling speaker, in a low-key rather than a rabble-rousing way. He speaks in simple, direct language about male-female relationships, tapping into contemporary fears and desires as adroitly as any writer for *Cosmopolitan* magazine. But in the next sentence he's soaring through the sublime heights of the *Tanya,* talking with heartbreaking sincerity about serving God with joy and humbling oneself through daily prayer. The combination—Chabad's special ability to infuse the commonplace with the divine—is riveting. Plus, the guy tells a good joke. What he conveys with a smile and a raised eyebrow is priceless.

Tonight, Friedman had a talk prepared on the ten *sefirot,* or aspects of the Divine, as understood by the Kabbalah. But the women have their own questions. What happens when we die? Does a fetus have consciousness in the womb? When the Messiah comes, who will be saved? That last question has particular relevance for this week's group. Ten of the twenty-three women are converts, past or potential. They've heard Friedman explain the traditional Jewish concept of the world-to-come, a time of universal immortality that will follow several hundred years of the preparatory Messianic Age. They know that, according to this belief, all nonrighteous people will die off during the Messianic Age, and the Jews and righteous Gentiles left alive at the advent of the world-to-come will be granted everlasting life. But how does one recognize a righteous Gentile? And what happens to the nonrighteous ones?

These women are worried about their non-Jewish parents and siblings. "Is my mother going to be in the world-to-come with me?" one worried convert from Texas wants to know. That's a tough one for Friedman. "Nonrighteous souls simply cease to be," he tells them. "But out of pure decency and respect, we should assume that your family is righteous and will be there with you."

Friedman doesn't shy away from discussing dybbuks, golems, reincarnation and other forms of soul-traveling, all of which are part and parcel of traditional Jewish belief, but that's not where he prefers to dwell. Judaism is about life in this world, he emphasizes. "If you concentrate on the world-to-come, you don't work hard enough to make this world better," he declares. Finding ways to inject holiness into the most mundane activity, elevating our awareness so that we serve God—and humanity—every waking moment, being true to ourselves and our partners—that's the goal, he stresses. And that's what Bais Chana's lessons on personal modesty, Torah, *Tanya,* and Jewish Law are meant to lead to, if they're understood correctly. It's not about worrying whether your wig is on straight, one instructor points out.

Friedman likes to talk about prayer, cutting through the students' preconceived notions of prayer as the rote repetition of Hebrew words they don't understand, presenting it instead the Hasidic way, as a difficult, heartfelt, sometimes excruciating process of approaching the Divine. Mouthing words you don't believe and directing them toward the Almighty is "like blasphemy," Friedman says. Hasidism demands that prayer come from the heart, always, no matter your mood. It's a conscious acknowledgment of God's presence in the world. The first prayer an observant Jew says upon waking in the morning begins *modeh ani,* "here I stand." It expresses the person's awareness that he or she is alive only because God so wills it, which knowledge should compel Jews to serve God in every action they perform. That's an awesome responsibility, Friedman points out.

This group of Bais Chana students is unusual. First of all, the large number of converts is atypical. Three of the converts are African-American women, two of them already wearing the *sheitels* that proclaim their status as observant Jewish wives. Several women are in their late fifties and early sixties. Two are still in high school. There's a massage therapist from Berkeley; a baby boomer English teacher from New Hampshire; a college student from Boston; a Queens native who learned her Bible in the church she joined with her first husband; five South American women, including an eighteen-year-old ballerina from Paraguay; and a recent immigrant from Moscow who used to produce the Russian-language TV version of *Who Wants to Be a Millionaire?* Only a handful are complete newbies to Judaism. Most have been studying for at least a year with their local Chabad rabbis and are here to see whether they're ready to take the next step toward leading an observant life. A few already consider themselves Lubavitchers. They nod their heads sagely as Friedman speaks, sometimes answering the other women's questions in his stead.

The next morning, the fifth day of the program, just seven of the women have managed to make the scheduled 8 A.M. breakfast call. The rest are too exhausted from last night's singing and dancing, which went on well past 2 A.M. Carol,* from Milwaukee, is debating whether to use

---

*The names of all the women in this section have been changed.

her Hebrew name for the rest of the program. One of the previous day's talks discussed the mystical benefits contained in a Jew's Hebrew name, which has to do with the kabbalistic significance of the Hebrew letters. *Ba'alei teshuva* routinely adopt Hebrew names, or a similar-sounding Yiddish name, when they join the Lubavitch fold. "Suddenly, this week, I've felt awkward using the name Carol," she muses. "But I won't ask my family to call me by my Hebrew name. That would be too weird."

Baila, also from Milwaukee, talks about feeling more distant from her family since she put on her *sheitel* and began identifying as an observant woman. "My sisters like it. They say it looks better than my own hair. They're very supportive. The distancing comes from me."

Twenty-six-year-old Yael is walking around the room, picking up used paper cups and plates. "Look at all the garbage we've created in the last twenty-four hours," she clucks. "I wish the Chabad Houses were more ecologically minded. When you have eight or ten kids, you can't just take, take, take from the environment." Yael is a New Age spiritual seeker from Berkeley. She studies massage and bodywork, prays with several Jewish Renewal congregations in the Bay Area, and became observant after a year in a Jerusalem yeshiva. Yael loves the praying, singing and dancing at Bais Chana but doesn't have a lot of patience for the classes. "I'm here more for the atmosphere," she admits. Although she walked out of the lecture on personal modesty, she approves of the practice. "I want people to see my inner grace," she states. Her week at Bais Chana has helped convince her to seek a career in the Jewish world and has further strengthened her resolve to "live within a Torah framework," but she's not about to make any major life changes. "Crown Heights is not for me," she declares.

Linda, who writes and teaches English as a second language at a university in New England, is wearing a loose-fitting long skirt, blouse, and head kerchief in soft earth tones. In her early sixties, she has almost finished studying for conversion with her local Chabad rabbi. "He doesn't call it 'conversion,' he says we're 'learning,'" she says. "He keeps me at arm's length. I never thought, as a longtime liberal, that I'd end up studying Judaism with a right-wing conservative Republican." Like a good number of the women in this room, Linda came to Judaism after a personal tragedy. Her daughter, a Peace Corps volunteer in Rwanda, saw her students massacred before her eyes by marauding guerrillas and later committed suicide. Linda found no solace in her local Unitarian church, or in the Christian God she'd grown up with. A Jewish friend took her to synagogue, and something in the words of Torah resonated. But it was a Reform congregation, which Linda found "too Christian—I sang in the choir."

Then she came across Chabad. "The rabbi is so amazing. He lives the Torah. He's totally focused on it." Several years later she keeps Shabbat, maintains a kosher home, and is ready for the next step. "I'm attracted to Hasidism," she admits with a gentle smile. "My Christian friends don't know what to say. My Jewish friends think I'm crazy. They say, 'What about being modern Orthodox? Why this?'"

Linda's love affair with Chabad isn't blind. She's critical of what she sees as the overeager attitude of some of the *ba'alei teshuva* to do whatever it takes to fit in with the Lubavitch community, worrying about the length of their skirts and insisting that no inch of Israel should be surrendered. She's also distrustful of all the talk about reincarnation and the Messianic Age. But that's not the essence of Chabad, she insists. You have to dig deeper, she says; you have to find the beauty in the Torah-committed lifestyle. She closes her eyes and smiles.

Rebecca, a twenty-four-year-old graduate student from Boston, is one of the few participants this week who fits the classic Bais Chana profile of the young Jew looking for her roots. Rebecca grew up in a nonobservant home, and her parents have not taken kindly to her decision three months ago to stop wearing pants. "They don't know I'm here at Bais Chana," she admits. It's hard to become more observant while living in the secular world, she says. That's why she came to all three sessions this summer at Bais Chana. She wanted to see what it would be like to live surrounded by Torah-observant Jews.

"These weeks have helped me understand what will make me happy, which is to lead an observant life. I know now that I want to keep Shabbat and *kashrut*. I want to be *shomer negiah* [respectful of the prohibition against touching members of the opposite sex outside of one's immediate family]. My family thinks it's selfish of me, but it's not, because I'm fulfilling a higher purpose. I'm doing what Hashem wants." Returning to her graduate school world will be a shock after three weeks in this religious cocoon. "I'm going to have a lot of challenges. But I've made the decision to pursue this. We're taught, 'Think good, and it will be good.' God doesn't give us any conflicts we can't handle."

After dinner, forty-year-old Rhonda sneaks out of a prayer session and comes into the kitchen in search of coffee. Finding only soy milk on the counter (dinner had been *fleishig,* i.e., meat-based), she makes a face. "I'm having a hard enough time with the long skirts, and now, no milk?" Rhonda is a vivacious, talkative, redheaded New Yorker who breezes in and out of the classroom at will. Her leopard-print miniskirt and black vinyl raincoat are at odds with the modest attire favored by the other students, but she would be shocked if anyone suggested she was trying to make a statement. This is who she is, she says.

Rhonda turned her back on her Jewish upbringing when she married a Catholic twenty years ago. Although she thought she'd "spontaneously combust" when she walked down the aisle at her wedding and saw a huge crucifix in front of her, that didn't stop her from following her husband to a Lutheran congregation, where she taught Sunday school. A year ago she had a Jewish reawakening, which she says was sparked by realizing that the Christian world had too many versions of the Bible. "Which one was true?" she wondered. At a Kabbalah lecture in Manhattan, a visiting Chabad rabbi suggested she light Shabbat candles, just to see how it felt. It felt good.

That Friday-night prayer over the candles was the only Jewish ritual Rhonda knew before this week. "I've learned more here in five days than in a year of Kabbalah classes. For a woman my age to find a place with so many other women in similar positions is phenomenal. It was like coming home." Rhonda is all fired up now to continue her Jewish education. Although she's just learned her first Hebrew blessings, she's already asked Rabbi Friedman whether she should move to Crown Heights. Friedman suggested she take it more slowly. "He said the Rebbe told us to cover every part of the world with *mitzvot,* so it's better for me to stay where I am, doing *mitzvot,* than to move into the [Lubavitch] community." Rhonda thought that was an "incredible" answer. Like a surprising number of students at this Bais Chana session, she had no idea that any authentic Jewish option exists outside Crown Heights. She was relieved to find out, as she says, that the Rebbe doesn't want her to leave Queens. "I thought I'd have to assimilate into their culture, but now I get to stay where I am."

Rabbi Friedman has dealt with plenty of Rhondas, Lindas, and Rebeccas in the thirty years he's been working with *ba'alei teshuva.* Bais Chana was first conceived by the Fellers as a way to use a campus Chabad House that emptied of students every June. In 1971, the Fellers and Friedmans sent out flyers to six nearby colleges, inviting women to come study Judaism for a few weeks that summer. "We thought we'd give classes from four P.M. to nine P.M. Eighteen women showed up—former SDS radicals, political activists, anti-Establishment nonconformists. They had a lot of energy. There was no way they were going to wait until four o'clock. They were angry, they hated the world, they didn't want sightseeing, and they weren't on vacation. They wanted to learn." That first summer Friedman taught eighteen hours a day. "I'd fall asleep on the carpet, wake up in the morning, and start again."

Their second summer, enrollment grew to 40, and was up to 104 the third year. In 1973 they added a winter session, and in the nineties they began offering special sessions for teenagers and couples. But no matter how the student body has changed, Friedman says that the core of what he teaches remains the same: *Hasidus,* or Chabad philosophy. He sneaks in a little basic Torah, of course, and sometimes he calls the course "Kabbalah," but it's really all *Hasidus.* It's about how to make Judaism work for these women in their everyday lives. "We're not interested in them becoming kabbalists. We're interesting in them being Jews."

Like many Chabad shlichim, Friedman likes to downplay his own credentials. "I never finished elementary school," he boasts. "I'm a dropout. I only learned English after I was married. That's why I have a Brooklyn accent." (He doesn't.) More seriously, Friedman fully supports the general Lubavitch disinterest in secular education. He acknowledges that shlichim lack breadth of knowledge, but they make up for it in sharpness of mind and the depth of their Jewish learning. "Anyone who goes to yeshiva is not starving the brain. The intelligence, the intellectual challenge, the brilliance, the insight, the depth, the wisdom—Shakespeare does not compare. The real question is, Why didn't Shakespeare learn *Hasidus?*" He also agrees with the Rebbe's distaste for the media. That doesn't mean a Lubavitcher shouldn't read newspapers or watch TV news at all, Friedman says. "It means that as a policy, as an ideal, it's unnecessary."

Television as entertainment is on another plane entirely. "It's unhealthy, destructive, and dangerous, not just for Hasidim, but for children and other living things," Friedman quips. "There is no good television. Years ago, the content was 'father knows best.' Now, it's 'your father is an idiot.'" But, he admits, "I watch it." And he listens to the radio, and he reads the newspaper headlines. No one's perfect. That's why we have *mitzvot,* he points out. Life is a process, a constant striving toward the good, without ever quite reaching it. The good comes with that striving.

And that's why unaffiliated Jews respond to Chabad, he believes. Chabad doesn't blame Jews for what they don't do, but rewards them for what they're trying to do, and accepts them as Jewish no matter what they do.

"Our entire outreach is based on the assumption that there is no such thing as an unaffiliated Jew. If you're Jewish, you're Jewish, even if you don't want to be. It's permanent. You're stuck. The Jew in you needs nurturing, not creating. You can't create a Jew. You already are Jewish, insanely Jewish." What caused the twentieth-century crisis in American Jewish life had to do with a young generation rebelling against parents and grandparents who told them they had to eat like a Jew, dress like a Jew, and pray like a Jew in order to be Jewish. "Something good, something true in their Jewish souls said, 'That can't be true.' And just to prove it, they stopped eating like a Jew and dressing like a Jew. And guess what? They're still Jewish." Friedman says he agrees "100 percent" with this youthful rebellion. "To suggest that a Jew is Jewish only on certain conditions is to undermine our whole existence and identity. I think people respond to Chabad because we agree on this very pivotal point."

Jews who feel comfortable with Chabad are not just responding to the movement's tolerance of their non-observance. "That's true, but that's not what does it. What does it is, we say, You're as Jewish as I am. This is what the Jewish soul wants to hear. Unaffiliated Jews, rebellious Jews, dropout Jews, born-again Christian Jews, they just want to hear one thing: You're very Jewish. They're starved for it. And once you tell them that, they say, 'So what do you want me to do, put on tefillin? Sure. Daven? OK.' It's not a gimmick. It's not a PR approach. It's not because we're nice people. It's getting to the heart of the Jews. This is our mission."

The love Friedman feels for the Jewish women who attend his Bais Chana classes and for the many, largely non-observant Jews who show up for his nationwide lectures shines from his face. You can feel it in his speech. It's not a squishy, anything-goes kind of love. It's a serious, bonding affection that suggests, We're on the same page. We are family. He treats his students with respect and the same kind of humility he teaches them about, listening carefully to the most naïve, even outlandish questions, and always offering a carefully reasoned response. But he's no pushover. He knows how to probe a sentiment he suspects is not heartfelt, and he can sometimes leave a questioner uneasy.

Friedman is not interested in quick promises or overnight conversions. "You have to go slow," he cautions. "This isn't the sixties, where you could drop everything, run to yeshiva, and grow a beard. Most *ba'alei teshuva* today are not as visible, not as identifiable. These are people who have settled lives, they can't make radical changes. They have wives, husbands, families, mortgages. So maybe they keep Friday night. They can't keep the whole Shabbos. And maybe they make their kitchen kosher, but they can't promise what they'll eat in the airplane. They're not the people who get interviewed, because they're not radical enough, but these are the real *ba'alei teshuva*. They've 'come back' to Judaism. These are the ones whose children will be Jewish."

CHAPTER 13

GOD'S LITTLE SOLDIERS:
Educating the Next Generation

In the darkened ballroom of the Brooklyn Marriott, between the roast chicken and the soy-ice-cream dessert at the annual convention of Chabad emissaries, a small boy steps up to the podium. Even stretching his neck, he barely reaches the microphone.

"My family and I are shlichim of the Rebbe in Salt Lake City," he begins. Then, with a cocky grin, nine-year-old Avremi Zippel delivers a stream of Borscht Belt one-liners, a pint-sized, squeaky-voiced, *tzitzit*-wearing Henny Youngman.

"In the entire state of Utah, there are just ten pair of *payes*. I have two of them." *Ba-da-boom!* "My teacher is a very nice woman. She also happens to be my mother. I don't get homesick when I go to school, because my school is at home." *Light touch of the cymbals.* "As you can imagine, life under these conditions is not exactly a piece of cake. They have no kosher cake in Utah."

Now that he has warmed up the crowd, Avremi introduces the evening's headline act in as booming a voice as he can manage. "Please join me in welcoming my fellow young shlichim, marching forward to greet Moshiach. Troops, forward march!" With great musical fanfare and rhythmic applause from the 1,400 seated emissaries, the doors to the main ballroom burst open and two lines of little boys begin marching in. More than 300 of them, all wearing identical blue T-shirts, their *tzitzit* peeking out from below. Some are so small that their adult-size yarmulkes cover their entire heads, reaching down to their forehead. These are the sons of the shlichim, boys eight to twelve years old. Some, like Avremi Zippel, live in remote Chabad outposts with their parents and are home-schooled by their mothers. Others have been sent away to Lubavitch schools in New York, Montreal, Detroit, or Los Angeles and come home only for holidays. This weekend is a rare chance for them to spend time with their fathers, even if it's just a few hurried minutes.

The music grows louder, the clapping intensifies, and young rabbis jump up here and there to snap photos. This goes beyond the usual kvelling of proud parents and grandparents. These kids represent the next generation, the future standard-bearers of Lubavitch activism. They will be the fulfillment of the Rebbe's dream, leading the Jewish world into the Messianic Age.

But hearing "Troops, forward march!" coming out of the mouth of a child is jarring. So are the words to the song the kids sing as they march into the room, a song that has them "marching forward to victory" in the Rebbe's service. Amid the friendly smiles and nonjudgmental acceptance of Chabad's outreach practice, there's plenty of militaristic terminology in the movement's literature and speeches. Chabad shlichim refer to themselves openly as "soldiers of the Rebbe." The Lubavitch-sponsored children's movement, established in 1980 and open to all Jewish children, is called *Tzivos Hashem,* literally, "the armies of God." Children join the movement as privates, and move up through the ranks as they obtain points for doing mitzvahs, eventually attaining the rank of general when they have amassed 1,000 points.

The Lubavitcher Rebbe set the tone early on for all this army talk, stating on numerous occasions that Chabad—indeed, all of Orthodox Judaism—is engaged in a "spiritual war" with the forces of secularism, atheism, materialism, and all the other "isms" that draw young Jews away from tradition. His shlichim were quick to adopt the terminology. "We are living in a time when we are fighting the battle for *Yiddishkeit* against overwhelming odds," declared Rabbi Moshe Feller at a Chabad women's convention in 1963. "In times of war, God forbid, homes are converted into hospitals and fortresses . . . for it is war!"

The language, of course, is used metaphorically, and the uniforms and marching are no different than what Boy and Girl Scouts do. There is no weapons training. The only "weapons" used in the battle for Jewish souls are persuasion and attractive programming. And the "enemy" is internal: the *yetzer ha'ra,* or "evil inclination" inside every human being that turns him or her away from doing good deeds. But children—and sometimes adults—don't always make those fine distinctions. Rivkah Slonim remembers how fired up she'd get as a Lubavitch kid in Crown Heights, where she learned a song at summer camp that was similar to what Avremi Zippel and his friends were singing:

> *From 770 we're marching out*
> *On to victory, without a doubt*
> *From the corners four we're marching happily*
> *Nation after nation we are conquering.*

"When you're a child, you have a very primitive idea of what that means," Slonim says. "You're going to come in, and you're going to give every single Jew Shabbos candles or tefillin, and you're going to change them. And you're going to conquer. I don't think that's what the Rebbe taught or wanted. I think it's the way in which it has been interpreted, and it's a very childish way of looking at what he wanted to do. He wasn't trying to change people from the outside in. He wanted to transform them from the inside out. And I don't think Lubavitchers always understand that themselves."

The label "Tzivos Hashem" comes directly from the Torah, where God refers to the Israelites he has just taken out of Egypt as his "armies," liberated from enslavement to Pharaoh's will and now free to devote themselves full-time to the service of God. That's how Chabadniks see themselves—as men and women guarding the outposts of the Jewish world, on constant watch against the incursions of secularism. The concept is central to the educational values they try to inculcate in their children through a carefully structured yeshiva system designed to turn out God-fearing young men and women, learned in Jewish Law, committed to the Hasidic lifestyle, and skilled in the Jewish outreach techniques they'll need in their future lives as shlichim.

Chabad *Hasidus* has always emphasized education. The first Lubavitcher Rebbe urged independent thinking among his Hasidim, telling them that each Hasid has to find his or her own way to God, using the rebbe as a guide and teacher rather than a crutch. That means constant, lifelong study for every Lubavitch man and woman.

The fifth Lubavitcher Rebbe established Chabad's first yeshiva system in 1896 in White Russia. The Tomchei Tmimim schools were a new phenomenon in Jewish life, a place where boys learned, along with the Talmud, mystical teachings and practices, such as setting aside time for individual contemplation before prayer, so that prayer truly comes from the heart. The sixth Rebbe extended the Chabad school system to girls by creating young women's study groups in pre–World War II Riga. When he moved Chabad operations to New York in March 1940, he immediately opened a yeshiva for young men. During the first months, when classes were held in a rented space in Brooklyn, there were barely two dozen students, many from orthodox but non-Lubavitch families. Within ten years Yosef Yitzchak Schneersohn had laid the foundation for what was to become the largest Hasidic educational operation in the country, a yeshiva system that also served many non-Hasidic children and young adults, thus spreading the Chabad message outside the Lubavitch community and, eventually, throughout the world. The first boys' yeshiva was joined in 1942 by the Beth Rivkah elementary girls' school, which opened with less than three dozen pupils in a Brooklyn storefront. A girls' high school was founded in 1955, and a teachers' training seminary in 1962. Other Lubavitch girls' schools eventually opened around the world, on the Beth Rivkah model.

Along with setting up an educational system for his own flock, the sixth Rebbe was instrumental in creating the Jewish day school movement, designed for the general Jewish population. During his first year in America he sent Lubavitch yeshiva students to New Jersey and Connecticut. These young men would speak in Orthodox synagogues, urging congregants to allow them to teach Torah and Hebrew to the boys and girls in their communities. At first that meant only a handful of pupils in two or three towns, taught by yeshiva students who would travel in from Brooklyn once a week by bus or train. Those early classes quickly mushroomed and took root, leading to the first Lubavitch-run day schools in Bridgeport and New Haven, Connecticut; Providence, Rhode Island; Newark, New Jersey; Boston, Springfield, and Worcester, Massachusetts; Pittsburgh, Pennsylvania; and Buffalo, New York. These were the precursors of the religious schools run by virtually every Chabad emissary couple today for the children of largely non-observant Jewish families.

But the Chabad school system designed for their own children, for the rearing of the next generation of Lubavitcher Hasidim, is much more rigorous and all-encompassing than the schools set up for the children of Chabad's clientele. It roughly follows the model set down in Eastern Europe in the nineteenth century, expanded to include girls. Formal education for the Lubavitch boy begins at the age of three, when a young boy's locks, allowed to grow untouched since birth, are shorn for the first time. On the morning of his first day at school, his father or rabbi-teacher puts a few drops of honey on his tongue as he pronounces the first few letters of the Hebrew alphabet, signifying a lifetime engagement in Torah study in a world in which learning is equated with sweetness. The young boy then begins *cheder,* where he learns Hebrew, the Torah, and eventually Mishnah and some Talmud until around bar mitzvah age, when he graduates to a *yeshiva gedolah,* a sort of "high school" that segues into "college."

Yeshiva study for a teenage Lubavitch boy is devoted almost entirely to the Talmud, supplemented by Hasidic texts that are virtually all discourses and talks of the seven Lubavitcher Rebbes. Yeshiva continues at the high school level until age seventeen or eighteen, when a successful student will move on to three or four years of what is still called yeshiva but is really a more intensive training for a future life as rabbi and shliach. During those "college" years, the young man will be shipped off for a year or two with a group of ten peers to a Chabad yeshiva far from his home turf, where he will continue his own studies while serving as mentor to the younger students. He typically spends each summer and holiday break in Chabad's Merkos Shlichus, or "Peace Corps," which may send him off to lead Passover Seders in Asia, or team him up with a fellow-student for two months of driving through Africa or the Midwest, visiting isolated Jewish communities to hand out books, *kasher* kitchens, put up mezuzahs, lead prayer services, and even officiate at bar mitzvahs. Following this period the young man headed for a life of shlichus will study for another year or so to prepare for his *smicha,* or rabbinical ordination. After that, it's marriage, perhaps another year of study in a *kollel,* a yeshiva for married men, and then on to Oshkosh or Athens with his new bride for a life of *shlichus* in the field.

Girls follow a similar path, minus the intensive Talmud study and the years of prerabbinic and rabbinic training. Lubavitch girls and boys attend preschool together, but at the age of three they're split up and the girls enter the Beth Rivkah school system, which all Chabad girls attend through twelfth grade. Ambitious girls then go on to seminary, which is loosely constructed to include at least one year of student teaching, with those destined for future lives as Chabad emissaries usually helping a shliach couple in a remote outpost. Formal study in the seminary lasts either one or two years, and can, if the young woman is so inclined, lead to a teaching certificate that will enable her to teach in non-Chabad Jewish schools (at least until she and her husband get their own Chabad school up and running). It is no longer typical for Lubavitch women to marry while still in seminary, although it does happen. Lubavitch boys, on the other hand, wait until they've finished their "college" years at yeshiva before approaching the matchmakers in search of a wife. More and more Lubavitch men wait even longer, getting their rabbinical ordination and studying or working for a further year or two before settling down to married life.

There is a fundamental reason why Lubavitch men and women are educated differently: Traditional Jewish teaching says that women are exempt from time-bound commandments, such as putting on tefillin and praying in a *minyan,* or prayer quorum, so that they can tend without interruption to their primary duties of home care and child-rearing. Whether or not that means women are actually prohibited from putting on tefillin or praying as part of a *minyan* or studying the Talmud that is the source text for all these laws and discussions is something that has been hotly contested in Jewish circles for at least 2,000 years. Many Orthodox rabbis still forbid Talmud study for women as "heresy," following the line set down by the second-century sage Rabbi Eliezer ben Hyrcanus, who stated, "If a man teaches his daughter Torah, it is as though he taught her obscenity." Other rabbis look for a more lenient approach, following the spirit of the teachings of Maimonides, who ruled in the twelfth century that a woman who studies Torah will receive a heavenly reward, but not as great as that given a man, for he is commanded to learn, while she is only doing it of her own desire.

As is the case with many issues of Orthodox belief and practice, Chabad has its own spin on the matter of women's education. Chabadniks proudly relate stories about the grandmother of the first Rebbe, whose command of the *Shulchan Aruch,* the multivolume code of Jewish Law, was so great, it is said, that she put to shame the men in her community. Shneur Zalman himself, we are told, studied Torah openly with his daughter.

"That women have to study has always been the case in Chabad, but what they study has changed," says Chana Gorowitz, dean of the Beth Rivkah teachers' training seminary in Crown Heights. "There's a more sophisticated study of *Hasidus* than when I was in school. When I was at Beth Rivkah, we studied *Chumash* [the Five Books of Moses] with a Hasidic twist, and *Tanya.* But there are many more volumes of the Rebbe's writings published now that weren't around then." While Jewish education in Lubavitch girls' schools today is certainly not nearly as rigorous as the education boys receive, it does go beyond what other Hasidic girls receive, mirroring a typical modern Orthodox girls' education: Bible with commentaries, a little Talmud, Jewish law and history, and the writings of the movement's leaders.

Chabad's outreach imperative is another reason why Lubavitch women are expected to keep up their Torah learning throughout their lives. Most shlichot in the field teach Bible classes to local women, and Lubavitch girls participate in the same kind of stop-you-on-the-street outreach as their brothers: the boys approaching men with tefillin, and the girls handing out Sabbath candles to women.

In some areas Lubavitch women are better educated than their husbands. Because Talmud study is so important for boys and anything that takes them away from it is considered a waste of valuable time, the typical Lubavitcher male's secular education ends at the sixth grade. Lubavitch girls continue their math, science, history, and literature classes through high school. This doesn't mean that Chabad men don't know about current events—they read newspapers and magazines, and listen to the daily news on the radio. But in the course of their outreach work they'll often defer to their wives on questions of American history, nineteenth-century novels, or the correct spelling of English words.

The rigid division between men and women in so much of Hasidic life, which takes the gender distinctions of Orthodox Jewish ritual and extends them tenfold, is pointed to by many critics of Hasidism as evidence of women's secondary status in this highly regulated world. But Chabadniks, not surprisingly, don't see it that way, and shlichim—especially the women—are often challenged to defend their way of life from charges of gender oppression.

Vivi Deren, a shlicha in Stamford, Connecticut, speaks regularly on the national Chabad circuit, usually about gender equality in Orthodox Judaism. Her argument has much in common with new feminist thinking, although she would probably be uncomfortable with that equation. Western society, according to Vivi, has artificially elevated the public sphere—career, money, social position—while devaluing the private spheres of home and family, which traditional Judaism considers of primary importance. The Jewish woman keeps the family together and transmits values to the next generation, thus fulfilling not just an important role, but the central role in Jewish society.

So what, Vivi says, if an Orthodox woman may not read from the Torah scroll during services? Real Judaism, the way Lubavitchers live it, is practiced every day, every hour, in the home, not just on weekends in the synagogue. Focusing on what women may or may not do in the synagogue, she says, places undue emphasis on what is really secondary in the Jewish scheme of things. Women get to bring new life into the world, she continues emphatically; nothing men can do could possibly compete with that honor.

Vivi has been battling stereotypes about Hasidic women for a long time. In 1972, when she was barely twenty and newly married, she spoke to a youth group from the Reform movement that was visiting Crown Heights. After her talk, one of the girls asked why Hasidic women are allowed to wear only black. "I just smiled. There I was, standing in front of her wearing a white dress with red polka dots. I kept smiling, but she didn't get it. There were other Hasidic women in the room in pastels and flowers. But this girl had read in a book that Hasidic women only wear black, and that was the image she had."

In 1974, Vivi and her husband, Yisrael, moved to Amherst, Massachusetts, to set up Chabad activities on the U-Mass campus. The women's movement had, she says, "reached a roiling boil," and Vivi was often asked to speak before Jewish audiences as a representative of the typical Hasidic woman. "The image was, you know, barefoot, pregnant, in the kitchen. Very condescending. If you could make chicken soup or bake challah, that was enough. It made me think of the slogan on the Beth Rivkah stationery when I was going to school: 'Raising the Jewish mothers of tomorrow.' I was always embarrassed by that, even though we didn't have courses on vacuuming or kugel. Raising the Jewish mothers of tomorrow actually meant we had to learn *Chumash* and Rashi and *tefillot,* materials of substance. It was a given: In order to be a Jewish mother, you had to have Jewish knowledge."

When Vivi talks, she is not justifying a way of life that she secretly fears is oppressive. Neither is she speaking naïvely, as someone who knows no other way of being. With great care she conjures up a world, the world she grew up in, where everyone's roles, men and women alike, are circumscribed by an all-encompassing set of rules called *Halacha.* It's not a case of men being allowed to do more than women, but a cosmic scheme in which man and woman, adult and child, Jew and non-Jew, each has his or her delineated function. "Growing up, it didn't occur to us to want [equal rights]," she says thoughtfully. "We lived with a Judaism that was for the most part genderless, but which had within it certain very limited, very prescribed roles that were specifically for men or for women. We all kept Shabbos and we all kept kosher and we all learned Torah and we all went to the Rebbe and we all davened and sang *niggunim.*"

It's somewhat ironic that Vivi is delivering this recitation while standing in front of her stove in Stamford, stirring a huge cauldron of soup for the upcoming Shabbat. (She is, however, neither barefoot nor pregnant.) Two of her six children are in the kitchen, talking to her at once. Twenty-six-year-old Mendel is flying out that night to Vienna for a friend's wedding, and then on to Moscow the next day to check out a job opportunity. Chani, twenty-one, is debating whether or not to drive with him to Kennedy Airport to catch the overnight flight to Brazil, so she can attend her cousin's bar mitzvah there the next morning. She'll have to fly back to New York right away, so as not to miss Friday morning's Open House at the Hebrew School where she teaches, but neither the ticket price nor the long hours in the air factor into her decision. She's only afraid she might be late for Open House. Anyone who thinks Lubavitchers are culturally isolated has only to look at this family's frequent-flyer mileage, typical of most shlichim. Shliach families are far-flung, making births, deaths, weddings, and bar mitzvahs all the more precious. From their early teens, Lubavitchers think nothing of hopping flights at a moment's notice to represent the family or lend a hand to another shliach. The Rebbe discouraged excessive expenditures, but as shlichim become further spread out, people's understanding of "excessive" has shifted.

This kind of travel was not common when Vivi was growing up in the

1950s in Nashville, Tennessee, the daughter of Chabad shlichim Rabbi Zalman and Risya Posner. Crown Heights was far away and rarely visited. Vivi knew from a very early age that she and her family were "different." There were other Sabbath-observant Jews in Nashville, but they were all elderly; she was the only observant child. Zalman and Risya never apologized to their children for making them grow up as miniature shlichim. On the contrary, Vivi says. "Being different was a fact of life. My parents communicated so effectively that it was not a burden." Vivi remembers walking to *shul* with her father and seeing other children point and laugh at his long beard and yarmulke. "My father was so totally not affected by it," she says. "It didn't touch him in the slightest. He didn't have to say anything to us, it was so clear he was proud of what he was and that anyone who didn't appreciate that was to be pitied."

Not only was he not embarrassed, Rabbi Posner also had a sense of humor about looking different. With his dark, untrimmed beard and swarthy skin, he bore a striking resemblance to a certain Latin American dictator. Once, while walking in the halls at Vanderbilt University's hospital, a man ran up to him to ask whether he was a well-known author scheduled to give a lecture that evening. "No, I'm Fidel Castro," Rabbi Posner replied quite nonchalantly, at which the man nodded and continued on his way.

Because they lived so far from any Lubavitch community, the Posners had to work overtime to make sure their children knew who they were and why they were doing what they were doing. Vivi recalls that, unlike Lubavitch homes today, where the Rebbe is a constant presence and children learn stories about him as soon as they can talk, Schneerson was a somewhat mysterious figure to her as a child. She and her siblings were brought up on stories about the heroic Lubavitcher Hasidim working underground in the Soviet Union. Their stories of secret mikvahs and harsh Siberian exile were bedtime tales for Chabad children in the 1950s and 1960s. "It was all very hush-hush. We were careful not to talk about anything that could endanger people still there. But they were real people doing real things." Still, Vivi always knew that the Rebbe was the reason they did those things. "The Rebbe was the one who was guiding, leading, showing the way. When my father got a phone call from the Rebbe's secretary, I saw the way he would act. It wasn't just a phone call, it was an event."

On the corner of Brooklyn and Lefferts avenues in Crown Heights stands a modern four-story building whose front archway is painted a cheerful lavender. This is Beth Rivkah, the cornerstone of Chabad's school system for girls. Home to nearly 2,000 girls, kindergarten through eighth grade, the $15-million, 125,000-square-foot school opened its doors in 1995, although final construction was not completed for another five years. About half the school's initial funding came from Revlon cosmetics tycoon Ronald Perelman.

Inside, girls dressed in regulation long-sleeved, high-necked blue blouses and mid-calf-length navy skirts, their hair short or neatly pulled back in ponytails, scurry between classrooms, chattering in English. (Similar banter in Chabad's Oholei Torah boys' school eight blocks away would more likely be in Yiddish.) The hallways are decorated with smiling photos of "students of the month," poetry from an English class, and letters written by some of the girls to then Israeli Prime Minister Ehud Barak urging more protection for Jewish settlers in the West Bank.

"Most of our families no longer speak Yiddish at home, so we have to introduce it as a second language," says school principal Chavi Altein. That reflects a sea change in Lubavitch life, testimony to their increased contact with the outside world and the numbers of *ba'alei teshuva* entering the community. It's a change that's become very apparent in the past ten years. Altein, a Crown Heights mother, says her first four children spoke only Yiddish at home, even though she, as a native English-speaker, had to make special efforts to keep it that way. By the time her eight-year-old was born, however, it seemed too awkward to speak what was essentially a foreign language in their home. That child had to learn Yiddish at school, in classes where most of the other youngsters were facing the same challenge. By the teenage years, Lubavitch boys are spending so much time with Yiddish texts that most of them are more fluent than the girls—another gender difference. And understanding Yiddish is critical for both sexes, Altein explains, for it's the language that links Lubavitchers to their rebbe. All of Schneerson's talks, carefully preserved on cassette and videotapes, are slowly being translated into Hebrew or English, but Lubavitch parents want their children to understand the Rebbe's words as he spoke them, in the original Yiddish.

Most Beth Rivkah students come from Lubavitch families in the neighborhood, but two busloads of non-Lubavitch girls are brought in from Flatbush every day. Daughters of shlichim posted in small towns or cities without Lubavitch schools begin showing up sporadically as boarding students from the fifth or sixth grade, but they are only a sprinkling until high school.

Beth Rivkah, like its boys' counterpart Oholei Torah, didn't always have such a high percentage of Lubavitch students. Chana Gorowitz, who graduated from the elementary school in 1955, estimates that just one-third of her classmates came from Lubavitch families. "Today, most of our girls are Lubavitch, because the other Jewish communities have started their own schools," she notes. She was in Beth Rivkah's pioneer high school class, which was founded, she says, because of the specific goals of the Lubavitch movement. "Our training at the time was, these are the girls that are going to go out to change the [Jewish] world. In those days, the [Jewish] world was wary of that. Lubavitch girls who went to other schools were constantly being challenged."

It's midmorning, so the Beth Rivkah girls are still learning their "Hebrew" subjects—Bible, Jewish Law, Hebrew, Yiddish, and teachings from the Rebbe. Hebrew subjects take up the first half of the school day, from 9 A.M. to 12:30. After a half-hour break for lunch, secular subjects, taught in English, take up the rest of the day until dismissal at 4 P.M. Those classes include grammar, literature, history, science, and math. "Jewish studies are our priority, but we try to keep an even balance," Altein says. Girls at the very youngest grades learn to read and write Hebrew not by using children's books, but by reading the words of the Hebrew Bible. By fourth grade, they're already moving on to the Prophets. Jewish Law is taught orally at the lower grades, but by sixth grade, the girls are tackling the *Shulchan Aruch*, or Code of Jewish Law, in the original Hebrew. Expectations are high. "An eighth-grader should be able to open a page of *Chumash* and give you the explanation of the *parasha* [that week's portion of the text] and Rashi's commentary," Altein says.

In one fifth-grade classroom, a young Lubavitch woman, just two years out of seminary, is teaching a class on Purim, which will fall during the next week. She stands in front of the class under a large portrait of the Rebbe, whose picture graces every room. As the teacher goes through the biblical story of Queen Esther, the secretly Jewish queen who saved her people from destruction at the hands of the evil Haman, she prompts the class with details from the story, and the girls finish her sentences with gleeful shouts.

"What does Haman want?" the teacher asks, wide-eyed, gesturing with her hands to tell the class she wants them to answer as a group. "Kill Mordechai!" the girls shout. "You know how hard it is to focus on something when you're thinking of something else, don't you?" the teacher smiles. "Yes!" the girls answer, giggling. "Last week, could you concentrate on your *Chumash*?" she asks. "No," they admit, playfully. "Why not?" the teacher asks with feigned innocence. "Because of the Purim party!" they shout. "That's right," the teacher continues. "And Haman, all he could think of was kill Mordechai, kill Mordechai. And what did King Ahashverus say to Esther? Raise your hands, girls."

Most of the girls raise their hands, a few more eagerly than others. The teacher calls on one girl, using her last name. In this class, as in every other one in the school, it's a necessity. Out of twenty-two girls in the room, ten are named Chaya Mushka, in honor of the Rebbe's late wife. At Oholei Torah, every other boy is named Menachem Mendel, after the Rebbe. It's customary among Lubavitchers to name children after previous rebbes and their wives, or biblical figures; since Schneerson's death, every young Lubavitch family has a Menachem Mendel and a Chaya Mushka.

"The king said, 'Whatever you want, I will give you,'" the girl responds. "That's right, but I want to hear the words of the Megillah [Book of Esther]," the teacher directs. The student obediently opens her Bible and reads the phrase again, in Hebrew. The teacher smiles. "Everything that happens in our life is what?" she asks. "Divine Providence!" the girls respond in unison. Yes, the teacher tells them, God always creates the medicine even before the disease it's meant to cure. She asks them to find proof of this in the text. They do. "God put Esther in the palace before the Jews needed her," one girl offers. "And God put the tree in the garden that Haman was hanged on later," another girl adds. The teacher nods approval. The concept of Divine Providence was one of the Rebbe's favorites, and it figures largely in Chabad videos and books for children.

Within fifteen minutes this teacher has covered all the major bases of a Chabad education. She's gotten the kids involved, both by asking them questions and encouraging them to work in groups, where they learn to help each other. She's taught them Hebrew, she's taught them Bible, and she managed to work in a key teaching of the Rebbe.

"We try to use any creative learning method available," Altein states. "Group work, cooperative learning, multiple-intelligence methods." Teachers are sent to frequent regional and national Chabad workshops, to be updated on the newest ways to keep kids interested while drumming information into their heads. At Beth Rivkah it seems to work. No girls are asleep at their desks. No one is talking back to the teachers. Discipline problems are not unknown, but are certainly much less frequent than in most schools.

Jewish history is a major focus of study at the school. In the lower grades it's taught mainly through Bible stories, which are read not as a spiritual guide, but as divinely ordained facts. To these girls Sarah, Rebecca, Rachel, and Leah are real people, treated like grandmothers whose stories form the early chapters of their family history. As the girls get older, Jewish history is taught more in context. They get their major dose of systematic Jewish history in sixth grade, which New York State law devotes to world history. But in Lubavitch hands, the sixth-grade world history curriculum is telescoped, becoming "What happened to the Jews when such-and-such was going on in the rest of the world?"

In one sixth-grade classroom at Beth Rivkah, the teacher is recounting the history of the Viking invasions of Britain. She's describing their great dragon-prowed sailing ships and is moving excitedly around the room, waving her hands in the air to show how large and elaborately planned were Viking war expeditions. "They came in, and they would plunder. They killed, they burned, wherever they went. People were terrified of them." That's pretty standard Viking fare for an American classroom. But now she adds the Jewish twist. "They plundered churches and synagogues especially. Why? Because that's where the gold, silver, and rich materials were. The Jews added a special portion to their daily prayers, asking Hashem to save us from the Vikings." Never mind that precious few Jews felt the Vikings' wrath in Dark Age Britain. To this teacher and this community—as in any community—world history is refracted through the lens of me and mine. The Roman Empire—was it good for the Jews? The Crusades—very bad for the Jews. European exploration of the New World—any Jews on the ships?

Beth Rivkah is a private, tuition-charging school, but it is certified by the State of New York, so it must adhere to certain teaching guidelines. They have to teach, among other things, biology and chemistry; U.S. and world history; English literature; and algebra, geometry, and trigonometry. Those girls wishing to teach someday in non-Lubavitch schools, or hoping to take college courses in, say, computer programming or early-childhood education—typical fields for a Lubavitch girl—must be prepared to pass the New York State Regents' exams in order to obtain a high school diploma recognized by the State of New York. This poses a moral dilemma for Lubavitch educators: They must teach subjects in ways that do not violate their ethical norms or religious beliefs while adhering to state law and preparing their girls for good jobs. This presents little problem in the early grades, in math, basic science, English grammar, and spelling. Even history and social studies aren't hard: Grades 1 through 4 learn civics and the history of New York City, and grades 4 and 5 study American history. None of that is particularly offensive to the Lubavitch point of view. Only the sixth-grade world history curriculum has to be rewritten, since the state-authorized textbooks focus on subjects like Greek mythology and Church history, which Lubavitch educators say they would rather not teach their children.

But when it comes to more advanced scientific disciplines, especially biology, there are glaring gaps between what the state wants children to learn and what Lubavitch Hasidim believe. "We have a problem with evolution, and with the solar system," states Altein. Chabad, like other fundamentalist Orthodox Jewish and Christian groups, takes a literal Biblical view of the time line of creation. The world was created 5,762 years ago, in seven days, by God, who created man and all the plants and animals in their present form. So who is this Darwin fellow? A theorist, nothing more. And scientific theories are changed all the time, whereas the Torah is true and constant.

Chabad's view on evolution comes straight from the Rebbe, who defended the biblical account of creation in a speech he delivered while studying at the Sorbonne in the late 1930s. The main points of that speech are contained in a letter he wrote in the 1970s to a newly religious young man troubled by the discrepancies between evolution and the Torah. In the letter Schneerson claims that there is no conflict between scientific theory and Torah, because the two disciplines operate in different arenas. "Science formulates and deals with theories and hypotheses, while the Torah deals with absolute truths," he writes. "It is small wonder that the various 'scientific' theories concerning the age of the universe not only contradict each other, but some of them are [also] quite incompatible and mutually exclusive." As to evolution, there is "not a shred of evidence to support it," he continues. Once one accepts the Torah and its notion of an all-powerful God, why not go on and further accept that He created dinosaur fossils for His own purposes within a relatively short period of time? Why is that more astonishing than the creation of the entire universe? "The question 'Why create a fossil?' is no more valid than the question 'Why create an atom?'"

So how do Beth Rivkah teachers deal with science textbooks that mention the Big Bang theory, the evolution of the planets, and what most of the Western world considers to be the real age of the earth? From first through fourth grade in New York, each science education module comes in its own small book, so Beth Rivkah teachers can pick and choose which booklets to give their students. From the fifth grade on, however, each year's science curriculum is printed in one large hardcover text, containing both offensive and nonoffensive material. So for those grades, the school simply doesn't buy the state-recommended texts. Teachers create their own loose-leaf textbooks by copying pages cannibalized from several sources, and they supplement them with classroom lectures. This is a labor-intensive method used by Chabad teachers all over the country, but particularly, and most systematically, at Beth Rivkah, the movement's flagship institution. The best lesson plans and cobbled-together "books" are saved from year to year, or even shared with other Chabad schools, to avoid reinventing the wheel each semester.

In high school, Beth Rivkah faces a different challenge. The state Board of Regents requires that teachers use specific science textbooks. "So the girls have their [biology] text, with evolution in it, and the teacher explains what the Torah says versus what their books say," Altein explains. "Where the book reads, 'The world was created millions of years ago,' we put a yellow sticker on the page that says, 'According to the Torah, we know the world is not millions of years old.'" In this way, older girls learn what the outside world believes, as they might learn a foreign language. If they take the Regents' exam in biology, which many of them choose not to do, they will usually leave evolution questions blank rather than write something they believe to be incorrect.

Sex education and the facts of human reproduction, on the other hand, are not avoided. They are, however, taught in the tenth grade rather than the eighth, which is the age recommended by state guidelines, because Lubavitch educators feel tenth grade is more age-appropriate.

Literature classes are also problematic. "We have our guidelines," Altein says. Romance between boys and girls is out, as is bad language or contemporary stories dealing with drugs and other social ills. "The truth is that in classical novels, it's such clean romance that it usually goes over the children's heads," she admits. "But because it's not something we encourage in our community, why do they have to read it?" Anything that talks about Christianity or other non-Jewish religions is dealt with carefully. "If it doesn't go against halakha, that's fine," Altein says. "Like a quote that says, 'Honor your father and mother,' even if it's not a Jewish person saying it, that's OK, because it's from the Torah."

Leah Jacobson is in charge of Beth Rivkah's secular curriculum. She reaches into a closet in her office and pulls out handfuls of novels, next year's offerings for several of the higher grades. Below the fifth grade, when students are still learning to read, she says the school doesn't censor the state-provided basal readers. "From the fifth grade on, we have our censorship code," she states. "We do it because we have no choice."

In some cases state-recommended books pass Chabad's critical eye in their original form. John Steinbeck's novel *The Pearl* is taught in eighth grade at Beth Rivkah, along with *The Miracle Worker,* William Gibson's play about Helen Keller. *Rebecca of Sunnybrook Farm* is considered inoffensive enough for sixth-graders, as is Mark Twain's *The Prince and the Pauper* at the seventh-grade level. But then there's *Heidi.* What could be wrong with this blue-eyed Swiss orphan girl? She's always talking about church and quoting the New Testament, Altein points out. On one hand, she says, what little girl doesn't grow up with Heidi? "But why do we have to expose our children to stories of the family going to church and celebrating Christmas? We want them to know that *goyim* must serve God in their own way, but we don't necessarily want them to know what that way is."

Charlotte's Web is also a no-no. Its talking spiders and barnyard animals contravene the Lubavitch prohibition on assigning human characteristics to animals. Wilbur the Pig is particularly problematic. Not only does he talk, he's not kosher. Schneerson specifically urged his followers to avoid children's toys and stories featuring nonkosher animals.

When you take books away in a school, you have to replace them with others. In recent years a handful of Jewish publishing companies have sprung up to fill the growing niche for ultra-Orthodox-friendly children's literature. These firms put out their own original books, as well as censored versions of great literature that is at least fifty years old and therefore no longer under copyright protection. Beth Rivkah's fifth-graders now read *Heidi,* for example, in a vetted version released by one of these approved Jewish publishing houses. "There has been a move towards understanding the needs of religious students that didn't exist when I started here fifteen years ago," Jacobson says. But the new religious presses have yet to produce an ultra-Orthodox Mark Twain or Louisa May Alcott.

Crown Heights educator Bronya Shaffer criticizes what she calls the "move to the right" throughout the Hasidic school system this past generation. "Women my age in Williamsburg can quote Shakespeare, but their children are appalled by it," she notes. (The Bard, by the way, is not part of the Beth Rivkah curriculum.) "There's this feeling today, 'Why do we have to go to the *goyim*? Why read Thomas Hardy when we have [religious author] Gershon Winkler?' There was no Judaic literature when I was growing up. Today, there's a lot, but it's almost all very poor quality." Shaffer teaches a twelfth-grade class called "Contemporary Issues" at Beth Rivkah, where she and the girls discuss the debate between science and Torah, the growing phenomenon of modern Orthodox women's prayer groups, and what Shaffer describes as preserving individuality in a society that values conformity. "You can't replace good literature with pap," she says. "It's a battle I've been fighting for years."

Like any private school, Beth Rivkah has a very close relationship with its students' parents and must satisfy the needs of the community it serves. That community, despite everything it shares, is not monolithic. Some parents don't want their kids touching Hans Christian Andersen. Others hire private tutors to teach their children about evolution. One Crown Heights mother, determined to open her kids' eyes to the world, reads Victor Hugo to them at night and takes each one, on his or her thirteenth birthday, to see *Les Misérables* on Broadway.

One Crown Heights mother in her late thirties (she asked that her name not be used) has an advanced academic degree but says she decided to send her daughters to Beth Rivkah and her son to Oholei Torah because what they get—a warm, safe learning environment and plenty of Jewish background—is more important to her than what they don't get. "We fill in the rest at home, with private tutors," she says. Another local woman (who also did not want her name used) says that not teaching classic literature or world history "is absurd." But she, too, keeps her children in the Lubavitch schools because she feels the trade-off is worth it. She gives her kids music and art lessons in the evenings, and she teaches them about history, "so they will know everything, as well as knowing how we Lubavitchers look at it; kids know when you're keeping something from them."

"There are different levels of stringency in the community," Altein points out. "We have to be delicate. It's not that we look at the outside world as taboo. We just pick and choose, to leave out the garbage."

The Beth Rivkah Division of Higher Learning, which includes Chabad's teachers' training program, is located on one floor of the cavernous Beth Rivkah girls' high school on Crown Street, a ten-minute walk from the elementary school. More than a hundred young women are enrolled here in one- or two-year courses in Bible, Jewish codes of law, Jewish history, Hasidic philosophy, Hebrew grammar, and educational techniques, courses that will prepare them to teach in Jewish religious schools as shlichot of the Rebbe.

In one room sixteen girls are waiting for their Hasidus class to begin. Like their younger sisters, they are modestly dressed, and although a few sport small earrings or discreet rings, most wear no jewelry, and there is no lipstick, eye makeup, or painted fingernails. These young women are nineteen and twenty years old, the age when most American Jews are in college. But few Lubavitchers go to college. Some, especially women, may take specific college classes in computers, psychology, or education, as vocational training for particular jobs. But very few will pursue a degree program. Schneerson, who himself was a university student, spoke out against college for his followers. The immorality on America's campuses would lead them, he said, away from a Torah lifestyle. Still, Schneerson never actually forbade college. That's not how he operated. He expressed his opinion, and his followers drew the logical conclusion. He didn't like college, so they don't go.

Again, Chabad is not monolithic. Everyone in Crown Heights knows "someone" with a college degree. Schneerson rarely discouraged *ba'alei teshuva* who were in the middle of pursuing a college degree—even a Ph.D.—from completing their studies. Now that these no-longer-newly-religious people have teenage children, they're more likely to send their kids to college, or at least not stand in the way if their children demand it. And with the Rebbe's physical presence gone and the central Chabad leadership no longer as visible, even some young *frum*-from-birth Lubavitchers are quietly studying law, medicine, and other professions their parents disdained. That doesn't mean they're any less Lubavitcher. They're just pushing the edge. And they're still in the great minority.

Chana Gorowitz says that the Beth Rivkah Division of Higher Learning was established forty years ago to provide teacher training for an American Jewish world that had a severe shortage of qualified religious school teachers. That's even more true today, she says, when modern Orthodox women, who used to provide the bulk of new Jewish day school and Hebrew school teachers, are going into professions such as law and medicine. "People who are more idealistically inclined tend to go into education," she believes. And no community idealizes the teaching profession more than Chabad, a movement in which just about every kid wants to be a shliach, and every shliach is, first and foremost, a teacher. Jewish leaders in many communities have expressed concerns that Chabad is exercising an undue influence on Jewish children because so many of the new teachers in non-Chabad schools are Lubavitchers. But whose fault is that? Sam Freedman says that Chabad is stepping in because no one else in the American Jewish world is prepared to do so. "In a way, they deserve to have that kind of influence," he says. "They're there, and we're not."

The students in Beth Rivkah's Hasidus class couldn't be more eager to fill those empty teaching shoes. Nineteen-year-old Feige, who grew up in Crown Heights, teaches Hebrew school at a nearby Chabad House and teaches a seventh-grade math class at Beth Rivkah. She says she hopes to become an elementary school teacher within the Lubavitch school system, although not necessarily in her home city of New York. Chani, also nineteen, from New Haven, teaches preschool five days a week and hopes to continue in the field once she earns her teaching certificate. "But wherever shlichus takes me, that's fine," she adds quickly. "Right," Feige chimes in. "I could end up in a different country, where they don't even speak English."

Rivka, twenty, comes from a non-Lubavitch family and was a student at Brandeis University when she decided to take time off to attend Chabad's seminary. "It's a natural desire to want to give over," she says. "When you believe in something, you want to share it with others." She now considers herself a Lubavitcher. "I always wanted to be more observant. From a young age, I wanted to wear a *sheitel* and take on more things not common in my community." Aidel, twenty, from a Chabad family in Detroit, says she, too, always wanted to go into education. In addition to being a full-time seminary student, she runs a bat mitzvah program for twelve-year-old girls in Long Island, studies Torah with elderly women once a week, and teaches a sixth-grade Beth Rivkah class every day after her own classes. "We live to give to other people," she declares.

To an outsider, this is an unusual group of nineteen- and twenty-year-old girls. They don't talk about boys—none of them is dating yet—they don't talk about TV shows, or movies, or the latest *People* magazine story. They talk about teaching, about "giving to others," about carrying on the Rebbe's work. From an early age they've been part of Chabad's cradle-to-grave mentoring system, a system set up by the Rebbe by which every Lubavitcher man, woman, and child is supposed to choose a *mashpiah,* or "person of influence." Throughout their lives, Chabadniks regularly consult their mentors on personal as well as religious issues. Should they marry this person? What should they do if their faith in God wavers? Can you explain this page of Talmud to me? Even the top movement officials and most distinguished rabbis all have their own *mashpiah,* someone to turn to in time of need.

The mentoring system is particularly strong within Lubavitch schools. Within the Beth Rivkah system, every pupil has a mentor and, if they're above bat mitzvah age, most also act as a mentor to someone. All of the teachers also function as primary or secondary mentors to the students. "We always had young teachers, just a few years older than ourselves, and they were able to teach us so much, to influence us," says Aidel. "They were young girls totally dedicated to what the Rebbe wants. It's inspiring." By seminary age most of the students have been mentors to younger girls since they themselves were thirteen or fourteen. Just as they look up to their own teachers as role models, so are they accustomed to being looked up to by younger children. "It brings out talents you didn't know you had in you," Aidel muses. "The girls call you up to ask questions. I'm constantly having to work on myself, to develop a constant awareness of what our purpose is. I can never lose sight of it."

"Right," agrees Leah, twenty, who grew up in Crown Heights with *ba'al teshuva* parents. Since she was in ninth grade, Leah has worked as a summer counselor in a Lubavitch camp for mainly non-observant children. "Me and the other counselor were the only religious people they'd see. However the campers looked at me, that's how they'll see Torah Judaism for the rest of their life. It's a big responsibility."

Chani and Feige both spent the previous summer as counselors at a Chabad overnight camp for non-observant children. "It makes you think about how you act and dress all the time," Chani says. "There are iffy skirt lengths and iffy necklines, things I might wear in my normal life, but as head counselor, you have to be more aware of how you come across." Feige nods, adding, "There are two hundred kids looking up to us." And it's not just at summer camp. The responsibilities of being a mentor and role model extend throughout the school year, Chani points out. "I teach at Beth Rivkah high school, and I was talking to a student about a book I'd read, *Tuesdays with Morrie*. She said, 'You read that?' She was shocked. Everything you do, you have to be so careful."

These young women don't look at it as a burden, but as a privilege. They've been groomed since birth to become shlichim, to open their hearts and arms to Jews who are less observant than they are, while remaining secretly (or not-so-secretly) proud of the greater religious responsibilities they themselves have assumed. Nine-year-old Avremi Zippel expressed it at the shlichim convention. So does twenty-year-old Leah, in her Beth Rivkah classroom, when she reflects on the social pressures of being a camp counselor: "I ended each summer so proud of who I am. I feel I had an effect on people's lives."

CHAPTER 14

WE WANT MOSHIACH NOW!:
Dealing with the Rebbe's Death

At the corner of Eastern Parkway and Kingston Avenue in Crown Heights stands the three-story red brick building known, by its street number, simply as 770. It has been command central for Chabad's international operations for the last sixty years. When Menachem Mendel Schneerson was alive, he worked out of a small ground-floor office to the left of the building's entranceway. His office was connected by a black rotary phone to the equally small office next door, where his key secretaries managed the day-to-day functioning of Chabad's central institutions.

During the years that the Rebbe occupied that office Chabad was far from a one-man operation, but the buck always stopped at his desk. He set the tone and policy for movement operations and kept firm tabs on his far-flung network of shlichim. He was the spiritual glue holding together a host of strong, sometimes clashing, personalities, all of whom subsumed their differences out of respect for their leader. "In the days of the Rebbe, if a shliach didn't get along with his head shliach, he'd have to move on," says one elder shliach, preferring to speak anonymously. "Today with the Rebbe gone, there's less central control."

Since Schneerson's death, Chabad has made an administrative shift to a more corporate structure, with policy and budgetary decisions made by the executive boards of Merkos L'Inyonei Chinuch (Chabad's educational arm), Machne Israel (the movement's social service branch), and Agudas Chassidei Chabad (the umbrella organization for the other two). The Rebbe set that transition in motion before he was incapacitated by a stroke in March 1992. His closest aides kept up the pretense of his being in control for the two years between his stroke and his death as much for their own comfort (they didn't want to admit that he wouldn't recover) as to maintain order in the movement.

Schneerson began the initial planning for his eventual passing on the afternoon of his wife's death in 1988, when he called Yehuda Krinsky, his driver and one of his secretaries, into his office to dictate a will disposing of his personal effects. Krinsky was named executor of that will, with Philadelphia shliach Avraham Shemtov as his alternate. Later that same year Schneerson called a meeting of the executive board of Agudas Chassidei Chabad and indicated to them orally that he wanted to move much of Chabad's decision-making from his hands into theirs. Between 1988 and 1990, Schneerson had the corporate papers for Agudas, Merkos, and Machne redrawn. He continued as president of all three divisions; his aide Rabbi Chaim Mordechai Hodakov was named vice president; Rabbi Nissan Mindel, another close aide, was named treasurer; and Krinsky was named secretary. Of those men, only Krinsky was still alive at the end of the decade.

Those were the sole documents left by Schneerson that dealt with the future of his movement. Other informal decisions he made—notably a handwritten note in 1985 naming Avraham Shemtov chairman of the executive committee of Agudas Chassidei Chabad, arguably Chabad's top administrative post—are still in effect. But, along with the so-called "second will" (an unsigned document drawn up by Schneerson's key secretaries in mid-1988), they continue to cause some uncertainty about who really speaks for Chabad today. In fact, no one speaks with the central authority that Schneerson did. Krinsky and Shemtov are acknowledged internally as the two most powerful men in the movement. The day-to-day affairs of Chabad's international operations are managed by the twenty-two-man board of Agudas Chassidei Chabad, a self-selecting board of rabbis whose members serve for life and who make decisions based largely on their interpretation of what the Rebbe would have wanted.

The Rebbe's downstairs office has been preserved as a pilgrimage site, but the locus of power has shifted to the building's second, third, and fourth floors, where a labyrinthine network of offices house the movement's administration, its editorial and educational arms, its outreach center, its library, and its publishing house.

In the basement of 770 is a synagogue. This was the Rebbe's *shul*, the cavernous room where he prayed and where he held his public *farbrengens*. His Hasidim would come at all hours of the day and night, crowding into the auditorium or the women's balcony, chatting, studying, singing, and craning their necks for a better view of their beloved leader. While the Rebbe was alive, this synagogue was Chabad's heart, as his office was its brain. The building functioned as a single organism. But today a jagged wound tears through the structure. Chabad's leaders don't come downstairs into the synagogue. Many who pray in the synagogue don't go to the offices upstairs. That same wound ripped through the streets of Crown Heights after Schneerson's death, setting family against family in the most serious division ever to have hit the Chabad movement.

It's called Moshichism, or messianism, a belief that spread among some Lubavitchers in the waning years of Schneerson's life that their Rebbe was Moshiach, the Messiah promised by the biblical prophets who would redeem Israel and usher in the world-to-come. It's an extraordinary claim, one that has done more harm to Chabad outreach—and to the movement itself—than any other single factor. While the numbers of Lubavitchers who promulgate this belief dwindle with each passing year, messianist strongholds still exist, to the chagrin of the movement's leadership and to the consternation of many in the outside Jewish world who remember the billboards and bumper stickers that proliferated in the early 1990s showing the message "Welcome King Moshiach" below the Rebbe's smiling face.

"What a waste," declares Dr. Norman Lamm. "They're doing so much good, why in heaven's name do they have to get latched onto this dreadful messianic business? There's an element of idolatry there that scares me very much. Imagine if they didn't have this messianic fixation, how much they could have achieved."

Miami filmmaker Jerry Levine makes promotional videos for Chabad and other Jewish organizations. He says that the rise of Chabad messianism in the early 1990s soured Chabad's relations with other groups doing similar outreach and remains Chabad's biggest PR problem today. "These people were my clients—Aish HaTorah, Torah Umesorah, the rest of the modern Orthodox world," he says. "Up until that point, there was a cold war between them. When the pronouncements starting coming out that the Rebbe was Moshiach, the cold war turned vocal. They couldn't hold it in anymore. They told their students how objectionable it was."

Chabad did not invent messianism. Belief in the Messiah, a man born into the ancient Davidic line who will lead the Jewish people out of the 2,000-year exile into the Land of Israel and into a universal age of peace and justice, is a fundamental tenet of Orthodox Judaism. It is one of Maimonides' 13 Principles of Faith, recited every day at the end of the morning prayer service. "I believe, with complete faith, in the coming of Messiah," the recitation goes. The Messiah "may tarry," but an observant Jew will continue to await his arrival "with every passing day."

Messianic hopes have waxed and waned throughout Jewish history, coming to the fore when Jews are oppressed, calming down again in times of peace and prosperity. False Messiahs have come and gone—Jesus is considered one of them—but the crashing failure of the most infamous among them, Shabtai Tzvi, a seventeenth-century Turkish Jew who convinced half of world Jewry that he was the Messiah and then converted to Islam to save his own neck, took the luster off messianic hopes for the next three centuries. "Raising messianic expectations is a very dangerous game," notes Lamm. "It gives hope, but it also encourages expectations. And if expectations are dashed, then along with it crashes the entire structure of Judaism."

Conservative, Reform, and Reconstructionist theologies define the messianic era in different ways, which do not necessarily include the arrival of a flesh-and-blood savior. Hasidim have no such scruples. But *be'as ha'Moshiach,* the coming of the Messiah, is a cornerstone of Chabad outreach: If a Jew's purpose in life is to do everything possible to expedite the Messiah's arrival, then encouraging others to obey Jewish laws and do good deeds becomes a divinely ordained activity.

Schneerson's mitzvah campaigns of the late 1960s and '70s were consciously motivated by a desire to do just that. Through the eighties, he spoke more and more openly about the Messiah, encouraging Jews to expect his arrival "at any minute." But in 1991, at a now-famous *farbrengen,* Schneerson shocked Chabad by announcing that he "had done all [he] could," and was now turning over the responsibility of bringing Moshiach to his followers.

The following March, Schneerson was felled by a massive stroke that left him wheelchair-bound and unable to communicate. Devastated by their rebbe's incapacity and roused to fever pitch by his increased emphasis on the need to "bring Moshiach now," many Lubavitchers began openly proclaiming that Schneerson was the Messiah and would soon reveal himself. This tendency had already existed within Chabad for at least ten years—children at Chabad summer camps in the early eighties were singing songs about "the Rebbe, our Messiah"—but the connection had remained primarily metaphorical. When he heard about such goings-on, Schneerson would put a stop to them. In the sixties, a Hasid in Israel reportedly went up in a helicopter and dropped leaflets all over the country proclaiming Schneerson the Messiah. Schneerson ordered the man to pick them all up, a task that took months. As late as 1988, he told an Israeli shliach who had been loudly promulgating the same message that he was "stabbing me in the heart," and a few months before his stroke he threatened to walk out of a *farbrengen* at 770 when someone began singing a messianist song.

But once Schneerson could no longer speak, the messianist faction among his followers was able to give full vent to its hopes. In 1992 they formed the International Campaign to Bring Moshiach, a group led and funded by Lubavitchers in Crown Heights, Montreal, and several other Lubavitch communities. Signs outside Lubavitch homes and offices, bumper stickers, billboards, and full-page ads in major newspapers proclaimed the aged, infirm Chabad leader to be the long-awaited Messiah. Some Lubavitchers would sleep with their clothes laid out on the bed, so they would be ready to greet the Messiah should he arrive when they were sleeping. A representative of N'shei Chabad, the international Lubavitcher women's association, wrote a letter to the Rebbe and addressed him as "King Messiah." When she received no formal rebuke, the woman announced to the Crown Heights community that the Rebbe had accepted the messianic mantle. Whenever Schneerson appeared in his synagogue, Lubavitchers began singing *yechi adoneinu,* "Long live our Rebbe, our master, teacher, and king Messiah, forever and ever," taking his half-conscious nods as indications of his approval.

Movement leaders tried to quash these public displays, but their efforts were hampered by their own ambivalence: If Jewish tradition holds that a potential Messiah is born in every generation, then who in this generation, they asked, was more fitting for the title than the Lubavitcher Rebbe? It may be inappropriate to declare so openly, but it would be equally inappropriate to decide, categorically, that he is not. Even today Yehuda Krinsky answers questions about Schneerson's messianic potential in talmudic fashion, turning the question back on the questioner, challenging him or her to name another individual who fits the messianic criteria as successfully as Schneerson. Still, even during the Rebbe's lifetime, Krinsky and the rest of the movement leadership opposed efforts to promote this message. "I personally feel the rebbe's Moshiach, but to go out and proclaim it? I don't think we should do that," longtime secretary Leib Groner told the *Jerusalem Post* in 1993. "If the Rebbe were actually revealed as Moshiach, you would know about it without having to place an ad in the paper."

Why didn't Schneerson himself put a stop to Chabad messianism? Some of his followers blame him for not doing so. Some even left the movement over it. But Lubavitch spokesman Zalman Shmotkin says that after March 1992, Schneerson had expressive aphasia and was physically unable to communicate his needs or wishes. "Every day after prayers, a bunch of guys would start singing *yechi*. The Rebbe finally started nodding his head to the tune. It was one of his favorite songs, but he'd always sung it without words. They added the words after he could no longer speak. It was one of the cruelest things I've ever experienced."

Any statements issued in the Rebbe's name during the final two years of his life were filtered through his closest aides, themselves divided as to how far they believed and were willing to push his messianic status. Krinsky came down on the side of discretion; Groner was more willing to hear the Moshichist viewpoint. Ari Goldman, who covered Chabad for the *New York Times* during much of the Rebbe's illness, recalls the "embarrassing spectacle" of Krinsky and Groner standing on either side of the Rebbe's wheelchair as they stood in the special balcony built for him in the 770 synagogue, "pulling and tugging at the chair" as if to drag Schneerson toward or against the crowd's messianic urgings. Lubavitch headquarters disputes this account, but other visitors to 770 in those years also remember it.

Messianic fever came to a head in February 1993, when Rabbi Shmuel Butman, director of Lubavitch Youth International and the self-declared head of the International Campaign to Bring Moshiach, attempted to hijack a celebration of the Rebbe's forty-third year in power by announcing to the world media that Schneerson would reveal himself as the Messiah during a "coronation" ceremony at 770. The event turned into an absurd charade. Butman organized a satellite hookup and stood downstairs talking to news media while the Chabad leadership pointedly remained upstairs during the celebration, descending only to stand by the Rebbe's side as he was wheeled into the synagogue for a brief appearance. Afterward, Krinsky met with reporters to downplay the entire evening. "Tonight was like every other night," he insisted. "The Rebbe just wanted to be with his people."

Several years later Chabad's leadership tried to fire Butman, sending him an angry letter removing him from his position, but Butman refused to step down. The decentralization that gives Chabad emissaries their maneuverability also makes it difficult to rein them in, particularly without the Rebbe to put on the brakes. Butman had developed his own private funding sources and his own board of directors. Through the spring of 1993 a surrealistic situation prevailed, whereby Butman sat in his Crown Heights office, sending out messianic proclamations on 770 Eastern Parkway letterhead, while Agudas Chassidei Chabad staffers sent out counterfaxes warning reporters and Jewish organizations to ignore all communications emanating from 770 not issued by themselves.

Chabad messianism grew through 1993 and early 1994, reaching a crescendo by June, as the Rebbe lay in a deep coma in Manhattan's Beth Israel Medical Center. Hundreds of Hasidim kept up vigils around the hospital, and the news media ran daily, sometimes hourly, reports on his health, seeking out young, grief-crazed Chabadniks eager to talk about how Schneerson would soon rise from his sickbed and lead them all to Jerusalem to rebuild the holy Temple. One reporter related a conversation he overheard in the hospital cafeteria, when a customer ahead of him asked the cashier what the heavy police presence was all about. "Oh, they've got the Messiah upstairs," she told him as she rang up his purchase.

Then, unbelievably, on June 12, the Rebbe died, sending an emotional shock wave through the movement. How could this happen? His frail, emaciated body was lovingly washed and shrouded in linen, wrapped in his prayer shawl, and placed inside a plain pine coffin, as thousands of Lubavitchers hopped on planes and rented vans to head to Crown Heights. Most knew they were coming to a funeral. But some hoped for more. Among the crowds of mourners crying and tearing their shirts as the funeral cortege passed down Eastern Parkway were small groups of Hasidim who seemed to be celebrating. They danced and sang with tambourines, in the desperate hope that, even now, their Rebbe would summon his superhuman will and rise from the grave to usher in the Messianic Age. One young woman who has since left Chabad because of the messianism was a high school student at the time, and she remembers driving down from Connecticut with her teacher and classmates to dance and sing at the Rebbe's funeral. "I was so crushed when he didn't reveal himself," she says.

The Rebbe's death moved the messianic squabble onto an entirely different plane. Normative Judaism holds that the Messiah will be revealed during his lifetime. Belief, on the other hand, in a savior who dies and is reborn to lead the way to salvation is a major theological distinction between Judaism and Christianity. "If they believe the Rebbe could have been Moshiach, fine, I agree," says Lamm. "Many people could have been the Moshiach, and he had a far better chance than most. But to say he's the Moshiach after he died? The whole polemic we've had with Christianity for two thousand years is that we say a Moshiach who did not accomplish world peace, who did not accomplish the redemption of Israel and the world, is not Moshiach. And here we're told that [the Rebbe] can be. If that's the case, why were we so reluctant to accept Jesus?"

Some Chabadniks point out that there are ancient Jewish sources, Hasidic and non-Hasidic, that do provide for a messiah to rise from the dead. Just because this belief is not part of normative Judaism today does not make it incorrect.

"The single most underappreciated thing in all this is that there are credible, traditional sources that allow the possibility for a *tzaddik* to be resurrected and become Moshiach," Zalman Shmotkin notes. "We can't come out and say the Rebbe or Moses or King David will not be the Messiah because we are simply not God. Only He can know." Not only that, Shmotkin continues, but the term "Moshiach" in Hasidus and Kabbalah refers to much more than the narrow legal or actualized Messiah. "When someone who learns Hasidus uses the word *Moshiach,* he is often talking figuratively about the redemptive and world-encompassing qualities of the *tzaddik's* soul, but the uninitiated may hear 'final actualized Moshiach.'"

What is incorrect is believing—or worse, telling others—that the Rebbe is, definitely, the Messiah. In 1998 the Central Committee of Chabad-Lubavitch Rabbis in the United States and Canada, Chabad's central rabbinic body, issued a statement denouncing this kind of messianism: "Belief in the coming of the Moshiach and awaiting his imminent arrival is a basic tenet of the Jewish faith. It is clear, however, that conjecture as to the possible identity of Moshiach is not part of the basic tenet of Judaism. . . . The preoccupation with identifying the Rebbe as Moshiach is clearly contrary to the Rebbe's wishes."

After the Rebbe's death many Lubavitchers who had loudly proclaimed him as the Messiah went through deep spiritual crises. Eventually, they faced the inevitable: Their Rebbe was dead and the Messianic Age had not yet come. Rabbi Moshe New, Chabad shliach in Montreal, had been one of the leaders of the International Campaign to Bring Moshiach and a vocal proponent of Schneerson as the Messiah before his death. The day the Rebbe died, New flew to New York for the funeral and returned home the next day, in a complete daze. "I couldn't stay for the shiva [the seven-day mourning period]," he says, his eyes filling with tears. "I just couldn't. For a week I couldn't do anything at all. Everyone was afraid that [my] Chabad House would fold. Then, over the course of a week, it started to sink in. We had a job to do. That doesn't change. I realized that I had no right to take the Rebbe's message beyond what he actually said. The Rebbe's message was that we are standing on the threshold of the messianic era, the world is evolving and becoming a more godly place, and we ought to do more mitzvahs to hasten that era. That was the Rebbe's message; not to promote him." A week after the funeral New called a meeting of his staff and major supporters. He told them that he had no explanation for the Rebbe's death, but he knew there was nothing to do but carry on. "I told them that we're going forward, and it'll be good."

Most Chabad shlichim reacted to Schneerson's death by doubling their outreach efforts, drowning their grief in work, and trying to fulfill the mission their Rebbe had left them. Los Angeles shliach Shlomo Cunin opened a new Chabad House in Malibu during the Rebbe's shiva. Detroit shliach Berel Shemtov announced plans to establish a new yeshiva in Schneerson's name, one specifically dedicated to producing shlichim. Salt Lake City shliach Benny Zippel took the red-eye to New York for Schneerson's funeral, stayed up all day, and flew back to Salt Lake overnight to perform a *bris* the next morning. There was no better way to honor the Rebbe, he felt, than to usher a new Jewish baby into the world. "It was very difficult to think in terms of what's going to be 'after,'" says Rabbi Yochanan Friedman, Chabad shliach in Santa Cruz, California. "But I don't think any [shliach] thought, Oh, this is the end of us. It wasn't that we had to think of new strategies or we'd fall apart. There was just something about the Rebbe that, after his passing, made us want to do more. It's like a child, when a parent dies. You want to do what he wanted."

But other Lubavitchers, including some shlichim, continued to proclaim Schneerson to be the Messiah even after his death. Books came out in 1994 and later, "proving" that the Rebbe was the Messiah, quoting page after page of Torah, Talmud, Maimonides, and Schneerson's own writings as incontrovertible evidence. Messianic conventions were held in Crown Heights and other locations, where Lubavitchers would watch videos of their beloved Rebbe and bolster each other's faith in his imminent return to earth. The *Beis Moshiach* (House of Messiah) magazine and Web site propounded the messianist line on a weekly basis, putting it forth as normative Lubavitch Hasidism. Movement leaders denounce this magazine as a fringe aberration, charging that it and other Moshichist publications fabricated quotes and sent out statements on forged 770 letterhead in a desperate attempt to seek legitimacy. The battle between messianist and nonmessianist grew ugly. More than once Brooklyn police were called to 770 to prevent the takeover of certain offices by what one movement official called "Moshichist gangsters."

The year 1996 marked the apex of post-Schneerson messianism. In January the International Campaign to Bring Moshiach put up a huge billboard beside New York's George Washington Bridge, proclaiming Schneerson the Messiah. In February the group held a convention at the New York Hilton. Organizer Shmuel Butman told reporters that they would soon "cover the greatest event in the history of mankind." This was all too much for Chabad's leadership, which struck out publicly against the messianism within its ranks, placing full-page ads in the *New York Times* and calling press conferences to distance the movement from what Krinsky and others called the messianist fringe. "It's embarrassing," Avraham Shemtov told a *Times* reporter. "It's reaching more people, and when it begins to reach more people, some aren't capable of sorting things out."

Eight years after Schneerson's death, Chabad still harbors a messianist wing. It has greatly diminished in influence and numbers, but the wounds it caused are deep. Chabad families check the messianist credentials of prospective brides and grooms before approving marriages, and there is virtually no "intermarriage" between Moshichist and non-Moshichist families. There is a town-gown split in Crown Heights, where a significant number of local residents still hold on to their messianic beliefs, while Chabad's administrative leadership does not. A Chabad scholar living in Crown Heights claims the split is largely a class issue. He says that many locals are poorly educated and live below the poverty line, struggling daily to make ends meet. "They are simple, naïve people who have so little they will do anything in their power to bring Moshiach," he says. "Those of us who are better off, more 'sophisticated,' are not Moshichist." That same split extends beyond Crown Heights to the larger Chabad world: most messianists live in Lubavitch communities; the overwhelming majority of Chabad shlichim are not messianist.

Lubavitch communities in Montreal and Safed, Israel, are among those known to be strongly Moshichist. Pittsburgh, Detroit, and Los Angeles are known to be strongly anti-Moshichist. Certain Chabad institutions propagate the messianist line: the Oholei Torah boys' school in Crown Heights, where students sing *yechi adoneinu* every morning; the New York branch of N'shei Chabad; a Chabad yeshiva in Safed. That doesn't mean that everyone who lives or works in messianist communities or institutions is a messianist, just that social pressure or institutional policies favor this line of thinking.

As a group, Chabad shlichim say they are saddened, as well as angered, by those who persist in these activities. "Who cares who the Messiah will be?" declares Avraham Berkowitz, Chabad shliach in Moscow. "If you personally feel so, keep it to yourself. Coming out with the statement that the Rebbe is the Messiah doesn't bring the Messiah closer."

Most disturbing of all to longtime Chabadniks, the Rebbe's *shul* at 770 Eastern Parkway is firmly in Moshichist hands. A *yechi adoneinu* banner is strung above the long table where Schneerson used to sit during *farbrengens.* A Kiddush cup is placed where he sat. The synagogue where Lubavitchers spent so many emotionally charged hours soaring with their Rebbe into the higher spheres is now off-limits to anyone not willing to countenance such reverential memorial displays. "It's the Israelis," sniffs one Lubavitcher woman who lives in Crown Heights and says she "never" goes to the main synagogue anymore. "I'm so embarrassed to go there and see how they've turned it into a place that makes people think we're nut cases. When the Rebbe was here, he knew how to keep them under control."

Some shlichim who clung to their messianist hopes after Schneerson's death began boycotting the annual Chabad shliachs' convention in Crown Heights to hold a separate convention down the block. Both conventions review Chabad House programming ideas and fundraising strategies, but the "alternative" group refers to Schneerson as the Messiah, while the official convention does not. By 1999 the breakaway convention was drawing only 70 participants compared to 1,500 at the official convention, indicating that the overwhelming majority of shlichim toe the administration's line. But some do not. Many of those who attend the messianist convention are not considered shlichim by the movement leadership. Chabad headquarters is much more concerned about messianism among the shlichim than on the streets of Crown Heights, because the former have a direct and damaging effect on outreach efforts. The administration is careful to weed out Moshichist candidates for new shliach positions, ensuring that new Chabad Houses will not be run by messianists, but those already working in the field are, for the most part, allowed to remain. Most have toned down or abandoned their messianist teachings—at least in public. But not all.

What does it mean to be a Moshichist? It's not a black-and-white question—is the Rebbe the Messiah, or isn't he?—but more a sliding spectrum of belief where metaphor weaves in and out between the lines of literal understanding. On one end of the spectrum are those very few Lubavitchers who state, *tout court,* that the Rebbe is not the Messiah. They say this quietly, in their living rooms, not on the street and certainly not in the newspapers. Next are those who acknowledge the Rebbe's death but say they don't know who the Messiah is—it could be the Rebbe as well as anyone else, and it's not for us to know. Most of the movement leadership, and the shlichim, fall into this category. Moving down the spectrum, one encounters those who acknowledge the Rebbe has died but remain unshaken in their belief that he is nevertheless the Messiah and will eventually reveal himself to be so. At the far extreme are those Lubavitchers who believe that Schneerson is the Messiah and that he is still alive.

It's difficult for some people to grasp the subtlety of a theology that states a *tzaddik*'s body and soul remain in closer contact after death than the body and soul of an ordinary person. And it's a short leap from that esoteric concept to believing that Schneerson's spirit is so close to his body that it still inhabits it, in some form or another.

One yeshiva student, fervently davening at the Rebbe's grave on a snowy March morning, says he firmly believes the Rebbe is alive and physically walking the earth. There's precedent for this belief in Jewish Law, the young man says. "The Talmud teaches that *Yaakov avinu* [Jacob the patriarch] never died." If Moses is Jacob's descendant, and if Schneerson was the Moses of our generation, the living incarnation of Moses' own soul, why then should he not be endowed with the same otherworldly powers? "The Rebbe is here, we just can't see him," the young man concludes. So who's in the grave? The student shrugs, uncomfortable yet defensive. "The Rebbe was never in that coffin," he states. "I didn't look in the box. Did you look in the box?"

When shlichim hear remarks like that, they sigh and shake their heads. Some have stronger reactions. One says, quite sharply, "They're kooks." Rivkah Slonim suggests that some of the messianists "are unbalanced souls," but acknowledges that "some very intelligent people" can also be numbered in their ranks. Moshe New says he's "mystified" by Chabadniks who continue to harbor messianist delusions, but he explains their position as more misguided than heretical. "It's a distortion of the truth," he states. "Souls do exist forever, all souls of all people, so the Rebbe exists as my grandfather and my grandmother also exist. But going beyond that and saying the Rebbe is here physically? I have *rachmones* [pity] on them."

Rabbi Eli Cohen, Chabad shliach at New York University, is one of those who continue to work as campus emissaries while proclaiming that the Rebbe is the Messiah. He downplays the significance of his stance and claims that most Lubavitchers agree with him. "Why else haven't they appointed another Rebbe?" he asks.

Chabad's leadership tries to deemphasize the number of shlichim who still hold messianist beliefs because they think it will hurt their outreach. Cohen disagrees, but other Lubavitchers claim that Cohen actually keeps his messianist beliefs under wraps on campus, knowing full well it would alienate many students.

One person who is deeply alienated is Brooklyn College Professor David Berger, an Orthodox historian who has made the issue of fighting Chabad messianism a personal crusade. He has written extensively on the issue, culminating with the 2001 publication of his book *The Rebbe, the Messiah, and the Scandal of Orthodox Indifference,* in which he outlines his case against Chabad and calls for its ostracism. In permitting its followers who still proclaim the Rebbe as Messiah to function as emissaries, rabbis, and teachers, the Chabad movement has placed itself beyond the bounds of normative Judaism, Berger says. And because Chabad is so big and influences so many other Jews, Berger believes that the Orthodox establishment has a religious responsibility to cut itself off from Chabad until the movement leadership declares once and for all that the Rebbe is not and cannot be the Messiah. He demands that, in the meantime, Chabad rabbis, teachers, and ritual slaughterers be dismissed from positions they hold within mainstream Jewish organizations.

Berger took initial steps toward that goal in June 1996, when he persuaded the (Orthodox) Rabbinical Council of America (RCA) to issue a resolution stating that "there is not and never has been a place in Judaism for the belief that . . . Messiah son of David will begin his messianist mission only to experience death, burial and resurrection before completing it." Even that resolution was intentionally inconclusive—it did not preclude someone rising from the dead to be Moshiach so long as he did not *begin* his mission before death, a loophole Lubavitchers enjoy pointing out.

Because of his very public campaign warning against Chabad messianism, Berger has earned himself the enmity of Lubavitch. Even mentioning his name to movement leaders brings scowls. But Berger insists that he is not hostile toward Chabad. "I've been a great admirer of Chabad all my adult life," he says. It's only the messianism that he wants to root out, and the irony is that this is the same thing that Chabad's own leadership is trying to accomplish. Berger remains unconvinced. "They can't stop it, because they're a minority," he states. "I think they do want to stop it, in terms of anything public. What's in their heart of hearts, I don't know."

Berger attributes messianist beliefs to the majority of Lubavitchers, a claim Lubavitchers say is patently absurd. Here everyone is treading on thin ice, for no one can know precisely how deep Chabad messianism goes. When Berger and other critics claim that it infects the majority of the Chabad movement, they have no greater statistical backing than do those who suggest that it is on the decline.

San Francisco shliach Yosef Langer believes messianism runs deeper than the administration wants to admit. "Every Chabadnik knows the Rebbe is taking us out of here," he says. "They may not say so openly, but we all tell each other that we believe it." Zalman Shmotkin, on the other hand, insists that Chabad messianism has been on the wane since 1996, and that those who head up the International Campaign to Bring Moshiach are motivated more by power and money than by religious sentiment. He points out that some of the leaders of the alternative shliach convention are the same individuals fighting Krinsky and Agudas Chassidei

Chabad in a New York court over the disbursement of a $12 million donation, and notes that some of them were embroiled in power struggles with their regional heads many years before messianism went public in the early 1990s.

If Chabad's leaders really oppose the grosser forms of messianism, why don't they stamp it out? Not so simple, Shmotkin says. The leadership is hampered in its struggle both operationally and theologically. Agudas Chassidei Chabad has made some moves to remove messianism from the public eye by taking down messianist banners in Crown Heights and using legal threats to stop the publication of ads proclaiming Schneerson as the Messiah. And Krinsky's office issued numerous statements between 1995 and 1998 that condemned the messianists' public activities. But as for casting out the messianists, that's "not the Chabad way," Shmotkin maintains. "Lubavitch never kicks people out." Yehuda Krinsky notes that throwing people out of the movement for such a belief would be like "throwing out the baby with the bath water." The Lubavitch approach, he says, is to love them and bring them to see the errors of their ways. While Shmotkin and others privately wish that 770 would take a stronger stand against messianism, they admit that the hands-off policy has worked and that messianism is on the wane.

Ultimately, it's impossible to know what every Chabadnik believes. It is doubtful that thousands of Lubavitchers who believed the Rebbe was Messiah during his lifetime would be able to wipe out that belief completely upon his death. Some say they were able to do so. Others simply no longer talk about it. "Are the messianists completely marginalized?" Norman Lamm wonders. "I can't get rid of the nagging suspicion that the difference between the messianists and the others is insignificant, or merely a matter of public [acknowledgment]."

But so long as the leadership continues to speak out against declaring the Rebbe to be the Messiah, and so long as the majority of new shlichim distance themselves from such positions and stop teaching it to outsiders, how much does it really matter? "In all my years dealing with Chabad rabbis, I have never heard a hint of the beliefs Professor Berger accuses Chabad of espousing," writes Dennis Prager, a Jewish talk show host in Los Angeles who took Berger to task in the February 2002 issue of *Moment* magazine. Rather than worrying about what "unnamed Chabad rabbis in Brooklyn" believe about the identity of the Messiah, Prager suggests that American Jews should thank Chabad for sending out its shlichim to spread Jewish knowledge. "Among those Chabad rabbis who believed this or who still believe it, this belief is entirely personal and plays no role whatsoever in the outreach work of Chabad. Chabad teaches Jews about Judaism, not about the Rebbe as Messiah."

The day after Schneerson died, television talk-show host Charlie Rose invited Ari Goldman onto his program to discuss Chabad's future. "I said Chabad cannot exist without a rebbe," Goldman recalls with a wry smile. "I held up my hand with all five fingers and said in five years they'll have a new rebbe. I thought some secret heir would emerge and claim the mantle. I was wrong, and I thought I knew the movement pretty well."

Almost a decade after Schneerson's death, no new rebbe has been appointed, and none is on the horizon. It's clear by now that the administration of the worldwide Chabad movement is in no danger of collapse. But so much of Chabad's strength and appeal came from the towering personality of Rabbi Schneerson himself. How will Chabad manage to convey the force of their Rebbe's personal charisma now that he is no longer here?

"I don't have an answer to that," says Krinsky. "Life goes on. The Rebbe's legacy, the Rebbe's work, is clearly apparent, and very much alive. Maybe more so than in his lifetime. It would be a grave error to think that our relationship with the Rebbe is now relegated to history."

Younger Chabadniks in particular have been engaged in a massive effort to keep the Rebbe alive by preserving his image and teachings in print, on video, and in cyberspace, thus managing a movementwide shift from personal devotion to a living *tzaddik* to veneration of his legacy.

In many ways this is nothing new. Chabad has been in the publishing business since the days of the first Rebbe, who wrote the *Tanya* mainly to make his teachings available to his Hasidim on paper so that they would stop clamoring for personal appointments. When Chabad Houses began opening in the 1970s and the Rebbe's outreach campaigns moved into high gear, Chabad headquarters stepped up the printing of books on Hasidic thought, in English, for the average American Jew in the street. Chabad was using the Internet by 1988, way ahead of the rest of the Jewish world; its Web sites today include Jewish holiday sites that reach millions of users and a live "chat with a rabbi" site that utilizes cutting-edge Web technology.

The Rebbe's death gave special urgency to these efforts. No longer rushing to keep up with the Rebbe's prolific output, Chabad is now scrambling to collect every last letter he wrote, every document he penned, every private picture, cassette, or videotape lurking in someone's desk drawer, every scribbled note jotted down by a yeshiva student at one of his public talks. And it's all being translated, printed, and distributed—poor substitute, perhaps, for the immediate appeal of the living man, but the only way that Chabad can pass on the Rebbe's legacy to the greater Jewish world and, just as important, to their own children.

One way Lubavitch children learn about the Rebbe is by writing letters to him, just as their parents do. During a recent convention of Chabad emissary women in Crown Heights, their eight- to twelve-year-old daughters spent three days at a concurrent convention held in the Beth Rivkah school. One morning was devoted to writing letters to Schneerson and then delivering them in person to his grave site.

"Now girls, we know that before we go to the *ohel* we don't just sit and write," advised their head counselor. "We have to put some thought into it. Every one of you now is going for her own private *yechidus* with the Rebbe. Hashem has the gates open and every girl can ask for whatever it is she needs."

Most of these young girls' letters were written as if to a beloved grandfather. "Dear Rebbe, I love you, let me tell you a few things I've been doing," one girl began. "Thank you for sending me to this convention, I'm having so much fun," wrote another. These girls are too young to have met the Rebbe, but they wrote as if to someone they know well. Their missives were filled with selfless wishes for world peace, good health for their parents, and the speedy arrival of the Messianic Age, as well as with touchingly naïve personal requests. "Help me get good grades this year," one girl wrote in purple crayon.

"I'm asking blessings for my sister-in-law and her baby, so it will come out normally," said eleven-year-old Malka Mushka Silberberg, daughter of Chabad shlichim in West Bloomfield, Michigan. "And so my older sister will get engaged. She's nineteen already." Malka was six when Schneerson died. "When I'm in trouble, or something's bothering me, it helps me to know that there's someone who can help, someone who can talk to Hashem."

Chabad educators are concerned about how to pass on the Rebbe's message to young Lubavitchers while steering clear of messianism. Chana

Gorowitz, the Beth Rivkah principal, says that after Schneerson's death her school instituted a weekly class in which the girls study a particular text from Schneerson's writings and then watch a video of him delivering that same text to his Hasidim. "It makes it alive for them," she says. "It's a tool, and we're going to make sure we use all the tools we have."

Shlichim in the field have always lived away from their Rebbe, but they would make annual family trips to Crown Heights, where their personal glimpses of Schneerson in action motivated them for the coming year. Now they have to depend on books and videos to provide that same motivation for their children. Detroit shlicha Bassie Shemtov makes it a point to refer to the Rebbe often during daily conversation. "The Rebbe is my life, and my children feel that," she says. "[My three-year-old] loves the Rebbe. I didn't tell him to; he sees that Levi and I love the Rebbe."

Pictures of the Rebbe are another way of keeping his memory ever-present. Even during his lifetime Lubavitchers hung portraits of Schneerson in prominent places in their homes and offices. Since his death the practice has assumed greater urgency. Lubavitchers use pictures of the Rebbe to teach their children about him. Some have their children kiss a picture of the Rebbe every night before going to sleep, much as a child would kiss a picture of a beloved but faraway grandparent. Lubavitchers also use these pictures to motivate themselves. One shlicha, speaking anonymously, says she hangs pictures of the Rebbe in every room in her house. "It strengthens me," she says. "Each one shows the Rebbe in a different pose. I talk to him a lot. I look at the Rebbe at times when I'm down. I ask the Rebbe to give me strength to face life's challenges."

Some shlichim insist that nothing has changed since Schneerson's death. Rivky Chazan, shlicha in Milan, Italy, talks to her children about the Rebbe in the present tense, to impress upon them that he is still in their lives. And she's proud that her children spend every Rosh Hashanah and Yom Kippur in Crown Heights, visiting the Rebbe's grave as their parents used to visit Schneerson in person.

Most shlichim, however, acknowledge that a lot has changed. One shlicha from the Toronto area, speaking to a group of her peers at the annual shlichot convention, spoke wistfully about her own memories of growing up in Crown Heights, at the epicenter of Lubavitch life. "Our children weren't in 770 like I was, growing up with the Rebbe. They didn't go to *farbrengens*, they didn't push, they didn't live it, they don't know what it is to walk up the street at six in the morning with a *Tanya* in your hand, and you know that you own the world, and you know that you're Lubavitch and the world starts at Eastern Parkway and it ends at Lefferts Boulevard and there's nothing beyond. You know! And your children don't necessarily know that. You have to give it to them, from the minute they're born."

The bulk of Lubavitch's publication efforts takes place on the top floors at 770. Computers whir, printing presses roll, and film is processed, all to churn out the Rebbe's teachings as quickly and comprehensively as possible. On the second floor is the main office of Chabad's Kehot Publication Society, which publishes works of Hasidic philosophy and mysticism, halachic texts, biographies, histories, and Jewish children's books. Kehot claims to have disseminated 100 million volumes of such material in twelve languages, making it the world's largest publisher of Jewish literature.

Kehot serves Lubavitchers, but the bulk of its materials is destined for the movement's outreach work. After Hebrew, English is the main language of publication, followed closely by Spanish, reflecting the growing scope of Chabad outreach operations in South America. Kehot began publishing simple Jewish textbooks and ritual guides in English in the 1940s, to serve North America's fledgling day schools and afternoon Hebrew schools. By the late 1950s, Kehot was publishing English translations of basic Chabad Hasidic works for adults. The *Tanya* was first translated into English in 1962, giving Chabad shlichim their first real text to use in adult educational outreach. In 1978, Kehot published its first prayer book with English translation for use in Chabad's "beginner" services. Kehot is now also trying to meet the demands of Chabad Houses who are attracting clients with more sophisticated Jewish backgrounds. In early 2002, Kehot launched the first volume of its Chasidic Heritage Series, consisting of discourses of various Lubavitcher Rebbes. The Hebrew text has vowels, making it easier for beginners to read, while the English translation is carefully footnoted "so you can sit down and study it like a yeshiva student," Kehot head Rabbi Yosef Friedman says.

Since Schneerson's death, Kehot has stepped up its pace. One-third of the company's English-language books have been printed since 1994, and there has been a particular push in the last seven years to find and publish all of the Rebbe's letters and speeches. One of the problems that has always plagued Kehot, and Lubavitcher Hasidim in general, is that in the early years Schneerson strongly resisted efforts to publish his talks [*sichos*] and the longer, more formal discourses [*ma'amarim*], preferring that Chabadniks focus on the writings of his predecessors. Because he disliked seeing people copying down his words, students and young rabbis would try to memorize his talks and re-create them afterward in group sessions, comparing notes to come up with the version they felt was closest to what the Rebbe really said. "When the Rebbe found out they were hiding tape recorders during his talks, he was upset," relates Shmotkin.

Unlike previous rebbes, who wrote out their own discourses either before or after delivering them, Schneerson never committed his to paper. Between 1950 and 1980 he edited only fifteen to twenty of his discourses, which had been compiled by others.

From 1950 to 1960, Rabbi Yoel Kahn, a distinguished movement elder and Schneerson's chief oral scribe, began typing out the Rebbe's discourses on his own initiative and distributing them by hand. From 1960 through 1976, the only discourses that were preserved were those compiled by individual students. Beginning in 1976 a more formal system of recording was instituted, but it was still carried out mostly by yeshiva students, and its success depended on the student body in any given year. Still, once or twice a decade some of the students would get hold of a copying machine and would print collections of Schneerson's discourses. Part of Kehot's challenge today is to collect and compare all those various versions and come up with authoritative editions to publish.

Much of that compilation effort takes place two floors above the Kehot offices, in the even smaller office of the Va'ad Hanachot b'Lahak, or Committee to Write Down the Rebbe's Talks in Hebrew. Chaim Shaul Brook and Rabbi Dovid Feldman have headed up this group since 1985. Since Schneerson's death the two men and their assistants have been collecting, translating, annotating, and publishing every bit of the Rebbe's private writings they can find, dating back to his marriage in 1928, including three notebooks they discovered posthumously among his belongings. By the end of 2002 they were up to the year 1956 and already had fifteen volumes published. They're also trying to publish every one of the 1,552 discourses Schneerson delivered during his lifetime. No records existed of 458 of them at the time of his death, but Feldman and Brook have since then collected notes from all but 49. Each week since

1998 they've put that week's findings on a free Web site in booklet form, for users to download, print out, and staple together.

Schneerson always spoke in Yiddish, and until 1981 that was the only language used to write down his talks. Brook and Feldman's team are now trying to translate everything into Hebrew. "Most of the community today writes and reads Hebrew, while Yiddish is dropping off," Brook notes. By 2002, Feldman and Brook's committee had put out several hundred volumes of Schneerson's unedited talks to accompany the thirty-six volumes of *Likutei Sichos,* weekly Torah talks Schneerson edited himself, and six volumes of discourses.

Other projects go on behind other doors. On the third floor, Rabbi Simon Jacobson, author of a popular daybook of Schneerson's aphorisms, runs the Meaningful Life Center, where he brings the Rebbe's teachings to the outside world with retreats, publications, and a weekly newsletter. In a nearby room Rabbi Yoel Kahn is embarked on the mammoth task of creating an encyclopedia of Chabad philosophy. One floor up, the Sichos in English office collects, translates, and prints Schneerson's talks in multivolume collections. Hundreds of them have been published so far.

Also on the fourth floor, Chabad's multimedia outreach efforts maintains its headquarters: JEM, the Jewish Educational Media video department; Lubavitch News Service; and Chabad.org, the movement's Internet department. Unlike other Hasidic groups, Chabad has never shied away from technology. Video, radio, satellite TV, and the Internet were always viewed as value-neutral tools that could be used either for good or evil. In the service of Jewish outreach, Schneerson taught, they were to be embraced. "The Rebbe taught that everything God created, He created for His glory," explains Chabad.org project supervisor Moshe Berghoff. "So we can take all his creations and use them for godliness."

Chabad made its first foray into the media world in 1960, with a weekly *Tanya* class broadcast on New York radio station WEVD. Schneerson, who edited the show himself, explained his positive view of radio's outreach potential in a 1966 talk: "There is a special advantage in using radio to teach Torah. Even if a person is not sufficiently motivated to go and attend a class, or even if he only turned on the radio to hear something else—the words of Torah reach him." In 1970, Chabad congregations in London, Israel, and Melbourne were connected to Crown Heights by telephone hook-up for the first live, intercontinental version of one of the Rebbe's *farbrengens*. By 1980, Schneerson's *farbrengens* were telecast live via satellite and cable TV. And in 1988, several years before the creation of the World Wide Web, the late Rabbi Yosef Kazen used Fidonet, an on-line discussion network distributed on several thousand nodes internationally, to spread Yiddishkeit. Kazen later digitized thousands of Chabad documents and posted them on the newly emerged Web, including an English translation of the *Tanya*. He created a Jewish Web library and an interactive "ask the rabbi" feature. Kazen saw the Internet as a way to get through to non-observant Jews who might be turned off by a rabbi in a black hat and long beard. The anonymity of the Internet allows people to ask questions they might not venture in person. To one young man who asked whether he could smoke marijuana on Shabbat morning, Kazen wrote back that "within Judaism, the concept is that prayer itself gives you the high."

When Kazen died in 1998, the *New York Times* called him a "Web pioneer," noting that the "Chabad in Cyberspace" Internet site he'd developed had become a model for other Jewish organizations looking to develop a similar Web presence. The site he left behind, Chabad.org, is now directed by Zalman Shmotkin and run by a few yeshiva students sitting in a room at 770 crammed with boxes and old computer parts.

By 2002, Chabad.org was getting more than 17,000 visits a day and had been completely redesigned to offer customized services for free to its subscribers. Visitors can sign up for daily lessons in *Tanya;* teachings from Maimonides; readings from *Hayom Yom,* a book of Hasidic aphorisms compiled by Schneerson in 1943; weekly mailings of the Torah portion; Midrash, Talmud, Hasidic stories, Kabbalah, and children's lessons; and a number of other offerings on a less frequent basis. The supersite includes news services, a lively weekly magazine, and holiday and ritual guides, and it is linked to sites devoted to the Rebbe and the history of Chabad, Websites for individual Chabad Houses around the world, and askmoses.com, a live on-line chat room where visitors can ask any Jewish or personal question and get a real-time response. Askmoses.com was developed by Rabbis Chaim Cunin and Simcha Backman at Chabad in Los Angeles, but the rabbis and teachers, male and female, who answer visitors' questions sit at computers all over the world. The site can thus operate twenty-four hours a day. As of early 2002, Cunin hopes to launch versions in Hebrew, Russian, and Spanish.

Chabad.org has garnered favorable reviews from such news organizations as ABC, CBS, CNN, Fox, PBS, *Time,* the *Village Voice* and the *Washington Post.* By 2001 close to 1 million visitors were logging onto its Jewish holiday sites each year. The Chanukah site grew out of live satellite hook-ups run out of Lubavitch World Headquarters from 1990 to 1994, when the organization broadcast outdoor menorah lightings from Paris, Jerusalem, Moscow, Melbourne, Hong Kong, and other major cities (including, of course, Crown Heights). Since 1998 those lightings have been streamed live over the Internet.

In addition to disseminating Jewish information, Shmotkin says that Chabad.org has created a worldwide cyber-community of Jews. He points to the hundreds of e-mail raves the site receives from readers. "We are already witnessing the amazing phenomenon of Jews living in the very furthest reaches of exile who no longer feel quite as estranged and lonely as they did just a few short years ago before the Internet revolution," he says.

Several doors away from Chabad.org is the office of Jewish Educational Media, Chabad's video division, directed by Zalman's younger brother Elkanah. Elkanah came to JEM in 1996, fresh out of yeshiva. The office was little more than an archive for hundreds of hours of uncut videotape from various *farbrengens* and public appearances Schneerson made over the years. Elkanah worked alone for three years, trying to piece together coherent documentary records of the Rebbe's teachings on various subjects. In 1999 he moved into his present space at 770, raised enough money to buy his own editing machine, and hired four people to help him. By 2002, JEM was producing a weekly series on the Rebbe and his teachings, which is distributed to subscribers on video and CD-ROM in six languages with an accompanying teachers' guide for use in the classroom. "Video has much more immediate impact than books," he says. "You can hear him and see him. That's something the Rebbe himself would appreciate." Elkanah's dream is to put together a video biography of the Rebbe. Considering that no written bio has even been published, that would be a landmark project for a Chabadnik. "I've spoken to [PBS documentary filmmaker] Ken Burns about it," he muses. "Maybe I need to do a ten-part series." He doesn't think it would be hard to raise money for such a project. "The Rebbe has a lot of fans," he notes. Elkanah's biggest challenge will be somewhat different—finding where to cut Schneerson's complex and long-winded speeches. "The Rebbe," he says ruefully, "never spoke in sound bites."

The books, Internet presence, and videos developed by Lubavitch World Headquarters are all powerful tools in keeping Schneerson's memory and message alive. The job remains, however, to ensure that these tools continue to steer clear of messianist overtones. When Lubavitch children write letters to the Rebbe's *ohel,* when they sing songs about how much they miss Schneerson and how they know he's watching over them, do they distinguish between a man alive in spirit and one alive in the flesh? And what are Lubavitchers really doing at the *ohel*? Moshe New insists that "no one's praying to the Rebbe—there are conversations with, or talking to, but no one's praying to him." But theological subtleties apparent to Yehuda Krinsky and Moshe New become muddled in younger minds. When a teacher in a Lubavitch preschool sings a happy tune about the Messianic Age while holding up a picture of Schneerson, few three-year-olds will grasp the metaphor. They only know what they see.

The people using all these educational tools have to be on the same page, or the message they convey can become twisted. Chabad's challenge now is to complete the *conceptual* shift to a post-Schneerson movement. Controlling messianist behavior is only the beginning. The Chabad leadership hopes that time will take care of much of the problem, as the years pass and a new generation of Lubavitchers who never knew the Rebbe grows up and takes control of the movement. "In time, the Moshichists will have to fade away," says Sam Heilman. "There's a limit to how long they can keep the excitement high."

CHAPTER 15

CHANUKAH, O CHANUKAH:
The Flap over Public Menorahs

On December 21, 2000, just after sundown, Rabbi Levi Shemtov, Chabad emissary in Washington, D.C., was perched high off the near-frozen ground in a cherry picker with then Deputy Secretary of the Treasury Stuart Eizenstat. The two men were poised to light the first candle of the "national menorah," a thirty-foot aluminum menorah right across the street from the White House. Eizenstat lit the giant wick with a flaming torch, and as it sputtered into life, Cantor Ari Klein of New York's Park East Synagogue intoned a Hebrew prayer. The TV cameras zoomed in, and Shemtov faced forward and said: "It is appropriate to celebrate Chanukah here, across from the White House, the center of executive leadership of the world's superpower. From here the message goes forth that the religious freedom we hold so dear is a freedom *of,* not freedom *from,* religion. The Maccabees' triumph recurs every year as we recall the victory of light over might, the few and determined over the many and oppressive, and truth over power." Hundreds of spectators clapped as the U.S. Marine Band struck up a lively chorus of "Heveinu Shalom Aleichem."

This lighting ceremony on the national Ellipse was covered live by every major TV network, and rebroadcast throughout the evening, along with local broadcasts of similar lightings of public menorahs in state capitals around the country. Virtually every one of those public lightings was sponsored by a local Chabad center. All in all that year, Chabad organized hundreds of public menorah lightings in forty-five states and Puerto Rico, and in close to sixty foreign countries. In New York City alone, Chabad lit thirty giant menorahs in highly visible outdoor locations, and an additional three hundred throughout the metropolitan area. In almost every ceremony, a prominent political figure—a mayor, governor, president, or prime minister, Jewish or not—helped the Chabad rabbi light the eight-branched menorah. The major international lightings—Paris, Melbourne, Washington, D.C., Jerusalem—were streamed live on the Internet by Chabad headquarters in Brooklyn, as was the movement's undisputed PR coup of the year—the almost surreal sight of Russian President Vladimir Putin helping to light a silver menorah at Chabad's new Jewish Community Center in Moscow, as he wished the Jewish people a happy and prosperous year.

Probably nothing Chabad does delights and annoys American Jews more than these highly public and highly publicized outdoor menorah lightings. Beginning in 1975 with a twenty-two-foot-high steel and mahogany menorah in Union Square, San Francisco, Chabad menorahs have stood every December outside city halls, in state capitol rotundas, in public parks, in shopping malls, along major highways from Alaska to Hawaii, from Santa Monica to Salt Lake City, and on New York's Fifth Avenue. The Jewish press calls the annual conundrum surrounding them the "December dilemma." In the midst of the holiday season, as plastic Santas overrun lawns and brightly colored Christmas lights are strung across downtown streets, the sight of a Chanukah menorah standing tall in a park or on a street corner can bring a welcome feeling of warmth to Jews, a reminder that December is their holiday season, too. But at the same time, there is a nagging thought at the back of American Jewish minds: What about the separation of Church and State? If there is something disturbing about public displays of baby Jesus in his manger, why should two-story-high menorahs be any more welcome?

To most Jewish groups in this country, they are not. Jewish organizations have figured prominently in the major legal and political battles against the public display of all religious items, Christian and Jewish, on state-owned land. But Chabad continues. "To Lubavitch, the public menorah balances out the public Christmas tree," writes attorney Marc Stern on behalf of the American Jewish Congress, which has opposed Chabad in many menorah lawsuits. "To the American Jewish Congress, the menorah on public lands clears the path for the crèche and the cross."

Whether or not the menorah stands on government property, Schneerson's point was that it should be seen by as many people as possible. Soon after he asked his followers to begin lighting public menorahs, Schneerson wrote to the Jewish Community Council of Teaneck, New Jersey, which was debating its stance on the question, urging that they continue the practice: "The Chanukah menorah . . . can, and *does,* bring many Jews back to their Jewish roots. I personally know of scores of such Jewish returnees, and I have good reason to believe that in recent years, hundreds, even thousands, of Jews experience a kindling of their inner Jewish spark by the public kindling of the Chanukah menorah in their particular city."

Chanukah commemorates the revolt, in 165 B.C.E., of a small band of Jewish warriors led by Judah the Maccabee against the powerful Syrian-Greek occupiers of ancient Israel. At the culmination of the Maccabees' stunning victory, so goes the tale, the Jews recaptured their Temple and tried to light the menorah inside it but found just one day's supply of sanctified oil. Miraculously, the Temple oil burned for eight days, long enough for more oil to be produced. This holiday glorifying military prowess and God's miracle-making was barely celebrated by non-Orthodox American Jews until the late 1940s, when the Holocaust, the founding of the State of Israel, and growing economic prosperity spurred a sharp rise in Jewish ethnic identity. Chanukah bushes and eight days of elaborate gift-giving were created in this country to combat Santa Claus and the Christmas tree, to give Jewish kids something to point to when their school friends were getting ready for Rudolph.

The Lubavitcher Rebbe appreciated that the present generation of American Jews, unlike their immigrant parents and grandparents who wanted to slip quietly into the American melting pot, were ready to respond with pride to public celebrations of "their" winter holiday. "You can see the Rebbe's vision," says Rabbi Yossi Greenberg, Chabad shliach in Anchorage, Alaska. "Intermarried families might not go to synagogue to fast on Yom Kippur, but they'll show up for Chanukah." Chanukah menorah-lighting was also a logical ritual for the Rebbe to seize upon as one of his outreach campaigns because the holiday itself demands that Jews publicize it. Jews are required to commemorate the Maccabees' victory by placing lighted menorahs in their open windows. In America, where Jews no longer faced persecution, Schneerson proclaimed that the mitzvah of publicizing Chanukah should be given new emphasis.

The Rebbe's shlichim rushed to put his latest outreach program into action. In 1974, Rabbi Avraham Shemtov put up a small wooden menorah next to Philadelphia's Liberty Bell, a symbolic gesture not lost on the nation's media. The next year legendary rock promoter Bill Graham sponsored Chabad's San Francisco menorah. Others followed, and in 1979 Shemtov decided that it was time for a Chabad menorah to go up in the nation's capital. In December of that year, a thirty-foot menorah was raised in Lafayette Park, practically on the White House lawn. "*Newsweek, Time* came, they took pictures," Shemtov recalls. "We got the White House to turn on their lights for the picture. One of the photographers was so engrossed he said, 'Could we move the menorah a little bit to the left so the White House will be in the middle?' I said to him, 'Why don't you get the White House to move a little to the right?'"

America was in the midst of the Iranian hostage crisis, and President Jimmy Carter had secluded himself for one hundred days in the White House. But he came out to dedicate the Chabad menorah. After the official lighting, Shemtov presented the president with a second, small silver menorah. It was the fourth night of Chanukah, so four candles were lit on the president's gift. Carter was unhappy, Shemtov recounts. He interpreted the four unlit candles as demonstrating that darkness still prevailed in the world, and he asked Shemtov to light the entire menorah. Shemtov hesitated. He explained that Jewish law provides for lighting an additional candle each night, but the president persisted. Eventually, Shemtov relented, telling himself that the commandment to publicize Chanukah was fulfilled by the giant menorah on the Lafayette Park lawn, which had the correct number of candles lit. This small silver menorah was ceremonial, and had been lit by an underage child, so it was not bound by Jewish law. In addition, the Talmud makes certain allowances for Jews who travel in government circles and have to show respect to political leaders. Why not do this small thing for the president? Later, Shemtov learned that the Rebbe was disappointed with his decision. "The Rebbe didn't say I did wrong, he said he expected more steadfastness. This labeled our contact with Washington: We need not compromise our principles in any way in order to be perfectly correct in our dealings with the government."

Through the 1980s, Chabad shlichim continued putting up Chanukah menorahs wherever they could. It is often the first action a new shliach takes when he moves to a town. Chabad's menorah-lighting ceremonies are festive and well attended. They receive prominent coverage from the Jewish and non-Jewish media, with Jewish parents quoted as saying how proud they are to show their children that Christmas trees aren't the only holiday decorations in their town. Some Chabad menorahs are placed in shopping malls or Jewish Community Centers, but most Chabad rabbis actively seek to put them on public property, to illustrate the Rebbe's point that in America, Jews and the Jewish religion enjoy full legal and governmental protection. Public parks and traffic intersections are sometimes used, but city halls, state capitols and courthouse buildings are better, signifying the highest levels of political approval.

As Chabad menorahs proliferated, so did the complaints against them. And the overwhelming majority of those complaints came from other Jews, primarily from Jewish organizations. There were two main lines of dissent. One held that Chabad's menorah lightings made public what should remain private, that they actually discouraged people from undertaking their own religious practice. But the most frequently articulated opposition to Chabad's public menorahs among Jewish groups is that they violate the establishment clause of the First Amendment to the Constitution, which lays out the fundamental principle of Church-State separation. "We don't think religious symbols belong on public property," explains Mark Pelavin, associate director of the Reform movement's Religious Action Center in Washington, D.C. "They convey the impermissible message of government endorsement and send a clear message that some religions are favored while others are not."

In 1986 a consortium of Jewish organizations, together with the American Civil Liberties Union, sued Chabad and the City of Pittsburgh, Pennsylvania, over that city's public menorah. Since 1981 the mayor of Pittsburgh had agreed to display a Nativity scene every December in the county courthouse, and a Chanukah menorah and Christmas tree on the steps of the City Hall. Chabad of Pittsburgh provided the eighteen-foot menorah, and the city was happy to put it up next to its forty-five-foot Christmas tree as part of a combined holiday display. After a tortuous three-year journey through the court system, Pittsburgh's Chabad menorah case landed before the U.S. Supreme Court, where it was joined to a similar lawsuit against the city's crèche scene. On July 3, 1989, the high court ruled in *Allegheny County v. ACLU* that the Nativity scene had to come down, as it sent a purely religious message advocating Christianity; but the menorah could stand, because its location next to a Christmas tree made it part of a display intended not as an official religious endorsement but as recognition that, in the Court's words, "both Christmas and Chanukah are part of the same winter-holiday season, which has attained a secular status in our society."

When the 6 to 3 decision in favor of the menorah came down, the media and Jewish organizations were astonished. How could the Supreme Court permit this blatant government endorsement of religion? A July 12, 1989, *New York Times* editorial decried the Court's "regrettable determination to knock down whatever remains of the wall" separating private religious faith and governmental authority. In fact, however, the Court's vote was not a victory for state-sponsored religion at all. The case squeaked by only because Justices Harry Blackmun and Sandra Day O'Connor, who were expected to vote against Chabad and the City of Pittsburgh, decided that a Chanukah menorah celebrates universal freedom, a secular message. Further, they decided, the context of this particular display, which included both a tree and a menorah along with a sign reading "A Salute to Liberty," effectively diluted any particularistic religious component.

Jewish organizations chafed at what they called the Court's "secularization" of Chanukah, and slammed Chabad for arguing the case at least partially on that basis. "It is ironic and troubling that Chabad . . . one of the most traditional observant Jewish groups, would argue that a Chanukah menorah is other than a religious symbol," wrote Anti-Defamation League national director Abe Foxman in a letter to the *Times*. "Lubavitch may win the right to display their menorah at the Pittsburgh City Hall, but only at the cost of secularizing this ancient and revered religious symbol." The national leadership of the American Jewish Congress, American Jewish Committee, the Union of American Hebrew Congregations and B'nai B'rith International all issued similar statements. Chabad stood alone.

But that didn't bother Nathan Lewin, Chabad's lead attorney on the Pittsburgh menorah case. A self-described Orthodox Jew who says he has "tried to facilitate and encourage religious observance by fellow Jews in the United States," Lewin says that he never claimed the menorah should be understood as a secular symbol, despite what the justices later wrote in their opinions. His argument focused on context. He handed the court a photograph of the eighteen-foot menorah as it stood next to the city's forty-five-foot Christmas tree, and told them that such a display did not violate the First Amendment's establishment clause, which was meant to protect against government imposition of a particular religion, because, he said, "You could hardly say this was propagating Judaism, when it was a relatively small menorah in contrast to the Christmas tree. Clearly, no one was trying to impose Judaism on the citizens of Pittsburgh."

The Court agreed, and Chabad won this case. But as Pittsburgh's Chabad rabbi was getting ready for Chanukah that year, newly elected Mayor Sophie Masloff—the city's first Jewish mayor—took office. She announced that if the Supreme Court says no crèche, then she says no menorah, either. Fair is fair.

Chabad fought back. On December 15, 1989, seven days before Chanukah, Chabad filed suit in district court to prevent the new city administration from interfering with what had now become the erection of a private menorah. This time Lewin took a different stand than with the Supreme Court. No longer arguing context, he turned now to defending the menorah on the grounds of free speech. Declaring the steps of a city hall to be a "public forum," he argued that Chabad's menorah amounted to a public expression of religious faith, which is protected as free speech under the Constitution. The founding fathers of this country, Lewin said—all deeply religious men themselves—wanted to ensure freedom *of* religion, not freedom *from* religion, a central point that has become twisted in the intervening two centuries.

Chanukah began that year at sundown on a Friday. On Tuesday, the U.S. district court accepted Lewin's free speech argument and ruled in favor of Chabad. The menorah could go up. Immediately, the city appealed to a circuit judge in Pittsburgh, who issued a stay of the district court's decision. The menorah could not go up. Chabad appealed to the Third Circuit Court in Philadelphia, which delayed its decision until late Friday afternoon, when it ruled against Chabad. At home, preparing for Shabbat, Lewin got the news and made a last-minute phone appeal to Supreme Court Justice William Brennan. Twenty minutes before sundown Brennan set aside the Third Circuit order. The menorah could go up. On Monday, the city tried one last time, appealing to the entire Supreme Court on an emergency basis, so it could take the menorah down before the end of Chanukah. The city argued that its City Hall steps were not a "public forum," thus not subject to First Amendment protection. By another 6 to 3 decision, the High Court upheld Justice Brennan, and Chabad's Pittsburgh menorah—which by now had somehow grown from a modest eighteen feet to a statuesque forty—held its position next to the forty-five-foot Christmas tree it was fast overtaking.

The Supreme Court had spoken, twice. But the menorah grumbling continued. Again, except for newspaper editors, most of the opponents were Jewish organizational leaders and rabbis. Few of them liked the Court's July decision, which subsumed the menorah's religious character in what Justice Blackmun blithely called the "winter holiday season." Fewer still were buying its December ruling, where Chabad's lawyers held up the icon of free speech. The controversy really turned on religious feelings, critics said, not constitutional principle. "It is disingenuous to suggest that the Jews and Christians who rallied round the menorah and the Nativity respectively were motivated primarily by a concern for free speech or an open public forum," wrote *Pittsburgh Post-Gazette* editorial page editor Michael McGough in the February 5, 1990, *New Republic.* "What they crave is government acknowledgment of their miracles."

So, and not so, counters Lewin. "It's not that I wanted the government to *acknowledge* the message of the menorah. I wanted it to *respect* the message of the menorah, to say that we are as good as anyone else." But he also admits that the case was important to him, and to many other American Jews, for personal reasons. "This whole enterprise, which the Lubavitcher Rebbe began, is an important aspect of pride in Jewish identity in the United States," he says. "Comes December every year, you go out in the street, and you're totally submerged in Christmas decorations—wreaths and stars and Christmas trees. Everything's all Christmas, and what are you going to do? I think the idea of putting up a huge menorah, in a public place, on the public forum, in front of City Hall, is really a sign that this is a place where Jews can hold their heads high." Marc Stern, who argued against Chabad in *Allegheny County v. ACLU* for the American Jewish Congress, finds that attitude problematic: "Lubavitch says, if you don't get Judaism endorsed by the government in equal measure with other religions, you send a message that Judaism is inferior. It's precisely that call for government approval that we find so objectionable."

Jewish opposition to Chabad's public menorah-lightings cuts across the denominational spectrum. In 1992, the UAHC, the congregational arm of the Reform movement, distributed a flyer to its member congregations outlining how Reform groups could outflank Chabad by holding their own menorah-lighting ceremonies. And while the Orthodox Union and Agudath Israel stay away from court cases challenging public menorahs, their leaders have stated that they oppose Chabad on this as well as other issues. "Ideally, we would prefer no displays of any religious symbols," then OU president Sheldon Rudoff told the *Forward* in December 1992.

The Supreme Court's decisions in the Pittsburgh menorah case were so narrow that they provided little guidance to other cities and judges confronting similar lawsuits. Public menorah cases proliferated across the nation, with courts ruling sometimes at cross-purposes. With the free speech and Church-State separation arguments all but closed to them, opponents of Chabad's public menorahs sought other ways to prevent what they continued to view as a dangerous state encroachment on private religious belief. The Supreme Court had stipulated that if a city permitted holiday displays on public lands, then it could not discriminate between which kinds of displays may be erected. But cities still had the power to declare that no displays of any kind could be put up, or that they may only be a certain size, or may only stand for a certain time period.

As the nineties dragged on, new lawsuits against Chabad menorahs began to invoke these kinds of local regulations. But the heart seemed to have gone out of the battle, and in the end, Chabad inevitably won. In Beverly Hills, California, a twenty-year struggle had raged between Chabad of the West Coast, headed by Rabbi Shlomo Cunin, and the ACLU, American Jewish Congress, ADL, and a host of Jewish residents opposed to Chabad's public menorahs. The annual contest generated such strong community feelings that several City Council candidates included their position on the menorah issue in their campaign platforms. Over the years, Cunin moved his menorah from one park to another in response to various suits, rode out a 1996 federal appeals court ruling that declared Chabad was receiving preferential treatment (its menorah was permitted in a public park denied to two other groups' winter holiday displays), and finally triumphed in 1997, when a federal district court struck down a city provision that limited any displays on city property to two consecutive days. That provision had been openly drafted as a last-ditch effort the previous year to prevent Chabad's menorah from going up. "Even Santa Claus knows that Hanukkah is celebrated for eight days," Chabad lawyer Marshall Grossman told the *San Diego Union-Tribune*. In December 1997, the ACLU of Southern California, along with the Jewish groups that had been suing Chabad for so many years, told the *San Diego Union-Tribune* that their fight in the courts was finished.

The same thing was happening across the country. Attorney Stuart Levey began working with Nathan Lewin in 1990 to defend Chabad menorah cases. He's still one of the country's main lawyers on the issue, and he sees only about six or seven cases a year. Virtually none of them make it to court. In 2001, Levey said it had been two years since he'd had to litigate a menorah case. "We've won all the important points," he says, and Chabad's opponents know that. When a case does come up, Levey says, "I write to the town attorney and say that we know our business, we will sue, and we will win." Levey had to deal with only three cases during Chanukah 2000, and each was resolved by letter. Money has a lot to do with it, Lewin adds. "When we win these cases, we not only get a judgment, but the town or city has to pay lawyers' fees of fifty-to-one-hundred thousand dollars. When towns know that's a prospect, they capitulate, quite frankly."

Stern says he gets "very few calls" from people looking to block public menorahs anymore. Invariably, he counsels those few callers to avoid bringing suit against Chabad. "In legal terms, there's relatively little that can be done," he says. He knows of "relatively few" instances where Chabad rabbis have not been allowed to put up their menorahs in public spaces. "Nothing stops them."

Meanwhile, what happened in Pittsburgh? Rabbi Yisroel Rosenfeld, still the head Chabad shliach there, says that a menorah goes up every year on the City Hall steps, but it's now owned by the city rather than Chabad. A Chabad representative helps light it, but since 1995, despite all the hoopla and the Supreme Court fight, Chabad of Pittsburgh has been erecting its own, separate menorah on *private* land. Rosenfeld says the ACLU "tried to stop" it several times but never returned to court. Sophie Masloff, who sent Chabad back to the Supreme Court in 1989, is no longer the mayor. Now, Rosenfeld says, she's a "good friend" of Chabad and even attends Chabad dinner functions. Not all of them, however. She didn't come the year that Nat Lewin was the guest speaker, which Rosenfeld says was probably best for everyone.

By the late nineties, the battle over Chabad's public menorahs moved from the courts to the political arena. No longer were lawsuits being brought before judges; now city councils were being asked to regulate what could and could not be displayed on their municipal property. A slew of cases cropped up in small New England towns. In Westborough, Massachusetts, the conflict had more to do with Chabad's operational style than anything else. In December 2000, Michoel Green, a Chabad rabbi in nearby Worcester, asked Westborough's board of selectmen for permission to erect a menorah on the town rotary, a central plaza that already hosted an annual "festival of lights" display featuring angels and a suspiciously Christmasy tree. His action raised hackles among the town's Reform and Conservative leadership, who felt Green had gone over their heads. "We didn't even know Chabad was in town," says Debra Hachen, rabbi of Westborough's Reform congregation B'nai Shalom. "They didn't send out a 'Happy Chanukah' or 'we're here,' they just went straight to the selectmen with their request." After a heated public meeting, the selectmen decided they would not permit the menorah that year, since it was already the week before Chanukah, but would review the situation and come up with a policy for the following year.

"That was probably the worst vote of my life," confesses Lydia Goldblatt, the only Jew on the town's five-member board of selectman and one of three who voted against the menorah in 2000. Westborough's selectmen felt uncomfortable having to rule on what they saw as a religious issue. After Green told them that the menorah is "never religious," but "a universal symbol for all people," the town's holiday-lighting committee called Hachen in to clarify: Is the menorah a religious object, or not? Yes, she told them. It's used in a religious ritual, which is sanctified with a Hebrew blessing. "But I told them that this is only my opinion, and Rabbi Green has another. I could see their growing discomfort."

All through the spring of 2001, Westborough's selectmen held meetings on the menorah issue, which had become a topic of conversation "in supermarket aisles," Hachen says. "People got the idea that the town had said no to the menorah. Christian kids wrote letters to the editor, saying they didn't think it was nice not to permit the menorah." The situation was blowing up. Green agreed to meet with Hachen and a few other involved individuals, and he apologized for creating such a ruckus. He was "really very nice," Hachen says, but she still didn't buy his argument. "He said if they allow it on the National Mall in Washington, D.C., then they should allow it here. I said, just because the government allows it doesn't make it right."

On June 26, 2001, Westborough's selectmen ruled to permit Chabad to erect its menorah every December on the town rotary. Lydia Goldblatt says she's pleased with the decision. "I'm from New York, I think it's good to have it up." Besides, she likes Rabbi Green. Hachen says she wasn't surprised at the town's ruling, but she disagrees with it. Her congregation does not advertise Chabad's menorah-lighting in its temple bulletin. "I told my congregation that those of us who believe in the separation of Church and State should make it a point not to attend this event, no matter how appealing it might be to sing Chanukah songs in public." But, she emphasizes, "I don't want any Chabad-bashing in my congregation. They have a right to ask the city for whatever they want, just as we do." Hachen, too, likes Rabbi Green.

Rabbi Green, for his part, is happy with the town's decision, and he also likes everybody. He says he "feels bad" for causing such dissension. When he and his wife arrived in Westborough in the fall of 2000, their only goal, he insists, was to serve the town's growing Jewish population. "We thought most of the Jews were unaffiliated, and we thought the best thing to do would be to put up a big Chanukah menorah. If there's one in Worcester, in Boston, and in hundreds of other places, we didn't think we'd encounter opposition." He was, he now knows, naïve. But he wasn't deliberately courting conflict. "I wasn't trying to make a legal point—I just wanted to put it up in the most visible place. In retrospect, I might have picked a different location, but once things escalated, I felt it would be counterproductive to back down."

Everything happens for a reason, Green says. Maybe it was best that the town turned down his initial request, because the resulting TV and newspaper coverage publicized Chanukah to a much wider audience than his menorah would have done. And although he doesn't like upsetting people, he doesn't mind standing up to the organized Jewish community in the Rebbe's name. "I know what the assimilation rate is, and I see how a public menorah excites people, how it brings them in. The fact that the town allows us to put up our menorah sends a powerful message to Jews who send their kids to public school. And if we upset some Jews along the way, that's the price we'll have to pay."

Throughout this fifteen-year legal and political battle over Chabad's public menorahs, the American people have been treated to the unsavory spectacle of Jews battling Jews, in courts and City Hall chambers, over what is essentially a matter of Jewish identity. Howard Sommer, the

Reform rabbi of Temple Beth Tikvah in Madison, Connecticut, describes how he was called in by his town's board of selectmen to debate his local Chabad rabbi over putting up a menorah on the town green. The scene dissolved into a bizarre situation, he says. "Here we were, this Lubavitch rabbi and I, arguing the history and message of Chanukah before two secular politicians." The menorah went up.

In some towns Chabad's public menorah creates such rancor between Jews that other rabbis boycott Chabad's lighting and stage their own instead. That happened in Great Neck, New York, where Chabad shlichim arrived in 1994 and erected a large menorah on the village green. "It polarized the Jewish community in an unfortunate and unnecessary way," says one of the other rabbis in town. "It resulted in vitriolic sermons and acrimonious accusations on both sides. Some of us were ready to consider a court case, but we were advised we would lose and would be held personally liable, so we dropped it." The following year, a dozen non-Chabad rabbis organized round-robin lightings of menorahs they installed at their own synagogues, "to demonstrate that it should be public, but not on public property," this rabbi recounts. But that cooperative effort only lasted for two holiday seasons. How long can rabbis continue to protest a Chanukah menorah, after all? "The Chabad menorah is still there, but the acrimony has long since subsided," he says. "There's no point anymore."

Sometimes, Chabad shlichim will bow to community opinion and will erect their menorah on private property, even when they are permitted to use public space. That's what they've done in Binghamton, New York, since 1985. "We chose a shopping mall and not City Hall because we didn't want to rankle the local bigwigs," shlicha Rivkah Slonim says. "Binghamton is a small town."

In most cases, however, Chabad shlichim feel that the good deed they do by placing a menorah on public land outweighs the grumbling of local Jews who don't understand the significance of the gesture but who will eventually come around. They may be right. Twenty, even ten years ago, few non-Chabad groups put up outdoor menorahs. Today, Reform, Conservative, and Orthodox congregations, as well as Jewish Community Centers, are lighting their own menorahs, more every year. Even if the original intention of these menorahs is to counter Chabad, and even if they are erected on private, not public land, Lubavitchers say the end result is the same: more public acknowledgment of Jewish identity. In Binghamton, the city's Reform temple began erecting a Chanukah menorah on its property soon after the Slonims' shopping mall menorah first went up. "In my heart of hearts, I can't help feeling it's a direct result of the Rebbe wanting menorahs to pop up everywhere," Rivkah Slonim asserts, adding with a twinkle in her eye, "I'm sure they'll interpret it differently."

In fact, they do. Jewish denominational leaders play down Chabad's effect on their ritual practice in general, and on public Chanukah menorahs in particular. But they don't discount it entirely. Marc Stern says he finds it "hard to take seriously Lubavitch's claim that so many people have been brought back to Judaism because they saw a menorah." He believes that the increased number of Reform and Conservative synagogues that light public menorahs today are responding to a "generational change" in their own movements, a growing comfort with public displays of Judaism. But he does admit that some of that is due to Chabad, to "the Lubavitch notion of public Jewish pride, that we shouldn't be ashamed." A *kippa*-wearing Orthodox Jew himself, Stern says Chabad deserves credit for eroding the American Jewish belief that religion belongs only in the private sphere.

Even those who fight Chabad menorahs on constitutional grounds find it hard to resist the menorah's tug on their heartstrings. Mark Pelavin notes that although the Reform movement he works for is a strong opponent of religious displays on public land, individual rabbis come to their own conclusions, depending on their circumstances. "It presents a real challenge to rabbis in smaller towns, especially," he says. "If there will be a Christmas tree in City Hall, and the city invites you to put up a menorah there, too, what do you do? That's not a decision I'd second-guess sitting here in D.C." Pelavin thinks about the issue differently now that he has children of his own. "I see how meaningful it is to them, how happy they are to see a menorah in a public place."

All in all, Chabad shlichim aren't too concerned with what the organized Jewish world thinks about their menorahs—or anything else, for that matter. Their target audience is the Jew in the street, the ordinary man, woman, and child whose spirit soars at the sight of a giant menorah lit in the town square, who secretly thrills to hear "Ma Oz Tsur," a traditional Chanukah song, broadcast on TV.

Some of the four hundred or so people who showed up for San Francisco's Chabad menorah-lighting in December 2000 said they weren't too sure about the legal principles involved, but they certainly loved what they were seeing. Fremont mother Brenda Golembo was standing on the edge of the crowd, holding a tiny lit candle and watching the rapt faces of her children, eleven-year-old Sharon and eight-year-old Eric. "It's fun," Brenda said. "There's a universal feeling of Judaism here. It brings Jews together from across the Bay Area." Brenda said she knows little about Chabad, and has no particular feelings about the group either way, but she appreciates their putting on this public show every year. "I think it's pretty good," Eric agreed. He and his sister said they would light their own menorah at home afterward.

Richard Fogel, a taxi medallion owner who represents Jewish war veterans on the city's Jewish Community Relations Council, was lounging at the foot of the giant Christmas tree that also stands in Union Square. His attention was fixed on Chabad Rabbi Yosef Langer, who had just finished lighting the menorah with San Francisco Mayor Willie Brown. Fogel has been coming to this Union Square ceremony every year since he first was introduced to Langer in 1978. "He's quite a guy," Fogel remarked. "This is the reason I'm an Orthodox Jew today."

It had been twenty-five years since Bill Graham sponsored San Francisco's first Chabad lighting, and this evening was a tribute to his memory. Along with the mayor, a bevy of city officials sat on the stage underneath the giant menorah. The police chief, the fire chief, the head of the city's public utilities, the director of Public Works, the city engineer, the heads of every major city government department—they were all there, singing or humming along, laughing politely when Langer presented the African-American mayor with a new Borsalino hat, to make him "a real Lubavitcher."

"I'm sure Brother Bill is lighting his Chanukah menorah up above tonight," Langer told the crowd. He recounted the Chanukah story in stirring detail, focusing on the holiday's message of freedom from oppression, and reminding the crowd that they, too, had the power to bring God's miracles into the world, just like the Maccabees did almost 2,200 years ago. "It's up to us to tap into that pure oil in each one of us," he proclaimed in a booming voice. "When tapped into, this miraculous light at our core lights up our homes and families, and brings peace to the Jewish people and to the entire world." He urged the adults in the crowd to reach into their pockets and give the coins they found there to their children, to teach them the importance of giving to others, in God's name. "The Lubavitcher Rebbe said that by going beyond our nature and reaching out to someone else, we can bring about a transformation of the entire world."

Then, with a beatific smile, Rabbi Langer motioned the band to strike up a Hasidic tune. He began to dance, his arms held high above his head, his eyes focused on the heavens. And the crowd danced with him, as the smell of frying latkes filled the air and four enormous candle flames shot up into the fast-darkening city sky.

CHAPTER 16

ADDICTS, INMATES, AND OTHER JEWS:
Serving the Underserved

Minnesota Chabad Rabbi Moshe Feller loves to tell the story about a great Hasidic rebbe (it's always a great Hasidic rebbe) who came from Israel to pay a courtesy call on the Lubavitcher Rebbe. The grand visitor swept into the Rebbe's room, followed by his entourage (great Hasidic rebbes always travel with an entourage).

Those fortunate enough to be in the room waited for the learned discourse that was sure to ensue. But Schneerson had another idea, Feller relates. "The Lubavitcher Rebbe asked him, 'What are you doing to curb promiscuity and drugs in Israel?' The visitor protested, saying, 'That's not a problem among *our* children.' The Rebbe looked at him very sternly and said, 'And which children are *not* our children?'"

In their efforts to reach those not always served by the organized Jewish community, Chabad shlichim have turned their attention to drug addicts, prisoners, orphans, the poor, and the disabled. Some of that work—dealing with drug problems in particular—was a natural outgrowth of Lubavitch street outreach in the 1960s and '70s. Chabad rabbis' overflowing enthusiasm for their work and their optimistic belief in the purity of every Jewish soul carries them into dark alleys where few other people choose to tread. It's not just Krasnoyarsk and Tierra del Fuego; Chabad shlichim are willing to go to East L.A. and downtown Detroit.

Some Chabad emissaries have built their shlichus around programs they've developed to serve these neglected segments of the Jewish population. Shlomo Cunin in Los Angeles set up a successful drug rehabilitation center in the 1970s that has helped thousands of clients, both Jewish and non-Jewish, and some of them very high-profile, kick their habits. A number of Chabad shlichim sponsor large-scale humanitarian projects in the former Soviet Union. Chabad's Children of Chernobyl program has brought more than 2,000 Jewish children from radiation-contaminated areas of Ukraine and Belarus to Israel, where they are housed, fed, and given medical care at Kfar Chabad. The program has also established a therapy center in a Minsk orphanage and one of the few mammography centers in the heavily contaminated area of northern Ukraine.

The Brooklyn-based Tzivos Hashem, Chabad children's organization, raises $1 million a year to run a food pantry in Dnepropetrovsk, Ukraine, that feeds two hundred needy families a week and a medical clinic for disabled children, Jewish and non-Jewish, in Zaparozhye, Russia.

All of these projects have generated considerable media buzz because of the celebrities Chabad has managed to attract to their fundraising efforts. Rabbi Cunin's annual telethon, carried live on public access television, raises $5-to-$6 million a year for his drug clinic. Tzivos Hashem raises the bulk of its budget through the Joseph Papp Children's Humanitarian Fund, which organizes star-studded gala dinner benefits in New York. The group's $500-a-plate dinner in May 2001 featured testimonials from Liza Minnelli and Mary Tyler Moore, and was cochaired by James Earl Jones and Mandy Patinkin.

Less well known are two other programs that also illustrate Chabad's propensity for serving the underserved: the Aleph Institute, a Miami-based advocacy organization that provides humanitarian and religious aid to Jewish prisoners and their families, and Detroit's Friendship Circle, which reaches out to special needs children and provides counseling for addicts.

The Friendship Circle is the brainchild of Levi and Bassie Shemtov, young Chabad shlichim in Detroit. Soon after their marriage in 1993, Levi was offered a part-time job counseling troubled youths by the Lubavitch Foundation of Michigan. While Levi was getting his feet wet in his new job, he and Bassie cast around for social work she could do. They made the rounds of Detroit's Jewish organizations, asking what was the community's greatest need. Supplementary care for special-needs children, they were told. Outside the public school system, nothing existed to help children suffering from autism, Down's syndrome, and a host of other emotional, mental, and physical disabilities.

Neither Bassie nor Levi was a trained therapist or physician, but they pinpointed an area where they could be effective: providing relief support for the parent-caretakers of these emotionally demanding children. Bassie came up with a scheme to match teenage volunteers with special-needs children, whereby the volunteers would visit these children in their homes several times a week in order to give their parents, most often a harried mother, a few hours of respite.

In 1994 she recruited a handful of teenagers from Detroit's Lubavitch girls' school and mailed a flyer advertising her free home-visitation service to a list of one hundred families with special-needs children that she got from Jewish Family Services. Only five families responded. When Bassie called some of the people on the list herself, she found that most thought it was a scam. Who would believe that this young rabbi's wife was offering to send them a free baby-sitter, with no strings attached?

The first few families who received Bassie's volunteers found they were getting much more than a baby-sitter. Whether it's the volunteers themselves, or the way Bassie keeps pumping them up by telling them how important their work is, the result is that by 2001, eighty-five families were being visited at least once a week by more than three hundred volunteers. Bassie recruits and trains the volunteers, coordinates their transportation, and monitors every case personally.

One Tuesday morning in March, Bassie is standing in the kitchen of her Oak Park home, juggling three telephones, four kids, and lunch for ten that she's preparing for Levi's lunch-and-learn Torah class the next day. A slight, energetic woman wearing sneakers and a gray sweatshirt with a matching drawstring-waist skirt, Bassie looks more like the teenage girls she works with than a rebbetzin of eight years' standing. She talks a mile a minute on two separate cellular phones, coordinating last-minute changes in that afternoon's home visits before grabbing her parka, backpack, and a toddler or two and racing out to the family minivan.

As she drives, Bassie talks about the program and the $4 million Ferber-Kaufman Life Town Center that's just broken ground on Lubavitch's new campus, a fifteen-minute drive away. When completed, the new facility will include eight standard therapy rooms, a gross-motor-skills room with special equipment, and sensory rooms filled with sand, water, and bean tables. Lounges for parents will allow them to relax while their children are receiving therapy from licensed staffers, and a separate lounge for the teen volunteers will be furnished with Ping-Pong tables, books, board games, and refreshments. But the most exciting part of the new Friendship Circle facility, she says, is the "Life Town," a scale-model city street that will include a restaurant, food store, general store, movie theater, and dentist office/beauty parlor where special-needs children will learn how to interact in "real society" without fear or embarrassment. On their Life Town visits, the children can shop for basic food, order and eat simple meals, have their hair done and their teeth "examined," and learn how to cross streets and greet strangers. The new facility will include a separate building for Levi's counseling work, the Daniel B. Sobel Friendship and Counseling Program. So far, seven donors have contributed $2.7 million, and Bassie is confident the rest will be raised on schedule.

Bassie pulls up to the home of fourteen-year-old Elana Kaminer at the same moment as the two Friendship Circle volunteers, Goldie and Freyda, arrive. Elana is waiting impatiently at her front door. "Bassie, Bassie, Bassie, Bassie!" she shouts, as she runs up to Bassie and the two girls, hugging them awkwardly and pulling them toward the house. Elana has dark curly hair pulled back in a ponytail and would be very pretty were it not for her slightly crossed eyes and unfocused smile. She has chromosome damage with attendant autism, which makes it difficult for her to speak and process information. Elana is irritable and headstrong, with the behavior of a child half her age. "She's a handful," admits her mother, Sheryl. "She doesn't have any friends her own age. These girls are her friends. She knows when they're coming and looks forward to it all day."

Elana has dragged the two girls upstairs to choose stuffed animals from the enormous collection that clutters her bedroom. Then they troop downstairs again, Elana chattering all the while, and head for the kitchen table, where Elana carefully positions five stuffed bears on one chair and sits across from them, ready to draw. She sits awkwardly on Goldie's lap, her hands clutched spasmodically, unsure where to begin. Freyda picks up a crayon and starts drawing one of the bears. "Elana, what did I forget?" she prompts, pointing to the drawing. "The tail? OK, what color shall I make it? Purple?" Elana nods. Purple is her favorite color, as Freyda well knows.

For the next two hours Freyda and Goldie draw, sing, and tell stories with Elana nonstop. They talk to her calmly, laugh a lot, and touch her continually, taking her hand as they walk or giving her a quick hug when she answers a question. Elana's eyes shine as she basks in their attention. She won't let her mother in the room while they're playing. These are *her* friends, the only thing she has for herself alone, and she guards them with fierce jealousy. Elana speaks with difficulty, forcing out each syllable through her nose and shaking her head violently when she can't make herself understood. The few hours a week that Bassie's volunteers come to visit are the only hours Elana's mother has to herself, to make phone calls, take an uninterrupted bath, read, or just sit quietly and shut her eyes.

Bassie has been sending Friendship Circle volunteers to the Kaminers for four years, always a pair of Lubavitcher girls. Although she now recruits her teen volunteers from throughout Detroit's Jewish community, she gives the toughest cases to Lubavitchers. "We grow up in large families, we're used to taking care of children and to the ethic of giving," she explains. On the drive home, Bassie reflects on the lifestyle choices that contribute to raising the kind of teenager who naturally gravitates to social work. Big families are certainly a factor, she says. So are the restrictions on dating and movies, which shield Lubavitch children from societal influences their parents consider harmful. "Watching a movie isn't going to change me. But it can have an effect on a teenager. People ask why we don't watch 'good' movies, like *Schindler's List*. But once you give a teenager certain videos, it opens the door and they want more."

That evening, after washing the dinner dishes and putting their children to bed, Bassie and Levi visit the Goldsteins,* parents of a cocaine addict Levi has been helping for several years. The Goldsteins are very well off, pillars of the local Jewish community. Their son David* was one of the first cases Levi dealt with in Detroit. David was in his late twenties when they met, a good-looking charmer whose drug habit kept him drifting from job to job. Levi started dropping by David's apartment without warning, checking up on him, sometimes spending the night to watch over him. He'd walk six miles to see David on Shabbat, waking him up at

---

*Not their real names.

noon to make sure he was still alive. One day, after months of these visits, David asked him in exasperation, "What do you want with me?"

"I want you to trust me," Levi answered. Levi sent David to one rehab center and then another. Each time David would stay clean for a while and then slip back into drugs.

The worst episode came when David had completed yet another rehab session in Florida and was living in Boca Raton. His parents hadn't heard from him in three weeks, and they were frantic. They called Levi. He said, "Let me see what I can do," and twenty minutes later the Goldsteins got a phone call from their son. "What the hell did you do?" he shouted. "I'm in the shower, and there's this guy with a beard banging on the front door, yelling at me to let him in." Levi had called Boca Chabad Rabbi Zalman Bukiet, who leaped into his car and went to check on David, a man he didn't know. When David, clad in a dripping towel, opened his door a crack, Bukiet slipped his foot in and said he wasn't leaving until David called his mother.

But the troubles weren't over. Ten days passed, and again David was out of touch. This time the Goldsteins called Levi and told him they knew something was terribly wrong. "I'll fly down there tonight," Levi promised. He hopped on the next Detroit-Miami flight, arriving after midnight, rented a car, and drove to David's apartment. Banging on the door, he roused Tom, David's roommate. The pair then went in search of David, whom Tom said had left a few hours earlier in search of drugs. Levi and Tom drove from place to place, following half-muttered leads, until one shady character directed them to a driveway across from a cemetery in Deerfield Beach, where a crowd of young men was gathered.

The rabbi and the roommate waited in the rental car until David drove up in a battered car, accompanied by a glassy-eyed fellow who, Levi relates, did not look like the best company. "Tom went to ask him to get out of the car, but he wouldn't, so Tom came back and said, 'Let's go.' It was the moment of truth. I was terrified. I got out of the car, walked over and said, 'David, come with me right now.'"

The Goldsteins shake their head as they picture the scene. "There's Levi in his *tzitzit* and yarmulke, at three in the morning, in the middle of this drug-dealing, knife-wielding crowd, and he just walks over and tells David to get out of the car." The man who was sitting with David took one look at Levi, turned to David, and said, "I think you better go with the rabbi." Levi broke down and cried. And David got out of the car.

Telling the story now, years later, David explains: "How could I disrespect him? He'd flown there just to rescue me. That's pretty impressive."

Once Levi had David in his car, he drove him back to rehab and promised to stay by his side. The next day Bassie and their eldest daughter, an infant at the time, flew down for a week so David would feel he had a family backing him up. David couldn't believe the love they were showing him. "Why would she come with her baby to spend a week with a drug addict?" he marvels. "Whenever I relapsed, they opened their doors to me. I lived in their house for weeks. It was an amazing feeling to be loved unconditionally. For the first time in a long time, I felt good about myself again."

Today at thirty-five, David doesn't know whether he'll be able to stay clean. He slipped again recently, but is back in a twelve-step program, encouraged all along by Levi. Levi harbors few illusions about the longevity of David's drug-free life, but refuses to give up on him. And it's not just Jews whom Levi helps. David relates the story of an African-American woman currently in prison who is dying of cancer. Her ex-husband won't bring her children to her on visiting day. Every month Levi picks up those kids and drives them two hours each way, so they can see their mother. "Levi doesn't see color," David says. "He puts other people's needs first, time and time again."

As for David's parents, their experience with the Shemtovs has changed the way they look at Hasidim. "My old impression of Lubavitch was of elderly people in long black coats and hats, knocking at my door to ask for money," says Mr. Goldstein. "That was before we met Levi and Bassie. These two people are angels. God clipped their wings and sent them down to earth to help people."

Back at the Shemtov home, it's midnight before Levi and Bassie have a few minutes to themselves. Levi, a burly man with a booming voice, takes off his jacket and sits in his shirtsleeves, while Bassie kicks off her shoes. Levi spends most of his days and evenings doing intervention work and follow-up counseling with drug addicts and compulsive gamblers. "I'm never scared going to an addict's house," he insists. "Bassie gets scared when guys call us at two in the morning, drunk, stoned out of their minds, and want me to go over and talk to them. But I go."

Levi considered getting a degree as a certified addiction counselor but decided against it for "strategic reasons," he says. He believes his clients open up to him in ways they wouldn't to a doctor or therapist.

Both he and Bassie feel they can do more as caring individuals than as medical professionals. They each keep long lists of physicians, therapists, and lawyers to whom they refer people, while keeping their own relationships strictly human-to-human. "We have degrees in friendship," Levi comments. "I get the most enjoyment out of knowing that we're doing something no one else can do."

Levi's work has brought him into close contact with other Detroit rabbis, and he says he takes pride in running a program that brings together Jews of all denominations. He says he's very close to a local Reform rabbi, who refers many drug cases to him. "Some Chabad rabbis become the Orthodox presence in their communities," he says. "The Rebbe preferred that this not happen. He didn't want anything to separate us from the total Jewish community."

Bassie admits that it took a while for her to accept that the work she'd chosen was a real shlichus. She missed the spiritual connection of turning people on to Judaism more directly, like through the street outreach she used to do as a teenager. "In the beginning, the Lubavitch girls I work with felt the same way. They said, this isn't *mivtzoim,* it's just helping people physically. Why are we putting this child to sleep? Why aren't we out teaching people how to light Shabbos candles? But the Rebbe felt so strongly about the need to help another Jew in any way. I tell the girls, just give them love. They will realize how special you are, and they'll want to do a mitzvah, to have the same connection to God that you do."

Levi doesn't teach Torah in any structured way to the addicts he works with, but he brings Judaism into every counseling session by talking about the value of life and what that person can contribute. "I explain to them that they're not nothing. They have value that comes from within, that has nothing to do with what they accomplish. I tell them, 'God created this world as an imperfect place. He implanted a piece of Himself in each one of us, and there's one part of this world that will not be perfect until you make it so. It's out there waiting for you.'"

Rabbi Mendy Katz is hurrying across the prison yard at a federal penitentiary in the American Southwest. It is eerily quiet. Dustballs blow across the ground, and the pink-and-purple desert hills loom in the hazy distance beyond the stark gray concrete buildings that house almost 1,500 inmates. Katz peers closely at a list of Jewish prisoners he was handed at the front desk, right under a large sign reading "All Visitations Cancelled Until Further Notice." The men have been in lockdown for two weeks, explains the prison chaplain. Apparently, a fight over a TV show erupted into a two-hundred-man riot. This morning is the first time they're being allowed to go to the canteen, and they're being given just an hour—the same hour Katz has scheduled his visit. "I don't think many of the guys on your list will show up," the chaplain comments. "You've got competition."

Katz is concerned. Director of prison programs for the Aleph Institute, a Chabad-sponsored nonprofit group that serves the approximately 4,000 Jewish men and women in America's state and federal prison system, he has taken the red-eye from Miami to visit the two dozen Jewish prisoners in this remote desert institution located halfway to nowhere. He's exhausted, and he has four prisons to visit in three days. He's here to talk Torah, offer spiritual guidance, maybe put on some tefillin, and in general make sure the men's Jewish needs are being met.

The prison is run by a private company, which means it may not be as efficiently run as those prisons under the control of the federal government. Katz has been getting letters from some of the Jewish prisoners complaining about the lack of kosher food. Federal law requires that prisons provide kosher food to Jewish inmates who request it, but no law says the food has to be hot, or even palatable. In one Pennsylvania prison, inmates on the kosher meal plan get a granola bar and a Slim-Fast shake, three times a day. In other prisons, the kitchen staff will simply remove the meat entrée from a prisoner's tray, leaving the side dishes, or will serve raw carrots and celery for weeks on end. Inmates with any kind of special request aren't overly popular with prison administrators.

At the prison Katz is visiting today, inmates report that the kosher meal plan has improved, but they suspect some tampering with the packaging, a common cost-cutting tactic. "The head of food services is a real anti-Semite," Katz mutters. "I told the warden, and he got mad. But I said, It's a free country, I'm entitled to my opinion."

Eight inmates show up for Katz's visit, which takes place in the prison's small chapel. Five of them are Jewish—three Israelis, a *ba'al teshuva,* and a guy who claims his mother sits on a Federation board. The other three men want to convert. The ratio of Jews to non-Jews at this meeting is not atypical. Word quickly gets around in prison that Jewish inmates get special books and food packages. And religious awakenings of all kind are common in the joint. If there are no atheists in foxholes, there are few in prison, either.

The men sitting in the chapel look like they're gathered for a synagogue board meeting—a group of middle-aged, nicely groomed, well spoken gentlemen who just happen to be incarcerated. "Don't be fooled," one of them remarks. "We're all convicted felons here."

Katz would like to get to the weekly Torah portion, but the men have another agenda: Friday night services. Within minutes it becomes clear that there are two warring factions within the prison's tiny Jewish population, one led by a Russian-born Israeli who conducts the services, and one that appears to consist only of one very vocal man who has grown a long beard and become religious in prison, alienating the others with his newly acquired "holier-than-thou" pronouncements. Katz has been asked to mediate the congregational squabble.

"So, what kind of services do you run?" he asks the Russian. "We light the candles, we say the prayers over the grape juice and the bread, we sing a little, and we talk about the Torah portion," the man responds. "What about *ma'ariv* [the evening service]?" Katz presses. The men don't want it, the Russian says. "I'm religious myself, but I'd rather have them all come and get something than stay away," he insists.

That sends Long Beard into a frenzy. "It's not according to Halacha," he charges. "I do Shabbat in my room, by myself. I don't go to their services." That's not right, Katz scolds gently. "Jewish law says don't separate yourself from the congregation, even if you don't like it. Put your feelings aside. I know it's difficult, but just come, open your book, and read." Long Beard looks down, chastened. "I'm doing my best, I'm not educated enough," he murmurs.

Katz turns back to the Russian. If the Jewish prisoners have put him in charge, why isn't he offering a real service? Chabad has sent booklets to the prison, with an abbreviated Shabbat service in Hebrew and English that takes just a few minutes. Because there's no *minyan,* the Russian protests. "You don't need a *minyan,*" Katz points out. "I prayed alone at a Texaco station on my way over here." The Russian replies that he's just following precedent, continuing the path laid down by previous generations of Jewish prisoners who also avoided leading prayer services. "Then it's time to change," Katz states. "When you make *kabbalat Shabbat* on Friday, you're connecting with millions of other Jews doing the service at the same time. If you don't do it, you miss out on that connection." The Russian tries one last time. "Once I did the whole service, and by the end, I was all alone in the room." Katz laughs. "So give out the challah and grape juice at the end. They'll stay, believe me."

Eventually, Katz gets around to his Torah lesson. Then he puts tefillin on the five Jews, hands out yarmulkes to everyone, and ends the session by getting the inmates to grab each other's hands in a spirited *hora* and a chorus of "Hava Negilah." The armed guard standing at the back of the chapel stares at the ceiling.

This is a typical prison visit for Katz, the kind of thing he does three or four times a week in Florida and several times a year on the road. The Aleph Institute was founded in 1981 by Rabbi Sholom Lipskar. It's still headquartered in his Bal Harbour Chabad House, and Lipskar chairs the organization, but the day-to-day operations have been handed over to a small staff headed by Isaac Jaroslawicz, a former commercial lawyer who acts as Aleph's director of legal affairs. Aleph also does outreach to Jewish military personnel, but the bulk of its efforts are directed toward helping Jewish prisoners and their families, from arrest through incarceration and rehabilitation. Aleph advocates alternatives to prison, suggesting proposals to judges in specific cases; gives social and other humanitarian support to prisoners' families; provides counseling and Jewish religious items to inmates, including rabbinical visits and food packages at Jewish holidays; and monitors the prison system for abuse, providing congressional testimony and supporting prison reform legislation dealing with religious rights. Their mission is to connect inmates with their Jewish souls, whether it be by mailing them Chanukah menorahs or stopping by to let them know they're worth visiting.

But this is no goody-goody troupe of singing nuns, Jaroslawicz is quick to point out. "I'm not an ACLU type," he insists. "To me we're not talking about innocent people who have been unjustly imprisoned. Unlike the typical criminal defense lawyer, I say that all of my clients are guilty, and I'm not here to get them off. We try to work out the best punishment that would satisfy society's needs without necessitating incarceration." Jewish tradition opposes imprisonment, Jaroslawicz explains. "It does nothing but put the person on hold, makes him bitter, makes him associate with other negative influences, and meanwhile, destroys his wife and children. We've watched families disintegrate under these pressures."

When Jaroslawicz or Lipskar is brought in after someone is arrested, he meets with the lawyers and the judge, suggesting alternatives to incarceration tailored to the specific case. They stay away from most violent crimes, but when it's a kid who has stolen credit cards or a real estate broker arrested for mortgage fraud, Aleph tries to work out a punishment that fits the crime, determining what kind of *teshuva,* or repentance, would be appropriate from a Jewish—and American—point of view. "It's not a cookie-cutter approach where everyone goes to Aleph School for two weeks," Jaroslawicz says. A financial crime would typically entail financial restitution, with a large fine. Aleph might suggest taking away a person's credit cards and monitoring his future finances through a court-appointed accountant. The organization has a host of professionals they can call in to help with a particular case: psychiatrists, social workers, forensic experts. Chabad rabbis may be called in to help monitor a client's probation, or drive him to court-ordered Narcotics Anonymous or Alcoholics Anonymous meetings.

Aleph deals with more than five hundred cases a year, and Jaroslawicz says their proposals are often adopted by the court. That may be because Aleph's suggested punishments are often tougher than the court's. "I've heard judges say to the defendant, after they read our proposal for alternative punishment, that if they were him they'd take the prison sentence," Jaroslawicz says.

Once a person is incarcerated, Aleph steps in to help ensure that his or her Jewish needs are met within the prison system. Jewish holiday packages take a large chunk out of Aleph's annual budget. The group spent $200,000 for Passover in 2001, shipping 6,000 pounds of matzah, 500 cases of grape juice, 4,000 cans of gefilte fish, and 1,500 jars of horseradish to 4,000 Jewish prisoners. At Chanukah they mail hundreds of presents to prisoners' children, with cards signed "Mommy" or "Daddy," and no indication that the gift really comes from Aleph.

The organization sends in Torahs, prayer books, and other Jewish religious materials, as prisoners request them. Chabad rabbis working with Aleph report that sometimes just requesting Jewish items can get a prisoner in trouble. "They'll roust you from your cell, and when you come back, all your stuff is torn up or missing," Jaroslawicz says. "And there are a lot of prison chaplains who don't allow Jewish books, because it's not the word of [the Christian] God." Aleph finds more serious, systematic discrimination against Jewish inmates in state penal systems than in federal institutions. In several Texas state prisons, Jaroslawicz says,

Jewish prisoners were thrown into "the hole," or solitary confinement, for fasting on Yom Kippur. "In worst-case situations, it appears [abuses] are based on malice," he wrote in the December 1999 issue of the *Cardozo Law Review.* "At best, sheer ignorance or insensitivity is coupled with a desire not to be bothered with the logistics involved [in satisfying] an extremely small—and often docile—percentage of the general prison population."

Aleph probably deals with more *kashrut* cases than anything else. One of Aleph's most difficult tasks is convincing prison officials that for a religious Jew, kosher food is not a luxury, any more than a low-salt diet would be for a hypertensive prisoner. They're somewhat sabotaged in that campaign by the many fraudulent requests prison administrators get from nonobservant Jews and non-Jews looking to get on the kosher meal plan. Any special treatment helps relieve the boredom of incarceration and is also a way of getting back at the system. "We get a lot of inmates who obviously never kept kosher before, wouldn't know kosher if it hit them in the face, but now that Aleph is there, they want kosher food," Jaroslawicz says. "We have a group of inmates in Michigan that want 'kosher-style' food."

Although Aleph makes it its business to seek out Jewish inmates and defendants, they help anyone caught up in the judicial system as far as their resources will stretch. Aleph's annual operating budget tops $900,000, and, like any other Chabad shlichus, is entirely dependant on fundraising. Jaroslawicz figures he raises about $750,000 a year, but can't bring himself to cut any of his programs. No other Jewish organization is standing by to take up the slack, he says. "I ask the Federation how much they spend on prisons, and they say, we don't. Their big donors like to see their names on hospitals and nursing homes and yeshivas. No one wants to see their name on a prison chapel." Marc Stern, of the American Jewish Congress, has battled Chabad vigorously in court on the issue of public menorahs but has nothing but praise for Chabad's prison work. "I send all my cases to Aleph," he says. "You can talk to the Federation till you're blue in the face. They're not interested."

Katz has been head of Aleph's visiting rabbis program since receiving his rabbinical ordination. He estimates that Chabad rabbis fill about 75 percent of the Jewish chaplaincy positions in the country's prisons, state and federal. In addition, he sends out five to ten pairs of volunteer yeshiva students each summer to visit Jewish inmates in prisons without permanent

Jewish chaplains. It's tough work for a nineteen- or twenty-year-old Brooklyn boy, wandering into a federal prison in Arkansas or Mississippi to argue for inmates' religious rights with gun-toting, good-old-boy wardens. Jaroslawicz, a modern Orthodox Torah v'Da'as and Yeshiva University graduate, says he's constantly amazed at what these young Lubavitchers choose to do. "I went to yeshiva all my life. You put your nose in the books, you don't get in trouble, you become a rabbi, and you're out of there. In Lubavitch, you have to get in those mitzvah tanks and annoy people on the streets, you have to go into hospitals, into prisons. That's something you don't see much of in the Orthodox community."

When Katz visits prisons, he acts as an advocate for the prisoners, but when he suspects he's being manipulated, he has no problem cutting someone off. When one inmate requested multiple copies of expensive Jewish books in order to sell them on the side, Katz caught on pretty quickly.

"I make it my business not to ask them what they're in for, but sometimes they want to talk about it," Katz says. Although there are very few Jews on death row in the United States, Katz has visited some of them. He says it's the hardest thing he does. "It's a very different ministry. You can't tell them there's hope, because that's rarely true." Unlike Catholicism, Judaism does not offer priestly absolution. "But we do believe in repentance and turning back to God," he says. If a prisoner is ready to tackle real *teshuva,* Katz counsels him first to apologize to his victim, or the victim's family, and make any appropriate monetary restitution. Only then may he turn to God to ask for heavenly forgiveness, which is something Katz can't guarantee he'll receive. "I can't tell a prisoner he's forgiven, because that's between him and God."

Back in the southwestern prison, Katz has finished with his hora and "Hava Negilah," and is now trying to hunt down the rest of the Jewish inmates on his list. Some didn't show up for his meeting, preferring to buy candy and cigarettes for the coming week. But five are in the prison's Segregated Housing Unit [SHU], what prisoners and movie directors call "the hole."

Katz is buzzed in through two steel-plated doors and asks a guard to direct him to the cell numbers he's been given. This is a new prison, and the rooms where ordinary prisoners live are called "units" rather than cells. But here in the SHU, it's cells and handcuffs and heavy metal doors with a three-by-ten-inch reinforced glass window at eye level and a knee-level metal slot for slipping food trays in and out.

This is only Katz's second visit to this prison, and he's still trying to determine who the Jewish inmates are. He wants to make sure he doesn't miss anyone.

Coming to the first cell on his list, he raps on the tray slit, and says, "Hi, are you Jewish?" A thin, dark-haired man in his mid-forties ambles over to the door and peers out of the thin window. "Yeah, why? Are you a rabbi?" He tells Katz he's been in the hole for six weeks. His family has sent him dozens of books and magazines, but the solitude is driving him crazy. It turns out he's in real estate, among other, shadier ventures, and he and Katz chat amiably about rising home prices in South Florida. As he talks, Katz casually unwraps his tefillin and places the leather straps on the metal shelf outside the food tray slot.

The inmate eyes the tefillin suspiciously. "So what's up? I see you have your agenda here," he remarks, grinning. "It's *your* agenda," Katz shoots back. "It connects you to God." The inmate laughs. "No it doesn't. Don't you read Einstein? God doesn't care about what we do." That's not true, Katz insists. "Do it anyway," he pleads. The man relents, rolling up his left sleeve. "I'm doing this for you, rabbi." Katz has to kneel on the cement floor and stick his arms through the narrow slot to wrap the man's arm by feel. Behind him, across the narrow hall, another inmate watches silently through his cell window as Katz twists uncomfortably to complete the awkward procedure. He says each word of the prayer out loud, and the Jewish prisoner repeats them easily.

"Thanks for stopping by, Rabbi," the man says as Katz folds up the tefillin and puts them back in their velvet carrying case. Katz nods, wishes him well, and walks quickly back down the brightly lit hallway, past two dozen faces peering out of two dozen other cells. He has to wait a minute for a guard to come and unlock the hallway door, which slams shut behind him with a heavy bang.

As he's leaving the prison, Katz is stopped by a white-bearded inmate who is working in what looks to be a library of Christian books and videos. "Hey, Rabbi, you're my hero!" he shouts, pumping Katz's hand vigorously. "I've been here for eleven years, and I can tell you, when the Bureau of Prisons guys hear your name, they shake. I love that!" Katz smiles politely, then takes another look at the inmate, and asks whether he's Jewish. "My mother is, but I'm not," the man says. Before the sentence is out, so is Katz's tefillin, but the prisoner backs away and shakes his head. "I converted, I can't do that anymore," he says, waving his hands at the literature in his little office.

"There's no such thing, come on," Katz insists, but the man refuses, until Katz sighs and puts away the tefillin. "You're a Jew, and you'll die a Jew, you know that, don't you?" he says quietly. The man nods. "I know."

EPILOGUE

Chabad-Lubavitch has spread all over the globe, but its heart remains in Crown Heights—for now. The small chunk of a largely African-American neighborhood that Lubavitch claims as its own runs seven blocks in one direction and four blocks in the other, anchored at one end by movement headquarters at 770 Eastern Parkway and at the far end by the Beth Rivkah girls' school.

Kingston Avenue is its commercial and political epicenter. From 770, one walks up Kingston Avenue past the $20 million Jewish Children's Museum, still under construction in 2002, and into a Lubavitch world. Small bookstores, clothing shops, and grocery stores catering to the local population crowd up next to the offices of Mivtza Taharas Hamishpacha, N'shei Chabad, and the Tzivos Hashem children's organization. The streets are filled with Lubavitchers running in and out of the Merkaz Stam bookstore, Judaica World, Raskin's fruit and produce store, Crown Bagel, and Kahan's Superette. One shop window displays frilly girls' dresses with high necks. Two shops sell men's hats. Kingston Pizza also sells falafel and several types of knishes.

This is not a wealthy neighborhood. Signs in several shop windows announce that the proprietor accepts food stamps. A run-down clinic and the Jewish Community Council headquarters advertise free vaccination days and workshops on financial aid. It's not a beautiful neighborhood. Lubavitchers are loath to criticize the urban setting their sixth Rebbe chose as his movement headquarters, but many privately admit they wish he'd picked somewhere a little less blighted, a little more green.

Still, it's Crown Heights. It's where Lubavitchers feel at home, it's where their Rebbe lived and died. Even Chabadniks who didn't grow up there feel a certain sentimental attachment to the place.

But something subtle has changed in the air since the Rebbe's death. People still come and go at all hours from 770, but there isn't the same sense of urgency. The crowds outside the synagogue entrance are smaller, more furtive. There isn't the same festive atmosphere on Friday evening; during the Rebbe's later years the women's section overflowed into the stairwell and clusters of yeshiva students spilled out onto Eastern Parkway through the early morning hours. The Rebbe's presence, which filled the air in Crown Heights with a constant, palpable expectancy, is very much subdued, felt more today at his grave site than along Kingston Avenue.

What will happen to Crown Heights now that the Rebbe is gone? During his lifetime the tremendous pull Chabadniks felt to go out on shlichus, as he urged them to do, was always tempered by their desire to remain near him. Those who chose to live in Crown Heights felt justified because it was also their Rebbe's home. Those who "went out" looked forward to their trips back, when they would replenish their emotional and spiritual bank accounts at the Rebbe's never-ending trough. Since 1994, that push-me–pull-you tension has weakened, more with each passing year. Virtually all Lubavitch youths today say they want to become shlichim and leave Crown Heights. They won't all do it, but that's the ideal.

Most Chabadniks say that their best and brightest young people will continue to move out of the neighborhood. Some, very few, dispute this characterization, saying it is demeaning to those who remain in Crown Heights. Indeed, some of the movement's best minds, and many of its most distinguished elders, live there. But will their children and grandchildren stay? The Crown Heights yeshiva no longer has the prestige it had when students knew they could spend every Shabbat with Schneerson. Other Chabad boys' yeshivas and girls' seminaries have opened around the world, drawing ambitious students out of Crown Heights. The Moshichist controversy continues to split the movement. When shlichim from the field visit Crown Heights, they try to ignore the few lingering "Welcome Moshiach!" banners fluttering from local balconies. Moshichism will die down as the years pass, but the emotional scars remain, as well as the memory that Crown Heights was its most fervent stronghold.

As Chabad's center of gravity continues to move out of Crown Heights, will the community itself survive? Or has the Rebbe's passing sounded the death knell for this Lubavitch neighborhood? "It's probably one of the most painful subjects for us today," says Rabbi Yisrael Deren, Connecticut shliach and one of the movement's national figures. It's "absolutely vital," he says, that Crown Heights continue to exist as a Lubavitch community. "You need a place to educate your children, you need a place to go to and draw inspiration from. You need a critical mass," he says. But it's difficult today to muster up the same enthusiasm for building a life and raising children in this Brooklyn neighborhood when the greater world of Chabad shlichus beckons.

"I am absolutely not worried about what's going on out in the field," Deren continues. "Pushed against the wall, I wouldn't say I'm worried about what's going on in Crown Heights or in any other Lubavitch community either, but . . ." He sighs. "What the Rebbe wants from somebody who's out, whether they're in Stamford or anywhere else, is clear. I wake up in the morning and I know exactly why I'm here. I know I am where I'm supposed to be, I'm out doing what I should be doing. For somebody who is not out on shlichus, the question of what does the Rebbe want from him or her is not as easily answered. And the possibility for mistakes is larger."

An emotional shift is one thing, but it seems unlikely that Lubavitchers will abandon Crown Heights en masse, at least not in the near future. Rabbi Jacob Goldstein has been chair of Crown Heights' Community Board 9 since 1980, and he says Chabad has sunk too much time and money into the neighborhood to pull up stakes now. Millions of dollars have been spent creating a communal infrastructure—yeshivas, girls' schools, homes, businesses—and no one's prepared to throw that away. "The upper ten percent could afford to leave, but they wouldn't have that infrastructure anywhere else," he says. "If you come from that background, you need that. Where would they go? Who's going to start building somewhere else? You can't build something like this overnight." Besides, Goldstein points out, the Rebbe told his followers not to abandon the neighborhood. He may be gone, but his wishes remain.

The Rebbe's passing has changed the dynamics of the movement's central administration. Schneerson's charismatic leadership gave him tremendous personal control. Even when he wasn't actively involved in a particular decision, the threat of his disapproval was strong enough to smooth over differences among his shlichim and his closest aides. Those aides are now running the movement, but much more as a corporate entity than as a movement focused around one leader. Rabbi Krinsky claims to see no diminishing of the movement's central authority, but some shlichim today operate with an independence that did not exist during Schneerson's lifetime. As the years pass and a new generation takes over the movement reins, they will undoubtedly move toward greater operational transparency and adopt more streamlined business methods. Chabad will look more and more like a multinational corporation.

It seems probable that as Chabad centers around the world move into their second and third generation, regional differences will continue to emerge. They might only be cosmetic. Yes, more Lubavitchers will go to college. Yes, more will become doctors and lawyers. Already Lubavitch women in the field are wearing more fashionable clothes, and some of the younger men are wearing turtlenecks under their suit jackets, but none of this has to affect Chabad's theological homogeneity. It hasn't so far.

Some Chabad watchers believe, on the other hand, that as Chabad continues to expand into the American Jewish mainstream and as more Lubavitchers come into daily working contact with non-Orthodox Jews, the movement itself cannot help but be affected. As more *ba'alei teshuva* come into the movement and their children and grandchildren grow up between two worlds, the lines in and out of Chabad will continue to blur. How long can Chabad congregations continue to be filled with Jews who don't know the Hebrew prayers and who don't eat kosher or observe Shabbat, without that influencing how outsiders view Lubavitch? Already, the definition of a Lubavitcher is widening to include Jews who support the movement but who don't wear black hats or sheitels. Will it further expand to include not-fully-observant Jews?

Forward editor J. J. Goldberg suggests that Chabad may one day fill the role currently filled by modern Orthodoxy, as a bridge between the observant and the non-observant Jewish worlds. New York University Professor Lawrence Schiffman, a longtime Chabad watcher, suggests that Chabad has already become a synagogue movement and will continue to increase its presence in the larger Jewish world. Both of those are compelling scenarios.

Predicting the future of Chabad has proved to be a perilous undertaking, but it's too tempting to resist. Whatever the future holds for Crown Heights, it seems safe to predict that Chabad-Lubavitch will continue to flourish, both as a worldwide Hasidic movement with a specific philosophy and practice and as a successful Jewish outreach organization. The teaching will continue, the Internet and print publication efforts will grow, and Chabad shlichim will continue to make their presence felt in the communities where they live and work.

Will there ever be a new Rebbe? Perhaps, perhaps not, but if so, not for decades. Will the last century's surge of interest in Jewish practice and identification continue into the new millennium? So far, that seems a safe bet. Will Chabad mysticism and philosophy continue to attract public attention and the interest of Jews from outside the movement? Will Chabad be able to hold on to its position as the dominant force in the new Jewish communities of Russia and Ukraine? The answer to both questions is, most probably.

Or perhaps Moshiach will come, and render all questions moot.

ACKNOWLEDGMENTS

This book grew out of an article on the Chabad movement I wrote for the August–September 2000 issue of *Moment* magazine. I must thank both Josh Rolnick, then managing editor of *Moment,* for assigning me the story; and Altie Karper, my editor at Schocken Books, for suggesting that I extend it into a full-length book. Throughout the eighteen-month research and writing period, Altie never wavered in her belief in this book. She edited the final manuscript with a sure hand and sensitive heart, and her extensive Jewish background enabled me to avoid countless errors.

I must acknowledge the many scholars, rabbis, and Jewish leaders who agreed to be interviewed, particularly Dr. Norman Lamm, president of Yeshiva University; Rabbi Eric Yoffie, president of the UAHC; Rabbi Jerome Epstein, executive vice president of United Synagogue of Conservative Judaism; Dr. Ismar Schorsch, chancellor of the Jewish Theological Seminary; Malcolm Hoenlein, executive vice chairman of the Conference of Presidents of Major American Jewish Organizations; Abe Foxman, national director of the Anti-Defamation League; Michael Schneider and Amir Shaviv at the American Jewish Joint Distribution Committee; Rabbi David Saperstein and Mark Pelavin at the Religious Action Center in Washington, D.C.; Marc Stern of the American Jewish Congress; attorney Nathan Lewin; and Professors Ari Goldman, Lawrence Schiffman, Alan Dershowitz, Bonnie Morris, David Berger, Samuel Heilman, and Arthur Hertzberg.

This book could not have been written without the trust and generosity of the many Lubavitchers who opened their homes and hearts to me, both in Crown Heights and around the country. I am indebted to Rabbis Yehuda Krinsky, Avraham Shemtov, and Moshe Kotlarsky for their patience and their frankness. I would also like to thank the following Lubavitchers for their time and hospitality: Bronya Shaffer, Hinda Leah Sharfstein, and Baila Olidort in Crown Heights; Rabbi Yisrael and Vivi Deren in Stamford, Connecticut, and Rabbi Yossi and Maryashie Deren in Greenwich, Connecticut; Rabbi Zalman and Risya Posner in Nashville, Tennessee; Rabbis Moshe Feller and Manis Friedman in Minneapolis, Minnesota; Rabbi Levi and Bassie Shemtov in West Bloomfield, Michigan; Rabbi Levi and Nechama Shemtov in Washington,

D.C.; Rabbi Sholom and Chanie Lipskar in Bal Harbour, Florida; Rabbis Moshe Denburg and Zalman Bukiet in Boca Raton, Florida; Rabbi Hirsch and Elkie Zarchi in Cambridge, Massachusetts; Rabbi Aharon and Rivkah Slonim in Binghamton, New York; Rabbi Yehoshua Harlig in Las Vegas, Nevada; Rabbi Binyomin and Chana Sharonne Zippel in Salt Lake City, Utah; Rabbi Shmuel and Shterna Notik in Chicago, Illinois; Rabbi Yisroel and Devorah Shmotkin of Milwaukee, Wisconsin, along with all their children; Rabbi Moshe and Devorah Wilhelm in Portland, Oregon; Rabbi Yossi and Esty Greenberg in Anchorage, Alaska; Rabbi Boruch Shlomo Cunin of Los Angeles, and all his sons and daughters in California, particularly Rabbi Chaim Nochum Cunin in L.A., Rabbi Yochanan and Baila Friedman of Santa Cruz, Rabbi Yosef and Hinda Langer of San Francisco, and Rabbi Levi and Chanah Zirkind of Fresno, California; Rabbi Avraham Berkowitz in Moscow, Russia; and the Kantors and Wilhelms, shlichim in Bangkok, Thailand, for the wildest Seder ever.

Many other Lubavitchers helped me in their professional capacities, far too many to be named here, although I must credit Moshe Berghoff and Dovid and Eliezer Zaklikofsky for locating and scanning photographs under extraordinary time pressure.

The financial generosity of my Aunt Joan and my late Uncle David Kasner gave me precious time to complete my research, and Faye Bittker's careful reading of the manuscript, along with her pointed suggestions, helped immeasurably. I am also grateful to Joel Smolen for taking the quite flattering photograph of me that appears on the book jacket.

Above all, I thank Rabbi Zalman Shmotkin, director of Lubavitch News Service and Chabad.org, for spending endless months digging up material for me, explaining arcane bits of Hasidus, encouraging other Lubavitchers to open their doors to me, and being a constant source of strength and friendship throughout the entire process. I know he'll be embarrassed to see his and his family's names in this book, for he was as eager to avoid steering me in their direction as I was to seek them out. Zalman and his wife Malya were my first Lubavitch friends, and I will treasure that always.

Finally, I am a reporter, not a scholar, rabbi, or Jewish theologian. I've reported here what I've seen and heard as best I could, and I apologize in advance for any errors or misquotations.

GLOSSARY

A pronunciation note: "Ch" is pronounced as a gutteral "h," as in Chanukah, and not as in "much" or "chat." Where relevant, both Sephardic and Ashkenazic pronunciations of the same Hebrew word are supplied, the Sephardic first and the Ashkenazic in parentheses.

Agudas Chassidei Chabad: Chabad's central leadership body, a twenty-two-man executive board that sets general policy for the worldwide movement.

ahavat (or, ***ahavas***) ***Yisrael:*** literally, "love of your fellow Jew." One of the Lubavitcher Rebbe's mitzvah campaigns, it fuels Chabad outreach.

Ba'al Shem Tov, Israel: The founder of Hasidism, who was born in 1700 in Poland and died in 1760; also referred to as the Besht, which is the acronym of his surname. The literal translation of his surname is "Master of the Good Name."

ba'al teshuva [pl.: ***ba'alei teshuva***]: a formerly non-observant Jew who has "returned" to the Orthodox faith and lifestyle.

bar mitzvah: ritual marking the onset of certain religious responsibilities when a Jewish boy turns thirteen. In 1922 a similar ritual for twelve-year-old girls, the bat mitzvah, was created by Rabbi Mordechai Kaplan.

bracha: a blessing.

brit (or, ***bris***) ***milah:*** circumcision ritual performed on an eight-day-old Jewish male.

Chabad, or ***Chabad-Lubavitch:*** Hasidic movement that follows the teachings of Rabbi Schneuer Zalman of Liady (1745–1813), the first of Chabad's seven rebbes, who is also known as the Alter Rebbe. Chabad is an acronym formed from the Hebrew words *chochmah* (wisdom), *binah* (knowledge), and *da'at* (understanding), human capacities that refer to three of God's ten mystical attributes as well. The movement is also called Lubavitch, after the White Russian town where four of its rebbes lived.

Chabadniks: adherents of the Chabad movement; also called Lubavitchers.

chalav yisrael: literally, "Jewish milk"; dairy products whose processing has been supervised by observant Jews from the milking of the cow to the sealing of the cartons or packages. These are the only dairy products a Lubavitcher will use.

Chanukah: the eight-day winter festival of lights. A nine-branched candelabra known as a menorah (or, more accurately, a *hanukiah*) is lit each night of the festival to commemorate the successful Maccabean revolt in 161 B.C.E. against the Syrian-Greek occupiers of ancient Israel.

cheder: an elementary school that, in pre–World War II Europe, was attended by Orthodox Jewish boys. In America today, it refers to a particular type of Jewish elementary school that is attended by ultra-Orthodox boys.

daven, davening: Yiddish for "pray" and "praying," respectively.

farbrengen [v., *farbreng*]: a Hasidic gathering led by a teacher or rebbe.

frum: Jewishly observant, religious.

halacha [adj., ***halachic***]: traditional Jewish law; the complex system of rulings derived from the Torah, Mishnah, and Talmud that govern an observant Jewish life.

Hashem: literally "the name," a euphemism for God used by observant Jews to avoid mentioning God's name when not in prayer.

Hasidism: an eighteenth-century religious movement founded by Israel Ba'al Shem Tov that stresses serving God through joy. Many different Hasidic offshoot groups originated in different European cities, each headed by its own rabbi, or rebbe. A Hasid (one who is a member of a Hasidic group; pl.: Hasidim) follows a strict interpretation of Torah law and is noted by distinctive dress, customs, and devotion to the rebbe who is the head of his group. Chabad-Lubavitch is one of many Hasidic groups.

Hasidus: Hasidic philosophy and teachings.

Havdalah: from the Hebrew for "separation," the ceremony marking the end of Shabbat at sundown on Saturday.

hora: Eastern European Jewish circle dance.

Kabbalah: literally, "that which is received," Jewish mystical teachings traditionally reserved for learned Jewish men over the age of forty, now taught in various translated formats.

Kabbalat Shabbat (or, **Kabbolas Shabbos**): prayer service welcoming the Sabbath on Friday evening.

kashrut (or, **kashrus**): the laws of keeping kosher, involving the strict separation of milk and meat and the complete avoidance of pork, shellfish, and other prohibited living things listed in the Bible. To kasher a kitchen means to perform whatever cleaning and/or purification procedures are required so that kosher meals can be prepared and eaten there.

kippah [pl.: **kippot**]: Also called *yarmulke*. A small round head covering traditionally worn by observant Jewish males.

Lag B'Omer: a festive day comemorating the thirty-sixth day of the forty-nine days between Passover and Pentecost. Lag B'Omer marks the end of a quasi-mourning period during which no weddings or other celebrations may take place.

l'chaim: literally, "to life," a traditional Jewish toast.

Machne Israel: Chabad's social service arm, one of the movement's three main institutions.

mashpia: the act of influencing another person. Used as a noun, it is the person a Lubavitcher chooses as his or her mentor, to be consulted in all matters personal, professional, and spiritual.

mechitza: wall or other barrier that separates men and women during an Orthodox prayer service.

Merkos L'Inyonei Chinuch: Chabad's educational department, which directs the movement's network of shlichim and other outreach activities.

mezuzah [pl.: **mezuzot**, or **mezuzos**]: a small parchment scroll onto which passages from Deuteronomy have been copied by a scribe. The scroll is then rolled up and put into a case. The cases are affixed to the doorposts in an observant Jewish home.

mikvah: ritual bath used for spiritual purification. A mikvah is used for religious conversion, for making kitchen utensils kosher, and by observant women every month on the seventh day following the cessation of the menstrual period. Many observant men go to a mikvah before Shabbat or Jewish holidays, and some Lubavitchers go every morning before prayers.

minyan: ten Jewish men thirteen years or older, who supply the quorum neeeded for group prayer in an Orthodox congregation. Non-Orthodox Jews count women as part of a minyan.

mitnagdim (or, **misnagdim**): Orthodox Jews who do not follow Hasidic practices, and in fact may be seriously opposed to them. Its literal meaning in Hebrew is "opponents."

mitzvah [pl.: *mitzvot*, or *mitzvos*]: Hebrew for "good deed." Positive precepts found in the Bible, the Mishnah, or other codes of Jewish law, which observant Jews are required to perform.

mivtzah [pl.: *mivtzoim*]: Hebrew for "campaign." The Lubavitcher Rebbe announced many "mitzvah campaigns," or *mivtzoim*, to encourage non-observant Jews to activate their Judaism through such actions as keeping kosher, lighting Shabbat candles, and putting on tefillin. Lubavitch youths typically go out on Fridays and on the eve of Jewish holidays to do *mivtzoim*, or outreach work.

mohel: One who performs a *brit milah.*

moshiach: Hebrew for "messiah." A descendant of King David who will be sent by God to usher in a new era of righteousness and proclaim the end of the Jewish exile from the Holy Land. *Moshichism* is a belief persisting among some Lubavitchers that the seventh rebbe, Menachem Mendel Schneerson, is the messiah.

neshama: soul.

niddah: the monthly period of physical separation of husband and wife, lasting through the menstrual period and for seven days beyond, ending with the woman's immersion in a *mikvah.*

niggun [pl: *niggunim*]: wordless Hasidic melody.

ohel: Hebrew for "tent." The term used for Menachem Mendel Schneerson's gravesite.

Passover (in Hebrew, *Pesach*): the eight-day spring holiday commemorating the exodus of the Israelites from slavery in Egypt, during which no leavened food products are consumed. Israeli Jews and Reform Jews throughout the world observe the holiday for seven days.

payos: side curls or earlocks left uncut by ultra-Orthodox men because of the biblical precept that prohibits cutting the hair at the "corners of the head."

Purim: spring holiday commemorating the foiled plot against the Jewish inhabitants of the Persian empire approximately 2,500 years ago, thanks to the intervention of the Jewish queen Esther. The *megilah* (or, scroll) of Esther, which tells the story, is read twice during the holiday.

rebbe: the leader of a Hasidic group, chosen by his disciples for his piety, learnedness, and/or lineage. Lubavitchers refer to their last rebbe, Menachem Mendel Schneerson (d. 1994), as, simply, "the Rebbe."

rebbetzin: wife of a rabbi or rebbe.

Rosh Hashanah: the Jewish new year, celebrated in September. Together with Yom Kippur, which follows ten days later, this period of prayer, introspection, and repentance is referred to as the High Holidays.

Seder: the festive meal celebrated on the first two nights of Passover, during which the Haggadah, the book that recounts the story of the exodus from Egypt, is read and various ritual foods are eaten.

Shabbat (or, **Shabbos**): the Jewish Sabbath, lasting from sundown Friday to sundown Saturday, during which no work may be performed.

sheitel: Yiddish for "wig," which is worn by Hasidic and other types of Orthodox women to cover their hair in public.

Shema: first word of the Hebrew prayer that proclaims God's unity, "Hear O Israel, the Lord our God, the Lord is One."

shidduch: match made between a man and a woman for the purposes of marriage.

shliach [fem.: **shlicha;** pl.: **shlichim**]: Hebrew for "emissary." A Lubavitcher who performs religious outreach to his or her fellow Jews.

shlichut (or, **shlichus**): a Chabad emissary's outreach mission; his or her permanent posting.

shochet: Jewish ritual slaughterer.

shul: synagogue.

Shulchan Aruch: Code of Jewish Law, compiled in the sixteenth century by Joseph Caro. Schneur Zalman of Liady, the first Lubavitcher Rebbe, wrote his own version, the *Shulchan Aruch haRav*, which is consulted by Lubavitchers for points where it differs from the original.

Sukkot (or, **Sukkos**): Feast of Tabernacles, a seven-day fall festival that begins five days after Yom Kippur and commemorates the Israelites' forty years of wandering in the desert following their exodus from Egypt and before their arrival in the promised land. To replicate the desert experience, meals are eaten in a *sukkah*, an outdoor hut that is covered only with tree branches, leaves, or bamboo poles.

taharat (or, **taharas**) **ha'mishpacha:** Hebrew for "family purity," the laws governing sexual relations between husband and wife.

Talmud: the heart of the Jewish legal system, a multivolume work consisting of the Mishnah, a code of Jewish law that initially had been transmitted orally, and the Gemarah, rabbinic discussions and commentaries on the Mishnah and on the application of Jewish law to everyday life. The Mishnah was codified in Palestine in the third century by Rabbi Judah the Prince. The Talmud was compiled by Babylonian and Palestinian scholars from the fifth through the seventh centuries.

Tanya: Published in 1796 by Schneur Zalman of Liady, it outlines Chabad's philosophy and is the major Hasidic text studied by Lubavitchers today.

tefila [pl.: *tefilot,* or *tefilos*]: prayer.

tefillin: phylacteries. The black leather boxes that contain portions of the Bible are wrapped around the left arm and the head with leather straps during morning prayers.

Torah: The first five books of the Hebrew Bible, also refered to as the Five Books of Moses. Also called the Chumash, derived from the Hebrew word for five. The Hebrew Bible consisits of thirty-nine books, including, in addition to the Torah, the twenty-one books of the Prophets, or Nevi'im, and the thirteen books of the Writings, or Ketuvim. The acronym Tanach refers to the complete Hebrew Bible.

Torah v'Daas: a non-Hasidic ultra-Orthodox yeshiva in Brooklyn.

tzaddik: a righteous or holy person.

tzedaka: charity.

tzitzit (or, *tzitzis*): fringes at the four corners of a prayer shawl (*tallit*, or *tallis*) and at the corners of a *tallit* (or, *tallis*) *katan*, the undershirt worn by religious Jewish men. Many Orthodox men tuck the fringes into their pants; some leave them exposed, following the biblical precept "and you shall see them."

yahrtzeit: anniversary of a person's death.

yechidus: a private audience with the Lubavitcher Rebbe.

yeshiva: a religious full-day school in which Jewish subjects are given emphasis that is either equal to or greater than secular subjects. Can be used to refer to elementary school, secondary school, or post-secondary institutions. A *yeshiva bocher* is a male yeshiva student.

Yiddishkeit: Yiddish for "Judaism," used by Lubavitchers to refer to the Eastern European, Ashkenazi-flavored Jewish beliefs and lifestyle they promote in their teachings and outreach work.

Yom Kippur: the day of atonement, spent in fasting and prayer.

SELECTED BIBLIOGRAPHY

Altein, Rachel, ed. *Out of the Inferno: The Efforts That Led to the Rescue of Rabbi Yosef Y. Schneersohn of Lubavitch from War-Torn Europe in 1939 40.* Brooklyn, N.Y.: Kehot Publication Society, 2002.

Avtzon, Sholom DovBer. *Likutei Amarim Tanya: Its Story and History from the Time When the Alter Rebbe Started to Prepare the Tanya Until Today.* Brooklyn, N.Y.: S. D. Avtzon, 1991.

Belcove-Shalin, Janet S., ed. *New World Hasidism: Ethnographic Studies of Hasidic Jews in America.* Albany: State University of New York Press, 1995.

Berger, David. *The Rebbe, the Messiah, and the Scandal of Orthodox Indifference.* London: The Littman Library of Jewish Civilization, 2001.

Buber, Martin. *The Legend of the Baal-Shem.* Princeton, N.J.: Princeton University Press, 1995.

———. *Tales of the Hasidim: Early Masters.* New York: Schocken Books, 1973.

Dalfin, Chaim. *Conversations with the Rebbe, Menachem Mendel Schneerson: Interviews with 14 Leading Figures About the Rebbe.* Los Angeles: JEC Publishing Co., 1996.

Ehrlich, Avrum. *Leadership in the HaBaD Movement: A Critical Evaluation of HaBaD Leadership, History, and Succession.* Northvale, N.J.: Jason Aronson, 2000.

Eisenberg, Robert. *Boychiks in the Hood: Travels in the Hasidic Underground.* San Francisco: HarperSanFrancisco, 1995.

Foxbrunner, Roman A. *Habad: The Hasidism of R. Shneur Zalman of Lyady.* Northvale, N.J.: Jason Aronson, 1993.

Freedman, Samuel G. *Jew vs. Jew: The Struggle for the Soul of American Jewry.* New York: Simon & Schuster, 2000.

Freeman, Tzvi. *Bringing Heaven Down to Earth: 365 Meditations of the Rebbe.* Vancouver: Class One Press, 1996.

———. *Be Within, Stay Above.* Vancouver: Class One Press, 2000.

Friedman, Yosef B., ed. *Sefer Hashluchim.* 4 vols. Brooklyn, N.Y.: Merkos L'Inyonei Chinuch, 1991.

Gurary, Noson. *Chasidism: Its Development, Theology, and Practice.* Northvale, N.J.: Jason Aronson, 1997.

Harris, Lis. *Holy Days: The World of a Hassidic Family.* New York: Summit Books, 1985.

Heilman, Samuel. *Defenders of the Faith: Inside Ultra-Orthodox Jewry.* Berkeley: University of California Press, 2000.

Hoffman, Edward. *Despite All Odds: The Story of Lubavitch.* New York: Simon & Schuster, 1991.

Jacobson, Simon, ed. *Toward a Meaningful Life: The Wisdom of the Rebbe*. New York: William Morrow & Co, 1995.

Landau, David. *Piety and Power: The World of Jewish Fundamentalism*. New York: Hill & Wang, 1993.

Levin, Feitel. *Heaven on Earth: Reflections on the Theology of the Lubavitcher Rebbe*. Brooklyn, N.Y.: Kehot Publication Society, 2000.

Loewenthal, Naftali. *Communicating the Infinite: The Emergence of the Habad School*. Chicago: University of Chicago Press, 1990.

Menachem Mendel of Lubavitch. *The Mitzvah to Love Your Fellows as Yourself*. Translated by Mangel and Z. Posner. Brooklyn, N.Y.: Kehot Publication Society, 2002.

Metzger, Alter B. *The Heroic Struggle: The Arrest and Liberation of Rabbi Yosef Y. Schneersohn of Lubavitch in Soviet Russia*. Brooklyn, N.Y.: Kehot Publication Society, 1999.

Mindel, Nissan. *The Philosophy of Chabad*. Brooklyn, N.Y.: Kehot Publication Society, 1985.

Mintz, Jerome R. *Hasidic People: A Place in the New World*. Cambridge, Mass.: Harvard University Press, 1992.

Morris, Bonnie. *Lubavitcher Women in America*. Albany: State University of New York Press, 1998.

Pickarski, Chana, ed. *Shlichus: Meeting the Outreach Challenge: A Resource Handbook for Shluchim*. Brooklyn, N.Y.: Nshei Chabad Publications, 1990 f.

Posner, Zalman. *Think Jewish*. Nashville, Tenn.: Kesher Press, 1979.

Rabinowicz, Harry M. *Hasidism: The Movement and Its Masters*. Northvale, N.J.: Jason Aronson, 1988.

Ravitzky, Aviezer. *Messianism, Zionism, and Jewish Religious Radicalism*. Chicago: University of Chicago Press, 1996.

Sachar, Howard Morley. *The Course of Modern Jewish History*. New York: Dell Publishing Co., 1958.

Sacks, Jonathan, adapter. *Torah Studies: Discourses, by Menachem M. Schneerson*. Brooklyn, N.Y.: Kehot Publication Society, 1996.

Schneerson, Menachem M. *On the Essence of Chassidus*. Brooklyn, N.Y.: Kehot Publication Society, 1986.

Schochet, Jacob Immanuel. *Chassidic Dimensions*, vol. 3 of *The Mystical Dimension*. Brooklyn, N.Y.: Kehot Publication Society, 1990.

———. *Mashiach: The Principles of Mashiach and the Messianic Era in Jewish Law and Tradition*. New York: S.I.E., 1992.

Scholem, Gershom G. *Major Trends in Jewish Mysticism*. New York: Schocken Books, 1974.

Sharot, Stephen. *Messianism, Mysticism, and Magic: A Sociological Analysis of Jewish Religious Movements*. Chapel Hill: University of North Carolina Press, 1987.

Slonim, Rivkah, ed. *Total Immersion: A Mikvah Anthology*. Northvale, N.J.: Jason Aronson, 1997.

Steinsaltz, Adin. *The Sustaining Utterance: Discourses on Chasidic Thought*. Northvale, N.J.: Jason Aronson, 1996.

Weiner, Herbert. *9½ Mystics: The Kabbala Today.* New York: Collier Books; Toronto and New York: Maxwell Macmillan, 1991.

Wiesel, Elie. *Souls on Fire: Portraits and Legends of Hasidic Masters.* New York: Touchstone Books, 1982.

Wineberg, Yosef. *Lessons in Tanya: The Tanya of R. Shneur Zalman of Liadi.* 5 vols. Brooklyn, N.Y.: Kehot Publication Society, 1982.

INDEX

Solomon, Jacob, 163, 168
Sommer, Howard, 296–97
Sorbonne, 73
souls, of departed people, 67, 272, 273
Souls on Fire: Portraits and Legends of Hasidic Masters (Wiesel), 75n, 76n, 77n
South Africa, 14, 190
South America, 188, 206, 209, 279
Soviet Union, 68, 72, 143, 190, 192, 248
  former, 8, 10, 13, 14, 110, 163, 171, 194, 209, 302
  Lubavitch books and, 197
  Siberian Gulag in, 143
Stamford, Conn., 124–25
Steinbeck, John, 255
Steinhardt, Michael, 165
Sterling, Ala., 141
Stern, Marc, 286–87, 292, 294, 298, 313
Stillman, Rabbi Yerachmiel, 226
Stone, Eileen, 203
Streep, Meryl, 167
street outreach (mivtzoim), 46–55, 61–63, 308
subway campaign, 56
sukkah, 55, 175
Sukkot, 109
summer camps, 259–60, 265
Supreme Court, U.S., 193, 289–92, 293, 294

taharat mishpacha (family purity), 150, 151, 152, 155, 158
Talmud, 61, 200, 270, 282, 288
  study of, 243, 244–45
Tanya, 18–19, 40, 82, 199, 230, 231, 245, 276, 279, 281, 282
Tashkent, 189
Tauber, Yanki, 58
Teaneck, N.J., 287
tefillin, 83, 145–46, 166, 204, 244
  campaigns, 45, 46, 48–49, 50, 51, 52–55, 61–63, 80, 99, 102, 241, 245
  Koufax and, 196–97
Tel Aviv, 215
telethons, 12, 166, 167, 178–82, 302

television, 236, 281–82
Temple Sholom, 130
Tenafly, N.J., 127
Ten Commandments, 52
Tenenbaum, Feigel, 107–8, 109, 110, 116
Tenenbaum, Rabbi Sholom Ber, 107–10
Tennessee, 112, 248
Thailand, 208–20, 222
Thatcher, Margaret, 69
Think Jewish (Posner), 80n
Tiferes Bachurim, 223
Tomchei Tmimim schools, 242
Torah, 20, 21, 22, 30, 46, 49, 105, 118, 150, 155, 164, 228, 234, 255, 270, 282
  Hillel vs. Shammai on, 191
  Lipskar on, 44–45
  mikvah and, 149, 150
  politics and, 190–91
  radio and, 281
  science and, 23, 253, 254, 256
  study of, 245
  tefillin and, 145–46
  Tzivos Hashem and, 241
  women and, 39
Toronto, 25, 60
Total Immersion: A Mikvah Anthology (Slonim), 156
Touger, Levi, 219
travel, 113–14, 247–48
Tuesdays with Morrie (Albom), 260
Turkish, Arthur, 35–36
Turkish, Ellen, 35
Twain, Mark, 255
tzaddikim, 67, 75, 80, 272
  Moshiach and, 268
  rebbes, 75–77, 80, 81
tzedaka, 6
Tzivos Hashem, 240–41, 302

Ukraine, 13, 302, 321
Union of American Hebrew Congregations (UAHC), 119, 123, 128, 290, 292–93

352   INDEX

Yom Kippur, 143
  Koufax and, 196–97
York, Michael, 166, 179, 180
Yostov, Zena, 105, 106
Young, Brigham, 202
Young Israel, 93

Zajac, Rabbi Shmuel, 32
Zalman, Rabbi Schneur (the Alter
    Rebbe), 18–19, 20, 21, 118, 245

Zarchi, Elkie, 102, 105, 106
Zarchi, Mendel, 32
Zarchi, Rabbi Hirsch, 102–3, 104–5, 106
Zippel, Avremi, 204, 205, 239–40, 241, 260
Zippel, Rabbi Binyomin "Benny," 201, 202, 203–4, 269
Zippel, Sharonne, 201, 202, 204
Zirkind, Chani, 131–32
Zirkind, Rabbi Levi, 131–32

Printed in the United States
by Baker & Taylor Publisher Services